Carole Haber's
Discriminating
TRAVELER

Carole Haber's
Discriminating
TRAVELER

An Insider's Most Treasured Travel Tips

FREUNDLICH BOOKS   NEW YORK

Copyright © 1985 by Carole Haber

Library of Congress Cataloging-in-Publication Data
Haber, Carole, 1942–
Carole Haber's Discriminating traveler.

Includes index.
1.Voyages and travels—1951–   —Guide-books.
I. Title. II. Title: Discriminating traveler.
G153.4H33   1985   910'.2'02   85-13169
ISBN 0-88191-036-8

Published by Freundlich Books
(A division of Lawrence Freundlich Publications, Inc.)
212 Fifth Avenue
New York, N.Y. 10010

Distributed to the trade by The Scribner Book Companies, Inc.
115 Fifth Avenue
New York, N.Y. 10003

Manufactured in the United States of America

10 9 8 7 6 5 4 3 2 1

TO BILL
YOU MAKE IT ALL POSSIBLE

Acknowledgments

I gratefully acknowledge the following people, all of whom have influenced my travels, thereby contributing to this book:

Bill Haber, my best traveling buddy.

George Kirgo, the Galloping Gourmet of Italy.

Miriam Rand, travel agent and adviser par excellence.

Mimi Schroeder, pour toutes mes études, qui continuent . . .

Margery Ramsdell, who'll follow me anywhere.

Marguerite Senechal, my mom, the gutsiest and most adventuresome traveler I know, in her sixties.

Everyone who has ever sent me a note or called me up to relate a travel experience, to recommend or advise, to refute or substantiate something I told them.

Countless unnamed people in cities and countries all over the world who have made my travels unforgettable.

Contents

About This Book

Fielding I'm not. I'm also not Fodor, Michelin, Nagel, Birnbaum, Pausanias, Frommer, Baedeker, Gault, Millau, or anyone else who writes extensively about traveling. I have a very small staff of one: me. Yes, I get a lot of input from a lot of people, which gets checked, doublechecked, and used or maybe not used. I don't have the time to go everywhere and check on everything; how I wish I did. That is why I call this a travel book, not a guidebook.

Even though there is a huge amount of information herein that is typical of most travel/guidebooks, this is still not a definitive book. No guidebook is. You'll need other sources and material. This is also a book about the art of traveling. I am not the ultimate authority on the subject; no one is. What you will read in this book is highly subjective and not too formal. Traveling is fun, and reading about traveling should also be fun.

This whole thing got started in 1970, when my suitcases began to go to work on a regular basis. After a trip to Hawaii, friends called me up for advice as to where to stay, to eat, to shop, etc. The next time I went away I got more phone calls, until it seemed as if the receiver and my ear were joining forces. To minimize these lengthy phone conversations, I began to type up, at first in outline form, whatever suggestions I had to make. Then, when I got the phone call, I had only to mail out my notes.

Pretty soon I had a stack of memos, which were being sent out to various people at various times. I began getting requests for them from people I didn't even know. After about five years of this, my husband suggested that I compile all the notes and have them published.

One thing about travel books—they take constant updating. I do that on a regular basis, but it's an impossible job for one person. This book is an orderly compilation of updated information from my travels. I hope you will enjoy reading it and using it as much as I have enjoyed the research and thousands of miles of traveling it took to write it.

To quote the title of one of my favorite movies, and "Now Voyager. . . ."

Impressions
and
Attitudes

There are some things that a traveler should not be without, but which cannot be packed in a suitcase. I'm referring to a good, kind, positive attitude, openness to people and situations of every kind, patience to get through trying moments, and a desire to return home enriched both intellectually and spiritually. Of course, if you're going to Hawaii or the Bahamas for three or four days of R&R, all this sounds very high blown, but the basic idea is applicable in almost all travel situations.

There are a few kinds of travelers that really drive me up the wall. One of them is the person who becomes irritated or even incensed that everything is not just as it is "at home." This person complains about almost everything, but mainly about customs that are foreign to him yet probably have been part of the visited country for hundreds of years. My advice is: if you want things to be just as they are at home, then stay home. If you travel abroad, then enjoy and take delight in those things that make a foreign country "foreign." Maybe you'll even decide its customs or system are better than yours.

Another pet peeve of mine is those people who have preconceived and unsubstantiated ideas about people and places they've never seen. They also tend to blame an entire nation of people for an incident or a political philosophy of a very few. How many times have you heard someone say something like, "Well, I wouldn't go there; I hear they treat Americans badly." Hearsay never stands up in court! Just because someone you know, or maybe only heard about, had a bad experience in India, don't cross India off your list. What you don't know, and may never find out, is what that person may have done to cause his own discomfort—often the reason people have unsatisfactory experiences with others. The best example I can give is the French: they have been bad-mouthed for years. I had to stop getting into arguments about it because I was going to give myself a heart attack. Most of the people who tell me how "bad" the French are have never been to France, or were there twenty years ago for a few hours, or have an uncle who had something negative happen, etc. I have been traveling to France on a regular basis for over fifteen years, and I have actually gone out of my way to notice any negative "attitude" or hostility toward Americans—or anyone else, for that matter. I've never seen it. People will argue that it's because I speak French, yet I know many who speak no French, or just a few words, who return from France totally enamored with the country *and* the people. Don't close yourself off or deny yourself the opportunity to have a really wonderful time, in any country or city, based on hearsay. One person's experience will not be the same as another's.

I almost never let politics enter into my decision as to where to go. If I did that, I'd never be able to go anywhere. There are some who cannot keep from letting the political philosophy of a few tinge their idea of a nation of people as a whole. The more I travel, the more I realize that people are people, no matter where they are, no matter what their government is saying or doing, no matter how rich, poor, or different they are. Everyone basically is trying to survive, get through the day, provide for their families, be healthy and happy, and find a little peace in life. Not everyone is out to "get" you or to "take" you. Most citizens of a foreign country are delighted to meet you, help you, speak with you (even if you don't speak the same language), laugh with you, and be gracious hosts. You must be a gracious visitor. You are an ambassador for the United States, for Americans, for Iowans, for the people in your town. It's your job to give a good impression, to pave the way for other Americans later. This can all be done naturally and simply, without any premeditation or conscious planning. Just be open, pleasant, understanding, gracious. It's amazing what one smile can do.

Those travelers who want everything to be just like it is at home, those who already dislike the Portuguese before ever getting to Portugal, those who complain about every small inconvenience: these are the ones I call the Ugly Americans. UA's, unfortunately, are everywhere. You can hear them coming, because they speak in loud voices; they will actually shout at the Italian who doesn't speak English, thinking that by shouting, they will be understood. UA's sometimes wear preposterous outfits; there's no way they're going to blend in with the crowd! UA's often travel in groups; if you're going to be obnoxious, there's safety in numbers. UA's make absolutely no effort to understand anything about a country, not even the monetary system (if you can count from one to ten, you can understand any monetary system; it only takes about ten minutes on the plane to figure it out). UA's are pushy, rude, undignified, and hazards to be avoided at all costs. There are also UJ's, UG's, UF's, UR's: every country has them. Don't be on the list. Don't believe anything they have to say; go in the other direction.

Try not to act like a tourist.

You only have one chance to make a first impression.

Do's, Don't's
and
Other Hot Tips

Handbags, Pockets, and Pickers Thereof

We all know what a good, sturdy travel purse is. Short, strong strap. Zipper on top. Something you can tuck under your arm with a death grip. But what about what you put *in* that great purse? Your best friend just gave you, as a going-away present, this handy all-purpose wallet: it holds all your money, credit cards, checkbook, traveler's checks, and passport. That's great for pickpockets—they can get it all in one neat grab. In fact, I think the Pickpocket Union manufactures those kinds of wallets. Diversify. Put all those things in separate places. Put your money in two or three places. Men, spread it out among all your pockets. Maybe they'll get it anyway, but why make it easy?

Suitable Suitcases

Now you have decided to get some cheap, tacky luggage, so the thiefs at the airport or the train station will take one look at it and decide it's not worth lifting. Wrong. The quality of your luggage doesn't seem to make any difference, according to the latest survey. Do something to your luggage, whether it's from Gucci or Sears, to make it stand out. Put a big, bright luggage strap all the way around it, one you can see a mile away. Also, don't let your bags out of your sight until you absolutely have to. Don't leave them sitting on a curb, unwatched, at the airport or in front of a hotel. Watch until all your bags are tagged; be sure it's with the correct tag. By all means *lock* your suitcase with a good, strong lock. Cheap ones are a joke.

Never pack money, credit cards, jewelry, or address books. Put these items in your hand luggage. Label your suitcases inside and outside with a business address or just a phone number.

Is There Any Weather?

What's the weather where you're going? Look in the weather section of your local paper every day for two weeks before you leave to see what the weather pattern is for the area where you will be traveling. That way you will get a pretty good idea of what's in store. Spot checks a day ahead can be misleading. And always pack an umbrella.

Copycats

Take your plane tickets, passport, credit cards, driver's license, and any other important documents that you are planning to travel with to a copy shop and make three copies of each item. Take one with you, give one to your traveling companion, and leave one at home where it can easily be found. If you lose or are robbed of any of those items, it will be much easier and quicker to get them replaced.

Take two extra passport photos. Do not keep any of the above in the same place as the originals.

Serially Speaking

Before you leave, go to the airport (or provide extra time for this at the time you take off) and register with customs anything that you are taking with you that has a serial number: wristwatches, cameras, clocks, lenses, tape recorders, etc. If you are taking good jewelry along, take a copy of a jeweler's appraisal, or the original sales receipt. When you re-enter the country and have these papers to show the customs people, you will not run the risk of getting nailed for paying duty on them. If you call a U.S. Customs office someone can tell you exactly where you have to go. It usually doesn't take very long.

Do-It-Yourself vs. Packaged Tours

I'm from the Do-It-Yourself School of Travel, whenever possible. I like the freedom of being able to choose where I go and when and how, what hotel I stay in and in which room, where I eat, with whom, when, and what. It takes a lot more work to travel on your own; it also costs more. When a professional guide is needed, I engage one through a local agency in the city or country in which I am traveling. So far I've been lucky and ended up with terrific guides, some of whom have become friends and pen pals. Naturally, my advice is: if possible, do your own thing.

Packaged tours have some advantages, I admit. You don't have to hassle with your own luggage, getting in and out of airports or around town. You don't have to think about where you're going to eat or make any reservations. Often you don't even have to decide what to eat, because you are not shown a menu and have to eat whatever it is that is presented to you. You don't have to decide what time to get up in the morning; you don't need to know much of the language; you don't need a map of the city streets; and there's always someone around to tell you what you're seeing, what to do, and when to do it. In some cases, you don't even have to think about where to shop, as you are herded into stores that are expecting you. OK. I admit, I am negative on the subject. Plusses are: packaged tours cost less than do-it-yourself trips. And if they are well organized and have a good guide, things will go smoothly and you will learn a lot without working too hard.

There are a few things to look for when booking a prepaid tour. How many people are in the tour? How many days do you get to spend in each place? How many "free" days or hours do you get? What are the hotels like? (There's often a gigantic difference between first-class hotels and deluxe hotels. Some first-class hotels aren't so first class.) Do you have any meals on your own? What are the credentials of the tour guide? How long has the tour company been in business? Is it possible to speak with more than one person who has taken the same tour? Do you get what you pay for?

There are some places that it pays to go on a tour: some Third World countries where traveling alone is tedious, if not dangerous. Safaris. Places like India, China, the Antarctic. I took an art history tour of Egypt (through the Los Angeles County Museum), and it was excellent. I never would have been able to see some of the sites I saw had I been on my own. There were thirty people in the tour, and that was enough. Twenty or less would have been better.

The quality of your experience is the bottom line. You have to do a little research and some serious thinking to make up your mind if you'll get that quality with a group tour or on your own. Each trip or case is a different story.

23 Days, 29 Cities

If you don't get anything else from this book, please get this point: don't try to do too much in too short a period of time. The worst mistake people make is trying to see everything in a week. Can't be done. You end up not remembering what you saw, where you saw it, what you ate, how it tasted, etc. You end up exhausted. You may think you'll never be in a particular country again in your life, so you better make this one shot count and go everywhere. Bad idea. If you go to Italy and you really like what you see in one or two cities, what's to keep you from going back and seeing more one day?

If you have two weeks and are going to Europe for the first time, forget about seeing London, Paris, Rome, and Madrid. See London and Paris, or Paris and Rome, or Paris, Rome, and Venice. Spend at least four nights in each of the main cities; that is the absolute minimum—a week is better. If you want to see countryside, do a day trip out of a major city.

If you have all the time in the world, you've got no problem; but how many of us can do open-ended traveling?

Another thing to think about, if you're driving yourself, is that it always takes longer than you think to get from point A to point B. The highways in Europe might be fabulous, but looking at a map and calculating distances doesn't take into account such things as cows on the road, stops at roadside stands, traffic jams in small towns, car troubles, and a million other things. One of the advantages of driving yourself is having the freedom and time to explore, go off the beaten track, follow your nose, get lost. Getting lost can be a great experience. That reminds me of one other thing: take the time to get off the freeways, autoroutes, and superhighways, especially in Europe. Whenever possible, follow the "scenic route," the small, country roads. Remember, it's quality, not quantity, which makes or breaks a trip.

Dr. Scholl, I Presume?

You have to travel with your feet, no matter how they feel. Without them, you're lost. Be nice to your feet; take good care of them. Don't expect them to carry you all over London or New York City if they are encased in a swell-looking but uncomfortable boot with a high heel. Finding comfortable walking shoes (the kind that can withstand four or five hours of use each day, on all kinds of surfaces) that are stylish and look good with your outfits is no easy job, but it's not impossible. Don't leave this crucial part of your travel wardrobe until the last minute. Take two pairs of walking shoes to trade off.

The Clothes Horse Syndrome

We all know how great you look in your gold jewelry and designer clothes, but leave most of them at home. Of course you want a certain number of nice things to knock 'em dead with here and there, but basically for sightseeing and doing the regular tourist things your best bet is to blend in. Think about taking comfortable, blend-in kinds of clothes. These days it isn't always a good idea to stand out in a crowd, whether at home or in a foreign country. Try not to *look* like a tourist.

Counting Calories

Go on your diet before and after, but not during your trip. Lose a few pounds before the plane ever takes off, and you can enjoy stuffing yourself all the more while you're away. It's my theory that a happy traveler is one who gains at least five pounds on a trip: that person has eaten and enjoyed. I always go for the extra piece of country bread, the ice cream cone about 4:00 P.M., the irresistible dessert, etc. Remember, once you're home, it's too late to sample all those goodies you passed up. Ah, but what about the guilt? Guilt schmilt. Have a good time. You'll walk off a lot of what you eat, anyway (unless you're on a cruise; then you could be in trouble). If you are on a trip lasting more than two weeks, you'll have to start watching it sooner or later, or you may have to fly home in your bathrobe. Always pack a pair of slacks that are too big; they'll probably fit fine by the time you go home.

Information, Please

I am going to say my piece about learning some of the language in a page or so. It wouldn't hurt to learn something, anything, about where you're going. History, culture, art, architecture—the basics. Even if you're going on a guided tour with a genius as a guide, know something before you go. Surprise him or her. Do you know how monotonous it is leading people around and explaining to them all sorts of things about what they're looking at, and seeing only blank faces staring back at you? Even if you don't want to know for yourself, give the tour guide a thrill. For one thing, it'll keep him or her on his or her toes if he or she thinks you have half a brain.

The Traveling Packrat

I always advise packing light, but I never practice what I preach and I'm always sorry. The less you can take, the better. If you need something that you left behind, you can always buy it when you get there. There are a few items you can take with you that don't take up too much space which can make your trip a lot easier:

An extension cord.   You'll be amazed at how handy this comes in. Most foreign hotels aren't equipped to handle anything stronger than an electric razor in the bathroom. That means if you want to use a hair dryer, electric rollers, or a curling iron, you have to use the socket behind a lamp or TV, and you find yourself on your knees in a dark corner with no mirror to do your hair. With an extension cord you will avoid this inconvenience. If you travel often in Europe, buy a cord there, as it will fit in all the plugs without an adapter; the adapter will fit in the end of the cord which doesn't go into the wall, and that's easier, too.

Adapters and converters.   Don't leave home without them. You never know when you're going to need them.

Flashlight.   Buy a very small one and throw it in, along with extra batteries. You'll do less stumbling around in the middle of the night in strange rooms.

Batteries.   Pack extra ones to fit your travel clock, camera, flashlight, flash attachment, calculator, etc. Batteries have a habit of wearing out at just the wrong moment; sometimes it's hard to find the right size in a foreign country, and they often cost more.

Crazy glue.   Traveling is hard on your fingernails, even though you don't have to do the dishes. Things break. A little container of crazy glue can be a lifesaver.

A deck of cards.   You never know when a one-hour layover will turn into a six-hour layover!

Pocket calculator.   Needs no explanation. The metric converting calculators are really great; but be sure you get one programmed for currency conversion.

Sewing kit, scissors, and buttons.   Naturally.

The portable desk.   Take along a few rubber bands, some paper clips, safety pins, a small pencil sharpener, a couple of extra pens, and a few yards of heavy twine. These take up no space and come in very handy.

Dear Abby.   If you are a heavy postcard writer, you can save a lot of time and monotony by taking along pre-addressed labels, the kind you peel off and stick on. This doesn't mean you won't also need your small, travel address book (which goes in your hand luggage, not your suitcase).

Taking notes.   Always carry a small spiral notebook on you. Jot down addresses, shops, good things you eat and where you eat them, places *not* to go again, places you visit. This doesn't mean you have to keep some fancy diary. Your notes will be of great value to you when you get home, especially if you're weeding through five hundred slides and can't remember where some were taken. You'll also be able to give more accurate advice to friends who are going next year.

Passing the bucks.   Go to the bank and get about 25 dollars in $1 bills; 50 dollars' worth, if you're going to a Third World country. They are really great for using as tips. I've never been anywhere where the American dollar wasn't more popular than the resident currency.

Rip van Winkling.   One of the most crucial things you need on a trip is your sleep. Take earplugs, eye blinders, and sleeping pills. Also take your travel clock with alarm, because you don't want to sleep through the whole trip.

Traveling medicine show.   Pack any prescriptions or medications you think you might need. This includes Band-Aids, aspirin, lip balm, vitamins, dental floss, antibacterial ointment, antacid, nasal spray, etc.

Singin' in the rain.   Always, but always, pack an umbrella.

Florence Chadwick fan club.   Pack a bathing suit, every time. Even if you are going to the North Pole. You never know when you'll run into an indoor swimming pool or a communal Jacuzzi.

The extra bag.   If you're a shopaholic like I am pack at least one, if not two, collapsible bags. There are some great ones on the market in all sizes. If you unroll them, they pack flatter. Even if you hate to shop, take one anyway. Conversions happen all the time . . .

The library.   Naturally, you would not go any place you'd never been without some sort of guidebook. So far, I've never found the all-inclusive book, which means you'll probably have to take more than one. If that gets too bulky, copy only the pages in the book that you think you will need. Then you can scribble on them as you go along, or throw them out as you finish with them. Take along any notes you may have made in advance, plus addresses and phone numbers. Get your hands on a map of the city streets (you usually obtain these after you arrive). If you read articles about a place, take notes, instead of the whole article. Talk to people who have recently traveled to the country where you are going; their advice can be of great value. Be careful with restaurant recommendations: know the person who's giving them! Someone who only eats dandelion fuzz and frogs' elbows isn't going to be much of an authority on a gourmet meal in Malaga. Restaurant tips from cab drivers generally don't pay off: they usually don't frequent the kinds of places you do and their tastes can be very different. Restaurant tips from hotel personnel can be good or not good: if their brother or second cousin owns a place down the block, they'll send you there, whether it's good or not (often there's a kickback involved). The more research you do and the more notes you have to compare, the better your chances are of having a great dinner, staying in the kind of hotel you really like, and seeing the places that matter to you. Even if five guidebooks in a row recommend the same restaurant, it doesn't mean it's the best one.

Some of my favorite travel readings are: *Gourmet* magazine; *Travel & Leisure* magazine (American Express); Voyager International, a newsletter, (Argonaut Enterprises, Inc., P.O. Box 2777, Westport, Ct. 06880); Passport newsletter (20 N. Wacker Drive, Chicago, Ill. 60606); World Status Map (Box 466, Merrifield, Va. 22116); La Belle France (1835 University Circle,

Charlottesville, Va. 22903); *Gault-Millau Le Nouveau Guide* magazine (31 cours des Juilliottes, 94704 Maisons-Alfort, France).

Plan Ahead

Whenever possible, make advance reservations for restaurants, special tours, operas, or plays, etc., as well as for your hotels. The really popular and well-known eateries are hard to get into at the last minute (a little bribe never hurts). If you don't like being locked into a schedule, you can still make the reservations and cancel when you get there. The concierge can take care of a lot of this for you, once you arrive. Your travel agent can usually dig up addresses for you before you depart, so you can write ahead. Be reserved.

Say Cheese: Photographers Unbound

Do you want to see England while you're in England, or do you want to see it when you get home on slides, videotape, or in 1,645 photos? Taking pictures is a good idea, providing it does not become all-consuming. Keep your photographer's trigger finger and equipment list in check, or you'll spend more time fooling with lenses and meters than you will enjoying the sights. Besides, once you see your pictures a couple of times, they'll end up at the back of the closet, rarely to be seen again. It's amazing how many people really *don't* want to see your home movies, even though they say they do.

Speaking
for
Yourself

You will probably get sick and tired of this subject as you go through this book, because I never let up on it. The subject is: foreign language. It doesn't take a rocket scientist to figure out that it's easier to travel through France if you speak French, or Greenland if you speak Greenlandise, or Mars if you speak Martian. (I really don't know what they speak in Greenland, but if I ever go there, I'll find out and learn some of it in advance. As for Mars, I'm not worried yet.) The point is: if you're going to go to all the trouble and expense to travel beyond the borders of your own country, then save a little more time and money to learn some of the words of the country being visited. Usually you need more time and less expense, and I know how busy you all are. If you have a cassette tape deck in your car, you have no more excuses.

Excuse Number One will be: if one is taking a package tour, complete with guides and translators, why should one bother to learn anything about the foreign language? Response: are you planning to spend every waking moment with this guide? Is this guide going to order a glass of water for you if you want one? What are you going to do if the phone in your room rings at 6:00 A.M. and the guide is two floors up and in another wing? What will you do if a strange person stops you on the street and says something to you in an excited voice? I guarantee you that even if you travel with a group, or one-on-one with a private guide, you are going to wish, somewhere along the way, that you knew how to say something.

I am not proposing that you become fluent in Italian if you are going to travel there for a few days; that's just silly. It will be of enormous help, not to mention fun, if you know a few words of Italian. I propose that

Speaking for Yourself

anyone can get by in any country with a passing knowledge of fifty words or less. That's not so many words to learn; you can do it while you clean up the dishes every night. You have to learn the right fifty words, though. I mean, you don't really have to know how to say things like aardvark, naval jelly, or vim. Here's a list of words that will come in handy (trust me): *hello; goodbye; good evening; good night; where is . . .?; how much is this?; my name is . . .; right; left; straight ahead; restaurant; hotel; telephone; the bill; waiter; please; thank you; yes; no; American; United States; I don't know; I don't understand; I speak English; help; I would like . . .; bathroom; taxi; passport; suitcase; arrival; departure; change; I'm sorry* or *excuse me; hot; cold; exit; entrance; good; bad; nice; pretty; delicious;* some numbers.

Of course, the best way to learn a foreign language is in a language class, of which there are many kinds. If you have the time and can afford it, go to a language school and take one-on-one lessons for a couple of weeks or more before your trip. If you don't want to or can't do it that way, go to a bookstore and buy one of several different language cassettes designed for travelers. They are inexpensive, and if you spend just a little time with them, you will learn something. I promise.

There are a couple more reasons for learning some of the language, other than making it easier on yourself when traveling. First, you will have a lot more fun. You will be more confident about striking out on your own, even for a short afternoon shopping trip. You will be able to get the gist of what someone might be saying to you, and therefore be able to respond, even if it's mostly by sign language and pointing. Most of all, you will create much goodwill and positive feeling wherever you go. You cannot believe how a waiter's eyes will light up the minute you attempt to say something to him in his own language, even if it's just a simple "thank you," pronounced all wrong. They just love it! Don't worry about mispronouncing the words: it's the thought that counts. (No, it is absolutely not true that the French will get insulted and/or be insulting if you stammer away in bad French. Ninety-nine out of a hundred will smile and help you say what you want to say.)

I believe it was Mr. Berlitz who said that a traveler can get by knowing only twelve words. Maybe he's right. Twelve are better than none. Do yourself a favor and make the effort; you won't be sorry.

The Best

Best dinner in Europe: Villa Lorraine, Brussels

Best airlines: Air France, First Class
               Air France Concorde
               Lufthansa
               Pan Am
               Regent Air

Best ice cream cones: Gelateria via Flaminia, Martinez, Argentina

Best lunch in Mexico: San Angel Inn, Mexico City

Best handbag store: Fine and Klein, New York City

Best chocolate truffles: Fauchon, Paris

Best place for breakfast in Mojave, California: French's

Best restaurants for skiers in Utah: Café Mariposa, Deer Valley; La Caille, Little Cottonwood Canyon

Most sumptuous portions of delicious food: Chez l'Ami Louis, Paris

Best small museum west of the Mississippi: J. Paul Getty Museum, Malibu

Best small museum east of the Mississippi: The Frick, New York City

Best museum for kids: The Air and Space Museum, Washington, D.C.

Best city transportation: The Paris Metro

Best macarons au chocolate: Carette Tearoom, Paris

Best hot apple tarte tatin: Auberge du Petit Val, near Giverny, France

Best packaged cookie: Delice-Choc, France

Best barbecue (churrasca): Anywhere in Brazil

Best airport: Charles de Gaulle, Paris

Highest, lightest soufflé: Dodin Bouffant, Paris

Best croissants outside of France: Vie de France, Santa Monica, California

Best almond croissant: Ludree, Paris

Best all-around shopping street in New York City: Madison Avenue between 60th and 86th streets

Best hamburger in Montana: The Grizzly Bar on the Madison River

Best language school in Los Angeles: Alouette Language Service, Santa Monica

Best hotel suite in southeast Asia: The Oriental Suite at the Oriental Hotel, Bangkok, Thailand

Easiest-to-read guidebooks: Green *Michelin* series

Best chocolate mousse: Chez les Anges, Paris

Best hot fudge Sundae: Serendipity, New York City

Best tropical paradise: Bora-Bora, Tahiti
            RUNNER-UP: Mana Island, Fiji

Best dessert menu for chocoholics: Chantecler Restaurant, Hotel Negresco, Nice, France

Best way to see a new city: walk

Best place to buy shirts: Alain Figaret, Paris

Cushiest ski resort: Deer Valley, Utah

Best ice cream in Rome: Giolotti's

Best ice cream in Paris: Berthillon

Best chinese food in Los Angeles: Chinois on Main, Venice, California

Best hamburger in Paris (if you must): Room service at the Concorde Lafayette Hotel

Best duckling: A tie between Villa Lorraine, Brussels and Alain Senderens-Lucas Carton, Paris (it's called Canard Apicuis, for two persons)

Paris
AND
Beyond

Paris

If I start telling you about how much I love Paris, we'll be here for days. One reason I haven't seen much of the rest of Europe is that I always go to Paris; I can't stay away. I think I must have been born with a metro ticket in one hand and a Michelin guide in the other.

"Why, oh why, do I love Paris?" It is without a doubt the most beautiful city in the world. Paris is romantic. Lovers smooching everywhere are a common sight. The cuisine is outstanding, even in the smallest, most inexpensive neighborhood bistro. Architecturally, historically, and artistically, it is never disappointing. The shopping is fantastic. And the people of Paris, bad-mouthed and maligned by so many who have never been there, are among the most gracious, helpful, and charming I have ever met. More and more, especially in the past two years, I have been hearing this from visitors, even if they don't speak French. The air is generally crisp and clean (I have rarely encountered smog), but you must always be prepared for rain.

What about speaking French? I have long maintained that not knowing the language is a terrible excuse for avoiding a place. Besides, it's no big deal to pick up a few of the basic words before you go. Everyone knows a little French already, n'est-ce pas? Don't be bashful or nervous about using whatever French you know, no matter how little. Smile and give it all you've got, and you'll probably be hard-pressed to find a Parisian who will not do his or her best to understand and help you.

I have been to Paris so many times that I've stopped counting. When I'm there, I feel as if I live there, and I guess I look like it, too, because I am constantly being stopped on the street and asked directions, even by Parisians. I love it. Living in Paris is a lot of fun. One of these days you'll have to call me long-distance if you want to reach me, because I'll be living there again.

So much for my love affair with Paris. Now let's get to some details.

A City For All Seasons

Question: When should you go to Paris? Answer: As soon as you can get there. Actually, as with all places, there are better times to go than others. I wouldn't want to be in Paris in August (hot and crowded), or January, February, March, and most of April (too cold). December would also be cold, but then you have the magic of Christmas to keep you warm. May and June are wonderful because spring is doing her thing, and even though you can still hit some very cold, soggy weather, there are flowers and blooming trees and some nice days. July can be hot and muggy, although one July when I was there, it poured every day and was very cold. September and October are gorgeous! The weather is warm and even balmy during the day, a bit crisp at night, and all the foliage turns to compete with an artist's palette. As I mentioned before, you should always be prepared for rain.

Tennis Shoes, Anyone?
"La vie est trop courte pour s'habiller triste."

What kind of clothes should you take to Paris? If you are from Southern California, you'll have to dress up a little more than you're used to, just for day-to-day sightseeing. You'll see people dressed in all kinds of things from tacky to chic, but Paris is a city where you want to look and feel chic. Compare it to San Francisco or New York. Most Parisians are well dressed, even when just going to the park or doing some shopping. That's one thing I've always admired about the French women—they always look terrific. That doesn't mean that they spend a lot of money on huge couturier wardrobes. Quite the opposite, in fact. They know how to put an outfit together and look as if they just stepped out of *Vogue* magazine, using a few well-chosen garments. Accessories are a big key to their success—knowing which ones to use and how to use them. A simple silk scarf draped a certain way can make all the difference. You don't have to rush out and buy a suitcase full of new clothes to go to Paris. Leave the blue jeans, tennis shoes, prairie skirts, and polyester pantsuits at home. Men should forget about plaid bermuda shorts, Hawaiian shirts, golf or fishing caps, etc. It happens to be true that you're likely to be treated better by shopkeepers and waiters if you're nicely dressed, but that's true wherever you may go. Someone once said something to the effect that life is too short to dress poorly. As for kids, they can get away with jeans and shorts during the day but should have something nicer for restaurants. If you really cannot decide what to take, take nothing and buy it all there. Shopping for clothes in Paris is one of the most fun things to do, and the clothes you buy there (and in Italy) will last you for years, stylistically. For daytime wear, be comfortable. Wear layers that can be peeled according to changes in weather. Above all—and I cannot emphasize this enough—take comfortable walking shoes! At least two pairs for trading off. Forget your chic high-heeled snake boots, except for going out to dinner. Walking in Paris and in most European cities is not easy. The streets are often cobbled, slippery when wet, torn up for repairs, with narrow sidewalks. Many museums and public buildings have hard marble floors. The parks have dirt, sand, and gravel. You'll encounter more stairs than you're used to, and you'll be walking more than you ever do at home. Be prepared! Remember: you want to blend in, not stand out.

Books

As for guidebooks, you'll need more than one. Of course, you'll have this book for starters, but you also must have the green *Michelin guide for Paris*. The Michelin people are very thorough about small details regarding museum hours, prices of admission, walking tours, etc., plus they offer some historical background. Along with that, you should have the blue *Michelin Paris Index Plan,* which shows even the tiniest alley. The thin, red, paperback *Michelin Paris and Environs: Hotels and Restaurants* book is a help for cross-checking references (you may have to pick this one up when you get to Paris). My favorite all-around book is the Gault-Millau *Le Guide de Paris* in French, or the English edition *The Best of Paris.* If you really want to know what you're eating, *The Taste of France* by Fay Sharman and Klaus Boehm (Houghton Mifflin, Boston, 1982) is a must. If you can't get it in your local bookstore, try specialty gourmet shops, or special-order it. Another food and wine dictionary which is not as complete but can nevertheless be helpful is the *Marling Menu-Master for France.* It's a small, pocket-sized book, and hard to find. The Berlitz *French for Travellers* is a handy, pocket-sized French-English phrase book, but also includes helpful travel hints. A small French-English dictionary, again pocket-sized, would also be useful if you are not fluent in the language. A wonderful book is *DuMont Guide to Paris and the Ile de France* by Klaus Bussmann. It's all about art, architecture, and history, beautifully organized and written. *The Food Lover's Guide to Paris* by Patricia Wells is fabulous.

To or From the Airports

You'll probably arrive in Paris at Charles de Gaulle Airport, especially if you're coming from the United States. You might be thinking about taking the airport bus from the airport into the city, if you are traveling on a budget. Forget it. By the time you take the bus, transfer to a cab, and get to your hotel, you've spent almost the same amount of money as for a cab, not to mention a lot of extra time. The cab fare from the airport to your hotel in central Paris should cost about 20 dollars including tips and luggage fees. If they hit you up for 30 dollars or more, you're probably being ripped off. Make sure you get a metered cab, and act as if you know where you're going, even if you don't. A lot of times it looks as if you're being given the "drive-around," but remember that many streets are one-way, and during peak traffic hours it is often faster to take a few back streets than the main drag.

If you arrive at the Orly airport, you may want to consider the bus, because the Orly bus goes to a different terminal than the Charles de Gaulle bus, and getting a cab is easier when you arrive. Your decision will probably be based on the amount of luggage you have, how tired you are, and if you're on a budget. Most cabs will only take three people. The drive from either airport into Paris takes about thirty minutes.

Francs and Dollars

Money, money, money . . . At the time of this writing, the poor French franc is worth less than 11 cents and still sinking (the exchange is 9 francs to the dollar). This is fabulous for the American traveler. Five years ago we were exchanging less than 4 francs to the dollar. But, you're mumbling, they probably upped all the prices. Not so. Prices in France will probably continue to be a bargain until the 1986 elections, so go and enjoy it while you can. When you exchange money in France, try *not* to do it at your hotel, an exchange bureau, or at the American Express office. Your best bet for a good rate of exchange will be at a normal French bank. Locate one near your hotel and compare exchange rates at several places before you change a lot of money. The exchange bureaus generally give lower rates than the banks, plus charge a fee. The hotels give the worst. American Express is sometimes good, but the last time I was in Paris, their rate of exchange was not as good as at a little bank I found around the corner. You may be charged a 1 percent fee for cashing traveler's checks, and you will get a slightly lower rate for cash. If you run out of francs while shopping, most storekeepers will take your traveler's checks, but often the rate will not be as good as the bank's. No matter where you are shopping, there is probably a bank nearby that you can run to. If you use a credit card, you will be charged the going rate for the day the charge arrives at your bank, which may or may not be to your advantage. Take along a small pocket or watch calculator. Don't cash huge amounts of money at one time. It's better to go several times and change smaller amounts (unless you feel the franc is going to zoom up for some reason). Be careful about weekends and holidays: plan in advance to have the cash to see you through. Otherwise you'll be stuck using the hotel cashier. (By the way, this advice goes for any country you're in.)

At the moment, VISA (Carte Bleu) and American Express are the two most widely accepted out-of-the-country credit cards. Some stores accept MasterCard. By the way, some stores and restaurants do not like to accept American Express because its discount rates are higher than other cards'.

The Detaxe

The *detaxe*: take advantage of it. You can save a lot of money. There is a tax (the TVA) put on all goods, including food purchased in restaurants, that everyone must pay. But as a foreigner you are entitled to get it back, if you follow the proper rules. The rebate, or *detaxe*, is anywhere from 15 to 25 percent (it seems to vary for reasons unknown to me). Note: you only get the *detaxe* on items you take out of the country.

1 • You must spend at least 800 francs (about 100 dollars) in one place before you can get the *detaxe* forms. This can be done on separate days; just keep all your receipts until you are done shopping in one place.

2 • Ask the merchant to fill out the *detaxe,* s'il vous plaît. Often they will offer, but sometimes you have to ask. They should all be prepared to take the time to do it. They will fill out one part of the triplicate form, and you will have to fill out the other part. Please note: you must know the name and address of your bank at home, plus the account number, so have this information with you. The merchant will give you a pink and green copy, plus a self-addressed, stamped envelope. You must have all of these to get your rebate.

3 • If you are shipping an item home, you cannot do the *detaxe* at the airport. However, the merchant should automatically take the tax off the top of the price you pay, so make sure he does that. (Remember, you have to spend about 100 dollars first.)

4 • Some stores will give you the *detaxe* right on the spot, but you still must take the form to the customs agent at the airport to have it stamped, or the merchant will get stuck for the tax. They may want to run the amount of the *detaxe* onto a credit card slip; then if you fail to get the form stamped, your credit card account will be charged for the amount. That's fair enough.

5 • Allow about an hour extra at the airport. Sometimes it takes less than that, but you want to be on the safe side. The last time I was there it took five minutes. Look for the sign that says "Customs," "Douane," or "Detaxe." There will probably be a line. A big sign is printed in English and French, explaining the procedure. On the sign it says that you *must* have the items that you purchased to show to the customs officer. I *never* had to show anything, until recently. They are getting fussy now about seeing what you bought, so if you have the time, do the *detaxe* before you check in. Otherwise, you may be "refused," as they say. You probably won't have to unpack your suitcase, just point to it, but just in case, keep the items you are declaring near the top of the pile. You should have, in addition to all your little pink and green forms and envelopes, your passport and plane tickets handy.

6 • After the official stamps the forms, he hands them back to you and you move out of the way and go sit down somewhere where you can concentrate. You keep the green form. You mail the pink form in your envelope. Don't put the wrong form in the wrong envelope! Mail them right there at the airport (the mailbox is usually next to the *detaxe* counter). Some customs officials will mail the pink forms for you.

7 • Within approximately three months, your bank or credit card account should be credited with your various rebates, depending on the speed of the shopkeepers.

8 • If you are leaving France by train, you can do the whole thing on the train. When the customs officer passes through the car to look at your passport, show your *detaxe* forms and ask him to take care of it. He probably won't offer, so be sure to ask. Once you leave France, it's too late.

9 • What a big hassle, you're grumbling to yourself. Well, it is and it isn't. It depends on your time, patience, and the crowds. It's certainly nice mentally to deduct 15 to 25 percent off all the items you see in shop windows, and it's even nicer when your bank sends you a letter informing you of your credit from France.

I understand there are similar rebates and procedures in England, Germany, Austria, Belgium, Denmark, Finland, Italy, Ireland, the Netherlands, Norway, Spain, Sweden, and Switzerland.

Transportation

How do you get around in Paris? Most tourists I know, at least the first time over, take cabs everywhere. Tsk-tsk. First of all, figure out how far it is from your hotel, or wherever you are, to your destination, and if it's a mile or less, walk it! Walk everywhere. The best way to see Paris (or any city) is to walk. I am totally opposed to cabs, except for going out at night, going to and from the airport, or if you are suffering from extreme exhaustion or your feet have turned to stubs. If it's too far to walk, or too rainy, take the metro. Absolutely you must learn to ride the metro. Not only will it save you tons of money and hours of time, but it is a lot of fun. The Paris metro system is the best in the world and will be your best friend in Paris. If you're traveling with a few friends, buy a *carnet*—a book of ten tickets. Then you'll always have them on hand and won't have to wait in line each time you want to ride the metro. Keep some tickets handy in a pocket. Don't bury them in the bottom of your purse; it's a hassle to dig them out and you'll be fair target for pickpockets.

It may take you a few times to get the hang of reading the maps and getting on the right trains. Figure out where you're starting from, where you want to go, and route yourself with the fewest number of changes *(correspondences)*. The signs in the stations are all according to the final destinations on a line, not according to the number of the line. For example, the main line running east and west through Paris, along the Champs-Elysées and the Tuileries, is the Pont de Neuilly–Château de Vincennes line (the end in each direction). If you are at the Place de la Concorde and want to go to the Louvre, you will be traveling east, or toward Château de Vincennes, so when you get into the station, follow the signs to that end. Along the way, on the wall, you will find all the stops listed. (By the way, the best stop to go to the Louvre is not the Louvre stop, but the Palais Royal stop.) Let's pretend you are again at Place de la Concorde and want to go to the Marmatton Museum (Muette metro stop). You'll have to change once. First, you'll take the Vincennes-Neuilly line, this time toward Pont de Neuilly (or Etoile). At Franklin D. Roosevelt, you'll get off and follow the signs to Pont de Sèvres (as this is the final stop on the line on which Muette is located). Then you'll get off at Muette. Once you get the hang of it, it's really easy. Ask for a "plan métro" at any ticket window and study it; carry it with you.

There are exceptions to every rule. Some trains go to two different final destinations, so you have to figure out which train is going to which one. In these instances, which are not many, the sign over the track will change as each train comes in, so you know where the train is going. Also, on each train, both on the outside of the car and on the inside, there will be a sign that will either change or be lit up. A perfect example of this dilemma is on the way to the Basilica of St. Denis, which I will explain when we get there.

The metro runs from 5:30 A.M. to 1:30 A.M. There are fewer trains running at night, on weekends, and on holidays, so it will take you a little longer. I don't recommend taking the metro at night if you are alone, or taking it to or from a noncentral neighborhood at night.

In some metro stations you'll see a sign which says "Cireur" which means shoeshine. The bathrooms *(toilettes)* in metro stations are usually very clean and safe. *Correspondences* means connections, and *sortie* means exit.

There are first- and second-class cars (marked with a 1 or a 2 on the outside). After 5:00 P.M. and on Sundays anyone can ride the first-class cars. Once in a long while an official will come through and check to make sure you have a first-class ticket if you are in the first-class car. If you're cheating (everyone does), you'll just have to change cars at the next stop.

The R.E.R. (Regional Express Network) consists of three lines at the moment, and is connected to the metro network. However, if you are on an R.E.R. train, it will not stop at every metro stop. It goes to only a specified few stops within the city, and then continues on to outlying areas. It's like an express. It's faster than the metro trains for this reason.

The Paris bus system is also very extensive, and many Parisians prefer it to the metro. I've never taken the time to learn the system, but if you're going to be there for any reasonable duration, it would probably be a good idea.

As for the taxis, I've already discussed using them to get to and from the airports. When using a cab to go to dinner, don't wait until the last minute to go out and find one, especially if you're in an out-of-the way area or a side street. The cabs are really busy during dinner hour and are sometimes hard to get. You can always try having your concierge call for one, but this can take time. If the doorman at your hotel isn't around, the best thing is to walk to the closest busy street and hail one. Better yet, go to a taxi stand and wait in line. A sign saying "tête de station" will tell you where the line starts—and don't try crowding in. That's a big non-non. Know the name and address of your destination and which of the arrondissements it is in (these are zones of the city). If you are at a restaurant and need a cab back to your hotel, and the restaurant is not located near or on a busy street, ask the maître d' to call you a taxi. You are generally charged for the round trip if the restaurant is out of the way. Also, the rates go up late at night, so it will cost you more to get home. You should add a tip to the fare.

A private hired car and driver is expensive, but nice. Be aware that no matter how much you pay, per hour, the chauffeur makes about $2, so tip generously.

Hotels

Whatever your budget, there is a charming room for you in Paris, be it a suite at the Ritz or a room in a small Left Bank hotel. Obviously I have not stayed in all of them, so will only comment on the ones where I have stayed or which have been given good reviews by people I trust. The prices I quote will vary according to the strength of the dollar. In all cases I would strongly suggest booking your hotel in advance, as there's nothing worse than trying to find a hotel after a thirteen-hour plane ride if you don't know the city and/or the language. You can always change hotels once you're there, if you're not satisfied. Generally a one-night deposit is required. All hotels serve breakfast *(petit déjeuner)*, which may or may not be included in the price of your room. Ask the concierge. The breakfast consists of coffee, tea, or café au lait, croissants and other breads, butter and jam. If you want anything besides that, there's an extra charge. When booking a hotel, always request a quiet room, one that is on a courtyard or a side street. Maybe you won't get it, but it doesn't hurt to ask. Also inquire about the cost of a small suite if you are staying in a small hotel. Small hotels usually mean just that: small! Or in some cases, postage-stamp-sized rooms. In many cases, a small suite is just a few dollars more than a teensy room and gives you a lot more space to move around in.

Use your concierge—that's what he or she is there for. Concierges can answer a lot of questions for you, get you tickets for plays, direct you to the metro stop or the bank, make restaurant reservations, etc. Always leave your room key with the concierge when you go out. Many concierges are seemingly curt, stuffy, or even rude. Don't be misled by this initial impression: underneath that facade there often lies a very nice person who is happy to help you, once he or she learns you aren't a pushy, obnoxious UA (Ugly American). If your concierge and/or doorman have been helpful, don't forget a nice tip when you check out.

Generally speaking, the larger, more luxurious, and expensive hotels are on the Right Bank, and the smaller, more quaint ones are on the Left. However, this is not a hard and fast rule. There are special charms about staying in the biggest, most expensive one, as well as in the family-run one located in a sixteenth-century converted house.

Right Bank

Atala,   10 rue Châteaubriand, 8e, phone 562–0162. 300–600 francs. A small hotel on a quiet street, near the Champs-Elysées. Garden, charm, good service, calm.

The Bristol,   112 Fg.-St.-Honoré, 8e, phone 266–9145. 940–2400 francs. Excellent restaurant. Great location.
This hotel is near the Place de Madeleine, and across from the President's Palace. The street it is on is *the* famous shopping street in Paris. It is a bit less lah-de-dah than the first three, and also a bit more relaxed. We had a beautiful large room, with the biggest and most luxurious bathroom I've ever encountered in any hotel (except for the Ritz). Our room, which had a large salon area, was about 200 dollars a night. Beautiful indoor swimming

pool on the top floor. Outstanding and very friendly staff. One of my very favorite hotels.

Castiglione, 40 rue Fg.-St.-Honoré, 8e, phone 265–0750. 750–800 francs.

Good location (near the Bristol) and small restaurant. Nice people. Inexpensive. I had a very small room, but it was quiet. There are better choices, but this is OK in a pinch. Nothing elegant about it, however.

The Crillon, 10 pl. de la Concorde, 8e, phone 296–1081. 1200–3600 francs. Excellent restaurant Les Ambassadeurs.

The Crillon is another "other best hotel in Paris," after the Ritz. Location: great! About a five-minute walk from the Ritz. Try to get a side-street or inner-courtyard room or suite. Recently remodeled. Slightly stuffy concierge, but the rest of the help was very friendly.

Georges V, 31 av. Georges-V, 8e, phone 723–5400. 1100–2000 francs.

This famous old hotel has "gone Arab," I've recently been told, but is still very nice. I haven't stayed there yet, and probably won't, because once again, I'm not crazy about the location. It's near the Plaza Athénée and the new, very garish Nova Parc Elysée.

Grand Hôtel, 2 rue Scribe, 9e, phone 268–1213. 700–1000 francs.

Large hotel recently renovated, good location but also noisy—right on the Place de l'Opéra. I would go for something smaller in a more quiet area.

Inter-Continental, 3 rue de Castiglione, 1er, phone 260–3780. 1000–1300 francs.

Big hotel with lots of activity, great location, a bit impersonal. Could be noisy if you were on the street.

Lancaster, 7 rue Berri, 8e, phone 359–9043. 800–1200 francs.

A popular, comfortable hotel where you're made to feel "at home." Just off the Champs-Elysées.

The Lotti, 7 rue de Castiglione, 1er, phone 260–3734. 800–1200 francs. Restaurant.

Great location: steps away from Place Vendôme. A bit more expensive than the Vendôme. I didn't stay there but met with some people who did, and they were quite happy.

The Meurice, 228 rue Rivoli, 1er, phone 260–3860. 900–1500 francs.

Recently renovated, great location, a well-known luxury hotel. Room 108 is the luxury suite. Be sure you do not get a room on the rue Rivoli.

Plaza Athénée, 25 av. Montaigne, 8e, phone 723–7833. Good restaurant (famous for lobster soufflé). 1250–3600 francs. Location: so-so.

Although the Athénée is in the same district as the Crillon, it really isn't anywhere near it. Unlike the Ritz, Crillon, and Bristol, this hotel must count its location as its main drawback. Many will argue that it's "right off the Champs-Elysées." But that's not very central. The Athénée is the big favorite of Americans, for what reasons I can't figure out. It's a beautiful hotel, to be sure, excellent service, etc., but in my opinion, for the money—go to the Crillon, the Ritz, or the Bristol.

La Pérouse, 40 rue La Pérouse, 16e, phone 800–1800. 800–950 francs.
Small luxury hotel near the Etoile, but quiet. Recently renovated. Excellent service. Small and good restaurant (l'Astrolabe). I prefer the Raphael, however.

Hotel Raphäel, 17 av. Kleber, 16e, phone 502–1600.
This is a beautiful, small and luxurious hotel about a block from the Arc de Triomphe. Reception rooms are panelled in boiseries, hung with nice paintings. My suite (room 403) was lovely, quiet and spacious with a big bathroom, for about $100 a night. Excellent service. Two drawbacks: no individual heat control in the rooms, and not a shower in the entire hotel. Small restaurant, beautiful bar.

The Regina, rue Rivolier 2 pl. des Pyradmides, 1er, phone 260–31–10. 490-1400 francs.
A lot of people know about this hotel, but no one I know has ever stayed there. It is on an extremely busy and noisy corner and you must insist on an inner room or you'll never get any sleep. The lobby is charming enough. I notice it's not recommended by Michelin, but then neither is the Vendôme, which I thought was just fine.

Residence du Bois, 16 rue Chalgrin, 16^e, phone 500–5059. 875–1000 francs.
Located about three minutes from the Arc de Triomphe, in a very nice neighborhood. This is one of Paris' best-known and most popular small hotels. Very friendly personnel, charming inner patio, small but pleasant rooms. We liked it very much except for the location.

The Ritz, 15 pl. Vendôme, 1er (meaning First Arrondissement), phone 260–3830. 1250–4500 francs. Two-star restaurant (Espadon). Location: the best.
How many times have you heard that name—the Ritz? I've read time and again over the years that the Ritz is the best hotel in Paris. I'll have to agree with that! It is exceptionally beautiful and lavish. The rooms are incredible. The most outstanding service I've ever encountered in a hotel, anywhere. Friendly personnel. We had suite 104—it was two stories, large and gorgeous, full of long-stemmed peach-colored roses when we arrived. I figured we'd taken a wrong turn and gone to heaven instead. That suite cost around 500 dollars a night. Extravagant? Yes. Worth it? Yes! Another suite, on another trip, was 700 dollars a night, and it wasn't as nice a room as #104.

Hôtel Royal Monceau, 35 av. Hoche, 8^e, phone 561–9800. 890–1500 francs. Good restaurant, especially noted for daily buffet lunches, brunch on Sundays.
This well-known old hotel is a bit out of the way for me, halfway between the Arc de Triomphe and the Parc Monceau. The neighborhood is very upper crust, however. When we were there, they were undergoing renovation and the

noise level in our room was intolerable. By now, however, all that work is done, and the hotel is most likely once again its elegant old self. For about 150 dollars a night we had a large, beautiful room on the inner courtyard. Japanese Embassy next door, so you see a lot of Japanese running around. Swimming pool and fitness club.

Scribe, rue Scribe, 9e, phone 742–0340. 800–1200 francs. Similar to Grand Hotel.

La Tremoille, 14 rue de la Tremoille, 8e, phone 723–3420. 800–1500 francs. Good restaurant.

Friends who have stayed at the Tremoille just loved it. It's owned and operated by the Athénée folks, sharing the same restaurant for room service. It's smaller, less expensive, and less chi-chi than the big brother next door. Again, I hedge on the location.

Hôtel Vendôme, 1 pl. Vendôme, 1er, phone 260–3284.

No restaurant, but breakfast included in the room price, and it is the best breakfast I've ever had in Paris, including the Ritz. A small hotel, fantastic location, less expensive, friendly staff. We had a marvelous suite full of antiques (#31–32) and we were completely happy. Our suite was about 130 dollars.

Left Bank

Hôtel Abbaye-St.-Germain, 10 rue Cassette, 6^e, phone 544–3811. 350–500 francs. Good location. No restaurant.

The hotel is housed in what was once an old abbey. The rooms are very small, but beautifully decorated. If you like quaint and cozy, this place is for you. Very popular. Breakfast. Staff can be stiff and stuffy, even rude.

Angleterre, 44 rue Jacob, 6^e, phone 260–3472. 250–400 francs. Former embassy of Great Britain. Good location. Some large rooms.

Colbert, 7 rue de l'Hôtel-Colbert, phone 325–8565. 230–600 francs. Small hotel with small rooms, but many have views of Notre Dame.

Hôtel Les Deux Iles, 59 rue St.-Louis-en-l'Ile, 4^e, phone 326–1335. 280–340 francs.

This hotel, and the next one, are not on either bank but right in the middle of the Seine, on the charming Ile St Louis. A little away from the center of things, but quiet; hospitable.

L'Hôtel, 13 rue des Beaux-Arts, 6e, phone 325–2722. 500–1600 francs.

Small, very popular hotel, very decorated. Lively bar, action, different.

Lutèce, 65 rue St.-Louis-en-l'Ile, phone 325–7976. 360–380 francs. Ditto the above.

Hôtel MontAlembert, 3 rue MontAlembert, 6e, phone 548–6811. 400–600 francs.

I have special thoughts about the MontAlembert, because it was the first hotel we ever stayed at in Paris, and we went back several times. The location couldn't be better, the staff is friendly, and the rooms are small but nicely done. But oh

—the noise! Impossible to get any sleep. If it isn't the traffic on the street, it's the churchbell next door. If not that, it's the couple on the other side of the wall going at it. Or doors slamming. Or the elevator, etc., etc. Too bad, because otherwise it's OK.

Hôtel Pont Royal, 7 rue MontAlembert, 7^e, phone 544–3827. 600–800 francs.

Stayed here once awhile back. It was much quieter than its neighbor next door. Beautiful marble bathrooms. Good location, large rooms.

Relais Christine, 3 rue Christine, 6e, phone 326–7180. 450–600 francs.

Nothing but rave reviews about this place from everyone who has stayed there.

Hôtel des Saints-Pères, 65 rue des Sts.-Pères, 6e, phone 544–5000, 350–800 francs.

Recently renovated seventeenth-century smallish hotel, lots of charm, great location. Bar, breakfast.

Hôtel Saint-Simon, 14 rue St.-Simon, 7e, phone 548–3566. 400–600 francs.

A small, family-run hotel in a recently renovated old townhouse. Lovely rooms and service. Get a room on the garden. Great location. Good restaurant next door.

Scandinavia, 27 rue de Tournon, 6e, phone 329–6720. 240–260 francs.

A small and beautifully decorated hotel, *very* popular for years. Advance reservations always needed. No restaurant, no elevator.

Hôtel de l'Université, 22 rue de l'Université, 7e, phone 261–0939. 300–550 francs.

For a long time this was one of the most popular of the Left Bank small hotels. I did a thorough check-out of the hotel. The location is great. The lobby is small and charming. The rooms are very small, but if you get the suites on the top floor, they are a bit larger, quieter, and have a modest view.

Hôtel de Varenne, 44 rue de Bourgogne, 7^e, phone 551–4555. 200–350 francs.

Good location near the Rodin Museum. Small, seductively charming hotel, patio, good service.

NOT RECOMMENDED

There are so many wonderful hotels in Paris that have tons of charm and great personal service, no matter how big they are, that it seems to me to be a mistake to stay in a large, chain hotel (such as the Hiltons, Concordes, Holiday Inns, Sofitels, Meridiens, etc.). The Meridien, by the way, is the pits and in a terrible location. No matter what kind of budget you are on, you can find real Paris atmosphere and charm more often in a nonchain hotel.

Dining Out

You're surely sick and tired of hearing that "it's impossible to get a bad meal in Paris." So far I've never had one and I'm inclined to believe it's true.

One of the great pleasures of traveling is eating, and one of the greatest places in the world to partake of that pleasure is Paris and all of France. Deciding which restaurants to go to during a given trip is nearly impossible. For every one you choose, you have to leave out twenty others. It's my biggest dilemma.

One thing is for sure: if you plan to go to one of the "biggies," it's a good idea to write ahead and make reservations. You can write in English if you must, but if you'd rather be très français, here's a form letter that you can use. If you write about a month ahead of your departure date, you'll probably get a letter back.

> *246 Mundane Avenue*
> *Nowhere, USA 00000*
>
> *Date*

Restaurant de Paris
357 rue Superbe
Paris, France 75005

Cher Monsieur:

Je serai à Paris pendant quelques jours en *month,* et je voudrais dîner chez vous. Puis-je retenir une table pour *number of people* pour le dîner *(or* le déjeuner) du *day, date, month,* à *time?* (Remember to use a 24-hour clock, so that 8:30 P.M. becomes 20 h 30.)

Je descendrai à l'hôtel *name of hotel (hotel phone number)* à partir du *date of arrival.*

Je serai reconnaissant de bien vouloir confirmer cette reservation au plutôt possible.

En vous remerciant d'avance, veuillez agréer l'expression de mes sentiments les meilleurs.

Your name

A ROUGH TRANSLATION OF THE ABOVE IS AS FOLLOWS:

Dear Sir:

I will be in Paris for several days in *month,* and I would like to dine at your place. May I reserve a table for *number of people* for dinner (lunch) on *day, date, month,* at *time?*

I will be staying at the hotel *name of hotel and (phone number)* from *date of arrival* on.

Please confirm this reservation as soon as possible.

Thank you very much, etc., etc.

Obviously, in order to fill in the blanks, you're going to have to get a French dictionary so you'll know how to spell the days and months. You can use the dictionary later when you get to France.

If you get a response, save the letter, take it with you to the restaurant as proof of your reservation, in case of a mix-up. It's also a good idea to phone the restaurant when you get to Paris and reconfirm (your concierge will do this for you if you aren't adept at Phrench Phones).

Most Parisians don't dine until around 9:00 P.M., and if you go earlier than 8:00 P.M. you'll probably be sitting in an empty restaurant. In nicer restaurants they dress very well, but not ostentatiously. Elegant, but conservative. Coats and ties for men in all better restaurants, although they usually don't turn you away if you come otherwise, providing you look neat and clean. I can't imagine sitting in Tour d'Argent wearing slacks and a sweater —I wouldn't be able to eat!

Lunch can be a big deal and a big meal, or no big deal, depending on where you go. In better restaurants, make a reservation and don't show up in blue jeans. It's best to eat around 12:30 to avoid the rush. At sidewalk cafés and neighborhood bistros, lunch is served from noon to around 3:00. After that no one is much interested in bringing you food, as they are concentrating on the bar business and getting ready for dinner. You are more likely to run into snippy waiters as the afternoon gets longer, especially if you eat in a touristy place. They have a tendency to seat tourists and women upstairs, or wherever the "in" room isn't. If you don't want to be seated in one of these areas, say so. (This doesn't apply to better restaurants.)

There is a 15 percent tax on all food, which generally is written into the prices you see on the menu. Rarely is it added at the bottom. A 15 percent tip is usually added to your bill, so you don't have to leave more than another 3 percent above that. If you're not sure about the tip being added, ask your waiter. Always add up your bill yourself. It's not uncommon to find "mistakes." (Italy is famous for this.)

Coffee is served as a last course. Don't expect to get it with dessert, unless you specifically ask for it, and then they'll look at you as if you're crazy. If you really want to stand out as a tacky tourist, order coffee with your meal. Better yet—don't. Order wine or mineral water. Local French wines are unbelievably cheap and pretty good.

The old custom of serving a salad after the meal seems to be out. I haven't seen it done for a long time. Cheese served before dessert is still very much in vogue.

If you are on a budget, check the menus posted outside the restaurant, so you know if you can afford it before you go in and eat. Often there is a "menu touristique," or "prix fixe" menu, which offers four or five courses at a considerably lower price than other choices.

I learned a wonderful lesson about dessert. In many better restaurants, when they bring around the dessert cart, you can order more than one, at no extra cost. The French do it all the time. And they don't necessarily give you smaller portions! So if you can't decide, take a little of each. Why not?

Butter is not automatically placed on the table in most places, so if you want some for your bread, you'll have to order it. French bread is so delicious, however, that you should make an effort to eat it without butter, as the French do. Think of the calories you'll save. Try some Dijon mustard instead, often found on your table in a little pot.

If you go to a bar and stand at the bar, your drink will be less than if you sit at a table. There is nothing tacky about doing this . . . it's very French. A café au lait is called a "petit crème" by those in the know.

Many restaurants do not serve what they refer to as "snacks"—that is, just a salad or just a sandwich. Three-course minimum lunches are the norm at most places other than bistros and brasseries. Check the posted menu before going in to be sure you can get the kind of meal you feel like eating.

Restaurants

Following is my list of restaurants. This is but a partial listing of hundreds of restaurants in Paris. One of the problems with being in the city for only a few days is deciding where to eat, having to leave out some old favorites for new adventures. It also tends to limit your inclinations to go out on your own and just walk into an interesting–looking place. Some of my favorites I found in just such a way, more or less by accident. If you have the time, by all means just drop into a neighborhood restaurant; often you'll be in for a nice surprise. If you went to Paris with no restaurant list at all and just went potluck, you'd get good food, if not great.

Prices are listed per person and include a moderately priced wine, tax, and 15 percent service charge. Michelin ratings (Mich) and Gault and Millau (G&M) ratings, based on twenty points max, are noted. (A top rating for Michelin is three stars.) Cl means closed. Restaurants are listed alphabetically within sections.

Chic and Expensive

Alain-Senderens-Lucas Carton (formerly l'Archestrate),   9 pl. de la Madeleine, 8e, phone 265–2290. Cl. Sat., Sun., 350–450 fr.

Recently relocating and changing the name, Senderens continues to serve one of the finest and most expensive dinners in Paris. Well worth it, however. Try canard apicuis, langoustines en papillote, medaillons d'homard, emincé d'agneau, sorbet chocolat amer, and the lobster in vanilla sauce. Dress up. Mich: 3 stars; G&M: 19/20

Beauvilliers, 52 rue Lamarck, 18e, phone 254–1950. Cl. Sun., Mon. lunch. Dressy. Elegant. 300–400 francs.

Service can be slow. Outstanding food. Exquisite room. Great duck with figs, chocolate cake. Romantic. Mich: 1 star; G&M: 17/20.

Le Bernardin, 18 rue Troyon, 17e, phone 380–4061. Cl. Sun., Mon. Semidressy. 200–300 francs.

Excellent food and service. Seafood. Berthillon ice cream. Mich: 2 stars; G&M: 17/20.

Le Bristol, 112 rue Fg.-St.-Honoré, 8e, in the Bristol hotel, phone 266–9145. Always open. 350–500 francs.

Beautiful restaurant (either the formal room or the garden room). Semicasual. Excellent food and service. You can get a truffled omelet here. Mich: 2 stars; G&M: 15/20.

Chiberta, 3 rue Arsène-Houssaye, 8e, phone 563–7790. Cl. Sat., Sun. Dressy. Expensive: 300–400 francs.

Outstanding service, food, decor. Steps away from the Champs-Elysées. One of our favorites. Mich: 2 stars; G&M: 16/20.

Le Crillon's Les Ambassadeurs, 10 pl. de la Concorde, 8e, in the Crillon hotel, phone 296–1081. Open every day. Dressy. 350–400 francs. Mich: 2 stars; G&M: 17/20.

Faugeron, 52 rue de Longchamps, 16e, phone 704–2453. Cl. Sat., Sun., 350–450 francs.

Beautiful, intimate restaurant serving outstanding cuisine with terrific service. Dressy, elegant. Best chocolate soufflé I ever had (order before dinner). Mich: 2 stars; G&M: 18/20.

La Flamberge, 12 av. Rapp, 7e, phone 705–9137. Cl. Sat. lunch and Sun. 300 francs.

Cushy room, elegant, creative cuisine, chic patrons. Mich: 1 star; G&M: 15/20.

La Grand Cascade, Bois de Boulogne, phone 506–3351. Cl. Sun. eve. and Mon. Dressy. 300–400 francs.

Beautiful pavilion in the forest; romantic; good food and service. Mich: 1 star; G&M: 15/20.

Le Grand Véfour, 17 rue du Beaujolais, 1er, behind Palais Royal, phone 296–5627. Cl. Sat., Sun. Dressy. 400–500 francs.

Outstanding service. Marvelous decor! Now has a new owner, M. Tattinger, and a new chef. Mich: 2 stars; G&M: 16/20.

Guy Savoy, 28 rue Duret, 16e, phone 500–1767. Cl. Sat., Sun. 400–600 francs.

One of Paris's best chefs. Small restaurant, very popular. Good service, excellent food. Mich: 2 stars; G&M: 18/20.

Jacques Cagna, 14 rue des Grands-Augustins, 6^e, phone 326–4939. Cl. Sat., Sun. Semidressy. 400–450 francs.

Lovely room. Fabulous food and service. Mich: 2 stars; G&M: 17/20.

Jules Verne, Tour Eiffel, 7^e, second level, phone 555–2004. Open every day; lunch and dinner. Dressy. 350–400 francs.

Exquisite restaurant in the newly restored E.T. Fabulous food and service. A must! Mich: 1 star.

Lasserre, 17 av. Franklin-Roosevelt, 8^e, phone 359–5343. Cl. Sun., Mon. lunch and dinner. Dressy. 400–500 francs.

Piano. The ceiling rolls back in good weather for a view of the stars in this very beautiful, romantic restaurant. Theatrical presentation of food. You go there for the whole experience, not just for the food. Mich: 2 stars; G&M: 17/20.

Laurent, 41 av. Gabriel, 8e, phone 723–7918, just off the Champs-Elysées in the park. Cl. Sat. lunch, Sun. Dressy. Elegant. Extremely expensive.

One of the round pavilions you see in the wooded area. Try warm lobster salad. Excellent food, service, ambiance. Mich: 2 stars; G&M: 16/20.

La Marée, 1 rue Daru, 8e, phone 227–5932. Cl. Sat., Sun. Dressy, expensive. 350–400 francs.

Outstanding seafood. Wonderful food and service. Great decor. Mich: 2 stars; G&M: 18/20.

Maxim's, 3 rue Royale, 8e, phone 265–2794. Cl. Sun. 400–500 francs. You don't necessarily go here for the food but to see and be seen in one of the most famous restaurants in the world. Dress to impress. Lavish late-nineteenth-century decor. The middle room is the most beautiful room and the bar is gorgeous. Maxim's has been greatly reduced to a tourist trap; best nights to go are Tuesday, Wednesday, and Thursday. Never go on Friday or Saturday. Mich: no mention; G&M: 17/20. Go for lunch so you can say you've been there.

Pavillon Elysées, 10 Champs-Elysées, 8e, phone 265–8510. Cl. Sat., Sun. Expensive. 310–450 francs.

Owned by Lenôtre of Pre Catalan. Mich: 1 star. Very new.

Le Pre Catalan, route de Suresnes, Bois de Boulogne, phone 524–5558. Cl. Sun. eve. and Mon. Dressy. 300–400 francs.

Fabulous and elegant lodge in the forest. Service is hit and miss. Good food and presentation thereof. Good Poulet de Bresse, hot apple crepes, tarte tatin. Romantic. Mich: 2 stars; G&M: 18/20.

Princesse Castel or just Castel's, 15 rue Princesse, 6^e, phone 326–9022. Cl. Sun. Dressy. 400–500 francs.

Also the most popular disco in Paris. Private club—you must be a member or have a connection to get in. Colorful dining room, late dining (9:30 P.M. is the earliest). Very good food; service was OK. The disco was hot, dark, smoky, crowded, and populated with young adults or old teenagers, whichever is worse. Mich: no mention; G&M: 15/20.

Ritz-Espadon, 15 pl. Vendôme, 1er, in the Ritz hotel, phone 260–3830. Always open. Dressy. 350–400 francs.

You can shop your way to the restaurant down the Ritz's unique shopping arcade. Excellent food and service; fresh fish tank. Good lobster bisque. Mich: 2 stars; G&M: 13/20.

Robuchon (Jamin),   32 rue du Longchamp, 16^e, phone 727–1227. Cl. Sat., Sun., July. 400–640 francs.

A young, creative chef, exquisite dining room, innovative cuisine, outstanding service. Try the chicken in pig's bladder (I'm not kidding). Great desserts. Also great lobster ravioli. Mich: 3 stars; G&M: 18/20.

Taillevent,   15 rue Lamennais, 8^e, phone 563–3994. Cl. Sat., Sun., Aug. Dressy. Expensive. 400–500 francs.

Outstanding service. Ditto decor. Ditto cuisine. Currently the most difficult reservation to get. Mich: 3 stars; G&M: 19/20.

Tour d'Argent,   15 quai de la Tournelle, 5^e, phone 354–2331. Cl. Mon. Open for lunch. Dressy. Expensive. 600–700 francs.

Specialties are duck and seafood. Don't get the pressed duck. Best table: the one in the front corner overlooking Notre Dame. Try to sit in the lower room (upper room is touristy). Everyone should go at least once, as it *is* one of the most spectacular restaurants you'll ever see. Service can be spotty. Mich: 3 stars; G&M: 17/20.

Very Nice and Moderately Priced

Al Diwan,   30 av. George V, 8^e, phone 720–8498. Open everyday and in the summer. 260 francs.

Lebanese cuisine in a beautiful setting, outstanding food and service.

Ambassade d'Auvergne,   22 rue du Grenier-St.-Lazare, 3^e, near the Pompidou Center, phone 272–3122. Cl. Sun. Lunch and dinner. Semicasual. 250–300 francs.

Regional food from the Auvergne, a bit on the heavy side; country and peasanty and delicious. Outstanding decor; good service. Lunch and dinner. Mich: no star; G&M: 15/20.

L'Ambroisie,   65 quai de la Tournelle, 5e, phone 633–1865. Cl. Sun. eve., Mon. Semicasual. 250–300 francs.

Tiny, ten tables only; modern decor. Outstanding food, charming service. Get poulet de Bresse, bitter chocolate cake, lemon feuilleté. Creative menu. Very popular. Mich: 2 stars; G&M: 15/20.

Le Bourdonnais,   113 av. de la Bourdonnais, 7e, phone 705–4796. Cl. Sun., Mon. lunch. 250–300 francs.

Near the Ecole Militaire. Small and charming restaurant, popular with locals. Excellent food. Mich: no mention; G&M: 16/20.

Le Carpaccio,   35 av. Hoche, 8^e, in Hôtel Royal Monceau, phone 561–9800. Cl. Sun. 300–400 francs.

Italian cuisine in newly opened restaurant. Mich: no mention; G&M: 16/20.

Caviar Kaspia,   17 pl. de la Madeleine, 8^e, phone 265–3352. Cl. Sun., from 100 francs without caviar, 300 fr. with.

I wouldn't go there unless you planned to eat caviar, since that is the specialty, although they also serve various types of smoked fish, soups, salad, etc. Upstairs from the famous Kaviar Caspia store, this is a small and very chic place to dine on the best caviar, washed down by a divine vodka. Desserts aren't too exciting. Mich: no mention. G&M: 12/20.

Chez les Anges, 54 bd. Latour-Maubourg, 7^e, phone 705–8986. Open every day. Lunch and dinner. Semi-dressy. 200–300 francs.
Wonderful food and service in a charming, well-known neighborhood restaurant. Don't miss the chocolate mousse! Mich: 1 star; G&M: 14/20.

Clodenis, 57 rue Caulaincourt, 18e, phone 606–2026. Cl. Sun., Mon. 250–300 francs.
Beautiful little restaurant, romantic, lots of charm, good food. Mich: no star; G&M: 15/20.

Le Divellec, 107 rue de l'Université, 7e, phone 551–9196. Cl. Sun., Mon. Semidressy. 600 francs.
Seafood tank (the specialty). Beautiful restaurant, excellent service (especially the sommelier). Fabulous caramel tart with Grand Marnier–soaked orange rind sauce. Great chocolate truffle cake. Mich: 2 stars; G&M: 17/20.

Le Duc, 243 bd. Raspail, 14^e, phone 320–9630 and 322–5959. Cl. Sat., Sun., Mon. Semicasual. 250–300 francs.
Simple decor. Excellent service. Seafood only. The best seafood I've ever had. Mich: 1 star; G&M: 17/20.

Duquesnoy (pronounced *doo-ken-wah*), 30 rue des Bernardins, 5^e, phone 354–2113. Cl. Sat. lunch and Sun. Dressy. 350–400 francs.
Lovely, newish restaurant; good food, service, and decor. They were extremely gracious to us even though we were forty-five minutes late without calling. Order the dessert plate of six different chocolate things. Mich: 2 stars; G&M: 15/20.

La Ferme St.-Simon, 6 rue St.-Simon, 7^e, phone 548–3574. Cl. Sat. lunch and Sun. Semidressy. 200–250 francs.
Charming decor. Nouvelle cuisine. Good food and service. Mich: 1 star; G&M: 15/20.

Le Galant Verre, 12 rue de Verneuil, 7e, phone 260–8456. Cl. Sat. lunch and Sun. 300 francs.
A very popular neighborhood restaurant; small, packed to the gills with noisy, happy people (always a good sign). Nouvelle cuisine. Try pigeon vinaigre de miel, and asperges feuilleté. Mich: no star; G&M: 15/20.

La Guirlande de Julie, 25 pl. des Vosges, 4e, phone 887–9407. Cl. Sun. eve. and Mon.
Alfresco dining, weather permitting. Located in the spectacular Place des Vosges. Lovely restaurant. Mich: no star; G&M: 14/20.

Jean-Claude Ferrero, 38 rue Vital, 16e, phone 504–4242. Cl. Sat., Sun. 350 francs.
Very charming and romantic little restaurant with excellent food; very modern decor. Mich: no mention; G&M: 16/20.

Jenny Jacquet,   136 rue de la Pompe, 16e, phone 727–5026. Cl. Sat. lunch and Sun. Semicasual. 200–250 francs.

Small, neighborhood place. Food was very good. Service was terrible, but it was probably just our waiter, who was a haughty, officious, swishy Englishman. Maybe he's been fired by now. Mich: 1 star; G&M: 15/20.

Lamazère,   23 rue de Ponthieu, 8e, phone 359–6666. Cl. Sun. 270–380 francs.

Regional (Gascony) cuisine. Well-prepared food. Mich: 1 star; G&M: 16/20.

Maison Prunier Traktir,   16 av. Victor-Hugo, 16e, phone 500–8912, closed Monday, 400-450 francs.

Casual, neighborhood restaurant with exceedingly friendly service and very good food. Request to sit upstairs, if possible. Specialties are seafood (excellent salmon). Also try pommes soufflés. G&M: 14/20.

Michel Rostang,   10 rue Gustave-Flaubert, 17e, phone 763–4077. Cl. Sat. lunch and Sun. Semidressy. Expensive. 200–300 francs.

Excellent service, excellent food. Order several items from the dessert cart. Mich: 2 stars; G&M: 18/20.

Morot-Gaudry,   8 rue de la Cavalerie, 15e, phone 567–0685. Cl. Sat., Sun. Semicasual. 250–300 francs.

Great view from this ninth-floor restaurant. Nice food. Get the dessert assortment—a giant plate with a little of everything. Mich: 1 star; G&M: 16/20.

Olympe,   8 rue Nicolas-Charlet, 15^e, phone 734–8606. Cl. Mon. Semidressy. 300–400 francs.

1920s decor. Food is good; service was horrendous when we went. Rude treatment on the telephone. Dominique is one of France's best-known female chefs. Mich: 1 star; G&M: 17/20.

Le Pavillon des Princes,   69 av. Porte d'Auteuil (Porte de Boulogne), 16^e, phone 605–6550. Open every day. 200–250 francs.

Decorated with plastic flowers and full of tourists, this rather stuffy place serves mediocre food with ditto service. I don't recommend it. Same owners as La Vieille Fontaine. Interesting people-watching on the drive to and from through the Bois de Boulogne.

Le Petit Bedon,   38 rue Pergolèse, 16e, phone 500–2366. Cl. Sat., Sun. Semicasual. 300 francs.

Getting some good reviews in other books, but I had a poor dinner there. Small, neighborhood restaurant; nice decor but not memorable. OK service, OK food. Specialty is smoked salmon. Mich: 2 stars; G&M: 15/20.

Pharamond,   24 rue de la Grande-Truanderie, 1er, phone 233–0672. Cl. Sun., Mon. lunch. 160–200 francs.

Been around for a long time; turn-of-the-century decor. Mich: 1 star; G&M: 13/20.

Au Pressoir,   257 av. Daumesnil, 12^e, phone 344–3821. Cl. Sat., Sun. 300–340 francs.

Creative cooking, modern decor. Degustation. Mich: 1 star; G&M: 16/20.

Prunier-Madeleine, 9 rue Duphot, 1er, phone 260–3604. Open every day. Semicasual. 250 francs.

Located in a beautiful old house. Nouvelle cuisine. Good fish, nice food, nice service. Mich and G&M: no mention.

Au Quai des Ormes, 72 quai de l'Hôtel-de-Ville, 5^e, phone 274–7222. Cl. Sat., Sun. 250 francs.

Nice decor, creative cooking. Mich: 1 star; G&M: 16/20.

Au Quai d'Orsay, 49 quai d'Orsay, 7e, phone 551–5858, and **Annexe du Quai,** around the corner at 3 rue Surcouf, 7e, same phone. Cl. Sun. 200–250 francs.

Well-known Paris restaurant; been around for a long time; big portions. Mich: no star; G&M: 14/20.

Le Récamier, 4 rue Récamier, 7e, phone 548–8658. Cl. Sun. Semicasual. 400–500 francs.

A very charming, small neighborhood place in a little alley near the Bon Marché department store. Popular for years. Alfresco dining in summer. Try chateaubriand, fresh tuna, panaché chocolat. The house Burgundy is excellent. Very friendly service. Mich: 1 star; G&M: 15/20.

Relais Louis XIII, 1 rue du Pont-de-Lodi, 6e, phone 326–7596. Cl. Sun. and Mon. lunch. Semidressy. 300–400 francs.

Wonderful and interesting sixteenth-century decor. Top-notch food and service. A bit touristy but don't let that stop you. Mich: 2 stars; G&M: 13/20.

Royal Monceau, 35 av. Hoche, 8^e, in the hotel, phone 561–9800. Always open. Semicasual. Buffet brunch every day. 200–280 francs.

Lavish array. Mich and G&M: no mention.

Le Toit de Passy, 94 av. Paul-Doumer (pronounce the "r"), 16^e, phone 524–5537. Cl. Sat., Sun. Semidressy. 350–400 francs.

Lunch and dinner, a different experience each time. Beautiful rooftop restaurant with a view of the Eiffel Tower. Excellent food and service; romantic. Nontouristy. Mich: 1 star; G&M: 15/20.

Le Train Bleu, Gare de Lyon (train station), 2nd floor, 12^e, phone 343–0906. Open every day. Casual. 200–250 francs.

Extravagant 1900s decor which you will not believe. It's worth a trip to this restaurant just to see the rooms. If you sit by the windows overlooking the tracks, you can watch the trains come and go. Food goes from medium to good, depending on which day you go. Service also. Mich: no star; G&M: 12/20.

Au Trou Gascon, 40 rue Taine, 12e, phone 344–3426. Cl. Sat., Sun., Sept. Semicasual. 250–300 francs.

A bit out of the way, but worth the trip. Charming decor. Well-known and popular small bistro. Dutournier is the chef. Mich: 2 stars; G&M: 18/20.

Les Ursins dans le Caviar, 19 rue des Ursins and 3 rue de la Colombe, Ile de Cité, 4e, phone 329–5480 or 329–5420. Closed Sun. 250 francs.

One of the most beautiful, small (12 tables), romantic restaurants in all of Paris. Excellent food and service. Go with someone you love.

Vivarois, 192 av. Victor-Hugo, 16e, phone 504–0431. Cl. Sat., Sun. Semicasual. 300–400 francs.

Decor is rather plain. Service was lax when we were there. Food was good but not great. Mich: 2 stars; G&M: 17/20.

Bistrôts and Brasseries

Allard, 41 rue St.-André-des-Arts, 6e, phone 326–4823. Cl. Sat., Sun. 230–250 francs.

A great old Paris bistro in one of the oldest streets in the city. Popular for years. Mich: 1 star; G&M: 15/20.

Au Clocher de Village, 8 bic, rue Verderet, 16e in Auteuil, phone 288-3587, casual. 400 francs. (Closed Sat. and Sun.)

A very authentic and romantic Paris bistro in both atmosphere and cuisine. Quaint, friendly, charming. Large helpings, rich food. G&M 11/20.

Benoit, 20 rue St. Martin, 4^e, phone 272–2576. Cl. Sat., Sun., Casual. 300 francs.

This wonderful bistro dates from 1912 and is perfect for lunch if you're in the Pompidou/Les Halles area, or for dinner no matter where you are. Delightful decor, great service, wonderful bistro fare. Mich: 1 star; G&M: 13/20.

Bistrôt de Paris, 33 rue de Lille, 7e, phone 261–1683. Cl. Sat., Sun. 300 francs.

Long-standing favorite with excellent bistro fare. Mich: 1 star; G&M: 15/20.

Bistro d'Hubert, 36 pl. du Marché-St.-Honoré, 1er, phone 260–0300. Cl. Sun., Mon. Casual. 350 francs.

Very popular neighborhood bistro; good food. Try emincé de boeuf, oysters and avocados, poulet de Bresse and peppercorn sauce, and especially feuillantine de fruits et carmalisée au fer. Mich: 1 star; G&M: 15/20.

Bistro 121, 121 rue de la Convention, 15e, phone 557–5290. Cl. Sun. eve. and Mon. 220–280 francs.

Long-time popular neighborhood bistro, classy clientele, good and creative cuisine. Mich: 1 star; G&M: 15/20.

Bofinger, 3 & 7 rue de la Bastille, 4e, phone 272–8782. Open every day. Casual. 150–200 francs.

Lovely turn-of-the-century decor. Oysters. A good stop for lunch if you are in the Bastille/Marais area. Mich: no stars; G&M: 12/20.

Brasserie Lipp, 151 bd. St.-Germain, 6^e, phone 548–5391. Cl. Mon. Casual. 180–200 francs.

A good place for lunch if you are in the St. Germain area. One of Paris' best and most well-known brasseries. Choucroute garni is the specialty. Reservations are not a must for lunch, but are for dinner. Mich: no mention; G&M: 13/20.

Chez l'Ami Louis, 32 rue du Vertbois, 3^e, phone 887–7748. Cl. Tues. Casual. 400–500 francs.

Very old bistro which is falling apart as you eat, but don't let that bother you. Very old chef. Very wonderful food, huge portions, great dining experience.

Don't miss the foie gras or any of the potatoes. Ask for green almonds. Boring desserts. Mich: no mention: G&M: 15/20.

Chez Francis, 7 pl. de l'Alma, 8e, phone 720–8683, always open, 250–300 francs.

A large brasserie near the Plaza Athenée Hotel, this is a good place to go for a late-evening dinner or snack. Notice the dragonfly chandeliers (how can you miss them?). Busy, casual, interesting crowd. No mention Mich. or G&M.

Chez Georges, 1 rue Mail, 2e, phone 260–0711. Cl. Sun. 100–150 francs.

A wonderful, very French, old bistro; no tourists. Hearty food, lots of atmosphere, good people-watching. Just off Place des Victoires, near Palais Royal and Beaubourg. Good for lunch. Mich: no star; G&M: no mention.

Le Coupe-Chou, 9 & 11 rue de Lanneau, 5^e, phone 633–6869. Open daily. 200 francs.

Intimate restaurant, excellent food. Mich: no star; G&M: 12/20.

La Coupole, 102 bd. du Montparnasse, 14e, phone 320–1420. Open daily. Very casual. 150–200 francs.

Largest of the Paris brasseries; original 1920s decor, lots of people watching and noise and very good food; good service. Mich: no mention; G&M: 12/20.

Dodin Bouffant, 25–27 rue Frédéric-Sauton, 5e, phone 325–2514. Cl. Sat., Sun. Semidressy. 250–300 francs.

One of Paris' best and most well-known bistros. Outstanding food and service. Be sure you get a soufflé for dessert—I've never seen or tasted anything like theirs. Mich: 1 star; G&M: 17/20.

Le Dôme, 108 bd. du Montparnasse, 14e, phone 354–5361. Cl. Mon. 200 francs.

Famous old seafood restaurant; great bouillabaisse. Mich: no mention; G&M: 12/20.

Julien, 16 bd. du Fg.-St.-Denis, 10e, phone 770–1206. Always open except in July. Casual. 180–200 francs.

A Gay-Nineties decor, but the real thing. Quite spectacular. Very good food, bustly, noisy, popular, fun. They have a bad habit of seating all the Americans together at a banquette along the wall; protest. Fabulous profiteroles. By the same owners and in the same vein are: *Terminus Nord,* 23 rue de Dunkerque, 10^e, phone 285–0515; *Brasserie Flo,* 7 rue des Petites-Ecuries, 10^e, phone 770–1359; *Vaudeville,* 29 rue Vivienne, 2^e, phone 233–3931. Mich: no mention; G&M: 12/20.

Au Pactole, 44 bd. St.-Germain, 5^e, phone 633–3131. Cl. Sat. lunch and Sun. 250 francs.

Well-known and popular old Paris bistro with excellent food. Mich: no star; G&M: 16/20.

Le Petit Zinc, 25 rue de Buci, 6e, phone 354–7934. Open every day. 200 francs.

Good food in a superb and friendly ambiance. Excellent coquillages. Wonderful attention to children. 1900s-style bistrôt. Mich: no mention; G&M: 13/20.

Au Pied de Cochon, 6 rue Coquillière, 1er, phone 236–1175. Always open. Casual. 160–200 francs.

In the Les Halles area not far from the Pompidou. Touristy, but tolerable. Alfresco dining, weather permitting. Specialties: shellfish and pigs' feet. Good onion soup and lobster bisque; also good frites, goat cheese, and desserts. If you go for lunch, arrive by 12:30 to get a table without waiting. Service can be slow. Mich: no star; G&M: 12/20.

Ramponneau, 21 av. Marceau, 16^{e}, phone 720–5951. Open every day. Semicasual. 500 francs.

A lively, fun restaurant retaining its old decor. Good food, friendly service. Large portions. Neighborhood favorite; nontouristy. Outstanding profiteroles. Mich: no star; G&M: 12/20.

Smaller and Less Expensive

Auberge des Deux Signes, 46 rue Galande, 5e, phone 325–4656. Cl. Sun. 300 francs.

Medieval-style decor, good food, near Notre Dame. Mich: no star; G&M: 13/20.

Au Châteaubriant, 23 rue de Chabrol, 10e, phone 824–5894. Cl. Sun., Mon. 180–200 francs.

French/Italian cuisine, good pastas. Popular, fun. Mich: 1 star; G&M: 14/20.

La Cafetière, 21 rue Mazarine, 6e, phone 633–7690, always open.

Inexpensive. Near Relais Christine. Charming bistro; ask to sit upstairs. Good chocolate mousse, poulet grillé, frisée au lardons, onion tarte. Very casual.

Chez Guy, 6 rue Mabillon, 6e, phone 354–8761. Cl. Sun. 200 francs.

Brazilian food, for a change. Mich: no mention; G&M: 12/20.

Chez Provost, 1 rue des Coulmiers, 14e, phone 539–8699. Cl. Sat., Sun. Casual. 200–300 francs.

A friendly neighborhood place, country-house atmosphere. Mich: no mention; G&M: 15/20.

La Closerie des Lilas, 171 bd. du Montparnasse, 6^{e}, phone 326–7050. Open every day. Semicasual. 250 francs.

A well-known restaurant frequented by Hemingway and his cohorts in their day. Now it has mediocre food and terrible service. Mich: no mention; G&M: 10/20. No surprise.

Concorde Lafayette Hôtel, 3 pl. Porte des Ternes, 17e, phone 758–1284.

Go for the buffet lunch or a hamburger; good for people traveling with kids. Mich: 1 star (Etoile d'Or).

La Coquille, 6 rue du Débarcadère, 17e, phone 574–2595. Cl. Sun., Mon. 300 francs.

Excellent coquilles St. Jacques; fresh fish plates plus nonfish items. Mich: 1 star; G&M: 13/20.

L'Epi d'Or, 23–25 rue Jean-Jacques Rousseau, 1er phone 236–3812. Cl. Sat., Sun. Lunch and dinner. Casual. 150 francs.

A short distance from Beaubourg and just around the corner from the round Bourse de Commerce. This is one of my "accidental finds." Walked in off the street one day and stayed for three hours, eating. Very old and old-fashioned Paris bistro. Huge helpings, great bistro menu. Rich, saucy food. Pleasant personnel. Homey, ancient decor. Noisy, fun, very popular. No tourists. Be very hungry when you go. Save room for the desserts, especially the tarte tatin and lemon tart. Good duckling, quenelles, frisée au lardons, frites. Mich and G&M: no mention.

Erawan, 76 rue de la Fédération, 15e, phone 783–5567. Closed Sun. 200 francs.

They say it's Paris' best Thai restaurant, and although it wasn't as good as some Thai restaurants in the U.S., it was still quite acceptable. Very good Tom Yam soup. Casual. Friendly service.

La Fermette du Sud-Ouest, 30 rue Coquillière, near Palais Royal, Cl. Sun.

Teensy, newish, darling, and features home cooking of the southwest of France. Charming owner/host/cook; good food. Inexpensive. No tourists—it's a neighborhood place. Mich and G&M: no mention.

La Fermette Marbeuf, 5 rue Marbeuf, 8e, phone 723–3131; open everyday; 225 francs. Casual.

Not far from the Plaza Athenée and Georges V Hotels. OK food and great dessert called Salade d'Oranges with chocolate ice cream. The main attraction is a Belle Epoque to the extreme dining room called the Salle 1900 d'Epoque, where you should insist on being seated. Or at least go have a look.

Le Grand Chinois, 6 av. de New York, 16e, across from the Seine and near the Trocadero, phone 723–9821. 250 francs. Casual.

A very show-biz type Chinese restaurant serving mediocre Chinese cuisine (although the pâtés imériaux are excellent as are the fried noodles. Forget the canard laqué charbon. Poor service. For tourists who don't know Chinese food.

Le Gosier En Pente, 5 rue Sauval, 1er, phone 260–2229. Cl. Sat., Sun. 200–300 francs.

Rue Sauval is a continuation of rue de l'Arbre Sec, which leads off from rue Rivoli by Samaritaine. All along these streets are adorable little restaurants, all enticing. I was enticed into this one and was thoroughly enchanted from the gorgeous cat sleeping on the chair next to me, through the delicious fresh fish entree, an outstanding salade aux trois fromages, and one of the best hot apple tarte tatins anywhere. Delightful decor and service. A good bet for lunch or dinner; near Les Halles. Ten tables only. Mich: no mention; G&M: 12/20.

Joséphine or Chez Dumonet, 117 rue du Cherche-Midi, 6e, phone 548–5240. Cl. Sat., Sun. 400 francs.

Southwestern French country cuisine, rotisserie, and grill, 1900s-style bistrôt, ample portions, charm. Mich: no mention; G&M: 14/20.

Ladurée, 16 rue Royale, pl. de la Madeleine (almost), 8e, phone 260–2179. Cl. Sun., open 11:30–4 P.M.

This is one of Paris' most popular tearooms and a great idea for a nice lunch. Better arrive between 11:30 and noon if you don't want to wait for a table. Seating also upstairs. When you're done with your main course, take your bill up to the patisserie counter and point out all the sinful things you want for dessert (they mark it on your bill and you return to your table.) It could be touristy but the day I was there, all customers were French (except me.) P.S.–The best almond croissants in Paris! Also excellent tarte d'abricots.

Lou Landès, 157 av. du Maine, 14e, phone 543–0804. Cl. Sun. eve. and Mon. lunch. 250–300 francs.
Belle Epoque decor; lots of fun, good food. Mich: no mention; G&M: 15/20.

La Marlotte, 55 rue du Cherche-Midi, 6e, phone 548–8679. Cl. Sat., Sun. Casual. 150–200 francs.
A very nice, old-fashioned sort of neighborhood place, full of locals. Mich: no mention; G&M: 13/20.

Le Moï, 7 & 14 rue Gustave-Courbet, 16^e, phone 704–9510. Cl. Mon. 150 francs.
Vietnamese cuisine, popular for a long time. Very small, casual. Mich: no mention; G&M: 14/20.

Pantagruel, 20 rue de l'Exposition, 7e, phone 551–7996. Cl. Sun. 200 francs.
Very nice food in a long-established and popular neighborhood restaurant.

Passy Mandarin, 6 rue Bois-le-Vent, 16e, phone 288–1218. Open every day. 200 francs.
Vietnamese/Chinese food; excellent dimsum, canard la quée (prix fixe menu), Peking beer, old linen tablecloths. Ask the maître d' to bring you a selection of items "à la vapeur." Also try roulezux impériale, fish, sake in the translucent marble cups, and beignets de pomme on bananes. Mich: no mention; G&M: 14/20.

Le Petit Montmorency, 5 rue Rabelais, 8e, phone 255–1119. Cl. Sat., Sun. 250-300 francs.
Popular, highly rated neighborhood bistro; creative menu. Mich: no star; G&M: 16/20.

Le Raccard, 19 rue Laplace, 5^e, near the Pantheon, phone 325–2727 or 354–8375. Open 7:30 p.m. to 2 a.m. About 180 francs.
Swiss specialties in a very decorated and quaint room, romantic, charming beyond expectations. The big deal here is the raclette, which you can have as many times as you want. Other good things to order are viande des Grisons (a dried meat appetizer), vin Fendant (the wine to go with the raclette), salade Saviaisane, fondue.

Across the street is another very cute place called l'Annexe and down the street yet another called Les Iles Philippines.

Le Relais Boccador, 20 rue du Boccador, 8e, phone 723–3198, closed Saturday. 180-200 francs.
Near Plaza Athenée Hotel. One of the best Italian restaurants in Paris. Try the scampi, ravioli, chocolate cake, profiteroles, hot crostini, pastas.

Le Seoul,   13 rue Montalivet,   8e, phone 266–1410. Closed Sat. lunch and Sun. 200 francs.
Excellent Korean food. G&M 13/20.

Tan Dinh,   60 rue de Verneuil, 7e, phone 544–0484. Cl. Sun. Casual. 150–200 francs.
Vietnamese. Small, popular. The owner and host, M. Vifian, couldn't be more charming. Consult him as to what to order or just let him bring it to you. Mich: 1 star; G&M: 14/20.

Very Inexpensive

Androuet,   41 rue d'Amsterdam, 8^e, phone 874–2690. Cl. Sun. Casual. 150–300 francs.
Androuet is basically a cheese shop, but on the first floor is a charming restaurant serving inexpensive lunches, the basis of which is cheese. In fact, you can get an all-cheese meal for 125 francs. A great place for lunch. About a ten-minute walk from the Opéra. Reservations recommended. Also open for dinner. Mich: no mention; G&M: 11/20.

Bistro de la Gare,   various locations around the city. Open every day. Casual. 80–100 francs.
Inexpensive prix-fixe meals; old 1900's-style decor. Food is good, considering the cost and atmosphere. Good frites and chicken. OK for a quick dinner, a cheap dinner, or with kids. Mich: no mention; G&M: no rating.

Bistro Romain,   various locations around the city. Open every day. Less than 100 francs.
Allied to Bistro de la Gare, with inexpensive yet good food, with an Italian flair. Mich: no mention; G&M: no rating.

Hong Kong Palace,   23 rue Paul Valery at rue Georges Villes, 16e, walking distance from the Arc de Triomphe, phone 501–6818.
This is a big favorite of all the locals who live in the neighborhood. Chinese cuisine, inexpensive, casual. Especially good deep-fried nibbles, canard lacqué, beignets de poulet au citron, shrimp toast, hot coconut or almond cakes and coffee ice cream.

La Petite Chaise,   36–38 rue de Grenelle, 7e, phone 222–1335. Open every day. Casual. 60–100 francs.
Opened in 1680, this is one of Paris' oldest (if not *the* oldest) places, and the same goes for small. Very popular, crowded, noisy. Good food and fun. Don't go during a heat wave; there's no AC. Mich: no mention; G&M: no rating.

Le Petit Niçois,   10 rue Amélie, 7e, phone 551–8365. Cl. Sun. Casual. 180–230 francs.
This is a teeny little neighborhood place which specializes in provençal fish dishes. Fabulous fish soup; good, sweet little mussels. Reservations. Mich: no mention; G&M: 10/20.

Le Soufflé,   36 rue du Mont Thabor, 1er, phone 260–2719. Cl. Sun. 150 francs.

For what else but soufflés? Lunch or dinner. Mich: no star; G&M: no mention. Reservations.

Vi Foc, 33 rue de Longchamp, 16e, phone 704–9681. Casual. Cl. Sat. lunch only. 120–200 francs.

Chinese and Vietnamese cuisine. Pretty oriental restaurant, popular with the locals in the neighborhood, very good food. Lunch or dinner. Take-out dishes.

Not Exactly Restaurants

Berthillon, rue St. Louis-en-l'Ile, Ile St. Louis.

Best ice cream in Paris. Many restaurants now serve it. They don't open until about 2:30 P.M., so don't go looking for an early-morning shot of coffee ice cream. Try the chocolate and the nougat. A scoop is called a "boule" and the cone is the "cornet." Around the corner from Berthillon, on rue des Deux Ponts, is *Cadmios,* which also serves their ice cream, but sometimes the line is shorter. The tearoom *Flore en l'Ile,* on the island, also serves it.

La Charlotte de l'Ile, around 22–24 rue St.-Louis-en-l'Ile, Ile St. Louis.

A marvelous little bakery and tearoom with out-of-this-world homemade goods you can't resist.

Poilane, 8 rue du Cherche-Midi.

The best bread in Paris. Many restaurants serve this dark, country-style bread.

Tearooms

have become very "in" and popular in the last two years. They are all over Paris, providing an alternative to sitting in a bistro or brasserie; usually the pastries are a lot better. Three of the most popular tearooms in town are Luduree (already mentioned), Carette at the Trocader (get macarons au chocolat), and Dalloyau at 101 Fg. St. Honore, 8^e, 69 rue de la Convention, 15^e, 16 rue Linois, 15^e, and Place Edmond Rostand, 6^e.

Out of Town But Not Too Far
(grouped by location)

L'Aubergade, Pontchartrain, approximately 28 miles from Paris, phone 489–0263. Cl. Weds. 200–300 francs. An exquisite restaurant in a garden setting; outstanding food and ambiance. Go in the summertime for a lovely lunch or leisurely dinner. Mich: 1 star; G&M: no mention.

La Belle Epoque, 10 pl. de la Marie, Châteaufort, 17 miles from Paris, phone 956–2166. Cl. Sat., Sun. 250–300 francs. Excellent food and service. Mich: 2 stars; G&M: 16/20.

Le Camélia, 7 quai Georges-Clemenceau, Bougival, phone 969–0302. Cl. Sun. eve. and Mon. Semicasual. 300 francs. About a thirty-minute cab ride from Paris, heading toward Versailles and Malmaison. Charming country inn decor with wonderful food. Worth the trip. Mich: 2 stars; G&M: 17/20.

Cazaudehore, 1 av. du President-Kennedy, St.-Germain-en-Laye, phone 451–9380. Cl. Mon. 250–300 francs. Garden restaurant in the forest. Mich: 1 star; G&M: 14/20.

Le Coq Hardi, 16 quai Rennequin-Sualem, Bougival, phone 969–0163. Cl. Weds. 400–500 francs. A thirty-minute drive from Paris. Very popular dining spot for a number of years. Beautiful restaurant along the river; country atmosphere. Extensive wine cellar. Everyone loves it. Mich: 1 star; G&M: 15/20.

Duc d'Enghien, 3 av. de Ceinture (at the casino), Enghien-les-Bains, 12 miles from Paris, phone 412–8000. Cl. Sun. eve. and Mon. 250–350 francs. Mich: 2 stars; G&M: 16/20.

Pavillon Henri IV, 21 rue Thiers, St.-Germain-en-Laye, 13 miles from Paris, phone 451–6262. Open daily. 300 francs. A place for lunch if you are sightseeing in the area. Mich: no mention; G&M: 13/20.

Les Trois Marches, 3 rue Colbert in pl. du Château, Versailles, phone 950–1321. Cl. Sun., Mon. 350–500 francs. The top-rated restaurant in Versailles. Mich: 2 stars; G&M: 17/20.

La Vieille Fontaine, 8 av. Gretry, Maisons-Lafitte, 13 miles from Paris, phone 962–0178. Cl. Sun., Mon. 350–450 francs. Go in the summer, in good weather. Excellent and beautiful restaurant. Mich: 2 stars; G&M: 18/20.

Before I continue, let me remind you:

Taxis are always around when you don't want them, and never around between 8:00 and 8:30 P.M., when everyone is trying to get to a restaurant. If you have an 8:30 dinner reservation, start working on a taxi by 8:00 or 8:10, or you'll end up walking, taking the metro, or being very late. When in doubt and if you can, hire a car.

Most of Europe runs on a twenty-four-hour clock, so when you make an 8:30 dinner reservation, you should say 2030. It takes some getting used to, but eventually you'll realize you're eating lunch at 13 hours and not 1:00 P.M.

Pet Peeve Number 678: the word "crèpe." It is *not* pronounced *craype,* as in "drape." It is pronounced *krep,* as in "schlepp."

If you're traveling with kids, the following restaurants would be amusing for them, or at least less boring than some of the others.

Au Pied de Cochon	Julien
Bistro de la Gare	Le Petit Zinc
Bistro Romain	La Petite Chaise
Concorde Lafayette Hotel (buffet)	Relais Louis XIII
La Coupole	Le Train Bleu
Jules Verne	

Open on Saturday Night

Ambassade d'Auvergne
L'Ambroisie
Androuet
L'Aubergade
Auberge des Deux Signes
Beauvilliers
Le Bernardin
Bistro de la Gare
Bistro d'Hubert
Bistro 121
Bistro Romain
Bofinger
Le Bourdonnais
Brasserie Flo
Brasserie Lipp
Le Bristol
La Cafetière
Le Camélia
Le Carpaccio
Caviar Kaspia
Cazaudehore
Au Châteaubriant
Chez l'Ami Louis
Chez les Anges
Chez Francis
Chez Georges
Chez Guy
Clodenis
Le Coq Hardi
La Coquille
Le Coupe-Chou
La Coupole
Le Crillon
Le Divellec
Le Dôme
Duc d'Enghien
Duquesnoy
Erawan
La Ferme St.-Simon
La Fermette Marbeuf
La Fermette du Sud-Ouest

La Flamberge
Le Galant Verre
Le Grand Chinois
La Grande Cascade
La Guirlande de Julie
Jenny Jacquet
Jules Verne
Julien
Lamazère
Lasserre
Laurent
Lou Landès
Maison Prunier-Traktir
Maxim's
Michel Rostang
Le Moï
Olympe
Au Pactole
Pantagruel
Passy Mandarin
Le Pavillon des Princes
La Petite Chaise
Le Petit Niçois
Le Petit Zinc
Pharamond
Au Pied de Cochon
Le Pre Catalan
Princesse Castel
Prunier-Madeleine
Au Quai d'Orsay
    and Annexe
Au Quai des Ormes
Le Raccard
Ramponneau
Le Récamier
Relais Louis XIII
Ritz-Espadon
Tan Dinh
Terminus Nord
Tour d'Argent
Le Train Bleu

Les Trois Marches
Le Vaudeville

La Vieille Fontaine
Vi Foc

Open on Sunday Night

L'Aubergade
Bistro de la Gare
Bofinger
Brasserie Flo
Brasserie Lipp
Le Bristol
Le Cafetière
Le Camélia
Cazaudehore
Chez Francis
Chez l'Ami Louis
Le Coq Hardi
La Coupole
Le Crillon
Le Dôme
La Ferme St.-Simon
Le Fermette Marbeuf
La Grande Cascade
Le Grande Chinois

Jules Verne
Julien
Maison Prunier-Traktir
Le Moï
Olympe
Passy Mandarin
Le Pavillon des Princes
La Petite Chaise
Le Petit Zinc
Au Pied de Cochon
Prunier-Madeleine
Le Raccard
Ramponneau
LeRelais Boccador
Ritz-Espadon
Le Seoul
Terminus Nord
Le Train Bleu
Le Vaudeville

Closed Monday

L'Ambroisie
Le Bernardin
Bistro 121
Brasserie Lipp
Le Camélia
Au Châteaubriant
Chez les Anges
Clodenis
Le Dôme
Le Duc
Duc d'Enghien

La Grande Cascade
Lasserre
Lou Landès
Maison Prunier-Traktir
Olympe
Pharamond
Le Pre Catalan
Au Pressoir
Tour d'Argent
Les Trois Marches
La Vieille Fontaine

Closed Tuesday

Chez l'Ami Louis

Closed Wednesday

L'Aubergade
Le Coq Hardi

Restaurants Open in the Summer

　　Even though the natives take to the hills and the Italian Riviera during the summer, the tourists are still in town to fill tables. Most restaurants are open in July, but many are closed in August. Here is the latest list of those places which *are* open in August. This list is subject to change, however, from one summer to the next.

L'Ambassade d'Auvergne
L'Ambroisie (part)
Androuet
L'Auberge des Deux Signes
Beauvilliers
La Belle Epoque
Bistro de la Gare
Le Bistro d'Hubert
Bistro Romain
Bistro 121
Bofinger
Le Bourdonnais
Brasserie Flo
Brasserie Lipp
Le Bristol
Le Camélia
Caviar Kaspia
Chez Francis
Chez les Anges
Clodenis
Le Coq Hardi
Le Coupe-Chou
Le Crillon
Dodin Bouffant
Le Dôme
Le Duc
Duc d'Enghien
Duquesnoy
La Ferme St.-Simon (part)
La Fermette Marbeuf
La Flamberge (part)
Le Galant Verre
Le Gosier en Pente
La Grande Cascade
Le Grand Chinois
La Guirlande de Julie
Guy Savoy
Jean-Claude Ferrero (part)
Joséphine or Chez Dumonet
Jules Verne
Julien
Laurent
Lou Landès
Maison Prunier-Traktir
Maxim's
Michel Rostang
Morot-Gaudry
Olympe
Au Pactole
Le Pavillon des Princes
Pavillon Henri IV

La Petite Chaise

Le Petit Zinc

Pharamond

La Piscine

Le Pre Catalan

Au Quai d'Orsay

Le Raccard

Le Récamier

Ritz-Espadon

Robuchon (Jamin)

Terminus Nord

Le Toit de Passy

Le Tour d'Argent

Le Train Bleu

Les Trois Marches

Au Trou Gascon

Le Vaudeville

Crazy Horse Saloon

This is not a restaurant, a saloon, or a place to go and dance. It's a strip joint, the most highly rated one in Paris, with supposedly the most beautiful girls. There are two or three shows nightly; no dinner. It will cost about 40 dollars per person, depending on how much you want to slip the usher for a good seat. It is full of mostly tourists who are mostly Americans. Music is canned, as is the singing. The girls, some of them, are gorgeous (at least from a distance). The dancing is more like squirming around to music. In my opinion, it is one gigantic waste of time and money. Better to go to the **Lido de Paris** and see a really good show. It's at 116 bis Champs-Elysées and open every night from 10:00 P.M. to 3:00 A.M. (phone 563–1161).

Hint: don't go with a bus tour.

One of the four top discos in Paris at 32 rue Tilsitt, 17e, at the Etoile. All night dancing in a very large, tiled, empty swimming pool on several levels. "Interesting" crowd, good music and effects.

Shopping

Nonshoppers shop in Paris. They can't help it. The presentation in the shop windows is always enticing and usually spectacular. Not only that, you see all sorts of wonderful little goodies you don't see at home, or at least don't notice. Depending on the franc, shopping in Paris can be very economical.

Certainly, perfumes and colognes are always much cheaper there than in the States. As for clothing, things you buy in Paris will last you for years, both in quality and style. I've never found clothing necessarily to be less expensive than at home; nor is it more expensive. The difference comes in the *value* you get for the money you spend. If you happen to hit a good sale or go to a couturier outlet, you can save a *lot*. Then there's the *detaxe*. If you take advantage of that, you save around 15 percent, depending on the article. French crystal, silver, and porcelain are a definite bargain, including shipping fees. Compare prices of what a piece of Baccarat costs at a store at home and what it costs at the Baccarat showroom in Paris. Same goes for Lalique, Daum, Christofle, Sèvres, Limoges, etc. You also have a much better selection: everything they produce.

Specialty food stores are everyone's major weakness. The range of items, their presentation, fantastic quality, and uniqueness are a true delight. Even the neighborhood charcuterie or boulangerie has the most wonderful-looking items you've ever seen. It's hard not to buy and eat something from every store. Instead of going to lunch in a restaurant, make the rounds of a few food shops and take a picnic into a park. Now that's fun! French cheeses, for which you pay a small fortune at home, are dirt cheap. A baguette of bread costs around 35 cents. A really good local French white wine can cost about 3 dollars; anything less is questionable as to its true drinkability.

If you are looking for antiques, you'll drown in the number of pos-sibilities. All you have to do is walk along a couple of streets, anywhere, and you'll get the idea.

If you can find a small, collapsible shopping bag to carry around in your purse, it will come in very handy. You never know when the shopping bug is going to bite, so be prepared.

As I mentioned before, try *not* to use traveler's checks in stores. You'll get a better exchange at a bank. And don't forget to ask for the *detaxe* form when you spend 800 francs or more.

Generally, shopping on the Left Bank will find you better prices than shopping on the Right Bank (not always, though). I find the Left Bank just plain more fun! Of course, you have to know where to go, which is what I want to get across in this section.

The old habit of closing for two hours during lunch seems to be fading away in Paris, but many shops still do it. Shopping is best beginning about 2:30 or 3:00 in the afternoon, as the stores are all open and stay open until about 7:00 P.M. Many stores do *not* open before 11:00 A.M., especially on Mondays.

If you're shopping on a budget, decide what things you can live without, or what you absolutely cannot find at home. Otherwise, my motto is "If you like it, buy it!" "Need" should not be part of the decision.

There's a little game to play when you enter a shop. Look around for the proprietor, smile, nod your head, say "Bonjour." She'll return the greeting and ask you if she can help you with anything. If you don't speak French, you won't know what she's talking about. Tell her you don't speak French (learn that phrase!), continue to smile, and get the idea across that you are just looking around, or point to an item if you want something specific. Most shopkeepers are more than anxious to be helpful. Whether or not you end up buying anything, be sure you say "Merci" and "Au revoir" when you leave the shop. If they offer to gift-wrap an item and it is indeed a gift, let them do it. Some of their wrapping is really charming.

Right Bank

The Avenue Montaigne and the side streets running off it are where many of the couturiers have their main showrooms and boutiques. This is the area where the Plaza Athénée, Georges V, and Parc-Elysée hotels are located. Look for the following streets: Marignan, Marbeuf, François 1er, Tremoille, Marot, Pierre 1er de Serbie.

Bab's is a great discount couturier clothing store, with a huge selection and often a good find. There are two stores, the main one being at 7 av. Marceau (near Place de l'Alma in the 16e), and the other one at 89 bis av. des Ternes, 17e.

Au Bain Marie, 20 rue Herold, 1er, is a beautiful store for housewares and gifts.

Boutique Daunou, 17 rue Daunou, 2e, near Place de l'Opéra, carries Pierre Cardin ready-to-wear at good prices.

No silk items, but lots of wool, sweaters, and high-quality polyester.

The Champs-Elysées is a good place to shop if you know where to go.

There are some beautiful *galeries* on the right-hand side of the street as you go toward the Arc de Triomphe (Galeries du Rond Point, next door at #26, and again at Galerie du Claridge at #74). These arcades have very nice stores and their prices are no worse than on St. Honoré. Much of the rest of the street is touristy, so you want to be a bit selective.

Galeries Lafayette, behind the Opéra, is Paris' nicest department store and one of the largest in the city, covering two city blocks and several stories high.

The metro stop Chausée d'Antin takes you to the door, and there's even an entrance directly into the store from the station. Inside, look up at the beautiful domed ceiling.

When you shop at the GL, save all your receipts, even ones you may get from the booths out on the street. Have the salesperson write on each receipt what you bought. At the end of your stay in Paris, take all these receipts to the *detaxe* counter (providing you have spent at least 800 francs), located on the street level. They have the whole thing down to a beautiful system.

If you decide to buy perfume here (a good idea), each salesgirl will lead you to another counter, and they keep track of what you're buying on one big sales slip. Then you only have to go to the *caisse* (cashier) once.

The first and second floors (meaning second and third, à la U.S. standards) are for women's apparel, including most major designer boutique lines. It's a good place to shop if you're short on time and want to see the latest styles, all in one place. Higher floors carry men's and children's items, and the basement is housewares heaven. Restrooms are also in the basement.

There is a branch *(succursale)* of GL located in the Montparnasse Tower, but it is a sorry second to the main store.

Les Halles, Beaubourg, Pompidou Center, and Forum les Halles,
These are all more or less in the same area, which is quite large.
The entire district has been undergoing extensive renovation for the past few years, luckily saved from total demolition. Many of the streets take pedestrian traffic only, only there always seems to be a vehicle passing somewhere. Most of the shops and boutiques are less expensive than in other areas of Paris. Many feature antique clothing, and the latest "in" thing with the young set. It all started out well and was looking as though it would become a really interesting and nice place to shop, especially the Forum les Halles. I regret to report that while it isn't even finished yet, it has already become very unpleasant: dirty, crowded, noisy, cheap and junky stores and restaurants (with one or two exceptions), and a very rowdy, unkempt crowd (mostly student types and Third World). Too bad. Maybe the city will do something about it before the entire area turns into a slum, while construction continues.

Next to the Pompidou Center there is a small shopping arcade called Galerie du Grande Horloge. That is nice. And don't miss the clock in the patio, at noon or 6:00 P.M. and 10:00 P.M., or on the hour at other times. (See the sightseeing section for more details.) For a nice lunch, go to l'Epi d'Or, Au Pied de Cochon, Pharamond, l'Escargot Montorgeuil, Benoit, or Le Gosier en Pente.

Le Louvre des Antiquaires,   Palais Royale.
For antiques of every kind in a beautiful, rather new building. Three floors, a city block square. You could spend days there. There is a café on the lower level, but you have to eat a complete meal. You can't get a quick bite ("Zees eez not zees znack bahr!" we were told after waiting twenty minutes for a table and ordering only a salad). If you want a snack, there's a marvelous little bar on the upper level.

Marché aux Puces is the giant and famous flea market of Paris, open Saturday, Sunday, and Monday. Take the metro all the way to Porte de Clignancourt, or better yet, take a taxi out and the metro back. The first few streets you walk on will be filled with a lot of junk, but every now and then you'll spot a good buy. WATCH YOUR WALLETS AND PURSES CARE-FULLY—this is Pickpocket's Paradise. The main reason to go to the Marché aux Puces is for antiques, and these you will find on the streets Biron (the best) and Vernaison. You'll have to deal with cash or traveler's checks at the Marché, and cash is best (providing it doesn't get stolen before you can spend it). There aren't any great places to eat in the area, but a decent lunch can be found at Le Biron, 85 rue de Rosiers by Allée Biron #1. Try the frisée au lardons and the profiteroles.

Miss "Griffes" at 19 rue de Penthièvre, 8e, near the Bristol hotel, is a small boutique carrying designer clothes with labels missing.
You have to fish around but you can get lucky. (How about a Givenchy silk dress for about 250 dollars?)

Place de l'Opéra is not the best place to shop, as it is totally touristy. One exception might be discount (so-called duty-free) perfume stores in or near the *place*.

Place des Victoires, 1er/2e, near Les Halles, is becoming a very nice little shopping area. Good lunch stop is Chez Georges, 1 rue Mail.

Rue de la Paix, between Place Vendôme and Place de l'Opéra. This is a short but very chi-chi street. For openers you have the principal *Cartiêr* store. Further on down is a store called *Alain Figaret,* which is a super place for shirts and blouses, both men's and women's. Also silk neckties. Fine, fine quality cotton, beautiful prints, great styles, and *cheap! Detaxe* form, no problem. Across the street at #22 is *Repetto,* a dance and leotard store, with some gorgeous exercise, dance, and work-out ensembles. Unusual leotard styles, gigantic stock, good prices.

The place to buy perfume is *Michel Swiss,* 16 rue de la Paix, 2nd floor (there's an elevator). They open at 9:00 A.M. Not only can you get every conceivable brand of perfume, cologne, after-shave, etc., you can also get makeup, cosmetics, scarves, purses and other leather items, sweaters, and crystal atomizers. Everything is discounted, with the best prices I've seen for such items. On top of their discount, you also get the 15 percent *detaxe.* One example: a Marcel Franck crystal atomizer selling in Beverly Hills for 125 dollars plus tax cost me about 27 dollars at Michel Swiss. Before you buy perfume anywhere else, try this. Salespeople speak English and are very helpful. It is obviously well known as it was crowded by 9:30 A.M.

The last time I was in Michel Swiss, I bought two crystal atomizers, one Nina Ricci leather bag, two after-shaves, and seven eau de toilettes or perfumes. I got a 40 percent discount on the perfumes and about 33 percent on everything else. The total came to less than 300 dollars. And they threw in a big carry-on flight bag to get it all home, plus lots of little samples.

The Passage Jouffrey, rue de Provence and rue du Fg. Montmartre, a large, enclosed gallery full of lower-priced shops. The name of the passages changes as you cross streets to Panoramas and Verdreau.

Another enclosed arcade is called *Vivienne,* corner of rue Vivienne and rue des Petits Champs, behind the Palais Royal. Some boutiques, and a darling tearoom called A Priori Thé.

Rue de Passy, in the 16e, not far from the Trocadéro, is a lovely shopping street where you won't see any tourists. Many nice, small boutiques; a daily street market for the neighbors; shops to fit any budget. Two exceptionally nice places to shop on this street are *Franck & Fils,* a large department store with nice-quality merchandise, and *Sephora,* one of Paris' best cosmetics stores. In Sephora you can find every color of nail polish, eye makeup, lipstick, rouge, etc., that exists, Rigaud candles, hats, scarves, shampoo and hair pins, costume jewelry, perfumes, etc.—it's a real treat. There's also a Sephora in Forum les Halles.

Rue de Paradis, 10e, not far from the Gare de l'Est. Metro stop Poissonnière.

This is *the* street for crystal, porcelain, china, etc. Some silver. At the Daum showroom you can see everything that is available, and then they will send you to stores on the street if you want to buy. At #31 bis, set back from the street, is the fabulous Baccarat showroom and museum. Even if you have no interest in buying Baccarat, you should go see this showroom. At the moment, prices are almost one-half less than what they are in the States. All along the street are many, many shops and stores, carrying the best of the French brands. Shipping is generally OK, especially from Baccarat. You might want to carry home purchases from some of the smaller places. Don't go to rue de Paradis on a Saturday or during lunch hours (12:30–3:00), as many places will be closed.

From rue de Paradis you can walk south along rue du Fg.-Poissonière and be in the furrier district. If you cut over to rue LaFayette and walk down, you'll end up at the Place de l'Opéra.

P.S. Another excellent store on Paradis is Club Paradis de la Table, on two floors, at # 38.

Pierre Alain Nemet Cosmétiques et Pharmacie, 4 rue de Rigny at Boulevard. Haussmann in the 8e,

is a good place for face creams, toiletries, and prescriptions. The personnel were extremely gracious, spoke English. I bought some face creams there for 6 to 10 dollars that I've been paying 30 dollars and more for in the U.S.

Rigodon, 31 av. Matignon, 8e, just around the corner from the Bristol hotel, has fabulous dolls, puppets, and masks. They are all handcrafted by local artists, and the larger pieces are signed. The dolls have porcelain hands, feet, and faces and are beautifully painted and lavishly clothed.

Rue Faubourg-St.-Honoré and rue St. Honoré (one and the same), extending east and west from rue Royale.

Even if you are only window-shopping with empty pockets, it's a treat to walk up and down this street and gaze in the windows. The shopping area is best between the Bristol hotel and the Place Vendôme. All the famous couturiers have stores there, and, yes, you will pay!

Rue Rivoli, from Place de la Concorde to the Palais Royale.

I mention this street, most of it under an arcade, because it is a good place *not* to shop. It is totally touristy, as you will quickly see when you walk by. If you want cheap souvenirs, sweatshirts, T-shirts, scarves, etc., this could be the place for you. In all fairness there *are* some nice shops here and there along the way. One is Eden Perfumes, #212. There are a couple of nice leather stores, too. W.H. Smith is an English bookstore at the corner of Rivoli and Cambon.

Roger Sakoun, 85 rue du Faubourg-Saint-Honoré, 8e.

There are so many gorgeous boutiques on this street that you might miss this one, which is in the block past the Bristol hotel. Beautiful couturier clothes, expensive, but some affordable items if you aren't on a major splurge.

Rue Royale, which runs from the Place de la Concorde to the Place de la Madeleine.

It is on rue Royale that you find the Lalique showroom on one side and Christofle on the other. Lalique is also very reliable for shipping. Their big problem is lack of salespeople. So many times we have walked in there with the intention to buy, and found two people to wait on twelve customers. Each transaction takes some time, too. Most of the other customers are Americans, it seems.

There are many nice shops along rue Royale, and the street crosses rue St. Honoré, which is *the* luxury shopping street of Paris. More on that later. Rue Royale terminates in Place de la Madeleine, dominated by a giant neoclassical church. Walk completely around the *place*, as this takes you by some of the best specialty food stores in the city. Not to be missed are Fauchon (two stores), Hédiard, and Caviar Kaspia. Be sure you go into Fauchon and browse around. In the candy department, you must get some of the truffles. They are expensive and exquisite—I think the best I've ever had. Their crystallized ginger is also great.

Samaritaine, at Pont Neuf on the Seine.
This is a *huge* department store that is really quite famous. It's so *huge* that I can never find anything to buy! You would need a guide, map, flashlight, overnight bag, food supply, and four pairs of shoes to get through all of it. Very inexpensive, lower-quality merchandise.

Two other discount-designer boutiques are *Mendés,* 65 rue Montmartre, 9e, and *Didier Ludot,* 24 rue de Montpensier, 1er, near Palais Royal.

For housewares, cookware, silverware, dishes, etc., you have terrific choices: *A. Simon* at 36 rue Etienne-Marcel and 48 rue Montmartre, 2e, *Dehillerin,* 18 rue Coquillière, 1er. Actually you have more choices than that, but these are the ones I can recommend. They are about two blocks apart in the Les Halles district. Shipping is OK.

For costume jewelry and fabulous fakes, go to *Ken Lane* at 14 rue de Castiglione, 1er. It's behind the Meurice Hotel and down the street from the Ritz.

More inexpensive costume jewelry can be found at *Agatha,* 8 rue de la Pompe, 16e. *Claude de Lupia* at 137 Fg.-St.-Honoré also had nice jewelry, but is basically an accessories (decorator's) store. "Bijoux fantasies" or fabulous fakes can be found in many shops all over Paris, at good prices.

Left Bank

Left Bank shopping is a different dish of ice cream from the Right Bank. While there are some expensive boutiques and antique stores, there are also many little inexpensive places on quaint streets and squares.

The area around the crossroads of St. Germain and rue de Rennes is a good palce to start. The small, twisting streets are full of boutiques on both sides of Boulevard St. Germain. It gets very confusing and you can get temporarily lost, but sooner or later you'll find yourself back on a main street. Look for the following streets: Dauphine, Mazarine, St. André-des-

Arts, rue de l'Ancienne Comédie, rue de Buci, rue de Tours, Cour du Commerce, Passage de la Petite Boucherie, Seine, Bonaparte, Four, Madame, Rennes, Sabot, Bernard-Palissy, Dragon, Canettes, Vieux-Colombier, Babylone, Mezières, Ciseaux, Sèvres, Raspail, Cherche-Midi, Chomel, and anything in between.

Anémone, 4 rue Bernard-Palissy, has great costume jewelry. Across the street is a nice little sit-down crêperie if you're hungry. Another Anémone is on St. Honoré by Place Vendôme.

Bon Marché, rue de Sèvres, is a large department store (the name means "cheap" but not everything they have is).

You can walk all the way down rue de Rennes and end up at the Montparnasse Tower, but the closer you get to the tower, the tackier the stores become. Shopping at the tower is not pleasant.

Au Caprice Maroquinerie, 19 rue de Sevres, is good for leather items, suitcases, handbags, etc.

Cerise, 1 pl. Alphonse Deville, 7e, just off rue de Sèvres near Bon Marché. Unusual and ethnic jewelry.

Au Chat Dormant, 15 rue du Cherche-Midi, is a shop for cat lovers. Nearby at #8 is *Poilane,* the best bread store in town.

Fabrice, 33 & 54 rue Bonaparte, has more costume jewelry and accessories.

Lupin, 17 rue Chomel (by Bon Marché department store), has beautiful knit items.

Ste. Placide, a street just off rue de Sèvres at the Bon Marché, is one long row of very drekky discount shops. If you are a real tried-and-true bargain hunter you may have the patience to dig something out of this jumble. I love a good buy, but I found Ste. Placide going just too far. The most popular store there is *Le Mouton à Cinq Pattes* at #8.

Brasserie Lipp on St.-Germain is good for lunch. If you can stand it, you can also eat at *Deux Magots* or *Bonaparte,* well-known brasseries. Or walk down to *Restaurant des Saints-Pères* at 175 St.-Germain. While you're in the area, do go in and look at the special little church of St.-Germain-des-Prés.

A short distance from the St.-Germain boutiques is another area known for its abundance of antique stores, many of which carry top-quality pieces at high prices. This area starts around rue du Bac and rue de Beaune, the streets Sts.-Pères, l'Université, Jacob, and Bonaparte.

Atelier 12, 12 rue des Sts.-Pères, 7e, is a very unusual gallery/boutique with items I find hard to describe. They are small sculptures of various materials, vividly painted, each one is unique, all made by one person. Not for everyone, but the items will appeal to many, and they're fun to look at, anyway.

At *Blanc Cassé,* corner of Bac and Lille, you can get discounted linens and towels, degrifféed.

Chacun Pour Toi, 58 rue de Bourgogne near the Rodin Museum, is a lovely little shop with unusual gift items, some of which can be personalized.

Changrila, 14 rue de Beaune, for gift items.

Demons et Merveilles, 45 rue Jacob, has unusual ethnic clothing and jewelry.

Fac Bazaar, 38 rue des Sts.-Pères, 7e, for beautiful sweaters for children and adults. Unusual styles and colors. Reasonable prices.

Galerie Sonkin, 10 rue de Beaune, has a great selection of country French antiques and furniture.

Jeanne Peral, at 17 rue des Sts.-Pères, has fantastic ethnic and costume jewelry; expensive.

Village Suisse is a nice little network of expensive antique shops located on avenue de la Motte-Picquet at avenue de Suffern. Open Sundays, closed Tuesdays and Wednesdays. Avenue de la Motte-Picquet is a nice shopping street itself.

Boulevard St. Michel (Boul. Mich.) from the Seine to the Luxembourg Gardens has shops on both sides of the street which would appeal to teenagers. All the latest hip stuff, whatever it happens to be.

Street Markets

One of the delights of Europe is the many colorful open-air markets that you come across from time to time. Many of them are daily affairs, others are scheduled only on certain days. There are so many of them in Paris (practically one for each neighborhood) that it would be impossible to list them all. The following are some of the main ones.

Rue d'Aligre, between rue Crozatier and rue de Charenton, 12^e, metro Ledru-Rollin. Not Mondays. Mornings. A huge neighborhood open-air market that goes on for several blocks. Sunday is best. It's great!

Rue de Buci, on the Left Bank every afternoon around 4:00 there is a nice little market. Not worth the effort to make a special trip, but if you are shopping in the area, you'll run across it.

Rue Daguerre, metro Denfert-Rochereau, late afternoons.

Rue Montorgueil, between rue Etienne-Marcel and St. Eustache Church, near Forum les Halles. Sunday mornings. Small.

Rue Mouffetard, one of Paris' oldest and best-known markets, on one of the city's most ancient and twisty streets. Go either in the mornings before noon, or late afternoons, after 4:00 P.M. Begin at St. Médard Church (go in and look at it first) and walk uphill all the way past Place de la Contrescarpe to rue Clovis. At that point turn left and you'll be heading downhill toward the Sorbonne. Immediately you'll come to St. Etienne du Mont, which you should go in and see (refer to sightseeing section). Other places of interest in the area, as long as you're there, are: Gobelins Tapestry factory, Arènes de Lutèce, Jardin des Plantes, the Sorbonne, and the Panthéon. You can really spend the better part of the day discovering this wonderful quarter of the city.

Porte de Montreuil, 20ᵉ, Sunday mornings.

Porte de Vanves, 14ᵉ, weekend mornings.

On Avenue Président-Wilson, across the street from the Museum of Modern Art of the City of Paris, on Saturday mornings there is a wonderful market. You'll wish you had a kitchen!

St. Denis Basilique, Don't go out of your way to go to this market, but if you happen to go see the basilica, which you should, you can wander into the town and see the market. Probably a good example of what a typical suburb market is all about, in a rather poor section. Not open on Sundays.

Shopping at Charles de Gaulle Airport.

Don't laugh! If you have a few francs you don't want to carry home or if you forgot a gift for someone, this is good to know about. I don't mean the duty-free shops, either. From the main floor where you check in, go downstairs. It is on this level that you will find stalls selling everything from goat cheese to designer earmuffs. Snack bars, magazine stands, etc., are also in this area. As for the duty-free shops, they are upstairs on the way to your boarding gate. If you want to hold out for duty-free items, better plan on extra time. Those counters are always a madhouse, not to mention confusing.

To Duty-Free or Not to Duty-Free

This decision depends on how desperate you are to save a few bucks, or francs, as the case may be. Certainly duty-free shopping is far from relaxing, you can't try anything on, you're usually in a rush, and contrary to popular opinion, you *do* have to pay duty on whatever you buy, back in the States. Do you really want to lug a fifth of Courvoisier all the way home, just to save 5 dollars? You have to decide if it's all worth it. There are so-called duty-free stores all over the city and you can often save some money by shopping in them. But not always. Many of them are very touristy. As with everything else, you should shop around and compare prices, if you have the time and inclination.

There are some items, such as perfume, that you should buy in Paris.

You really do save a lot. Then you have the problem of carrying it home; bottles of perfume are heavy and take up space. In Paris you can get gorgeous hosiery in all sorts of colors and textures, for 3 to 8 dollars a pair, and you probably won't see the same thing when you get home. If you have a baby, want to have a baby, know someone who has a baby, or know someone who might have a baby someday, you'll want to buy baby clothes. You'll see what I mean when you look in the shop windows. The baby clothes in France and Italy are so adorable you'll find an excuse to buy some. Believe it or not, at the PrisUnic and UniPrix department stores (similar to Thrifty or SavOn), you can sometimes find beautiful baby clothes at dirt-cheap prices. If you like Rigaud candles, buy them in Paris (again you have a weight and space problem).

Always, but always, pack one or two collapsible suitcases in your suitcase, especially if you are a shopper. If you go through those, you can always get another one at a sidewalk stand or a department store. Somehow you'll get it all home, and be glad you did. It helps to ship as much as possible.

I find it's a good idea *not* to carry receipts home with you, like in your wallet. This includes *detaxe* receipts. If you are really anxious to keep some receipt for future reference, mail it home to yourself. One exception to this would be a receipt for anything you are having mailed to you. Also, mail yourself credit card receipts.

By the way, a drugstore in Paris is not a drug store. What I mean is, it's more like a minidepartment store. If you want drugstore items à la U.S.A., you must go to a "pharmacie."

If you forget to pack an extension cord, go into a hardware store *(quincaillerie)* and ask for a "ralongeur." If they don't carry it, they'll probably send you to a store that carries electrical items.

Sightseeing

One can go sightseeing in Paris by walking down any street. So far I've yet to find one that didn't have at least something vaguely interesting on it, and most of the time you don't know where to look first. Sightseeing, by my definition, doesn't necessarily mean going to see a monument or a museum. True sightseeing includes people-watching, window-shopping, park sitting, strolling, as well as the out-and-out cultural trips.

Paris is a cornucopia of art, museums, monuments, parks, bridges, statues, fountains, flowers—it never ends. Visitors who are in the city for only a brief period will be hard-pressed to make choices as to what to see and what to eliminate. If you are a first-timer *(débutant),* or if you are on limited time, look at the first few items on my lists, as these are the ones everyone should see. As you scan further down the list, you'll find less famous places to see, but not necessarily less interesting. I've found that the lesser-known, more out-of-the-way places are often the most exciting or charming. This is true wherever you go.

I won't attempt to mention every detail (time schedules, admissions, etc.) except in some cases. For this up-to-date information, refer to the green Michelin guide. It somehow manages to stay on top of all the little changes in scheduling that go on.

Monuments, Squares, Boulevards, Parks, and Anything That is Not a Church or Museum

L'Arc de Triomphe. If you're already on the Champs, take the underground walkway to avoid being killed and get over to the Arc. If you go up to the top, you'll get a great view of the area and understand why it is also called the Etoile, meaning star. There's an interesting museum inside which deals with the construction of the monument. On French holidays, there is generally some ceremony at the Tomb of the Unknown Soldier, and it's usually quite impressive.

Balzac's home, at 47 rue Raynouard is open daily for Balzac fans. It's rather small and contains old manuscripts, engravings, and items that belonged to one of France's and the world's greatest writers. The neighborhood is in the *Passy* section, a very pleasant area with expensive apartments, some nice shops on rue de Passy. Nearby is the *Clemenceau Museum,* at 8 rue Franklin. The walk from Balzac's house back toward the Eiffel Tower is quite attractive, along the river bank, rue de Passy, or avenue Paul Doumer. You'll end up at the *Palais de Chaillot*, no matter what. In the opposite direction, along rue de Passy, you'll come to a nice little park, beyond which is the *Marmatton Museum.*

Bâteaux Mouches is what you call all those tour boats you see going up and down the Seine. You can get on them at various points along the river (mainly around the Eiffel Tower). You're probably resisting the urge because you think it's silly and just for tourists, etc., but forget that because if you've never done it, it's a great way to see part of Paris. It's especially lovely to go on a warm evening around 9:00, as all the major buildings are illuminated. I think the last tours go before 10:00 P.M., so don't wait too late. Don't go if it's rainy or if the Seine is extremely high, as they can't negotiate some of the bridges and you won't get the whole tour.

Beaubourg, or Pompidou Center, Forum les Halles.
You could spend an entire day in these few square blocks. Within the Pompidou Center is the wonderful *Museum of Modern Art,* third and fourth floors. Many other rooms have temporary exhibits. Just to the north of the Pompidou, almost on the corner of rue St.-Martin and rue Rambuteau, is a shopping gallery called Passage du Grand Horloge. If you walk through the gallery into the inner courtyard, turn right and look up, you'll see a most unusual clock, *Le Defendeur*

du Temps. On every hour the clock comes to life and enacts a little scene, and at noon, 6:00 and 10:00 P.M. it does extra moves. A real delight for everyone; a must for kids. At the extreme opposite end of the Pompidou Center, between it and the Church of St. Merri, is a large pool in an area called *Place Igor Stravinsky.* This pool is full of unusual and wonderful water fountains, all moving, each one dedicated to one of Stravinsky's works. Another must for kids. The *Church of St. Merri* is also worth looking at and into.

The Pompidou Center structure is a marvel to see, even if you don't like very modern architecture. The large square in front of the building comes alive from about noon on, with all sorts of people doing crazy things. Some of the performers are really good and have gained a certain popularity; other acts range from the ridiculous to the really ridiculous. In any event, it's great people-watching.

Near the Pompidou Center is a *Museum of Holography.* (Refer to the museum list for details.)

A short walk from the Pompidou Center leads you to the former Les Halles area, now being completely renovated. Here you will find the new and modern shopping area—*Forum les Halles*—one of Paris' oldest and most impressive churches, *St. Eustache,* several well-known old eateries offering onion soup and shellfish, and the round Bourse de Commerce building. In view of that building, at 23–25 rue Jean-Jacques Rousseau, is another favorite restaurant, *l'Epi d'Or.* A couple of doors from that is an old, wooden, and beautiful *galerie*, *Galerie Ver-Dodat.*

The Bibliothèque Nationale (or National Library), behind Palais Royale, is indeed a library, and not all the rooms are open to everyone. The architecture is eighteenth and nineteenth centuries. On the first floor, in what is called the Mazarin Gallery, are temporary exhibitions. In the same area is a large room displaying coins, medals, Greek and Etruscan art—a real mishmash of very interesting items.

The Bois de Boulogne is a gigantic park, forest, or woods, whatever you want to call it, located at the west end of Paris. If you travel west from the Etoile down avenue Foch, you'll arrive at the Bois. In the Bois itself are the race track, several excellent restaurants, a garden in which are grown many of the flowers used elsewhere in Paris, some museums, lakes, an amusement park for children (*Jardin d'Acclimatation*), and various gardens (rose, French, Japanese, rock). You can go bike riding, jogging, pique-nique-ing, horseback riding, driving, walking, birdwatching, horse racing, and to the zoo. The museum is the *National Museum of Popular Art and Traditions,* concerned with the environmental, technological, industrial, agricultural, and folk aspects of French life. Bois de Boulogne is pronounced *Bwah-Duh-Boo-Lone-Ya.*

Buttes Chaumont Parc is another of Paris' very large parks, off the beaten track for tourists. It's hilly, with a lake and a small canal and some good views. It's near the St. Martin Canal.

The Canals in Paris are usually a surprise to most people. Yes, Paris does have a canal system, complete with locks and barges. The best time to view all the activity is during the week, as on weekends there isn't much going on. If you go to metro Juarés you can go to St. Martin's Canal, which is the best known and in the prettiest area.

For a cruise through the canals contact La Patache Seine cruise at 874–7530 and ask about their Eautobus cruise. They do not operate in the winter.

The Catacombs are a real treat. Great for kids. Take your flashlight and flash attachment for your camera. Go to metro Denfert-Rochereau and the entrance is on one side of the square. What are the catacombs? Well, they are underground passageways, which were at one time quarries, that go on for blocks. During the eighteenth century, when more land was needed for the living, many cemeteries were dug up and the bones of the inhabitants therein were removed, cleaned, and neatly stacked in the corridors of these quarries. Not stacked just any which way, mind you, but in very creative designs. During the war the Resistance used the catacombs as headquarters. The catacombs are open Tuesday through Friday from 2:00 to 4:00 P.M., and weekends from 9:00 to 11:00 A.M. and 2:00 to 4:00P.M. A line begins to form about a half hour before they open. When they open the doors everyone goes in at once, but it doesn't stay crowded because the people spread out as they walk along. It takes a little over an hour to go through them, and believe me, you'll love it! It's one of the largest and last surviving ossuaries in the world.

The Champs-Elysées.
No matter how often you go to Paris, you end up on the Champs sooner of later. You'll notice right away how touristy it is. But what a magnificent boulevard this is just to look at! For a real thrill, walk along the Champs in the evening after dinner, when the Arc de Triomphe is lit up and there is lots of activity. Sit in one of the sidewalk cafés (*Le Fouquet's* is the biggest and one of the most famous; there's also *Le Drugstore,* which is not sidewalk). The *Tourist Information Bureau* is on this street, as are most of the airline offices. The *galeries* have been spruced up over the past few years. At the end of the Champs furthest from the Arc, just where the trees begin, is a circle called Pont Rond. At that corner you will see a shopping *galerie* called *Rond Point des Champs-Elysées.* If you go in, you'll come face to face with a delightful, large clock and waterwheel device. This would be especially interesting for kids. Another such treat is to be found in the courtyard of the *galerie* next door, at #26. Believe it or not, there's a large and unusual waterfall in the courtyard which does a series of orchestrated moves. You have to hang around about five minutes to see the whole thing. A good idea for lunch is *Prunier-Elysées,* which looks onto this waterfall and provides alfresco dining in good weather. Further up the street at *Galerie du Claridge* (#74) you'll find an interesting clock which tells the time by various vessels continually filling up or emptying out water of different colors. Another OK restaurant serving 24 hours a day is *Quick Elysées,* 144 Champs-Elysées (upstairs). Also recommended is Flora Danica.

The Conciergerie is an imposing building dominating the Seine from Ile de la Cité, between Pont Neuf and Pont au Change (two bridges connecting the island to the Right Bank). The Conciergerie is an old prison, and its chief claim to fame is being the place where all guests of the guillotine awaited their final hour. Most famous names from the Revolution (on the side that lost) spent time here, the most well-known being Marie Antoinette. There are guided tours through the prison, but only in French. Even if you don't understand the language, it's still of interest to take the tour, as you can't see the interior on your own.

Crypte Archéologique, Parvis Notre Dame.

If you walk away from Notre Dame to the far end of the square in front of it, you will see an underground entrance to the Crypte. You are in for a big surprise. Underneath the square, beautifully excavated, is a part of Roman city, plus remains of an older part of Paris. There are beautiful displays, explanations in English and French, interesting lighting. You really have to see this.

The Egouts, or sewers of Paris, have provided fun and games for sewer rats of all kinds throughout the ages. But seriously, folks, there is a rather unusual and interesting one-hour "tour" of this massive underground system. You have to descend at the Quai d'Orsay at Pont de l'Alma (left bank). Open every Monday and Wednesday, and the last Saturday of the month, from 2:00 to 5:00 P.M. The tour is in French, but they give you headphones in English. No, you do not go on a boat or need to know how to swim, and it doesn't smell bad. (Doesn't smell good, either!)

Nicholas Flamel's House, at 51 rue de Montmorency is supposed to be the oldest house in Paris. It is now a restaurant, recently remodeled, but I can't comment about the cuisine. I've heard it's so-so; the main attraction is the atmosphere. The house dates from 1407. It's not far from the Pompidou Center, going north on rue St. Martin. Another old house in the same area is at 3 rue Volta.

The Gobelins Tapestry Factory *(Manufacture des Gobelins)* is really fascinating. The tour is only in French, but for non-French speakers it is still worthwhile as you get to see artisans actually working on some of those incredible tapestries. Located at 42 avenue des Gobelins (metro to Gobelins), the factory tours are only Wednesday, Thursday, and Friday from 2:00 to 4:00 P.M. They are still making the tapestries the same way they did in the seventeenth century. You will see old as well as new works, and you'll definitely leave with a greater appreciation of all tapestries, not just Gobelins.

When you leave Gobelins, walk up avenue des Gobelins, cross Boulevard de Port Royal/Boulevard St.-Marcel and continue a short way to the small church *St. Médard* and *rue Mouffetard,* described earlier.

Hotel des Invalides and Napoleon's Tomb (Tombeau).

There are two museums within this old veterans' hospital *(Military Museum* and *Museum of the Ordre de la Liberation),* plus a church wherein are buried several French military heroes, including Napoleon. His tomb is very impressive, as are the others. Tickets are obtained in the gift shop to the left of the entrance to the church. The military museum, *Musée de l'Armée,* is interesting for kids. *The Rodin Museum* is near the Invalides.

The Hôtel de Ville is the town hall, but what a town hall! Recently cleaned, it is now gleaming white (especially beautiful at night, when illuminated). It dates from the 1800s and is neo-Renaissance in style. There are guided tours of the interior on Monday mornings. The interior contains some very sumptuous rooms. The tour starts at 10:30 A.M. Go to 29 rue de Rivoli.

Ile St. Louis is a small island in the Seine behind Ile de la Cité (the island on which Notre Dame stands). The Ile St. Louis is one of the city's most charming areas, very exclusive, highly desired as a place to live, impossible to get an apartment there. Most of the houses are sixteenth to eighteenth century. The streets are narrow, with views in every direction. If you stroll through Ile St. Louis, including along the *quais* (riverbanks), and read the plaques over the doors, you almost get a history lesson. On rue St.-Louis-en-l'Ile you'll find the ornately decorated *Church of St. Louis.* Further down on the same street is the well-known *Berthillon* ice cream shop. Nearer the church is a marvelous tearoom and pastry shop called *La Charlotte de l'Ile.* Around the corner from Berthillon is another ice cream stand, serving the same product, called *Cadmios* . A popular tearoom and ice cream shop facing the bridge leading to Notre Dame is *Flore en l'Ile.*

One outstanding place to see on Ile St. Louis, which you must not miss, is the *Hôtel de Lauzun,* 17 quai d'Anjou, a block or so from Pont Marie leading from the Right Bank. It is currently open on a regular basis during peak tourist seasons, and only at special times or for groups during the rest of the year. This is by far the most lavish, lush, and almost unbelievable private seventeenth-century house I've yet to see in Paris or anywhere. It's a real jewel. It gives new meaning to the word overdecorated.

Luxembourg Gardens (Jardins) is a large and beautiful garden, rivaling the Tuileries. In the gardens is the *Luxembourg Palace,* formerly and briefly the palace of Marie de Medici. The palace is open for tours on Sundays from 9:30 to 11:00 A.M., and again from 2:30 to 3:30 P.M. Don't miss the Medici Fountain, which shows up on postcards and in practically every picture book about Paris.

Place de la Madeleine.
Another very interesting *place,* especially for shoppers (Lalique, Christofle, rue St. Honoré, many chic boutiques) and food freaks (Fauchon, Hédiard, Caviar Kaspia). The church in the middle of the square, modeled after the Parthenon, is more impressive outside than inside.

The Marais, one of Paris' oldest and formerly one of its most chic areas, allowed to fall into complete decay, is now being slowly renovated. Wonderful, narrow streets with fabulous old buildings. Many of these large old homes are called "hôtels" and are open to the public, usually housing some collection or other. Among the best are:

Hôtel de Béthune-Sully, 62 rue St. Antoine, with guided tours to visit some of the apartments.

Hôtel Carnavalet, 23 rue de Sévigné, home of the Museum of the History of the City of Paris, which is very entertaining.

Hôtel Guénégaud, 60 rue des Archives, housing the *Museum of Hunting* (Musée de la Chasse et la Nature).

Hôtel de Lamoignon, 24 rue Pavée, housing the Historical Library of the city of Paris.

Hôtel Libéral-Bruand, 1 rue de la Perle, where you'll find the Lock and Metalwork Museum (*Bricard Museum*).

Hôtel de Rohan, 87 rue Vieille du Temple, housing temporary exhibitions in many rooms, some of which are in original condition.

Hôtel Salé, 5 rue de Thorigny, now being prepared as the Picasso Museum.

Hôtel de Sens, corner of rue des Nonnains d'Hyères and Quai des Celestins, now housing the *Forney Library.* This hotel is one of the three remaining medieval private houses left in Paris. The facade and the inner courtyard, as well as the garden, are especially interesting to architecture fans.

Soubise Palace, 60 rue des Francs-Bourgeois, wherein are the National Archives, beautifully and carefully displayed and very interesting. You can also visit some of the lavish apartments.

One of the highlights of the Marais is the exquisite *Place des Vosges.* Even if you don't have time to see any of the above-mentioned *hôtels,* be sure you don't miss Place des Vosges. It may be the most beautiful *place* in Paris. There are now some antique shops and decent restaurants beginning to appear in the arcades. Here you can visit the apartment of Victor Hugo, #6, now a lovely museum.

Rue de Rosiers is the heart of the Jewish quarter. Many of the buildings here are extremely old. Read the plaques over the doorways for a sobering experience.

Rue St. Antoine, leading to *Place de la Bastille,* is on the outer limits of the Marais. This is a fun street to walk on, as it also has many old buildings. Often you'll find sidewalk vendors and open-air shops. See the Hôtel de Sully, built in 1624, at #24 (temporary exhibitions).

One church, not really in the Marais but close enough, which you should not miss is the *Church of St.-Gervais-St.-Protais.* The facade is pure classical style and the first of its type to be built in Paris. The interior is flamboyant Gothic. Stand back from the church at the end of the parking lot and get a good look at the facade. If you turn around, you'll see the back of the Hôtel de Ville.

The Memorial de la Déportation is a sobering and small memorial to the thousands of French deported by the Germans during the Second World War. It's located at the tip of Ile de la Cité, where Notre Dame is. Go all the way around behind the cathedral to the very end of the island.

Parc Monceau, about a half mile from the Arc de Triomphe, is my favorite park in Paris. It is so beautiful and so romantic. Located in one of the nicest parts of town, its chief attractions are its wonderful landscaping, flowers, grottoes, ponds, statues, people, kids, ducks, and pigeons. Take an hour and just wander through it. There's a small snack bar in the park where you can get hot, fresh waffles *(gaufres),* among other things. Two museums in the park, which are high on my list, are the *Musée Cernuschi* housing a collection of Oriental art, and the *Musée de Nissim de Camando,* which I advise you not to miss. A third museum, also excellent, is about five minutes away on foot and is called the *Musée Jacquemart-André.* (More on these three museums in the Museum section.)

Montmartre, with its gleaming *Sacré-Coeur,* can also be seen from many points in Paris. Montmartre had its heyday in the twenties. Unfortunately much of its charm has now been buried under tons of tourists and tourist-trappers. Still, a trip up to the top is on everyone's agenda, at least once. My suggestion is to go in the morning, by 10:00 A.M., on a clear day. The worst time to go up there is on a weekend, especially Sunday afternoon. If you go by metro (by now you should be going everywhere by metro), go to either Abesses or Anvers and follow the signs to the Funicular. Another metro ticket for this will take you to the top. If you're looking to burn off the calories from your morning croissant and café au lait, you can go up the stairway. There's a great view of Sacré Coeur from the bottom of this stairway, and a great view of the city from in front of Sacré Coeur. Be prepared for crowds.

Be sure you see the interior of Sacré Coeur and wander inside the little church next door called *St. Pierre.* Next to St. Pierre is the famous and much painted and photographed *Place du Tertre.* It must have been quite charming way back when; now it's more or less a *cauchemar* (nightmare), as you will see. Nevertheless, if you've never seen it, hang on tight to your purse and mosey through.

Find some extra energy and spend an hour walking through some of the old and twisty streets of old Montmartre: look for *Place Emile-Goudeau* (where Picasso used to live), and streets such as rue Ravignan, rue Norvins, rue des Saules, rue St.-Rustique, Place du Calvaire, avenue Junot, and rue Lepic. See the **Lapin Agile** at the corner of rue St. Vincent and rue des Saules; this was the tavern where all the artists used to hang out. Across the street you'll see the Montmartre vineyard, still producing. On rue Lepic you'll see the last two surviving windmills of Montmartre, which used to be all over the hill. One of those windmills is the famous **Moulin de la Galette,** which inspired so many painters and was the site of a former popular dancehall. At 12 rue Cortot visit the **Musée de Montmartre,** which used to be home to Renoir, Dufy, Utrillo, and others. In the cemetery (across from the Lapin Agile) you can visit the tombs of Zola, Berlioz, Gautier, Dumas, Degas, Offenbach, Stendhal, and Greuze. In the Montmartre area is also **Place Pigalle,** horribly named "Pig Alley" during the war, but the name sort of fits now, unfortunately. In the next *place,* Blanche, is the **Moulin Rouge** (the old one.) For Gustave Moreau aficionados, see his atelier and *Museum* with an enormous amount of his works, also in the area.

The Montparnasse Tower, just mentioned dominates the area. Underneath this huge tower is a large shopping mall, a major metro station, and some fast-food places. A branch store of the Galeries Lafayette is here, but it's small, crowded, hot, and not at all like the main store behind the Opéra. The best thing about the Montparnasse Tower is the view from the top! Don't bother if it's not a clear day or evening, which reminds me—the best time to go to the top is around sundown (in the summer, this means between 9:00 and 10:00 P.M.). I must say, the view from this, the tallest office building in Europe, is spectacular and well worth your time and *argent* (money).

Rue Mouffetard is a nice little one-hour stroll. The street is one of the oldest and most charming in Paris. Unfortunately, many of the old buildings are being spruced up too much, but you can still get an idea of what it used to be like. Start at the bottom at the *St. Médard Church* (go inside and look at the church, of course). Don't go between noon and 4:00 P.M. as the delightful street market that occurs there will be shut down for lunch. If you walk all the way to the top, you'll come to rue Clovis, where you'll turn left. There you'll see the church of *St. Etienne du Mont,* which you should not miss. Both the outside and the inside are exceptional. Be sure you go into the cloister to see the stained glass. Across from the church is the *Panthéon* and down the street a ways you'll come to the *Sorbonne.* Also in the area is Paris' largest mosque, *Le Minaret de la Mouffe,* at 1 rue Daubenton.

A second route you can take from rue Mouffetard will lead you to the *Arènes de Lutèce,* what's left of an old Roman arena. To get there, turn right into the quaint Place de la Contrescarpe, go to the left up rue du Cardinal Lemoine just a few steps, then right on rue Rollin. Cross the busy rue Monge and just beyond you'll come to the arena. It's not exactly the Colosseum and is used now by groups of men playing *boules* (bocce ball). Not far from the Arènes de Lutèce is the *Jardin des Plantes,* or the botanical gardens, where you'll also find the *Museum of Natural History.*

Place de la Concorde. This is a particularly beautiful square, for in each direction is a beautiful view. The obelisk in the center was brought from Egypt by Napoleon. Crossing the *place* can be tricky business, so watch what you're doing. From this *place* you can walk in any direction and end up somewhere terrific!

Place de l'Opéra is a large square dominated by the very impressive Opéra, one of the largest theaters in the world. If you can get inside the Opéra to see the theater area, you'll find it's very beautiful. Don't miss the Chagall ceiling. The best way to see the inside is to go to an opera. Behind the Opéra is the Galeries Lafayette department store. *The Café de la Paix* is a famous restaurant and outdoor café. Unhappily, this lovely square is jammed with tour buses and tourists. The exchange bureaus located here, as well as most of the little shops, are *not* the best place to do business. Tourists everywhere, lines, hiked-up prices, etc. The metro stop here is one of the largest ones, taking you in just about any direction. A few steps off Place de l'Opéra, on boulevard des Capucines, is the *Cognacq-Jay Museum,* a little gem. A good restaurant nearby is *Chez Pierre,* Place Gaillon, phone 265–8704.

Palais Royale is a busy area adjacent to the Louvre. This seventeenth-century palace is now the location of government offices. The large garden in the interior is quite lovely, with some shops under the arcades. As you face the Palais, on the left is the *Comédie Française,* with a wonderful interior. To the right is a *huge* antique store called the *Louvre des Antiquaires.* It goes on forever. I think there must be one of everything ever made in there. Even if you aren't looking to buy anything, you should go in there, as it's almost a museum in itself. The entrance to the *Musée des Arts Décoratifs,* in the Louvre building, is close by. To the rear of the Palais Royal past the gardens is the *Bibliothèque Nationale* (library), and one of the oldest and best of Paris' restaurants, *Le Grand Véfour.* A short stroll down rue St. Honoré will take you to the church of *St. Roch,* known for its seventeenth- and eighteenth-century art.

Père Lachaise Cemetery is great fun for the living. It's tremendous in size and the whoozwho of France is buried here. The monuments and tombs are jammed practically one on top of the other, and you really could spend hours or days wandering through them. At each of the main entrances a guard will offer you a map, directing you to famous tombs. For this he'll want a franc or two. If you're tired of doing what everyone else in Paris is doing, take a walk through Père Lachaise. It is especially magnificent on a sunny day in October or November.

Pont Alexandre III, which crosses the Seine down from the Grand and Petit Palais, is Paris' most ornate bridge. It's gaudy to some, romantic to others, but the views of and from the bridge are some of the best in the city, especially with a colorful sunset.

Rue Rivoli runs along the Tuileries from Place de la Concorde to the Marais. This is a heavily traveled street, noisy, fumey. Under the arcades are shops and boutiques, but except for a few, they are really touristy. If you want a T-shirt or sweatshirt from Paris, you'll find plenty of them here, along with every conceivable sort of doodad and gewgaw. There are some hotels located along this street, but I'd only stay in one of them if I didn't care about sleeping.

The Sorbonne, Panthéon, and Boulevard St. Michel area is the Westwood of Paris. You all know what the Sorbonne is so I won't bore you with an explanation. You can walk into this giant old school and look around all you want. *Boul. Mich.* (pronounced "bool meesh"), the short form of Boulevard St.-Michel, is the Westwood Boulevard of Paris. Full of students and more students, and a lot of shops and boutiques that would appeal to teenagers. If you want to find some dirty streets in Paris, you'll more than likely find them around here. The metro stop St.-Michel is usually a disaster area. If you are standing in Place St.-Michel by the Seine and looking away from the Seine, to the left will be some very small, twisty, and fun streets (rue de la Huchette, rue de la Harpe, rue des Prêtres St.-Séverin, rue St.-Séverin, rue du Chat qui Pêche, the last supposedly being the narrowest street in Paris). Along the streets are many ethnic food shops and restaurants. We've eaten at some in the past; the food has been passable and cheap. You go there mainly for the crazy atmosphere. There are two interesting churches in the area—*St.-Julien-le-Pauvre* and *St.-Séverin* (see church section).

Back at Place St.-Michel and with your back to the Seine, to the right are some other small and wonderful little streets, and if you continue to work your way to the right (rue St. André des Arts, rue Danton) you'll end up in the Left

Bank shopping area, where I've spent a major amount of time and francs. Boul. Mich. crosses Boulevard St.-Germain, and at that point you're but a couple of blocks from the area called *St.-Germain-des-Prés*.

As for the *Panthéon,* this great structure contains in its crypt the burial places of many of France's famous citizens (Voltaire, Hugo, Zola, Rousseau, Braille, among others). You can take a guided tour of the crypt, and part of the rest of the Panthéon is open from 10:00 A.M. to 6:00 P.M., Tuesdays excluded.

Before you leave this area, be sure you visit the marvelous church on the square, *St. Etienne du Mont* (see church section). If you walk around behind the church on rue Clovis and turn right on rue Descartes, you'll end up on *rue Mouffetard,* described earlier.

St.-Germain-des-Prés is the heart of the Left Bank. This is the area to the north and south of Boulevard St.-Germain and between rue des Sts.-Pères and rue de Tournon. Some of the best shopping is in this area, plus some famous sidewalk cafés (Deux Magots, for one). You'll also find a marvelous church called *St.-Germain-des-Prés,* what else? Also there's a large church called *St. Sulpice,* worthy of a visit. One of Paris' best-known theaters, the *Odéon,* is in this area, as is the *Palais* and *Jardin de Luxembourg.* To the rear of St.-Germain-des-Prés church is the lovely *Place de Furstemberg,* which ends up somewhere in every French film ever made. In Place de Furstemberg is the *Delacroix Museum* and *atelier* (studio or workshop). There's always a late-afternoon street market on *rue de Buci.* If you go all the way down rue de Rennes you'll arrive at the *Montparnasse Tower.*

Tour Eiffel was *the* star until the Pompidou Center was built. The great thing about the Eiffel Tower is that you can usually see it from anywhere in the city. It does require close-up viewing, however, to really understand what this giant tinker toy is all about. If you have the time, take the ride to the very top for a panoramic view. At the second level you can get off, as there are viewing platforms, a restaurant, and shops, including the outstanding restaurant *Jules Verne*. Let's consider the front of the Eiffel to be on the Seine side. Therefore, the long field at the "back" is called the *Champs de Mars*, ending at a group of buildings which are the Ecole Militaire. Opposite the "front" and across the Seine is the *Palais de Chaillot,* in front of which is the *Trocadéro.* One of the very best views of the tower, especially at night, is from the Trocadéro. In the Palais de Chaillot you'll find four museums *(Maritime Museum, Museum of French Monuments, Museum of Man, Cinema Museum)* and a *Film Library.* (More about these in the museum section.) Also you'll find a freshwater downstairs in the park on the left, aquarium and one of Paris' largest theaters.

The Tuileries is Paris' version of Central Park on a smaller scale. Beautiful in the spring when chestnut trees are blooming, and equally so in the fall when the leaves are turning. In the Tuileries are a couple of snack bars serving all sorts of yummy goodies. If the weather is nice, it's delightful to sit and snack on a Crêpe Bretonne and a glass of wine, and watch the kids, pigeons, and people. The snack bar on the Left Bank side of the park usually has a better selection of items than the one on the Right Bank side. The wonderful Impressionist museum, Jeu de Paume, is located at the Place de la Concorde end. Eventually a part of this collection will be moved to the Musée d'Orsay, now being prepared. Just opposite the Jeu de Paume is a twin building called the Orangerie, which has just reopened after several years of renovation and houses a permanent collection of post-Impressionist works that will not be going to the Musée d'Orsay. At the Louvre end is a round pond popular with children for sailing boats. If you have kids with you, they might enjoy this pastime. On certain days a man shows up with a cartful of big sailboats and for a small amount of money you can rent one. The kids can spend all afternoon sailing these boats, while you go shopping or doze off nearby. The view from the Louvre end of the park up to the Arc de Triomphe is nothing short of *formidable!,* as the French would say. It's an especially thrilling view at sunset. On the Right Bank side of the park, at the boat pond end, there are public *toilettes;* they look menacing, but they really are OK.

Place Vendôme, home of the Ritz Hotel, is a masterpiece of seventeenth-century architecture. It is the sight of the *Colonne Vendôme,* well-known boutiques, and formerly the square on which a few famous people lived and died. If you walk out of Place Vendôme on rue de la Paix, you'll pass the main Cartier store, and what you'll see in the windows will knock your socks off. Just past Cartier you'll come to Place de l'Opéra. If you leave Place Vendôme by rue de Castiglione, you'll cross rue St. Honoré, the famous shopping street (turn right to get to Place de la Madeleine), and will arrive at rue de Rivoli, bordering the Tuileries.

Parc de la Villette, 19e, now being created, will be a huge cultural center even larger than the Pompidou. Scheduled to open in 1986, the 136-acre park will have a major science and technology museum, a theater, restaurants, a canal, and lots of open green space.

Churches

The Dome Church at the Invalides is often overlooked because people are too busy looking at Napoleon's tomb. So when you've seen Napoleon, be sure to take a good look at the interior of the church.

The Madeleine, which looks like a Greek Temple, commands rue Royale and the surrounding *place.* As mentioned earlier, this church is much more interesting on the outside than on the inside, so don't break your leg getting across the street to see it. It does have an interesting history which you can read about elsewhere.

Le Minaret de la Mouffe, 1 rue Daubenton, is a large Moorish-style mosque which will give you a little relief from the other religious edifices you've been seeing. There are guided tours, lasting about fifteen minutes. This is the largest of over sixty mosques in Paris.

Notre Dame, is one of the great cathedrals of the world. There are plenty of things to do at Notre Dame after you walk around the inside and take photos of the rose windows. They have a *Museum* across the street (#10), open

Saturdays and Sundays. You can also go up a long spiral staircase and walk around the towers, getting good views of the city, the towers, gargoyles, etc.

If you stand in front of the cathedral (place du Parvis), which used to be a tacky parking lot, turn your back on the building and walk to the end of the square, you'll see on the right a sign saying *"Crypte Archeologique."* This is described in the last section and you shouldn't miss it.

Also described previously is the *Memorial de la Déportation,* located behind the Cathedral at the tip of the island.

You must walk completely around the building to properly see it. Good views are from the Left Bank and Ile St. Louis.

On Sunday afternoons at 5:45 there is a forty-five-minute free *organ concert.* Sometimes there is some other sort of musical presentation before this. Immediately following the concert is evening mass. To be assured of a seat, you should arrive around 5:15 or so; often it's SRO by the time the concert begins. To avoid the crush of people leaving at the end, stay seated and listen to the beginning of the mass—it's very nice with the choir and all.

The public *toilettes* in the Parvis in front of Notre Dame are OK.

Notre Dame du Travail, 59 rue Vercingétorix, 14e, entrance on rue Guilleminot. Two metro stops from Gare Montparnasse (to metro Pernety) and then a short walk to see this very unusual church, the inside of which is done in the ironwork style of old Les Halles and the turn-of-the-century train stations. A bit out of the way and the neighborhood is on the seedy side, but a must for churchaholics.

Sacré-Coeur and St. Pierre, adorning Montmartre (the former is visible from almost anywhere in the city), are semi-interesting on the inside, so as long as you're there, you may as well go inside and look around. There are marvelous views of the city from the steps of Sacré-Coeur and also from the top of the dome, which you can get to during certain hours of the day. Entrance to the stairway is on the north aisle. The public *toilettes* down the steps from Sacré-Coeur are OK.

St. Alexander Nevsky Cathedral at 12 rue Daru is a stone's throw from Parc Monceau, and is interesting in that it is the Russian Orthodox Church of Paris. It is rather elaborate inside. See the write-up on Parc Monceau for other places to see in the same area.

La Sainte Chapelle is a three-minute walk from Notre Dame on the same island, located in the Law Courts building. As you approach the very ornate gates, you'll see a guard standing out front and it all looks so imposing that you might think you can't get in and leave. I've seen tourists do this, without even asking about entry. Just walk right on through the gates and go to the left, down the driveway. You'll be at the back of this very ornate, old, small church. Walk around to the front and you'll see a ticket window. If the upstairs room is not open, don't bother going in. They have just spent almost two years cleaning and restoring the windows and they should be more exquisite now than ever, if that's possible. Try to go on a sunny day. When you enter the Chapelle, after looking at the main floor room, take the small winding stairway in the corner up to the second level and be prepared to have your mouth drop to the floor. Being moved to tears is not the least bit unusual. If I had to recommend one church in all of Paris or most of Europe to see, aside from the "biggies," this is the one.

St. Etienne du Mont, already mentioned a couple of times in the previous section, is across the street from the Panthéon, up the street from the Sorbonne, and at the top of rue Mouffetard. You really have no excuse for not seeing it. The facade and interior are both remarkable. At the back of the church where they sell a few postcards, there's a door leading into the cloister, where you can see some wonderful stained-glass panels close up, and get a good look at the detail and craftsmanship that really goes into them. The roodscreen in the church is very unusual, as most of them have been removed from other churches. This church is also important as it contains some relics of Ste. Geneviève.

St. Eustache is the immense church dominating the Les Halles area. If you are at the Forum les Halles you can't miss it, and you should take the time to go over and pay a visit. It's one of the oldest and most beautiful churches in Paris and has been undergoing restoration for a number of years.

St.-Germain-l'Auxerrois is a jumble of five architectural styles, with an unusual porch. Inside are some fine wood carvings, statues, and glass.

St.-Germain-des-Prés is *the* oldest in Paris, Romanesque or medieval in style, and very, very charming. You can really feel its antiquity when you're inside. This is one not to miss.

St.-Gervais-St.-Protais, located behind the Hôtel de Ville, was the first church in the classical style built in Paris. Stand at the end of the ugly parking lot to get a good view of the facade. Inside you'll find flamboyant Gothic. One of Paris' more entertaining churches.

St.-Julien-le-Pauvre and St.-Séverin are on the Left Bank, across from Notre Dame. The former is as old as Notre Dame. The view of the cathedral is very nice from the garden. What a contrast between the two! It's really a surprise to go from Notre Dame to St.-Julien-le-Pauvre.

St.-Séverin is just around the corner from the other, and is interesting for its architecture, windows, and concerts given once a week. The streets around St.-Séverin are fun to walk through, being narrow, colorful, and full of eye-popping ethnic food shops and restaurants.

St.-Louis-en-l'Ile, on the island with the same name, is quite decorative on the inside.

Ste. Marguerite, 36 rue St.-Bernard, has a remarkable interior and small cemetery, where Louis XVII is supposedly buried. The stained glass in the church is modern and some of it is beautiful, commemorating World War I heroes. I would not go out of my way to see this church, but if you go to the rue d'Aligre streetmarket, it is just a couple of blocks away.

St. Médard is the quiet little church at the bottom of rue Mouffetard which you should visit before you start your journey up the street.

St. Merri is the small flamboyant Gothic church next to the Place Igor Stravinsky next to the Pompidou Center, and is interesting on the inside for its woodwork and windows.

St. Roch, on rue St. Honoré near Palais Royal, while lost in the shuffle of the busy street on the outside, is quite interesting on the inside for its works of art, mainly dating from the seventeenth and eighteenth centuries.

St. Sulpice, on rue Bonaparte on the Left Bank, is gigantic. Inside are some frescoes by Delacroix and his friends, plus a very unusual altarpiece. From St. Sulpice you can head off down rue Vieux Colombiers and into the best of the Left Bank shopping areas.

Museums

Musée de l'Arc de Triomphe, located in the Arc, has already been discussed in the Monuments, etc., section.

Musée de l'Armée, located in the Invalides, where you'll also find Napoleon's tomb in the Church of the Dome, is just what its name implies—the museum of the army. Within you'll find armor, weapons, uniforms, and memorabilia of French military history. A good place to take kids.

In the same building you'll find the *Musée des Plans-Reliefs,* and the *Musée de l'Ordre de la Libération,* 51 bis bd. de Latour-Maubourg, commemorating the heroes of World War II.

P.S. A good restaurant in this area for lunch or dinner is Chez les Anges (see the Restaurant section). And don't forget that across from the Invalides is the Rodin Museum.

Musée d'Art Moderne de la Ville de Paris, or Modern Art Museum of the City of Paris, 11 av. du Président-Wilson, right on the Seine near the Tour Eiffel, in the Palais de Tokyo. While not on a par with the Modern Art Museum at the Pompidou, this museum does have a nice collection of post-Impressionist to contemporary art, along with temporary exhibitions.

On Saturday mornings on avenue Président-Wilson, there's a really good open-air food market.

Artcurial, 9 av. Matignon, just off the Champs-Elysées at Point Rond, is actually a print gallery, but on display you'll find decorative arts and paintings by contemporary artists.

Musée des Arts Africains et Océaniens, 293 av. Daumesnil, not only displays art and artifacts of Africa, but also has a tropical aquarium downstairs.

Musée des Arts Décoratifs, 107 rue de Rivoli, near Palais Royale and in the Louvre building, features decorative arts from medieval times to 1900 and is quite extensive. During the past few years the museum has been undergoing major renovation, and at this time I'm not sure how much of it has reopened. There are always temporary exhibits as well.

Baccarat Museum, 30 bis rue de Paradis, is adjacent to the Baccarat showroom and you can visit it while you're buying your Baccarat. The museum, which is small, has fine examples of practically everything that Baccarat has ever made.

Musée Bricard, Hôtel Libéral-Bruant, 1 rue de la Perle, in the Marais. Five rooms displaying locks, keys, hinges, knockers (of doors), door handles, and everything you can think of pertaining to locks and keys. Allow one hour.

Musée Carnavalet, 23 rue de Sévigné in the Marais, is open on Tuesdays, so now you have a museum to visit while all the others are closed. Not only is this a beautiful building to see, but the collection is quite fascinating, as it is the museum of the history of Paris.

Musée Cernuschi, 7 av. Velasquez, practically in Parc Monceau, is around the corner from the Camando. The house has a large collection of Oriental art, both antique and modern.

Musée de la Chasse et de la Nature, located in the lovely seventeenth-century hôtel Guénégaud in the Marais area, contains items pertaining to the hunt, including paintings. Great for old kids as well as young kids.

Musée du Cinema, Palais de Chaillot. This is a very large film museum donated by Henri Langlois. You get a one-hour tour, in French, which is really a two-hour tour. The first half-hour is interesting, but after that, unless you are a devout French-speaking movie buff, it becomes a B picture.

Musée de Cluny, 6 pl. Paul-Painlève, corner of Boulevard St. Michel and blvd. St.-Germain, has two attractions other than its fabulous collection of medieval and Roman works. The building is actually a wonderful old manor house that belonged to the Abbots of Cluny, all built over the remains of third-century Roman baths, the walls and other parts of which are still visible and visitable. The famous tapestry series, *Lady and the Unicorn,* is in the rotunda on the first floor. Cluny is pronounced *Clew-nee.*

Musée Cognacq-Jay, 25 blvd. des Capucines, a few steps from Place de l'Opéra. It is a townhouse with period rooms, furnishings, many wonderful paintings, and engravings by famous artists. It doesn't take a long time to visit this museum, it is *never* crowded!

Musée Delacroix, 6 rue de Furstemberg, St.-Germain-des-Prés area behind the church. If you like Delacroix you'll enjoy this small museum, located in his former *atelier* and containing many of his smaller works.

Musée d'Ennery, 59 av. Foch, has a private collection of Oriental art and is a must for you netsuke fans. Located in a private townhouse.

Musée Français de l'Holographie, 15–21 Forum les Halles (1st level). Featuring one hundred or more holographs on all sorts of subjects. Great for kids.

Le Grand Palais is a palace, not a museum, but this is where the top temporary exhibitions appear. There are always one, two, or even three exhibits here, and they are usually all terrific. Be sure you find out what's at the Grand Palais as soon as you hit town. For especially popular shows, there's always a line, and I suggest arriving by 9:30 A.M. to get in when it opens at 10:00.

Musée Grévin, 10 blvd. Montparnasse and in the Forum les Halles.

This is a giant wax museum with over fifty lavish displays, beautiful sets, costumes, portraying famous people throughout history. There are also a hall of mirrors, two small theaters, and exotic decor. Do not go on a weekend or holiday. Best to arrive at 3 P.M., when they open, as by 4 P.M. it's already mobbed. Great for kids. The one in Forum les Halles features Belle Epoque scenes. Allow two hours.

Musée Guimet, at pl. d'Iéna contains Far Eastern art from Cambodia, Tibet, Nepal, Pakistan, India, China, Korea, and Japan. Not only is the collection enormous, it is of very high quality and beautifully displayed. Be sure you visit all three floors. Allow at least two hours, maybe more. Even if you are not into Asian art, you can't help but appreciate and get lost (mentally) in this collection.

Musée de l'Histoire de France, or the National Archives, 60 rue des Francs-Bourgeois, is found in the beautiful Soubise townhouse in the Marais section. The documents here are well organized and displayed, and you can really get carried away with them. French history in a large nutshell. Also available to see is part of the house, partially renovated, and some fine tapestries.

Musée d'Histoire Naturelle at the Jardin des Plantes, 57 rue Cuvier, displays gems, bugs, butterflies, several gardens, greenhouses, a herbarium, minerals, etc. Good for kids, too.

Musée de l'Homme (Museum of Man), Palais de Chaillot, is anthropological and scientific in nature, with displays and materials about man from prehistoric times to more recent. The collection includes artifacts from cultures from all over the world. The upper floor is of special interest.

Victor Hugo's House, 6 pl. des Vosges in the Marais, contains rooms taken from various homes where Hugo lived. In the rooms you see his furniture, many old photos, the famous standing writing desk, and his paintings. Much of the furniture he designed himself. It's really a nice little museum and a must for Hugo aficionados.

Musee Instrumental du Conservatorie National Superieur de Musique at 14 rue Madrid has over three thousand types of musical instruments in its collection.

Musée Jacquemart-André, 158 blvd. Haussmann, is a five-minute walk from the two above and is also located in a sumptuous private residence. You'll find paintings by famous artists in period rooms with period furniture. By the way, Haussemann is pronounced *Ohs-mahn,* not *House-man.*

Note: to see all three of these museums in one day, you'll have to go in the afternoon, as the Jacquemart-André is not open in the mornings. You'll also have to go Wednesday through Sunday, as two of them are closed Monday and Tuesday. And don't forget St. Alexander Nevsky Cathedral, also in the neighborhood.

Musee Jeu de Paume is located in the Tuileries at Place de la Concorde. This is called the "Impressionist Museum" for obvious reasons. It is always crowded, always hot and stuffy inside. This will be somewhat alleviated in the future with the opening of the Orsay Museum, where part of the collection of nineteenth-century French art will be moved.

Le Louvre. Where do you begin? First of all, don't expect to make even a dent in it in two hours. You need an entire day to do a quick run-through, and then some. I must have spent over thirty hours in the Louvre and still haven't seen it all. It always seems to be crowded, and rightly so, considering the astonishing collection. You'll probably have to wait in a long line out the side door, which is slow because it leads to the ticket window. Once inside, however, you'll notice 90 percent of the people are standing in line for one window, while there may be two or three other ones open, and no one in line. So take a good look and see if one of the other windows has shorter lines or no lines. Hint: go on Wednesday or Sunday and it's free, which eliminates the line. Sundays, however, are the most crowded. If it's really hot you could possibly pass away while in the Louvre, as it seems to be stifling on even cold days, at least in some of the more popular galleries.

Everyone who goes to the Louvre for the first time rushes to see (a) Mona Lisa, (b) Venus de Milo, and (c) Winged Victory (which you can't miss, if you go up the Grand Staircase). So after you've run around and seen them, you can be more leisurely about the rest of the place! The green Michelin guide has a very good and detailed section on the Louvre, and I send you to them. Being a museum freak, I find every room in the Louvre exciting, but you may want to be more selective, especially if you are on a time schedule. Don't miss the first-floor galleries with decorative arts (furniture, etc.). Don't miss the Egyptian rooms; the Greek rooms, the Far Eastern antiquities, or the crown jewels, or . . . see what I mean?

There is a snack bar on the first floor (remember the first floor is really the second floor) and bathrooms in various locations throughout the museum. Some of these bathrooms are small, crowded, and not too tidy at times. Carry some tissues. Fortunately the Louvre is in the process of being reorganized, so these situations will change in the near future.

P.S. The best metro stop for the Louvre is not the Louvre stop, but Palais Royale. This museum and most others are closed Tuesdays.

Le Louvre des Antiquaires, located on one side of the *place* at Palais Royale, is not a museum, but it could be. As mentioned in the shopping section, it is an immense antique store covering three floors and a very long block. Chock-full of every type of antique you can imagine.

Musée de la Marine in the Palais de Chaillot, pl. du Trocadéro, across the Seine from the Tour Eiffel, has the largest collection of its type in the world. The collection ranges from fabulous model ships to all sorts of marine equipment to paintings. Films are shown in the auditorium; model-ship builders come on the second Sunday of the month in the morning to demonstrate their art. A great museum for kids. Beautiful displays. Allow one and a half hours.

Located in the same building is the *Musée de l'Homme,* the *Musée des Monuments Français,* the Trocadéro freshwater *aquarium,* the *Henri Langlois Cinema Museum,* and a *large film library.*

Musée Marmatton, 2 rue Louis-Boilly, is in the Passy or Chassée de la Muette area of Paris, metro Muette. In a very chic neighborhood next to the Bois de Boulogne is where this lovely old house is to be found, exhibiting a wide-ranging collection of furnishings, tapestries, and other items, but best known for its Impressionist collection, most especially Monet. It's second in line after the Jeu de Paume, at the moment, in the number of Impressionist works. The house, collection, park, and whole area make this a nice outing. From the museum you can walk down rue de Passy to the Palais de Chaillot. You can also go see *Balzac's house,* which is in the area.

Musée de la Mode et du Costume, 10 av. Pierre-1er-de-Serbie in Palais Galliera, is a fashion and clothing museum with a beautiful Belle Epoque collection, as well as fashions for all ages and from all ages, from the eighteenth century to the present. Allow thirty to forty-five minutes.

Musée de la Monnaie, 11 quai de Conti, is not only for coin and medal collectors. The seventeenth-century building (Hôtel des Monnaies) is well worth a visit by anyone interested in architecture, interior design, or just beautiful buildings. Temporary exhibits will sometimes replace the permanent collection.

Musée de Montmartre, 12 rue Cortot, Montmartre, is located in an old house where a few famous artists, writers, and composers used to rent space. The museum contains memorabilia pertaining to Montmartre and the artists who made themselves and the area famous. Lovely garden in the back. If you are in Montmartre, drop in. Allow thirty minutes.

Musée des Monuments Français, Palais de Chaillot, is one of the best museums in Paris and no one ever goes. Entire facades and portions of medieval cathedrals and buildings are in this vast, astonishing museum. The upper floors have entire frescoed chapels; all is twelfth to fifteenth century. Allow two hours. You shouldn't miss this one.

Musée de Gustave Moreau, 14 rue La Rochefoucauld, 9e.

If you like Moreau you will enjoy this small museum, crammed with drawings and many large, unfinished paintings. The latter are interesting because they give you an idea of "work in progress". The apartments that the museum occupies were Moreau's at one time. There is a marvelous spiral staircase leading from one floor to the other. Unless you want to delve for hours into the trays of drawings, you can go through this small museum in thirty to forty-five minutes or less.

Musee de la Musique Mecanique, Impasse Berthad, 3e, (Metro Rambuteau) near the Pompidou. This museum, as the name implies, has all sorts of mechanical musical instruments. Great for kids. Open Saturday, Sunday, and holidays only from 2 to 7 P.M.

Musée National d'Art Moderne, Pompidou Center, or the National Museum of Modern Art, is the largest museum of contemporary art in the world. Located on the third and fourth floors with a viewing terrace on the fifth floor, this museum covers the period from the end of the Impressionists to the most contemporary. Even if you aren't into "modern art," you should make yourself go see this collection. Kids really like this museum!

For other things to do while you're in this area, refer to the earlier writing about the Pompidou Center.

Musée National des Arts et Traditions Populaires, described earlier in conjunction with the Bois de Boulogne, is located at 6 route du Mahatma Gandhi. Displays are environmental, technological, industrial, agricultural, etc. Closed Tuesdays. Take metro Sablons.

Musée National des Techniques,   270 rue St.-Martin, has thousands of items and displays regarding technical and scientific advances in France's history. Everything from toys to cars. Good one for kids.

Musée Nissim de Camando,   63 rue de Monceau, is around the corner from Parc Monceau and is probably my favorite of the small museums. This one, plus the next two, can all be visited in one afternoon, along with the lovely *Parc Monceau* and the *St. Alexander Nevsky Cathedral* (Russian Orthodox Church). The Camando is extremely intimate, being housed in a luxurious townhouse, with the eighteenth-century rooms in original condition. Inside is a wonderful collection of furniture, tapestries, paintings, silver, porcelain, all displayed in period rooms with views of the park.

Musée de Notre Dame,   10 rue du Cloître-Notre-Dame, by Notre Dame, relates to the history of the cathedral.

Orangerie des Tuileries is the twin building to the Jeu de Paume and stands opposite it at Place de la Concorde. This museum was just reopened after several years of renovation, and contains a permanent collection, belonging to two people, of post-Impressionist works, all beautifully lit and displayed. It's a must. Works by Renoir, Cezanne, Derain, Soutine, Laurencin, Matisse, Rousseau, Utrillo, Modigliani, Picasso, Monet, Sisley. Allow one hour. It's not crowded like the Jeu de Paume, either with people or paintings. A small treasure.

Musée d' Orsay will complement the Jeu de Paume, as it is being built to house all nineteenth-century French art, plus some temporary exhibitions. It isn't really being built from scratch but constructed within the walls of the old Gare d'Orsay, a train station of the late nineteenth century. It was rescued from the demolition crew and has been undergoing extensive renovation. The plans and models for the finished museum suggest that it will be quite wonderful. It is meant to be the museum link between the Louvre and the Modern Art Museum in Pompidou. The opening date keeps getting pushed back: I've heard everything from 1983 (didn't happen) to 1988. You can see the Gare d'Orsay very well from the Tuileries by looking across to the Left Bank.

Palais de la Découverte,   av. Franklin-Roosevelt in the Grand Palais, is the museum of science, including a planetarium. The displays are all in French, but kids and scientific adults will still find it interesting.

Le Petit Palais is across the street from the Grand Palais and houses the Museum of Fine Arts of the City of Paris. It is sort of a mini-Louvre, although that's being generous. There are some very good things to see in the collection, ranging from Etruscan and Egyptian to Flemish and Impressionist.

Musée Picasso,   in the Hotel Sale, 5 rue de Thorigny in the Marais area. The museum is in a 17th century mansion, and is open from 10 a.m. to 5:15 P.M. every day except Tuesday.

Musée Postal, 34 blvd. de Vaugirard, covers the history of the P.O., and would be especially interesting for stamp collectors.

Musée de la Publicité, 8 rue de Paradis and a few doors from the Baccarat showroom, is a poster museum, with posters of every kind. Some are extremely valuable, many are by famous artists. The entrance through the driveway has some beautiful tilework on the walls and ceiling.

Musée Rodin or Hôtel Biron, 77 rue de Varenne, next to the Invalides. This is a fabulous townhouse containing a Rodin collection which you won't believe, plus other pieces by some of his contemporaries. The large gardens in the back are very pretty (that's where the *toilettes* are located). As you come through the front gates, to the immediate right is another gallery, usually with a temporary exhibit. Even if Rodin is not your cup of café au lait, you will enjoy this museum.

Out of Town, But Not Far: Sightseeing "Environs" de Paris

Versailles

Whatever you've heard or read about Versailles is true: it's fantastic. It's huge. It takes two days to see it all. It's mobbed with tourists. It needs more furniture in it (a huge amount of the furniture that wasn't destroyed during the Revolution went to England, and has subsequently been dispersed around the world).

There are several ways you can go about seeing Versailles. One of them is to do it on your own. You can hire a cab or a limo to get there, at some cost, needless to say. Or you can take the metro to Pont de Sèvres, get off and go upstairs and catch bus 171, which will take you to the square by the château. (Double-check with the bus driver, in case the bus number has been changed.)

You can also take an organized tour with Paris Visions, or one of the other private tour companies in Paris. These tours are reasonably priced, include a lunch stop, and have a guide.

In any case, don't miss Versailles.

Restaurants in Versailles which are good are:

La Boule d'Or, 25 rue de Mal-Foch, phone 950–22–97
Le Potager du Roy, 1 rue du Mal-Joffre, phone 950–35–34
Rescatore, 27 av. St.-Cloud, phone 950–23–60
*Trianon Palace,*1 blvd. de la Reine, phone 950–3412
Les Trois Marches exceptionally good), 3 rue Colbert, phone 950–
    13–21.

You'll probably want to break the day up a bit, so if you see the main château in the morning, have lunch, then see the gardens and/or the *hameau* and/or the Petit and Grand Trianons in the afternoon, you may get through the day in one piece. If possible, try *not* to go to Versailles when it's raining (which means you may never get there!) because you really cannot enjoy those incredible gardens, and the fountains won't be working.

Musée Bouilhet-Christofle is in another suburb called St. Denis, at 112 rue Ambroise-Croizat. If you like silver, you'll love this. Christofle is a well-known and old master manufacturer of silver, and the museum displays examples of its work from the eighteenth century onward.

Chantilly is a delightful, lovely château about an hour north of Paris. You can get there on the train from the Gare du Nord or take a day tour from Paris. Not much farther on, still on the train, is the museum and château of *Compiègne*, and between the two (sort of) is the *Senlis Cathedral*. You could do all three in a day, if you moved. A good restaurant near Chantilly is *Tipperary*, 6 av. du Mal-Joffre, phone 457–0048; or *Relais Condé*, 42 av. du Mal-Joffre, phone 457–0575.

Chantilly is pronounced *shawn-tee-yee;* Compiègne is *comb-pen;* Senlis is *sawn-lee.* They all have nasals.

Chartres Cathedral is another one you shouldn't miss. Often it is part of the Versailles package tour, when you go with one of the charter tours. Unfortunately, each place has so much to see that it's impossible to do them justice in the same day. Chartres is too far out of town to get to on a bus. If you rent a car, it's freeway all the way, but do yourself a favor and take the country roads if you have the time, at least one way.

When you get to Chartres, check the lecture time by the Englishman Malcolm Miller. He's famous now, and has made it his life's work to study and give tours at Chartres. I've taken three of his tours and each one has been completely different.

A lunch stop in Chartres could be at *Restaurant Henry IV*, 31 rue du Soleil d'Or. Also *Le Grand Monarque*, 22 pl. des Epars, or *La Vieille Maison*, 5 rue au Lait.

Chartres is pronounced *Shart.*

Fontainebleau Château and forest *(fôret)* is an all-day trip, which should also include a stop in Barbizon, home of the famous school of art. If you don't have a car, there are bus tours that go daily, leaving from central Paris. We took one of these and it was quite satisfactory, except that the Barbizon stopover was very touristy and commercialized. This is a major château and you really ought to see it on one of your trips to Paris. It's a very interesting contrast to Versailles, as well. The forest and surrounding areas are really beautiful. By the way, Fontainebleau is pronounced *phone-ten-blow* (not fountain-blue!).

Giverny (pronounced *Jee-vair-nee*) is where Monet's home is located. It's about eighty miles from Paris and it takes an hour to get there, either by car or train. If you don't have a car and don't want to pay for a limo (probably at least 200 dollars), you can get to Giverny on the train from one of the main stations in Paris (ask your concierge to find out exactly which one). If you take the train, a taxi will take you from the Giverny station to the house and you can arrange for the driver to come back at a certain time and pick you up.

Giverny can be a half-day trip from Paris, unless you include lunch. If you go in the morning, arrive there before noon, as the gift shop, which is located in his atelier, closes for a long lunch.

For lunch, I've heard that five miles away in a town called Gasny there's a place that's pretty good, called *Auberge St. Eustache*. Friends ate at a restaurant called *Château de la Corniche* and said it was terrible. An excellent lunch stop is Auberge du Petit Val (25–27 av. de l'ile de France, Vernon, phone 325–1185). Superior trate tatin. Open noon to 8:30; closed Monday evenings and Tuesdays.

Malmaison was the home of Napoleon and Josephine, more hers than his, and she died there. You can go to Malmaison the same day you go to St.-Germain-en-Laye; there's a bus that runs from one to the other. If you go to Malmaison directly from Paris, take the metro/R.E.R. to La Défense and from there take bus 158. Tell the driver you want to get off at Malmaison. It's about a three-block walk from the bus stop to the house. There are one-hour tours of the house in French only, but there is a leaflet in English you can get at the entrance. The house is quite lovely and rather an intimate look at two of France's most famous people. Don't go at lunchtime; it's closed.

Musée National de la Renaissance in the Château d'Ecouen is new. It's about a half-hour drive from Paris. I've read it is quite marvelous. Check with your concierge for an exact address.

Musée de Neuilly is a mechanical toy museum for all ages. Neuilly is a suburb *(banlieue)* of Paris and easily reached by metro. The museum is at 12 rue du Centre. Automatons, or mechanical dolls, have their original parts and costumes, and sometimes in the afternoon, after lunch, some of them are allowed to perform. A real delight for kids, even old ones. (Neuilly is pronounced *Nuh-Yee*.)

Reims, with the cathedral Notre Dame, is definitely an all-day trip from Paris, and you may even want to spend the night, although that's not absolutely necessary. Reims and its very important cathedral, plus museums, not to mention the famous champagne cellars, provides many hours of exploring and surprises. Don't miss the Palais Tau or the Basilic St. Remi. The tour of the Pommery Champagne Cave is very good. It's imperative that you have lunch at the beautiful three-star hotel and restaurants called Les Crayers, or Boyer (64 Bl. Henry-Vasnier, phone 26–82–80–80). Advance reservations. A lovely place to spend a night, as well.

By the way, you pronounce it *rance,* but make the "n" nasal, and swallow the "r".

Sèvres Porcelain Factory and Museum (Musée de Sèvres et Manufacture), 4 Grand Rue, Sèvres. Closed Saturday, Sunday, and holidays. Open 9:30 to 12:30 and 1:30 to 5:30. Take the metro to the end of the Pont de Sèvres line. When you exit the station, go out the side that says "Côté Boulogne," cross the bridge, and follow the signs to the Musée. In the room to the left on the main floor you get your ticket for the tour, which isn't a tour, but it's free and interesting. It takes about fifty minutes; you see a very good film about how Sèvres porcelain is made, and then in another room you see four or five people demonstrating some of the techniques of throwing and decorating. After or before all this, you buy a ticket at the main counter and see the National Porcelain Museum of France, which is through the door to the right and also on the first floor (upstairs through the glass doors). It's a very interesting way to spend an afternoon, see a *banlieue* (suburb) of Paris, and learn something.

Basilique de St. Denis is the first great Gothic edifice in France and the necropolis of kings and queens. Take the metro to the end of the line Basilique St. Denis. There is a small catch to this, however, which you must be aware of. At the stop called La Fourche the track splits. The conductor will announce whether he's going to Basilique St. Denis or to Asnières-Gennevilliers. If you can't understand what he's saying, look in your car at an illuminated sign at either end. It should be lit up behind the direction that train is going. You do not want to go to Asnières-Gennevilliers. If your train is going there, get off and wait right there for the next train, which should be going to the Basilique. It will say on the outside of the train and also on the sign over the tracks. If, for some reason, you get fouled up, get off the train, backtrack to La Fourche and try again. This is the voice of experience speaking . . .

Now let's assume you arrive safely at the Basilique and are ready to go in. First of all, don't go on a weekend, if possible, as there is nothing going on in the town and nowhere to eat. During the week everything is open and there's a big marketplace just down the street from the basilica. So if you arrive and find part of the basilica closed for lunch, you'll have something to do. Once you survey the remarkable facade of the church, go in and down the right-hand aisle. About two thirds of the way back is a ticket window. Get a ticket and go to the rear of the church, where you will see some of the most outstanding and interesting funerary sculpture in the country. If you have the green Michelin guide, it will explain some of what you are looking at. Over on the left-hand side there is a stairway descending into the crypt, some of which is twelfth century. It is there that you can see the tombs of Marie Antoinette and Louis XVI. Many other kings and queens of France were at one time buried here, but they didn't make it through the Revolution. If you are interested in church architecture or sculpture, you really want to see this.

St.-Germain-en-Laye is a wonderful day trip from Paris. You can easily get there on the metro/R.E.R., generally with one train change. The countryside is beautiful. When you get there you'll find a very charming, small town, dominated by a fabulous château and magnificent park, affording views of Paris in the distance, on a clear day.

The château has a terrific museum, *Musée des Antiquités Nationales.* This is largely archaeological in nature, but also has some Greek and Roman collections.

A good restaurant in town is *Pavillon Henri IV,* 21 rue Thiers, phone 451–6262. Also *Cazaudehore,* 1 av. du President-Kennedy, phone 451–9380; and *La Petite Auberge,* 119 bis rue Léon-Desoyer, phone 451–0399.

Vaux-le-Vicomte is very near Fontainebleau and is a much-advertised and well-known château, popular with tourists. You can take charter tours there also. Some combine the two, although that's a bit much for one day. Still, if you are on limited time . . . (Pronounced *voh-l-veecomt.*)

Vincennes can be reached by metro quite easily. It's another nice half-day trip from Paris. There are two things to see when you get there: the remains of a fourteenth-century château (the highlight is a tour of the *donjon,* or keep) and its chapel, and the zoo. If you want to spend all day at Vincennes, there's a large forest with various gardens and two museums (Musée des Transports, and Musée des Arts Africains et Océaniens). You'll also find a children's garden, a lake, riding club, Buddhist Center, and a theater. Vincennes is pronounced *Van-Sen,* the first syllable is nasal.

Beyond Paris

If you listen to me long enough you might begin to think that Paris *is* France, but it's not true. In the past few years I've concentrated more on the City of Light, but believe me, France is a great big, wonderful country, and almost anywhere you go within its borders will be a delight. The only "iffy" area is to the north and east of Paris, which is more industrial, but there are exceptions there, too.

Getting around in France is easy. You can always fly if you're in a big hurry, but you'll miss it all. The rail system is one of the best in world, and at least you can see the countryside whizzing by as you go along, even though you can't smell it, touch it, or eat in it. The best way to go is by car (*not* bus tours!), so rent a car, get a map, and take off. The autoroutes are terrific, with rest stops every thirty or forty miles; most of them are large, clean, and provide every service. Autoroutes are speedy, but you are still going to miss a lot. So get off the autoroutes and take those little roads that show up as teensy black lines on your map. Now you'll have a real adventure!

There are some books you should not be without as you travel through France. As far as hotels are concerned, would you like to stay in a Holiday Inn or an eighteenth-century castle? I thought so. For manor house–hotels, château-hotels, country inns, and regional restaurants, you can't go wrong with a little soft-cover book called *Relais et Châteaux,* published annually and available at any French Government Tourist Office or bookstores in France. I've had nothing but marvelous experiences in these hotels and they aren't necessarily expensive. For the more popular ones in highly traveled areas, try to book your room in advance. The second-best book for hotels and restaurants is the current edition of the Gault-Millau *Guide France.* The English version is called *The Best of France.* A cross-reference to this book is the hardcover red Michelin *France,* current edition. And for every area you go to, get your hands on the pertinent green paperback *Michelin guide.* Unfortunately, not all of them are in English. (If you live in Los Angeles, the bookstore on Westwood Boulevard called Cité des Livres carries all these books.)

It's been a while since I've been to some of the provinces, so I will only mention what I know to be still valid.

Loire Valley and Châteaux

You can see the Loire quickly in three days, but if you have five days it's better. It's not difficult to visit two or three châteaux each day. They're all different and all wonderful, in my opinion. Most of them have guided tours, and even if you don't understand French, take the tours—at least you'll get to see the inside.

Not only does the Loire have all those romantic castles, it also has gorgeous countryside, wonderful inns and restaurants, and fascinating, historic towns.

You can take charter bus tours from Paris, but unless you are unable to drive yourself, don't do it. Rent a car and do your own thing. The driving is easy and fun.

Orléans (pronounced *or-lay-an,* with a nasal "n") is a nice little town about halfway between Paris and Tours and not too far from Chartres. The city's most famous temporary resident was Jeanne d'Arc, and once a year on her saint day they have a big celebration. (Joan of Arc, remember her?) Anyway, it's a good jumping-off place for the rest of the Loire. A good restaurant is Auberge St.-Jacques, 72 quai du Châtelet (I'll never forget their hot fudge sauce, but that was a long time ago). Also good is La Crémaillière, 3 rue Notre-Dame-de-Recouvrance. For hotels, check your other guides.

Four châteaux that can be seen in the same day between Orléans and Amboise, are: *Chambord* (the largest), have lunch; *Cheverny* (the "hunter's château"); *Blois* (feudal); and *Chaumont-sur-Loire,* where Catherine de Medici passed many unhappy years. See the stables, also. (P.S. If you want to read about an interesting bunch of people, read about Catherine de Medici, her husband/king, and his mistress.) Of course you will have to get an early start and you won't get into Amboise until early evening, so be sure you have made advance reservations. You really shouldn't miss any of these châteaux, even if it means doubling back to one of them.

How do you pronounce them? In order of appearance: *Shawm-bore, Sheh-vair-nee, Blwah, Show-moan-sir-lwar* (with a nasal "n").

Amboise is a good place to spend the night, because the château is one of the biggies, and a short walk from the castle is *Clos Luce,* the house where Leonardo spent his last years and died. Take tours of both places. A good hotel in Amboise within walking distance of the château is Le Choiseul, 36 quai Ch.-Guinot. It's small, full of antiques, and has a lovely dining room overlooking the river. We got some delicious fresh river salmon there.

Two more châteaux coming up on your route are *Chenonceaux* and *Loches.* Two more opposite types of châteaux are hard to find. The first is a gorgeous and very romantic château built over the river (this is where Catherine de Medici's husband/king let his girlfriend live all those years, while Catherine was shut up in the smaller one). Loches is a feudal castle and only part of it remains. Views from the castle look out over the valley and the town, much of which is very old.

Now you're getting nearer to *Tours,* where there are a lot of hotels, but just outside the town is an excellent choice: the extremely popular (advance reservations are a must) *Château d'Artigny,* Route d'Azay-le-Rideau.

More pronunciation, starting with Amboise: *Ahm-bwoz; Cloh-loose; Sshh-non-so; Lowsh; Tour; Dahr-tee-nee.*

The next five châteaux coming up are *Azay-le-Rideau* (pronounced *ah-zay-l-ree-dough*), *Villandry (vee-land-dree); Langeais (lahn-jay;* the "n" is nasal and the "j" as in the second "g" of garage); *Ussé (ooo-say);* and *Chinon* (*she-known;* the second "n" is nasal). My advice is—don't pass up any of them. Chinon is totally in ruins, but is very important and very interesting, especially for Jeanne d'Arc fans. Azay-le-Rideau is almost totally surrounded by water in a very beautiful setting. Villandry has magnificent gardens, planted intricately in various patterns. Langeais is a fortified château, one of the best-furnished. Ussé is said to have been the inspiration for Sleeping Beauty's Castle.

There are several beautiful château-hotels in the area. One in particular that has been very good and popular for a number of years is in a town called Chenehutte and is called *Le Prieuré.* Part of this hotel is six hundred years old and at one time was a religious retreat. Located right on the river and having its own restaurant, as many of them do, this is really nice. You pronounce it *pree-ure-ray.*

There are several other châteaux in the area to see, such as the ones in Angers and Saumur, not far from the Prieuré. The Michelin guide can be your guide for them.

The Dordogne

You aren't going to believe this and no self-respecting guidebook would dare to do this, but I am now telling you to go to a place I've never been. The Dordogne. It's a region south of the Loire Valley. You've probably heard of the famous cave paintings of France, most notably the caves of Lascaux—they're in Dordogne. It's a river valley with steep canyon walls, old fortresses, beautiful scenery, delightful villages and towns, wonderful country inns, etc. I know several people who have stayed in the Dordogne anywhere from one to four weeks, and they've all loved it! If you're driving way down to the south of France from the Loire Valley, spend a couple of days in the Dordogne. I'm sure you won't be sorry. It's pronounced *door-doanya.*

Carcassonne

Carcassonne is almost in the Pyrenées, southeast of Toulouse, not far from the Mediterranean. If you are anywhere remotely close to this place, you've got to go! It's an incredible, double-walled, medieval city, one of the very few of its kind in the world. You'll probably want to stay the night nearby and spend a few hours touring the city. Be sure you take a guided tour in English.

There are a couple of hotels within the city walls, which you'll think you should stay in. Wrong. They are full of tour groups. Instead, stay at a really wonderful old manor house about three miles away, out amongst the vineyards. Part of this hotel dates back to Charlemagne. It's called the *Domaine d'Auriac,* route de St.-Hilaire, in Auriac. Advance reservations are a good idea. Restaurant in the hotel. The drive from this hotel to the city gives you a fabulous view of the latter.

Marseille

Everyone will tell you not to go to Marseille because it's dirty and rough, etc. Don't listen. It's true that it's busy, and in places a rather dirty port city, but it does have its saving graces. One of them is a very lovely, small, romantic hotel with great views of the bay, called *Résidences le Petit Nice Marina Maldormé,* on Corniche J. F. Kennedy. If you have to spend a night in Marseille for any reason, this is a good bet. The hotel has a fine restaurant. There are other nice hotels in the city, plus several excellent restaurants. If you ever dreamed of bouillabaisse Marseillaise, this is the place to get it. Marseille is pronounced "mar-say," but Marseillaise is "mar-sayez."

The South of France

The "south of France" encompasses a wide area, but generally refers to the whole area east of Carcassonne to the Italian border, including the French Riviera (Côte d'Azur). The weather is a chief attraction for the area, as it is generally much sunnier and warmer than anywhere else in France. There is so much to see, to do, to eat, to absorb in the south of France that you'll have to read several sources. Believe me, there's a lot more to the French Riviera than topless sunbathers in St. Tropez or the film festival in Cannes (please pronounce it properly: *kahn*), or the fancy yachts and casinos in Monte Carlo. There are many outstanding museums throughout the area, lovely small towns in the hills, fabulous restaurants, and breathtaking vistas.

Provence is the area northeast and northwest of Marseille, and is good for at least two or three days, especially if you are interested in Roman ruins and architecture. *Nîmes* (pronounced *neem*), *Arles,* and *Avignon* are especially interesting. The *Camargue* area is beautiful, as is *Aix-en-Provence.* Let's clear up the difference between Provence and province. The first one is pronounced *pro-vawnce;* the second is pronounced *pro-vance.* A province is just what the name implies, a province; similar to a state in the U.S.A. Provence is a city and an area.

Les Baux-de-Provence is one place you should definitely not miss. Book in advance and stay at the very famous *Oustau de la Baumanière;* if you can't get in there, stay at their annex down the road, *Relais Cabro d'Or.* Whichever place you stay, don't fail to eat in the marvelous three-star restaurant at the *Oustau.* The lamb en croûte and strawberry soufflé are especially memorable. As for sightseeing, the entire area is very unusual, as you are surrounded by almost pure white mountains, pocketed with rectangular bauxite mines. Some of the mines are accessible and are now used as wine-tasting cellars. Walk down into one; it's very interesting. And don't miss walking through the old destroyed city. It's fascinating and affords wonderful views of the valley.

For the *Côte d'Azur* (meaning blue coast), you'll have to make decisions as to where you want to stay, as each little town is famous or semifamous. The cities of Nice and Cannes are usually very crowded, and you may opt for one of the more picturesque seaside resorts. We were very happy with *La Réserve de Beaulieu* at Beaulieu-sur-Mer; the hotel is gorgeous and the dining room is too, serving terrific food from its two-star restaurant. Another good hotel in Beaulieu is *Le Metropole,* also with an excellent restaurant. Beaulieu is nicely located about halfway between Nice and Monte Carlo. In St.-Jean-Cap-Ferrat stay at the outstanding *Voile d'Or* and eat at *Le Provençal,* 2 av. Denis-Semeria in the harbor.

If you're driving around the area, don't just stick to the Petite Corniche, the road that runs along the beaches. Get up on the Grande Corniche or even the Moyenne Corniche; the views are spectacular.

In *Nice,* the *Negresco* is a gorgeous hotel with an excellent restaurant called the *Chantecler* (phone 93–883–951). Their chocolate desserts were to die for—a whole page. One place you do *not* want to stay in Nice is the *Meridien.* While sightseeing, don't miss the old part of town—you'll swear you're in Rome or Florence. I'm referring to the area behind Place du Palais, along rue Prefecture and streets surrounding it. The Opera House is also interesting to see, as well as some of the less-traveled residential and shopping areas. Let's face it—the whole place is really touristy, but you can get away from it if you want to.

The Great French Balloon Adventure:
Ballooning Over Burgundy With The Bombard Society

And now for something completely different. Leave the noise and fast lane of the city behind and head for the beautiful wine country of France: Bourgogne. Go hot-air ballooning over sleepy villages from the fourteenth century, perfect patchworks of green farmlands, romantic châteaux, and some of the world's most famous vineyards.

The Bombard Society was begun in 1976 by Buddy Bombard, a sort of Renaissance man when it comes to traveling and enjoying outdoor activities. He has organized an extremely classy operation which functions from May to October in some of the most beautiful countryside of France. His staff is young, dynamic, experienced, and fun. His chefs can compete with many in the best restaurants. The itinerary is exciting, diverse, and definitely different!

Your week starts when you are picked up in Paris in front of a designated hotel and driven to a hotel in Saulieu or Beaune, depending on whether you're on the three-day or the six-day trip. Take the six-day trip; you'll get more out of it because you have the time to get more into it. After three days at Saulieu you are driven to Beaune, where you are put up at the *Hôtel de la Poste,* which is quite nice and has an excellent restaurant. In the mornings you have plenty of time for sightseeing in the area; there is a lot to see and do!

You will be taken to wonderful little villages, ancient churches, wine-tasting cellars, private vineyards and caves, private châteaux for tours, Roman ruins, shopping, etc. Of course you can opt to sleep in and miss all that, if you are not interested.

Then in the afternoons, after a fabulous lunch or *pique-nique* some-where, you go ballooning. To try to explain this experience is impossible —it would take several pages, every superlative adjective in the dictionary, and a lot of pictures. It is very safe, very quiet, very thrilling, very beautiful, and I can't think of many ways to see a countryside that can compare. You very much become a part of all of it. The balloons take on certain personali-ties after a while. This is romance and adventure! No two days are the same; in fact, no two moments are the same.

This adventure is not for everyone. It is only for people who enjoy doing something different, who love good food and wine, who can marvel at exquisite countryside, cows, smogless skies, who enjoy meeting the people of the country (who could not possibly be more charming and gracious), who love walking through ancient churches, towns, and castles, who can't wait to have a good time.

P.S. It's a bit expensive.

Clothing

The Bombard Society will send you a list of things to wear. Read it and follow advice! You absolutely *do* need some good waterproof boots which can withstand cowdoodoo, streams, mud, thorns, and other interesting adventures. You also need a warm sweater, a windbreaker or jacket, and jeans. For evenings, when dining in the restaurants, you will want to dress up a little—a dress, skirt and blouse or good slacks and blouse. Men will want a sportscoat and even a tie. Take lots of film.

The grape harvest, which occurs at the end of September and early October, lasts only about ten days. This is a very exciting time to be in Bourgogne, so you may want to plan your trip around it.

You can get more information and brochures from a travel agent, or contact The Bombard Society, 6727 Curran Street, McLean, Virginia 22101 (phones: 800–862–8537 and 703–448–9407). Buddy is now also ballooning over Salzburg, and the Loire Valley. They also do combination barge/bal-loon trips.

Some Bits on Burgundy

Whether you travel through Bourgogne with the Bombard Society or on your own, here are a few suggestions.

If you are going to the area, be sure you have a good travel guide with you and read it in advance. The green Michelin guide on Bourgogne is in French, so if you don't speak French you'll have to find another book. The area is very rich in history, the architecture is diverse and totally wonderful wherever you go, and of course you should know something about the wine industry there.

Vezelay

Vezelay is a fabulous medieval town of about 400 people. The *Hôtel de la Poste* is beautiful, with a good restaurant. If you eat there, order *fromage blanc* for your cheese course. This is a regional dish which is akin to skyr in Iceland. Quite unusual and delicious.

Shopping in Vezelay is not too complicated. There are a few touristy-type souvenir places and only four clothing stores. One of the latter happens to be the most incredible sweater store any of us had ever been in. It is the first store on the right as you go up the hill into town and is called *Atelier Jacques d'Aubres.* The d'Aubres family make all the things you see in the store, which is huge: she makes all the sweaters and he makes all the jewelry. The shop itself is in an old church and if you look around you'll see pieces of ancient capitals, sculpture, and beams, etc. The couple completely renovated the church, which was in ruins when they acquired it. They live upstairs and a peek up the stairway reveals old beams and vaulted ceilings. The prices are high but fair, the quality of the work is tops, and you'll go bananas. P.S. You can't get a *detaxe* form here as their wares are considered arts and crafts.

A bit up the street next to the Post Office is another, smaller sweater store. Selection was limited, prices were lower, and quality did not seem as good, but there were a few nice things.

Restaurants So far as we could see there is only one decent place to eat in Vezelay and that is at the hotel. However, there were some local, "cute" sort of places up in town, none of which we tried. Nightlife is carried on at only one place—a bar called Boucainville. Nearby, however, in a charming little town called St. Père there is a three-star restaurant called *l'Espérance,* which is also an inn.

Sightseeing The *Basilique de la Madeleine* is important—not just in size but historically. Be sure you have some information about it, especially regarding the sculpture.

You would also want to walk around the old walls and ramparts of the city and to see the view of the Cure Valley from behind the basilica.

There is a cross erected on the hillside below the Porte Ste. Croix, marking the spot from which St. Bernard preached during the Second Crusade in 1146.

The town of *St. Père,* down the road, is charming. There is a small but gorgeous Gothic church there, across from which is a small museum. The custodian of the museum can direct you or take you a short distance out of town to the remains of *Roman baths,* which have been dated to the Mesolithic period.

One of the best things to do, if you have a car, is to drive casually around in the area, as the villages, towns, and people are all wonderful.

What to Eat Burgundy is famous for many dishes, cheeses, and wines. The local cheeses, especially the *chèvres* (goat cheeses) are fabulous. Also be sure you try Brillat de Savarin, Epoisses, and *fromage blanc.* Burgundy is also noted for its beef and its sauces—rich and heavy for the most part—coq au vin, escargots, jambon persillé, and mushrooms. When we were there in October we feasted daily on wild blackberries along the roadsides.

On the Road from Vezelay to Beaune Don't take the autoroute. Get on those little, narrow, twisty roads that wind through farmlands and villages. Stop along the way and poke around in places that interest you. Don't be in such a rush.

There are lots of charming towns along the way. Read your other guidebooks to find out which ones have churches, museums, or things you are interested in. *Pouilly-en-Auxois, Ste. Sabine,* and especially *Châteauneuf* are of interest. Châteauneuf can be seen from the valley as it dominates the area from high on a hill. The town itself is a national monument and is virtually unchanged from the fifteenth century. The château is now being repaired so you may not be able to get into it. There are also other châteaux along the way which you can visit. We went to *Commarain* and had a tour; it is one of the nicest, best preserved châteaux I have seen.

You can have a leisurely drive, sightsee, and still arrive in Beaune by early afternoon in time for lunch!

Beaune (pronounced bone)

Hotels There are two good ones here, *Hôtel de la Poste* and *Le Cep.*

Restaurants The restaurant at the *Poste* is popular, well known, and good.
In *Chagny,* a nearby town, there is a three-star restaurant, folks. But

book well in advance. It's called *Hotel Lameloise* and it's almost impossible to get in there at the last minute.

Ermitage de Corton is a one-star restaurant near Beaune. The people at the hotel can direct you.

In *Auxey-Duresses,* a small town about ten minutes away, there is an absolutely charming restaurant with wonderful people and delicious food called *La Crémallière.* Reservations are probably a good idea on weekends.

Shopping Beaune is a fun town for shopping. The streets are often cobbled and there is a large square ringed with many nice little shops. I've never seen so many candy stores in one town.

On rue Maufoux there is a boutique called *Monique Rigeot.* She had some great things.

Sightseeing There's so much to see and do in Beaune and all the surrounding countryside that it's hard to list everything. The best idea is to "Beaune-up" on the area before you begin and decide where you want to go.

In Beaune is one of the most famous and interesting structures in all of France, the **Hotel Dieu,** also known as the **Hospices de Beaune.** You absolutely do not want to miss this; try to take a tour through. Don't miss the small museum housing their masterpiece, Rogier van der Weyden's polyptych of the Last Judgment.

There is also a **Museum of Wine of Bourgogne** in town. Many, many "caves" (wine cellars) are there to visit, where you can go tasting. You can also go out of town to the famous châteaux (Meursault, Pommard, etc.) for tours and tasting. Beware some of the more commercial or touristy places.

Hôtel de la Rochepot is a gorgeous château a bit out of town, from which we launched our balloons one day and behind which we picnicked in the forest. You can take a tour of this château.

Sully is probably one of the most beautiful châteaux of any we've ever seen. We saw it from the air, which is the best way. It is privately owned and inhabited and you can't go in. If you are in the area, however, you should drive by and just take a look. One of our balloons came down in the garden in front of Sully; the sister of the owner came running out and invited the entire group in for champagne and a private tour. Anything can happen when you fly with Buddy Bombard!

Normandy

If you go to Giverny (Monet's country home—see the Out of Town section), you are officially in Normandy. You have entered into one of France's most beautiful regions, with an intricate and rich history extending from before the time of the Norman conquest up to World War II. You need at least five days to do a quickie tour of Normandy; if you have a week or more, you can include Brittany, which some think is even more beautiful. You can get from Paris to Rouen in two hours and to Honfleur in three hours. Here's a brief run-down of some of the places we found particularly interesting:

Alençon

This town is famous for lace making. You can stop here and see the lace museum, showroom, and factory. For lunch try *Au Petit Vatel,* 72 pl. de Desmeulles.

Audrieu

Near Caen, with a fabulous hotel, the *Château d'Audrieu.* One of the most beautiful I've ever had the great pleasure to stay in. Wonderful restaurant, swimming pool, forest, scenery—you may never want to leave.

Avranches

Another small town with a Jardin des Plantes, lovely in itself, but the main reason to stop here for a few minutes is to get a great long-shot view of Mont St. Michel.

Bagnoles De l'Orne

An odd little mountain town with a small lake where you can rent paddle boats, etc. It seems to be a weekend retreat for Paris people and older folks. It's somewhere between quaint and corny. There's a cute little hotel there called *Bois Joli,* 12 av. Philippe-du-Rozier, which is within walking distance of the little downtown area and the lake. From here to Paris is about a three-hour drive.

Bayeux

This is a small town famous for its tapestry, *Tapisserie de la Reine* (also called the Bayeux Tapestry). Be sure you see it, located in the Place des Tribunaux in the Baron-Gerard Museum. Get the audio-tour, which lasts about twenty minutes. The cathedral across the street is very old and beautiful.

D-Day Beaches

These are of particular interest. Drive along the little road right next to the beach, which is not the main road. There are many small monuments and markers along the way, little signs explaining what happened at a certain spot. You'll see some wonderful old beach homes, many of which have never been repaired. Go as far as Point du Hoc. Along the way you'll pass all major beaches, including Omaha and Arromanches, plus the American cemetery. It's an all-day drive if you stop to take it all in, but certainly worth the time. Even kids will enjoy it, as there are many abandoned army vehicles, artillery, and bunkers along the way. At Arromanches there's a popular museum and film, usually crowded and closed for lunch.

Deauville

A short drive from Honfleur. The *Royal Hotel* is gorgeous, right on the beach, has beautiful rooms and service, a lovely dining room with so-so food. Other major hotels in the area are *Golf, Normandy,* and *P.L.M. Deauville.*

Dinan

This is a spectacular, perfectly preserved medieval walled town with a couple of good restaurants, great views of Brittany, and an interesting walk. The restaurants are *La Caravelle,* 14 pl. Duclos, and *Avaugour,* 1 pl. du Champs-Clos.

Honfleur

This is a famous and picturesque (that's an understatement) seaside village, generally mobbed with tourists. The most popular and charming hotel is called *La Ferme St.-Siméon,* but there are few rooms so make advance reservations. Restaurant in the hotel.

Mont St. Michel

The highlight of a tour through Normandy. I won't go into all its history, but you must read up about it a bit before you venture out onto this island-fortress. Kids will love it. You can only get there at certain times of the day, due to the extreme tides, which by now you will have no doubt noticed, especially if there is a full moon. Be sure you take the English-version conducted tour of the Abbey.

Have an omelet for lunch. You can spend the night on the Mont, which would probably be enormous fun; you'd have the whole place almost completely to yourself, all the other zillions of tourists having left. The best hotel is *Le Bussy.* The famous restaurant is *Mère Poulard,* but you better have some advance reservations; phone: 33–60–1401.

Pleven

This town is so small it barely shows up on a map. Technically it's in Brittany. The main reason to go to Pleven is to stay at a wonderful old farmhouse/hotel called the *Manoir Vaumadeuc.* It has only nine rooms so be sure you book in advance. Lovely dining room and regional food. A short distance from the hotel are the remains of an old fortress; ask at the hotel how to find it.

Pleven is near a town called Plancoët. I had a terrible time getting directions because I was pronouncing the word all wrong. It's pronounced more or less *plahn-kwet.* There happens to be a good restaurant there called *Chez Crouzil,* with regional dishes.

Rouen

Don't miss this wonderful old city. Be sure to walk through the old section: see the three main cathedrals, the square where Jeanne d'Arc met her death, rue du Gros Horloge, the Musée des Beaux-Arts. You can have a pretty good walking tour and see everything in three hours. Restaurants for lunch or dinner are: *Les P'tits Parapluies,* 46 rue Bourg-l'Abbé; *L'Ecu de France,* 1 rue de la Pie; and *Le Tournebroche,* rue Crois-de-Fer. *La Couronne* is one of the oldest inns in France and has great food.

If you want to buy *faience* (ceramic ware) of Rouen, better buy it while you're there. You won't see much of it elsewhere, and if you do you won't find a big selection and the cost will be higher.

St. Malo

An interesting old seaside-fortress city. The old section and ramparts have been reconstructed, but you can still enjoy the feeling of what the old fortress used to be like. There are some nice little streets for browsing with shops and restaurants. The beaches, when the tide is out, are quite nice and the swimming is good.

Normandy is famous for a lot of things and places, and I've only mentioned a few. Take along the green Michelin paperback book on Normandy, and the Gault-Millau *Guide France* for further hotel and restaurant ideas.

One thing you'll love about Normandy and Brittany is the food! The best butter you'll ever eat, coming from cows as big as elephants. Shellfish, especially clams, oysters, and mussels, are the specialty (you'll pass lots of oyster beds). *Cidre bouchée* is a kind of alcoholic apple cider; one step up is the famous Calvados. Anything made out of apples is popular. Big buckwheat crêpes called *galettes* are served everywhere, with all types of fillings. The ones with ham and cheese are my favorite, but sometimes they're a little dry; you can fix that with butter or mustard. Naturally, the cream is the creamiest. You can easily gain a pound a day in this part of France without trying too hard. Oh, but it's worth it!

Italy

Italy

There's something about Italy which cannot be put into words. The more you try to describe it, the more you realize you can't, really. You can read all about where to stay and what to eat, but until you go there, you cannot imagine what it's like and no one can explain it. You leave Italy a little wiser, a little happier, and probably a good deal fatter than before you went; but that's not what I'm getting at. If you have even the remotest feelings for art and history, you cannot help but be moved and awed by what you will see there. Italy is good for your soul.

I love Italy. I can't wait to return. At the same time, I would not choose to live there for any extended period of time (I'll save that for France!). After three weeks in Italy I have to get out for a while. Italy is *not* organized. Besides intense joy, you'll feel great frustration: at the constant need to be watchful about your personal belongings, about the graffiti sprayed all over the most magnificent antiquities, at the overcrowded and dimly lit museums, at the sometimes littered and dirty streets, at the frenetic pace in the cities.

Before going to Italy, do your homework. Learn a few Italian words, by all means. Learn something about the ancient Romans, the Renaissance, about Italian sculptors and painters and musicians, about the architecture. This is not a monumental task. One good book about the country is all you need. You will miss so much if you don't do this. Try not to take an organized tour, no matter how inexpensive it is. Italy is not hard to get around in on your own, and you will see it so much better if you are not in the midst of thirty other Americans trailing behind a guide. If you must, hire a guide in each city or take guided tours of museums and ruins. In the cities, use your feet, not a bus or a taxi. Don't be forced into eating in the "tourist section" of restaurants, where you'll be surrounded by only more Americans and be offered the tourist menu (*never* accept a tourist menu!). Take maps and guidebooks and a little dictionary along with you, and a lot of film. Plan to do a lot of shopping! Take an extra, collapsible suitcase. Wear a money belt. Take very comfortable walking shoes. Don't wear a lot of expensive jewelry.

Unfortunately, crime in Italy is a national pastime. If you aren't extremely cautious and aware, you may be one of the victims. The police aren't too helpful (in fact, they are sometimes collaborators). I'm not just making all this up; I know very few people who have come home from Italy without some story to tell, and it never has a happy ending.

When in Rome do as the (wiser) Romans do:

1. *Never walk with the flow of traffic, but against it.*
2. *Never take your eyes off approaching motorbikes.*
3. *Never carry cameras on neck straps (unless you want to be garrotted by teenage hoodlums on motorbikes).*
4. *Never wear heavy necklaces, flashy earrings, or neck-chain medallions.*
5. *Never carry shoulder-strap bags or big handbags (carry passport and money in pockets of jacket or pants).*
6. *Never lunch or dine with cameras or handbags on tables placed next to open windows or at curb of sidewalk restaurants.*
7. *Never display more than minimal cash when changing dollars or traveler's checks, paying bills in shops or restaurants, or while purchasing tickets of any kind.*
8. *Never approach any cluster of young men with motorbikes or near bars.*
9. *Never be drawn by curiosity into any crowd of demonstrators.*
10. *Never drive or hire luxury cars with "foreign" licenses.*
11. *Never leave luggage or possessions in sight inside unguarded car no matter how securely locked. (My idea: park in front of police stations when possible.) Don't trust the police, either.*
12. *Never walk at night next to walls and doorways, but at the curb.*
13. *Never walk in daytime along curb, but next to walls.*
14. *Never turn your back day or night to sidewalk when unlocking doors or searching for names on doorbells.*
15. *Never be too proud to run if frightened.*
16. *Never be slow to scream or shout if attacked.*
17. *Never forget—going anywhere alone after dark may be courting disaster.*
18. *To these I would add: Never allow yourself to be surrounded by groups of children, especially if they are holding large pieces of cardboard. Watch out for women with children who are begging; while you are dealing with the woman, her kid is behind you dipping into your purse or pocket.*

As for *guidebooks,* I'm disenchanted with the ones I've been using so can only advise you to browse through some at your local bookstore, and possibly wait until you get to Italy to pick one up, as they seem to have an abundance of them there that are not available in the U.S. I do not like the green Michelin for several reasons (its organization is confusing and the facts are few, for two things). The red Michelin (restaurants and hotels) is good for cross-reference but not as a bible. The *Guide Bleu* is good. For restaurants, in Italy find *I Ristoranti di Veronelli.* Rely a lot on recent magazine and newspaper articles, and recommendations from friends.

A few more bits of advice:

Even the best hotels seem to be locked into forty-watt light bulbs. If you have a traveling illuminated makeup mirror, take it.

Even the best hotels aren't equipped to handle the voltage from your hairdryer or curling iron. Take transformers, adapters, and an extension cord. Plug larger appliances into the TV outlet to avoid blowing the electricity on the whole floor.

Take a nice-sized bar of soap; many times you'll get one teensy little cake for the whole week.

Take your own facial tissues; they're often non-existent in hotels.

Be prepared for shaky restroom facilities, not to mention really revolting, at times. Take seat covers and tissues into restrooms, even in restaurants. Only in Morocco did I encounter worse bathroom conditions.

Don't buy film there—it costs a fortune.

Save all receipts when you cash traveler's checks. Without them, you cannot cash in your lire when you leave the country.

Take a very sturdy handbag with a short shoulder strap, one that allows you to grip the purse in your armpit. Be sure it fastens securely—the more complicated, the better. Don't put everything in one place: spread your money, passport, airline tickets, credit cards, and traveler's checks around: in your wallet, in zippered compartments in your purse, in a money belt, in a compact, in a tissue packet (don't throw it out by accident), in your eyeglass case, etc. Men should not casually put any such items in a back pocket or in a single pocket.

Lock all valuables in hotel safe when you're not using them.

If you are going to take a train, get your seat booked well in advance. They oversell the trains and you could end up standing in the aisle for three hours. Book only in first class. Watch your luggage carefully at each stop. Don't dally getting off the train; they don't give you much time, and if you have a lot of luggage, you'll have to be organized. People getting on the train don't care how desperate you are to get off, and vice versa.

If there is a strike on while you are there and you can't get into a museum or monument, go visit something that belongs to the Vatican: a church, museum, catacomb, etc. The Vatican is separate from Italy and does not adhere to the same rules.

Make reservations in restaurants, both for lunch (if it's a well-known restaurant) and for dinner. Make some of these before you leave home, as the famous places fill up in advance. Have your concierge confirm them for you when you arrive at the hotel.

Study the monetary system a little before you go. They deal in thousands of lire and it can be confusing. Take a pocket calculator.

While you're shopping and negotiating, taking a photo, or reading a guidebook, don't leave your purse agape. Your wallet will be missing.

Rent a car and get out into the countryside. Yes, city driving is pure madness, but once you're out of the city, it's wonderful. Italian highways are beautifully marked and maintained, with rest stops every few miles. Driving around Italy is a real treat, especially if you have the time to venture off the main roads and explore a hill town you've never heard of. Renting a car is expensive, so look into it before you go; your travel agent can arrange the best deal for you. Hiring a car and driver is extremely expensive, but if you can afford it, it can be a good idea for half-day or day trips.

Allow yourself equal time for sightseeing, shopping, and eating. In Italy, each is an experience you don't want to miss. Let's take these one by one.

Sightseeing could fill every minute of the day and night, if you let it. I generally find it's better to do it in the morning, while you're fresh and full of energy, instead of a lot of pasta. The problem with sightseeing in Italy is that there's so much to see, and you have to make choices. That's why it's important to do your homework before you go, so you'll know which monuments, antiquities, churches, and museums you really want to see, and which ones you can afford to miss. If you have enough time and plan carefully, you can see them all. I visited twelve churches, five museums, and all the main archaeological sites in five days once, plus did a lot of shopping. I admit I'm a fanatic. Be careful about the lunch hour, or hours—most places are closed from noon until 2:00, or from 1:00 until 4:00, etc. Find out before you go. Even the churches close for lunch.

Shopping is a lot of fun in Italy, because the stores are so interesting and full of wonderful goodies, and all the famous labels are right there. If you can, take even more money than you think you'll need; once you get into it, you'll go crazy. Clothes are a very good buy in Italy, especially in Rome and Milan, because the styles will hold up for years. Again, you need to do your homework on this, so you know where to go for leather, ceramics, or sausages.

Ah, and now for the best part: *mangiare!* If you've never been to Italy before, you do not know the true meaning of the word "pasta." Even if you've eaten in the best Italian restaurants in New York, you don't know. You will feel guilty at first for having pasta for both lunch and dinner, along with all the other things you order; this will pass. Just remember one thing —once you leave the country, you can't get that pasta anymore, so go for it!

Italy also has very good country breads. The fresh green salads are fabulous—they usually make them at the table with all sorts of unusual greens, and they're safe to eat. This is the place to get *bufalo* cheese (fresh mozzarella), either in a salad or by itself. Be sure the balls of cheese are in water or they'll be dry. Ice cream is of prime importance; you must have some every day. Capuccino was invented here. Order a dessert called *caffè affagato*—it's ice cream with hot espresso poured over it, at table. Also order *tartufo* for dessert. French-fried artichokes *(carciofi alla giudia)* are delicious. Try the local wines, especially the whites. Many of them never make it out of the region you're in. If you want decaf coffee, ask for *caffè hag* (pronounced *ahg*). If you want just a quick snack for lunch, go to a bar and order a *tost,* which is a grilled ham and cheese sandwich. Get a cappuccino to go with it. Above all, eat slowly, eat all you want (you're going to walk it off, right?), savor each bite. You'll dream about it for months after you're home.

Here's one of the best pieces of advice I can give you. Pick a sunny afternoon; then pick a nice piazza—it doesn't matter how big or small it is. Then pick a nice sidewalk café in the piazza and go there around 4:00 or 5:00. Sit down and order a glass of wine or your favorite libation. Let the world go by in front of you. Sit there for a very long time. Listen to all the sounds. Watch all the people. Don't think about anything else. Promise yourself you will return to Italy one day.

Rome

I doubt if all roads lead to Rome these days, but yours should. Rome should be the jumping-off place for your trip to Italy, especially if it's your first. It's a big city, initially confusing, dirty in many places, more dangerous than other Italian cities, crowded, polluted, and fantastic! For a first visit, allow yourself at least five days, but a week is better. If you're going for a good hotel and the best restaurants, reserve in advance. Find out what the weather is and plan accordingly. You can be quite casual during the day, but the beautiful people come out at night and you'll want to get dressed for dinner.

Hotels

Albergo d'Inghilterra,   Bocca de Leone 14, phone 672161
In a great location, at the bottom of the Spanish Steps, and what's better, next door to Valentino. Small hotel, small rooms, good service, not expensive.

Cavalieri Hilton,   via Cadlolo 101, phone 2151.
There's a panoramic view from the restaurant, La Pergola, and the hotel has undergone a recent facelift.

Hotel Giulio Cesare,   287 via degli Scipioni in the Prati District, phone 310244.
A very nice small hotel just across the river from Piazza del Popolo. Doubles are about 100 dollars a night, which includes a marvelous buffet breakfast, served in the rooftop bar/restaurant on nice days, to savor the view of Rome. Quiet street, excellent service.

Hassler Villa Medici,   piazza Trinitá dei Monti 6, phone 679–2651
The best hotel in Rome, at the moment. The location at the top of the Spanish Steps is great. We found the rooms to be a bit on the tacky side and typically

Roman in decor. Terrific service. Rooftop restaurant has panoramic view of the city.

Lord Byron, via de Notaris 5, phone 3609541.

Another popular, small hotel. It boasts a Michelin one-star restaurant called Le Jardin.

The other popular and better of the large hotels are *Le Grand Hotel,* via Vittorio Emanuele Orlando 3, phone 4709, recently renovated and the *Eden,* via Ludovisi 49, phone 4742401. The Eden has a rooftop bar and restaurant with great views. Also recent renovations. The *Excelsior* seems to have fallen out of favor.

Restaurants

On my last trip to Rome I was disappointed in the food. In general, the pastas had slipped, the main courses had declined, and the desserts had died. Not in every restaurant, mind you, but in many. I've had better luck with pasta recently in New York. Let's hope this condition was unusual and not the status quo. To help you in your restaurant decisions, get a book called *I Ristoranti di Veronelli.* Don't rely too much on Michelin. Ask the local gentry of your economic and intellectual level where they like to eat.

Don't take any chances—always have advance reservations. It's possible to get a table at the last minute at lunch in some places, but don't be surprised if your favorite place is all booked up (it's probably everyone else's favorite, too).

Dress in most Italian restaurants is on the casual side. Only in the very expensive, chic places do you really have to dress to impress. On the casual side, in my book, does not mean you can wear jeans (only tacky UA's wear jeans anymore to restaurants).

Alberto Ciarla, piazza San Cosimato 40, in Trastevere, phone 588668.

Seafood, chic, very good.

Al 59 (Cinquantanove) Ristorante da Giuseppe, via Angelo Brunetti 59, phone 3619019.

Cesarina, formerly of Cesarina, now shares her wonderful recipes in this new kitchen; nontourist, all local Romans. Simple decor and sensational food.

Alfredo's alla Scrofa, via della Scrofa 104, phone 6540163.

Home of the original fettucine Alfredo. Everywhere else that you order this dish, it's known as fettucine with cream sauce.

Dal Bolognese, piazza del Popolo 1, phone 3611426.

A nice little place with an enclosed porch. *Bollito misto* (boiled meats with sauces) is their specialty. Other dishes were good but not great. OK for lunch.

Caffè Grecco, via Condotti near the Spanish Steps.

A very old and well-known coffee house. Go for tea. You have to go to the pastry counter yourself and select your goodie; drinks are served at the table (if you can get one).

Capriciosa, Largo Lombardi.

A wild and crazy place, lots of noise and cheery Italians. Inexpensive and casual.

Cecilia Metella di Graziani Roberto, via Appia Antica 125–127, phone 5136743.

Good bet for lunch if you're visiting the catacombs. Alfresco dining in good weather.

Cesarina, via Piemonte 109, phone 460828.

The owner, Cesarina, moved on to Al 59 and sold this place to Arabs, so I was told. It used to be outstanding but who knows now? Roman friends told me not to go.

Cicilardone, via Merulana 77, phone 733806.

Inexpensive and great for pasta.

L'Escargot, via Appia Antica near the Catacombs.

Very small, sort of country-French atmosphere. Lots of charm and character.

Fontanella Borghese, Largo Fontanella Borghese 86.

A very popular place where we had a very lousy meal. Can't recommend it. The service wasn't so great, either.

Galeassi, piazza di Santa Maria 3, in Trastevere, phone 583775.

Alfresco dining, weather permitting, on the same piazza as Sabatini. Go for lunch.

Gelateria Della-Palma, via della Maddalena 20–23.

Another best bet for ice creme, near Giolitti's. Soon to be a worldwide ice cream chain.

Giggetto al Portico d'Ottavia, via del Portico d'Ottavia 21, near Teatro Marcello, phone 6561105.

Nontouristy, popular, inexpensive, good for lunch.

Da Gino, via della Lungaretta 85, phone 5803403.

Small place for fish; inexpensive.

Giolotti's, via Uffici del Vicario 40.

You're at the Pantheon. Turn your back on the front of it and walk down the street which leads off the piazza. This will lead you to Piazza della Maddalena (by all means go in and look at the church). Continue through this piazza and down the street on the right. When it deadends, turn right, and you will arrive at Giolotti's, where you will get some of the best ice cream you'll ever eat. Get a cash register receipt before you order. You can eat it there, but better to lick slowly as you walk through the streets of Rome.

Girarrosto Toscano, via Campania 29, phone 493759 or 490604.

Very pretty and popular restaurant; get grilled meats; the pasta was forgettable. Great antipasto. Casual.

Grotte di Livia, via Tiberna 1, in Primaporta, about a twenty-minute drive from the heart of Rome.

Local, neighborhood place in a grotto (cavelike) atmosphere. Lots of charm and color. Grilled meats are the specialty. Pasta was mediocre. No one speaks English, which makes it better.

Harry's Bar, via Vittorio Veneto 150, phone 4745832.

Go for drinks but don't stay for dinner.

Hassler Villa Medici Hotel rooftop restaurant, piazza Trinità dei Monti 6.

Great views of the city; elegant. Food is OK.

Hostaria dell'Orso, via Monte Brianzo 93, phone 6564250.

In a palazzo where Dante used to live, or so they say. Elegant, formal, a bit expensive.

Il Drappo, vicolo Malpasso 9, phone 657365.

Local place, good food.

La Pergala, via Cadlolo 101, phone 3151; on the terrace of the Hotel Cavaliere Hilton. Open late.

Nouvelle Italian cuisine. One of Rome's best.

Al Moro, vicolo delle Bollette 15, phone 6783495.

Romans in the know think this place is mediocre. My friend George loves it for the spaghetti carbonara and baby lamb. I thought it was good.

Nino, via Borgognona 11, phone 6795676 and 6786752.

Popular, noisy, crowded, fun place, good food, great grilled meats and bean soup.

Open Gate, via San Nicola da Tolentino 4, phone 4750464, open 9 PM–1:30 AM, closed Sunday.

Luxurious and expensive restaurant/nightclub. Dancing til 4 A.M. Very popular and excellent food.

Osteria dell'Antiquario, Piazzetta San Simeon 27, phone 659694.

Popular restaurant serving classical dishes; inexpensive.

Da Pancrazio, piazza del Biscione 92, phone 6561246.

A taverna decorated in old Roman. Interesting.

Passetto, via Zanardelli 14, near Piazza Navona, phone 6543696.

A star awarded from Michelin (although I don't pay much attention to Michelin in Italy). Expensive but very good food.

Piccolo Mondo, via Aurora 39, phone 4754595.

Very popular, especially at lunch. Good.

Piperno, Monte de Cenci 9, phone 6540629.

Michelin gives them a star. Very good food. Try the *carciofi alla giudia* and *fettucine al salmone*. Lunch or dinner.

Ranieri, via Mario de'Fiori 26, phone 6791592.

Same idea as Sans Souci and El Toula.

Sabatini, piazza di Santa Maria 13, in Trastevere, phone 582026.

Good alfresco dining in nice weather. Good food, service, charming restaurant, interesting neighborhood. Don't walk around the area at night.

Sans Souci, via Sicilia 20/24, phone 493504.

Expensive, elegant, but very good food.

Scolio di Frisio, via Merulana 256, phone 734619.

A wild decor is an understatement. They tried to make this seafood restaurant look like the bottom of the sea. It doesn't work but it is amusing. Very charming people, good food, lots of atmosphere. Many big families for Sunday lunch, which makes it fun.

Sibilla's   in Old Tivoli, about an hour's drive from Rome.

When you visit Tivoli Gardens, you go here for lunch. A very charming country restaurant with a view of the ancient temple of Sibilla. Excellent food. Try fresh trout and ravioli.

Tentativo,   via della Luce 5, phone 5895234, in Trastevere.

Frequented by locals, good food, inexpensive.

El Toula,   via della Lupa 29, phone 6786471.

Same idea as Sans Souci.

Trattoria Ambasciata d'Abruzzo,   via Pietro Tacchini 26, Parioli district, phone 878256.

If you want to eat a lot of food and get off really cheap, this is the place for you. It used to be better. It has become too touristy for me. You don't order off a menu—they just bring you platters of food for about two hours. Four people can stuff themselves here for less than 45 dollars. Good bread and sausages; some antipastis are OK; pasta and main course were forgettable; desserts were lousy. But cheap! Some atmosphere.

Tre Scalini,   piazza Navona 28–31.

Best for lunch on a sunny day or dinner on a summer evening, but always a must. Excellent pasta, main-course crêpes, antipastis, and their special *tartufo* dessert, unlike any other. The location in the Piazza Navona couldn't be better.

Vecchia Roma,   piazza Campitelli 18.

Great place for lunch near the Forum and Campidoglio. Nontouristy.

Sightseeing

If you stayed in Rome about a year, you might cover the basics. There's so much to see there that it almost seems defeating at the beginning. Your list, which you have made up in advance, is very long. With your Michelin guide in hand, your map of city streets, camera, best walking shoes, and all the energy you can muster, you set out to discover the wonders of Rome, which number far beyond seven.

Ancient Rome and Other Sites

The Arch of Constantine currently being restored, is the famous triumphal arch in Rome. You'll automatically see it when you visit the Forum or the Colosseum.

Caracalla's Baths are gigantic and well worth a tour. You can see them on your way to or from the Catacombs. Operas during the summer.

The Castel Sant'Angelo (Hadrian's Fortress) is quite fascinating if you have the time. You can rent an audio cassette in English.

The Catacombs on the via Appia Antica should not be missed and are a good place to go when everything else in the city is shut down, since they are under the auspices of the Vatican. The relics of St. Sebastian can be found in the church next to one of the catacombs. There are several different catacombs, and you can usually count on getting into at least one of them. They offer guided tours in English, which is the best bet.

The Colosseum will probably be next. You can go inside part of it but are not allowed to roam around anywhere you want. Ongoing restorations.

The Forum is about as good a place to start as any. You should have some sort of map of the Forum with you, with explanations, so you are not stumbling around wondering exactly what it is that you're seeing. If you can find a tour in English, so much the better; they had no such thing when we were there. Be sure you go up to the Palatine (top of the hill) as part of your tour. The Forum will take you at least half a day. Ongoing excavations.

The Janiculum is the highest hill in Rome, affording wonderful views. It is there that you can visit San Pietro in Montorio and the Tempietto.

Knights of Malta Piazza Aventino area. If you're in this neighborhood, stop in the piazza and take a look through the keyhole (I'm sure someone will point it out to you). Very famous view.

The Pantheon (Rotunda) is an architectural wonder and you can't miss it. It's also where Raphael is buried. Read about the Pantheon before you go—its construction, history, etc. Near the Pantheon is Piazza della Maddalena with a wonderful baroque church, and near that is Giolotti's ice cream store (see restaurant section).

The Piazza dei Campidoglio is famous because Michelangelo designed it. Architecturally it is beautiful. It's where you'll find the Capitoline Museum.

The Piazza Navona is, for me, Rome's most beautiful piazza. You could spend hours in this piazza doing nothing more than watching the people. Lunch at *Tre Scalini* is mandatory (sit outside).

The Piazza del Popolo is another beautiful piazza, but unfortunately you can barely get an idea of its beauty because of the jillions of cars constantly parked there. It shouldn't be allowed. Two good churches on the piazza and a couple of good restaurants.

The Piazza di Spagna and Trinità dei Monti (Spanish Steps area) is a wonderful place to go sit and people-watch. The views from the top are very good, and Rome's most chic shopping street leads off from the bottom. It's especially beautiful in the spring when they put the azaleas out.

The Piazza Venezia is recognizable because of the dominating presence of the memorial to Victor Emmanuel II, more commonly referred to as The Wedding Cake. I suggest that a drive by will suffice.

The Pincio is a pretty area with views of the city, especially of the Piazza del Popolo. If you go up to the top of the Spanish Steps and walk downhill, you'll be on the Pincio.

The Teatro Marcello is a not-so-small theater which you can't get into, but it's interesting to walk around it. The surrounding neighborhood is full of bits and pieces of antique architecture peeking out from the modern world, plus a few wonderful hideaway restaurants that most tourists don't find.

Tivoli Gardens (Villa d'Este) are about an hour's drive from Rome and make a wonderful day trip (more like two thirds of a day). The gardens are famous for their magnificent fountains. The drive through the countryside is quite pleasant, once you get outside the Roman suburbs. Be sure you stop for lunch at *Sibilla's,* where you'll see the charming, ancient temple of the same name. If you want to go to Hadrian's Villa, or what's left of it, it's also in the area.

The Tomb of Cecilia Metella is within walking distance of the catacombs along the famed Appia Antica. That road, by the way, is narrow and the cars go ninety miles an hour, so be careful as you walk along, especially if you have young children.

Trajan's Forum and Column you will pass as you go to the Forum or Colosseum. There's not much to do here except just look at them, and try to conjure what ancient Rome must have looked like. New and exciting excavations and discoveries being made.

Trastevere is the name of an entire section of Rome located "across the river Tevere." A fabulous neighborhood to wander in; some great restaurants and an extremely old church.

The Trevi Fountain was made famous by people singing and throwing three coins into it back in the fifties. It's a major tourist attraction but very beautiful, both in the daytime and when lit at night.

Museums and Palaces

I'm putting these two categories together because most of the time the museum is in the palace, or the palace is full of wonderful frescoes. Churches are also museums of a kind, but I'll list them separately.

The Borghese Gallery is in the Borghese palazzo in a beautiful parklike setting leading off the Pincio. Magnificent sculpture and paintings. Recent renovations.

The Capitoline Museum, in a seventeenth-century palazzo, is located in two buildings on the Piazza dei Campidoglio, mentioned earlier. Some famous and breathtaking ancient pieces.

Museo delle Terme (National Museum of Rome at Diocletian's Baths).
This museum is located in the restored baths and beautiful peristyle garden of Santa Maria degli Angeli. Before entering the museum you can go into an exhibit of recent and ongoing excavations, very nicely presented. Inside the museum are many, many ancient Roman sculptures, and some wonderful Greek pieces. Don't miss the room on the first floor (second to you) which has all the frescoes from Livia's villa at Primaporta.

While you're in the area, go see Santa Maria Maggiore. From there you can walk to Santa Maria della Vittoria, Santa Susanna, San Carlo alle Quattro Fontane, and Palazzo Barberini.

Palazzo Barberini, via delle Quattro Fontane.

This palace was built in 1627 for the family of Pope Urban VII. It now houses a *pinacoteca* (picture gallery) that is pretty dark and dismal, despite some good works on the walls. The chief attraction here are the series of apartments, maintaining their original wall paintings and some furnishings. It's just one little unmarked door which leads to these rooms, so if you don't find it, ask. Allow one and a half to two hours.

Down the street from the palazzo are three churches, mentioned above, which you should not miss. They are all closed from noon until 4:30, so time your visit accordingly.

Palazzo Farnese dates from the sixteenth century and is only partially open on Sundays from 11:00 to 12:00 A.M. You can only see the garden and inner court.

The Vatican Museums should be at the top of the list, actually, because they should be seen above all others. Get there the minute they open in the morning (9:00), because they close at 1:00 P.M. for the day. Be prepared for impossible mobs of people, especially noisy, screaming groups of students (you'll find these everywhere, unfortunately). Struggle your way to the ticket window and push along with the crowd. You will be herded through corridors full of wonderful things and end up at the *Raphael Stanze* (rooms), which you must not miss. Here you can rent an audio–phone, and when you enter each room you must stand in a circle in the floor to get reception. Of course, the big attraction for most people is the *Sistine Chapel,* and seeing is believing. But there is so much more to the Vatican Museum than most people see. It's huge and contains some of the most outstanding sculpture, antiquities, paintings, tapestries, apartments, etc., in the world, collected through the ages by the popes. Be sure you see the *Pio-Clementine Museum,* the *Picture Gallery, Library, Borgia Apartments, Raphael Loggias,* and *Tapestry Gallery.* It'll be nearly impossible to do everything in one half day.

When you finally stagger out of the museum with your head swimming and heart pounding, you can find your way right over to St. Peter's.

The Villa Giulia is in the same park and a short walk from the Borghese Gallery, past the zoo. It is the former summer home of Pope Julius III and now houses the Etruscan Museum. If you're not familiar with the Etruscans and their art, you should be; they had a fascinating society and their art and artifacts are captivating. The most outstanding collection of Etruscan art I've yet to see. Don't cut yourself short on time for this one.

Villa Farnesina is a Renaissance-style (sixteenth-century) country mansion, open from 9:00 a.m. to 1:00 p.m. weekdays.

You can tour this magnificent villa, which contains some beautiful frescoes and retains its original wall decoration.

Churches

That saying about all the art of Europe being in the churches is probably truer for Italy than anywhere else. It's almost impossible to walk into any church without stumbling happily upon some fabulous fresco by a famous artist, or an exciting altarpiece, pulpit, or piece of sculpture. I used to have a motto about never passing a church without going inside. It got out of hand; but I still think it's a good motto and I do my best to stick with it. I've never been disappointed.

Basilica San Giovanni in Laterano is Rome's oldest church, dating from Constantine.

Basilica of San Paolo Fuori le Mura (St. Paul's Beyond the Walls) is Rome's second largest basilica, after St. Peter's. It's huge, with an impressive interior and mosaics.

St. Ignazio is near Piazza Venezia and contains an impressive baroque ceiling painted by Pozzo.

St. Peter's is, of course, Il Grandissimo. You need a couple of hours here to see it all: the piazza, the crypt, the interior, and a climb up to the roof—as high as you can go—for an unbelievable view.

San Clemente is a famous basilica built on the ruins of an ancient Roman temple, dating from around the fifth century. The lower part closes for lunch, so be sure you time your visit not to miss it. The upper rooms have beautiful mosaics.

Santa Maddelena in Piazza della Maddalena, a short walk from the Pantheon, has a great baroque interior.

Santa Maria del Popolo in Piazza del Popolo has two very famous Caravaggio frescoes and a side chapel designed by Raphael.

Santa Maria in Trastevere is very old, with fine mosaics. If you eat at Sabatini, you'll be just across the piazza.

Santa Maria della Vittoria is possibly my favorite church in Rome or anywhere. The interior is an explosion of color and movement. The altarpiece, *St. Teresa in Ecstasy* by Bernini, is quite marvelous. Best time to get in is late afternoon.

Santa Maria Maggiore is another of Rome's basilicas and is quite large and spectacular, especially some of the baroque side chapels, the mosaics, the elaborate ceiling.

San Pietro in Montorio is up on the Janiculum, a little walk from Trastevere. It is here you can see Bramante's famous Renaissance temple, the Tempietto.

San Pietro in Vincoli (St. Peter in Chains) is a short walk from the Colosseum. The church itself is not all that exciting, but what's in it is: Michelangelo's *Moses*.

Scala Santa is a small church across from San Giovanni in Laterano and contains a wooden staircase, supposedly from the house of Pontius Pilate. They say that Jesus walked up this staircase before he was judged.

The *Gesù Church* has some very sumptuous altarpieces.

This is but a partial list, but I think you'd be glad if you visited any or all of these churches. I thought I was making pretty good headway doing churches in Rome until I read an article which stated that there are over 360 churches in the city. At least I'll have something to look forward to . . .

As for dress in the churches, the standards have been somewhat relaxed in the past few years. Women can enter wearing slacks.

Shopping—Hello Gucci, Valentino, Missoni, Fendi, Bulgari, Ferragamo, And Friends!

If you're going to be visiting several cities in Italy and don't know where to spend your money, I can advise you that for wearing apparel, Rome is your best bet. You'll have a larger selection and better prices than in the other cities. Milan is also good for clothes and shoes, but Rome is more fun.

My favorite area for shopping is around the bottom of the Spanish Steps—the via Condotti and all its side streets. The Condotti will cross the Corso, which is another good street, although it's quite busy with traffic and moving around is more difficult. The Corso is less expensive than the Condotti section, which is where you'll find top designers and names.

Two inexpensive department stores are Coin, Piazzale Appio, and the old standby, Rinascente, on the Corso. Bargains available.

For knits and sweaters, go to Annette, piazza di Spagna 35. A good place to buy very inexpensive sweaters is Anticoli al Gambero, via del Gambero 35–36; there are other locations in the city.

A good men's tailor is Angelo's, via Bissolate, off the Veneto.

For gloves, scarves, bags, ties, belts, wallets: go to Anticoli Gloves Factory, piazza Mignanelli 22, just off Piazza di Spagna.

Wherever you shop, have a good time. Watch your purse and your money. If you like it, buy it! You may not see it anywhere else. The quality and styles of clothing and accessories in Italy are topnotch, equaled only by those in France.

Rome is the kind of city you can visit, do nothing, and see almost everything. If you hate shopping, hate museums, hate sightseeing, love to sleep in, you'll still get a lot out of Rome. All you have to do, really, is just go walking in any direction, down any street; then sit in any piazza. You can't go wrong.

Florence

With a little imagination you could look at the view of Florence from the Piazzale Michelangelo and think you were back in the fifteenth or sixteenth century. The giveaways are the buses in the parking lot and the people wearing jeans, instead of tunics and tights. Despite the passing of time and the encroachment of more recent centuries, Florence has retained much of the look of past ages.

To get the most out of your trip to Florence you should know something about the Renaissance and the Medici, so go to your local library and get a good book on the subject before you ever leave home. Even if you only read about Michelangelo, you'll be somewhat attuned to what Florence is all about.

As in Rome and most cities, the best way to see Florence is by extended use of the bottoms of your feet: in other words, walk a lot. It's not a very big city and you can get almost everywhere on foot. The architecture is something you don't want to miss.

There's so much to see in Florence that you'll need at least four or five days, especially if you want to venture out into the surrounding countryside, which is gorgeous. Save enough time to savor this unique city.

Hotels

The Excelsior, piazza Ognissanti 3.
A grand hotel and also quite popular. It's had a good rep for years. More expensive than the previous two and not as charming overall. 209 rooms.

Grand Hotel Villa Cora, out of town at viale Machiavelli 18.
Quiet, beautiful rooms, terrific restaurant; transportation into town.

The Lungarno, borgo Sant'Jacopo 14.

Very popular also, with 71 rooms and a view of the Arno from the other side. It's more modern and less charming than the Principe, but a good hotel.

The Principe, lungarno Vespucci 34.

A very small and very elegant hotel with only 21 rooms. Very popular, so reserve in advance. Ask for a room with a view of the Arno. We had the attic rooms, which were like dollhouses, with a view from the patio you couldn't beat. Room 12 is one of the larger rooms.

There are several other good hotels in Florence of various sizes and prices, but I've never spoken to anyone who didn't stay at one of the four I just mentioned.

Restaurants

Al Girarrosto, piazza Santa Maria Novella 9.

For grilled cuisine; casual, inexpensive.

Boca dell'Orafo (don't have an exact address or phone number).

A tiny, "in" place, and if you don't get there around noon, you probably won't get a table. It's in a small alley between the Ponte Vecchio and the end of the Uffizi; off lungarno Gen. Diaz. I've heard it's terrific. Casual, inexpensive.

Buca Lapi, via del Trebbio 1, phone 213768.

One of several of Florence's popular steakhouses. Florence is supposed to be famous for its steaks and beef; however, we never did have a good steak there, especially not at Buca Lapi, where it was noisy, crowded, smoky, and touristy. If you want to try a steakhouse anyway, try *Buca Mario,* piazza Ottaviani 16, which I've heard is better.

Cafaggi, via Guelfa 35, phone 294989.

Our "secret" place for lunch. I think we were the only tourists they'd seen there in a year. We went in because we were hungry and the place was overflowing with happy Italians, all stuffing themselves (good sign of a good restaurant). We were not disappointed. This is definitely a neighborhood hangout, with its faithful habitués. Very inexpensive and casual. Best chocolate ice cream, made on the premises, that I will probably ever eat.

Cammillo, borgo Sant'Jacopo 57, phone 212427.

A wonderful Florentine trattoria; small, popular, not too expensive.

Doney, via de' Tornabuoni 46, phone 214348.

Around for years, this restaurant is very well known; also elegant and expensive. I've heard it's a little stuffy but that the food is good. Haven't been there myself, as I prefer something a little less chic.

Enoteca Pinchiorri, via Ghibellina 87, phone 242777.

A new one on me, but I just read that it has two Michelin stars, which is unusual for Italy (they usually give one or none). It's probably very good, and I base that opinion on other two-star restaurants I've dined in. Reservations a must.

13 Gobbi, via del Porcellana 9, phone 298769.

One of the city's best. Again: atmosphere, not too expensive, well known, great food.

Harry's Bar, lungarno Vespucci 22, phone 296700.

Needs no introduction. It's OK. I prefer the Harry's Bar in L.A., if you want to know the truth. If you're sick of pasta and dying for a hamburger, you might like to go here.

La Loggia, piazzale Michelangelo 1, phone 287032.

A very nice place to go for lunch. On Sundays you'll share the room with many of the Italian families from the neighborhood. Reservations a must. Moderate prices. After lunch be sure you see the vista from the edge of the piazza, then drive around the neighborhood to see some marvelous private villas.

Mama Gina, borgo Sant'Jacopo 37, phone 296009.

One of our favorites. Small, *molto* atmosphere, outstanding pasta. Great for lunch or dinner. Casual, inexpensive. Best *paglia e fieno* (straw and hay) I ever ate.

Otello, via Orti Oricellari 36, phone 215-819.

Our favorite on the last visit. Be sure you are given the regular menu and not the tourist menu. It's a lively and popular place, across the street from the train station, but don't let that last detail deter you. Reservations are a must. Not too expensive. Fabulous pasta!

Ottorino, via Sant'Elisabetta 6, phone 218747.

Superb food at moderate prices with contemporary decor.

Paoli, via dei Tavolini 12, phone 216215.

A beautiful restaurant with plenty of atmosphere, supposedly in the style of the thirteenth century. Good food, not expensive. A short distance away is Dante's house, and in the other direction is a good ice cream store called Per Che No?

Sabatini, via de' Panzani 9/a, phone 282802.

Quite expensive, very elegant, somewhat stuffy and noisy, and the food is OK. It's been popular and well known for years, so it must have something going for it. We prefer the more quaint restaurants with better atmosphere and better food.

Ristorante Taverna Machiavelli, viale Machiavelli 18, in the Grand Hotel Villa Cora, phone 2298451.

Wonderful food; expensive.

Sightseeing

Museums (You don't want to miss any of them.)

The Accademia.

This is where you go to see Michelangelo's *David* (no, the one in the Palazzo Vecchio is *not* the real *David,* only a copy). The museum also contains other Michelangelo works, plus some primitives.

The Archaeological Museum.
Contains antiquities, including an Etruscan collection.

The Bargello Palace and National Museum.
Another spectacular building housing sculpture and decorative arts. Wonderful, wonderful! Another two hours, at least.

The Museum of San Marco.
Here you'll see the famous and so beautiful frescoes of Fra Angelico. The *Annunciation* and the monks' cells are on the second level.

The Palazzo Medici-Riccardi.
Home of the Medicis for almost one hundred years and a beautiful Renaissance building. It has a small museum and a very famous frescoed chapel.

The Palazzo Vecchio.
Not really a museum, but sort of fits into the category. The interior has many gorgeous rooms, full of magnificent artworks; some exhibitions are temporary. There is an entrance for students in the Piazza Signoria, but if you go around to the side entrance, you'll avoid their noisy, smelly, crowded confusion.

The Pitti Palace.
Something to see, although the collection can't compare to that of the Uffizi. Be sure to see the Royal Apartments, which are not always open. The Silver Museum wasn't all that exciting. You'll need about three hours for everything. The Boboli Gardens are behind the Pitti, but when we were there, the gardens were really tacky, dirty, and unkempt.

The Uffizi.
I won't even try to describe it. I think I cried five different times on my first visit. Just plan on three to four hours for an overview trip through one of the world's greatest museums.

Churches

In Florence, you don't want to pass a single one without going inside. There is always a treasure to discover.

The Baptistry.
Across from the Duomo. It's possible to go inside at certain times to see the mosaics. The chief thing to see, of course, is those bronze doors by Ghiberti.

Orsanmichele.
An unusual church with well-known sculptures in the niches on the exterior, plus della Robbia roundels.

Santa Croce.
Contains many famous tombs. Nearby is the very famous Pazzi Chapel, a jewel of the Renaissance; also more beautiful cloisters and a small museum. Don't miss this one.

San Lorenzo.
Famous for the Medici Chapel, Medici tombs, the Laurentian Library with its entry by Michelangelo. You don't want to miss any of these. About an hour.

San Marco.

An interesting interior, the main attraction being the museum (already mentioned).

Santa Maria del Carmine.

This should be at the top of your list because of the famous Masaccio frescoes. I couldn't believe I was actually seeing them in person. The church also contains many other beautiful frescoes. It's a short walk from Carmine to Santo Spirito, and beyond that, the Pitti Palace.

Santa Maria del Fiore (the Duomo).

You can't miss it. Simply astounding exterior. Unexciting interior, but with a Michelangelo *Pietà* near the back. Climb to the top of the very, very famous dome for a wonderful view of the city.

Santa Maria Novella.

Note the remarkable facade by Alberti; inside are fabulous frescoes, some by Giotto. Don't miss the Sacristy and the lovely Cloisters. Don't leave Florence without seeing it.

Santissima Annunziata.

Renaissance on the outside, baroque on the inside, with a beautiful atrium and the tomb of Cellini.

Santo Spirito.

A beautiful, serene, purely Renaissance church.

The Synagogue.

Very Moorish in design, this is an interesting contrast to the churches you've been seeing.

Other Places of Interest

Casa Bounaroti, via Ghibellina 70.

Not exactly where Michelangelo lived, but where some of his family lived. It's quite charming inside, and worth the time for the short tour.

Casa Guidi   piazza S. Felice 8.

Once the home of Robert and Elizabeth Barrett Browning.

The Loggia dei Lanzi.

Located in the Piazza della Signoria, along with the Palazzo Vecchio. In the Loggia are some important sculptures, the most famous probably being Cellini's *Perseus* and the *Rape of the Sabines* by Giambologna.

The Ospedale degli Innocenti   (Foundlings' Hospital).

In the Piazza Santissima Annunziata, this contains a gallery, some frescoes, and medallions by Andrea della Robbia. The piazza is also where you'll find San Marco, so you can really spend an afternoon here.

Piazzale Michelangelo.

This has already been mentioned a couple of times, but in case it didn't sink in, this is where you go to get The View of Florence. The surrounding neighborhood has lush villas.

The Ponte Vecchio.

Unavoidable; you'll cross it several times going from one side of the city to the other. It's full of jewelry shops, but I wouldn't be too quick to buy anything very expensive in any of them.

The Strozzi Palace.

Very beautiful Renaissance palace.

Out of town, but only five miles:

Fiesole.

A charming, old hill town, dating to Etruscan times, with archaeological ruins, a wonderful view, Bandini Museum, the lovely Monastery of San Francesco, and the cathedral. It's a popular spot on weekends and can be crowded. Makes a nice half-day trip. The *Villa Michele* in Fiesole is recommended as a wonderful hotel, but not its restaurant. For dining, try *Trattoria le Cave.*

In the area near Fiesole there are some important villas, which are open at various times: *Palmieri, Poggio a Caiano, Medicea, Villa della Petraia.* Check at your hotel for conducted tours leaving from Florence.

Other day trips you can take from Florence, although I advise going and spending the night or you'll be very rushed: Ravenna, Pisa, San Gimignano, Lucca.

Shopping

Florence is a lot of fun for shopping. The streets are narrow, old, and romantic; the boutiques are charming; the choice of items to buy is large and enticing. A great place to buy jewelry, providing you know what you're doing and deal with a reputable shop. Also a good place for leather goods. Here are a few shops I found:

La Botteghina, via Guelfa 5.

Wonderful ceramics.

La Cuccuma Boutique, piazza Pitti 29, across from the Pitti Palace.

Great store for buying hand-knit sweaters at good prices.

Emilio Paoli, via Vigna Nuova 26.

Unusual straw items.

John F., lungarno Corsini 2, near Ponte Vecchio.

Good for leather items; large selection.

Lakis, lungarno Acciaiuoli 82.

A jewelry store in which I bought a wonderful oxblood coral ring. The stone turned out to be authentic, but the 18-karat gold turned out to be about 10-karat with a lot of other stuff in it. I didn't care, though, because I was going for the stone.

La Menagère, via dei Ginori 8.

It's a hardware store, but I found that hardware stores in Italy carry all sorts of wonderful goodies at very reasonable prices.

Leone Leandro, via Santa Trinità 22.

Go upstairs and ring the bell to get in. For jewelry; beautiful things, good prices, reliable.

S.E.L.A.N., via Porto Rosso 107.

I can't recommend this, although most of the other guidebooks do. They have a marvelous selection of ceramics, but the people are very snobby and rude. Expensive and supposedly reliable for shipping.

The Straw Market.

An outdoor market. Very touristy, fun, inexpensive, a good place to buy gifties to take home. Near San Lorenzo.

Street Markets.

Appearing in various streets on certain days, they're always a good bet for browsing, as you'll usually find some bargain you can't live without.

Venice

There are two ways to come into Venice: from the airport via water taxi, or from the train station if you've arrived by train or car. If you come in through the train station, do this (especially if it's your first trip to Venice): take a water taxi to your hotel via the Grand Canal, even if it means going out of your way. Sit in the front of the boat, if possible, even if it's raining. You'll never forget it. If you come from the airport, you'll end up at Piazza San Marco and the approach to that is almost as spectacular.

There's no adequate way to describe Venice—you just have to go there and see for yourself. Forget all the negative remarks about the odor, the crowds, the garbage, etc. If you run into any of it, just ignore it. Venice is unreal; you half expect to walk around behind a building and see that it's only a cardboard prop. It's all too good and too real to be true.

If it's your first trip to Venice you'll need at least three days; four is better. You'll also need an umbrella, unless you are there in the dead of summer (not good planning, if you are).

Don't spend all your time just going to the main tourist attractions. Take a walk down any little street and see where it leads you. Once you get away from the crowds, you'll find another side of Venice that is very charming.

Hotels

Cipriani, isola della Giudecca 10.
Another expensive but highly rated luxury hotel. People rave about it. You have to *vaporetto* (or water-taxi) every time you want to go to the main islands, however.

The Danieli,   near Piazza San Marco.
The other top-notch hotel; expensive, luxurious rooms, great views. Don't miss lunch on the rooftop, but only on a sunny day. Ties required for men.

Des Bains,   lungomare Marconi 17, on the Lido.
This is where they filmed *Death in Venice,* so if you've seen that movie, I need say no more. It's a great, old hotel to go *look* at; however, unless they've done some renovating since the last time I paid a visit, I wouldn't want to stay there.

Excelsior,   lungomare Marconi 41, on the Lido.
About twelve minutes by boat over to Venice. This is a large and beautiful hotel right on the beach, which is full of wonderful seashells. Might be good if you have kids who are tired of sightseeing and just want to go swimming.

La Fenice et Des Artistes,   near the Opera House.
A popular, small hotel. What it lacks in elegance is made up in charm. Inexpensive.

The Gritti Palace,   on the Grand Canal.
As good as it gets. Sure, it's expensive. Room 111 was gorgeous. Room 113 is supposedly where Hemingway stayed. Have lunch on the veranda. If you're going to save up for one splurge on your whole trip, save it for the Gritti.

Hotel Saturnia e International,   calle larga 22 Marzo 2398.
A fourteenth-century house; medium priced; small but charming rooms; excellent service. Good restaurant.

Locanda Cipriani,   on Torcello.
Supposedly *the* place to stay, if you're not staying in Venice proper. Again, you have to taxi over every time. Haven't stayed here yet, but I will soon, as I'm sick of hearing from every one else about how great it is.

Restaurants

Al Graspa de Ua,   calle dei Bombaseri 5094, near the Rialto Bridge.
One of the best restaurants in Venice. Casual, medium prices, don't miss it.

Antica Trattoria Poste Vecie,   Pescheria 1608.
This is a really cute restaurant in the corner of the main fish market. If you go to Palazzo Pesaro (and even if don't), this is perfect for lunch. See the fish market in action before lunch. If you walk across the Rialto Bridge from the San Marco side and go toward the canals, you'll find it.

Antico Martini,   Campo San Fantin 1983, also near Teatro La Fenice.
Excellent.

Da Arturo,   San Marco 3656, near Teatro La Fenice.
Small, neighborhood trattoria; gracious service; nontouristy.

La Caravella,   in the Hotel Saturnia e International, calle larga 22 Marzo 2398.
Specializes in seafood. One of the city's best.

La Colomba,   piscina di Frezzeria 1665.
This gets a lot of good reviews. However, the night we were there, everything was wrong. I can't recommend it for that reason, but it must have better days or it wouldn't get so many returnees.

Gritti Palace restaurants.

There are two. One is inside and formal, for dinner; it's OK. The other is outside on the deck, so you can almost dangle your feet in the Grand Canal. On a sunny day you can't beat it for lunch and atmosphere.

NOTE: About every ten minutes, in Venice, you'll swear you've died and gone to heaven.

Grotta Azzurra,   off Piazza San Marco.

A touristy place where you can go for drinks and listen to opera singers. They also serve food, but you're better off with just drinks. Local color? (If it's serious opera you want, go to La Fenice Opera House.)

Harry's Bar,   calle Vallaresso 1323.

Maybe the most famous and "in" place in Venice; did not measure up to the hype the night we were there. Maybe it's where the beautiful people hang out, but all we saw were families on vacation. It was very expensive and the food was not memorable. It could be that we hit an off night, though, because too many people come home raving about it.

Locanda Cipriani,   isola della Giu decca 10, phone 707744

A great idea for lunch or dinner; an outing. Beautiful, rustic setting. Famous. It's also a hotel.

Noemi,   calle dei Fabbri 909.

Excellent restaurant, medium priced.

Quadri and Florian's,   in Piazza San Marco.

These are the two well-known tearooms which tend to vie with one another across the piazza. In the afternoon you'll be serenaded in a good, old-fashioned way. It's forbidden to go to Venice and *not* spend at least a couple of hours in the late afternoon at one establishment or the other. Between 4:00 and 6:00 P.M. is ideal. The best therapy for whatever it is that ails you. They are also good for after-dinner ice cream treats.

Royal Danieli rooftop restaurant

A must for lunch, but only on a sunny and warm day when you can sit outside. Ties for men are required (so carry it in your pocket and put it on when necessary). Get the *fettucine buranella,* olive bread, spinach bread, and baba au rhum. Take your camera. Take your money. Take your time.

Taverna La Fenice,   San Marco 1938, behind Teatro La Fenice.

A beautiful restaurant with excellent food and ambiance. Somewhat expensive, but not a wallet buster. Dressy. Special.

Todaro,   just across from the Doge's Palace, on the canal.

Not a restaurant—it's an ice cream shop. The ice cream is very good.

Shopping

If you're going to be in Rome, save your serious shopping for there. Shopping in Venice is verrrrrrry touristy, so watch your prices. The same items on the San Marco side of the canal often cost twice as much or more as on the Accademia side.

Jesurum.

Over a bridge behind San Marco. Used to be a lace-making factory and now a very chic and expensive boutique with clothes and linens. Worth a visit just to look, if nothing else. (P.S. We had a fabulous gondola ride which commenced just in front of this place.)

Luigi Oreffice.

San Marco 1656 and 2013 (one near Teatro La Fenice and one on Frezzeria). Antiques, gifts, gadgets. Unusual and wide selection, moderate prices.

Pauly and Sons.

Main showroom behind San Marco. Glass factory and distributors. Supposedly the best of the Murano glassmakers and reliable for shipping. Ask them to take you upstairs to see everything. Act interested in buying or they may not take you. What they have upstairs would astound even Louis XIV.

R. Siffi, Campo San Zaccaria 4683.

A glass shop which was nice; good prices; seemed reliable.

Rigattiere.

Between Campo Sant'Angelo and Campo San Stefano. If ceramic is what you want, this is the place. Goes on forever.

Sightseeing

There's nowhere in Venice that *isn't* sightseeing. Everywhere you go, even if you aren't going anywhere in particular, is marvelous.

Museums

Accademia. Crème de la crème for Venetian paintings. Shouldn't miss it.

Correr Museum, located at the entrance of Piazza San Marco. A beautiful, large, well-lit museum with a little bit of this and a little bit of that. Worth a visit.

Peggy Guggenheim Museum, located in what was once her private home. Contemporary and modern art, a sharp contrast to what you'll see in most of the other museums. Should go.

Churches

San Giorgio Maggiore.

Also shows up in many pictures and paintings of Venice. It's located on an island and is most visible from the Doge's Palace.

San Marco is, of course, the *gran formaggio* here. Go when it's sunny. The mosaics are incredible. You'll want to buy a ticket to see the Pala d'Oro, which is behind the altar; be sure you have a guide explain it to you. The same ticket will get you into the museum, which is on the right as you enter the basilica. Now, you *do* want to go to the museum, because it has some interesting things to see and also because you can get up very close to the mosaics. You can go outside on the balcony, which affords you a wonderful view of the piazza. The famous bronze horses on the balcony are not the real ones (maybe one of them is), because they took the original ones down and put them indoors for preservation purposes.

San Moise. A wonderful baroque exterior, but inside it's blah. You'll pass it often as you stroll around the city.

San Pantaleon, near the Scuola San Rocco. You should run in and look at the ceiling.

San Zaccaria in a piazza a short walk away from the back side of San Marco. It has some interesting frescoes inside.

Santa Maria della Salute. This shows up in practically every painting of Venice. You'll see it daily just across the canal from San Marco.

Santa Maria Glorioso dei Frari, near Scuola San Rocco. You'll see fabulous, monumental tombs and sculpture, plus a Bellini *Madonna* and some Titians.

Santi Giovanni e Paolo, also called *San Zanipolo,* in Campo Santi Giovanni e Paolo, a marvelous piazza with a beautiful school in the Renaissance style. A very famous equestrian statue called Bartolomeo Colleoni by Verrocchio was located here, but at one point it was removed for a tune-up and I don't know if it's been put back, or moved permanently indoors for safekeeping.

Other Sites

Ca d' Oro.
On the Right Bank on Strada Nova. The best-known and most beautiful of the renovated palazzos that are open to the public.

The Doge's Palace.
Just smashing! Be sure you go on a sunny day because the lighting inside is terrible. Notice the capitals on the columns surrounding the porticoes.

Gondolas.
To Gondola or Not to Gondola, there *is* no question! Go once on a sunny day and once on a moonlit night. Maybe the gondolier won't sing your favorite Italian love song, but you'll still be enchanted. It's not so expensive—30 dollars should get you at least a forty-five-minute trip. Settle on the price before you get in. If you don't take a gondola ride in Venice, they revoke your passport when you get home.

The Lido.
A resort on the Adriatic a short boat ride from San Marco. There's nothing much to do there except look around. There are a couple of big hotels. If it's a trip to the beach you want, this is where to do it. A nice half-day trip, with lunch.

Palazzo Pesaro.
on Calle della Regina, Left Bank. Not renovated but it does house the more "modern" art collection of Venice. I wasn't impressed.

Palazzo Rezzonico.
A renovated palazzo and worth a visit.

Palladian Villas Tour.

A one-day trip by motorcoach, including lunch, you visit four of Palladio's masterpieces. Thursdays only. Write or call Contessa Maria Pia Ferri, San Marco 2814, Venice 30121, phone (041) 85343.

Piazza San Marco.

Needs no introduction. It's worth the time and possible hassle to go to the top of the Campanile; the view is the best you'll get. Be sure you take notice of the *Clock Tower* when it chimes, because it's been doing it for over five hundred years. The *Doge's Palace* and *Correr Museum* are also located here. Best thing to do in Piazza San Marco is go sit at one of the outdoor cafés and spend a couple hours in never-never land.

The Rialto Bridge.

Very famous and for that reason you need to walk on it.

Scuola San Rocco.

Contains fifty-six works by Tintoretto. It is astounding. You must see this. Before leaving, walk around behind the building and see the house with the windmills.

Teatro La Fenice.

A jewel of an opera house and one of the most famous in Europe. If you're in Venice during the season, by all means get tickets through your concierge.

Milan

I spent a very brief time in Milan, just enough to get a taste. It is a city where I would like to spend more time. Milan has a completely different flavor than Rome, Florence, or Venice. It's very businesslike and less charming or romantic. However, it's terrific for shopping, and there are good museums, great restaurants, a magnificent cathedral, and perhaps the world's most famous fresco.

If you are traveling on a budget, you can take the airport transporter bus into Milan for about 2 dollars. The exact same ride in a taxi will cost you between 30 and 40 dollars. Same road, same AMount of time. Even if you aren't traveling on a budget, this sounds hard to beat.

For hotels, you'll have to go to another source, since the one I stayed in was really awful (Flora Majestic). The best hotel in town is supposed to be the *Principe e Savoia;* also good are the *Excelsior Gallia,* the *Palace,* and the *Hilton International Milano.*

Restaurants

Alfio, via Senato 31.
A neighborhood hangout, casual, inexpensive, very good, and fun.
Savini, galleria Vittorio Emanuele 11, phone 8058343.
Very chic, rather stuffy, very expensive, and the food is good. Nothing unusual, however.

Recommended by friends are: *Scaletta,* piazzale Stazione Porta Genova, phone 8350290 (Michelin two stars); *Bagutta,* via Bagutta 14, phone

702767; *Boeucc,* piazza Belgioioso 2, phone 790224; *La Nos,* via Amedei 2, phone 8058759; *Giannino,* via Amatore Sciesa 8, phone 20135, Michelin one star; *El Toulà,* piazza Paolo Ferrari 6, phone 870302; *Gualtiero Marchesi,* via Bonvesin de la Riva 9, phone 741246, Michelin two-stars; *Da Aimo,* via Montecuccoli 6, phone 416886, Michelin one-star; and *Casa Fontana,* piazza Carbonari 5, phone 6892684, Michelin one star.

Sightseeing

The Biblioteca Ambrosiana, not far from piazza del Duomo.
A library within a palace; besides the library, there is a small gallery on the first level containing works by some of Italy's most famous artists.
The Brera Palace and Gallery, via Brera.
Here you'll see a fine collection of works, mainly by northern Italian artists, such as Mantegna, Bellini, Carpaccio, Tintoretto and Tiepolo. Also frescoes.
The Duomo.
This is hard to miss. It's really magnificent. Be sure you make the effort to go up and walk around on the roof.
Galleria Vittorio Emanuele.
This extends from the cathedral to La Scala. It's a beautiful galleria with shops and restaurants.
Il Salumaio di Monte Napoleone.
A smaller version of Peck and also very good, gastronomically speaking.
Peck, via Spadari 9 and via Hugo 3 and via Cesare Cantu 3.
Milan's answer to Fauchon, Zabar's, and Dean and DeLuca. It's actually four stores in one, embracing a deli, cheese shop, gourmet store, liquor store, etc. You can snack there, or take out.
The Poldi Pezzoli Museum, via Morone.
In a refurbished manor house with works by Italy's greatest.
Sant'Eustorgio.
A church in the Romanesque style, containing the famous Portinari Chapel, which you shouldn't miss.
Santa Maria delle Grazie, in piazza San Ambrogio.
Home of Leonardo's *Last Supper.* The fresco is not always on view, so check in advance. There are other frescoes to see as well, plus the chapel itself and its cloisters.
La Scala Opera House.
Not generally open for public consumption other than during performances. Of course, if you are in Milan during the season, you will go to the opera. Otherwise you can view it from the piazza.
The Sforza Castle, on foro Buonaparte.
Contains a small museum with works by such artists as Michelangelo, Bellini, Correggio, Magnasco, and Lotto.

A Day Trip from Milan:
Lake Como

About an hour out of Milan you are in the Alps and can visit one or more of the lakes. Como is the quickest and easiest to get to and makes a wonderful all-day trip. When you get to Bellagio take the ferry across to Cadenabbia and head back down to Milan. Plan your day so that you can have lunch at the *Villa d'Este* no later than 1:30; reservations are a good idea. You will also want to see the *Villa Carlotta* and its gardens. Take a sweater —it can be cold in the hills.

Northern
Italian Towns

Assisi

Don't miss this. Spend the night here, if you can get in a hotel. Find
a guide, preferably one of the monks, to give you a tour of the basilica. Hold
on to your hats if you are a fresco freak, because you are in fresco heaven.
Be sure you see the crypt and the tomb of St. Francis. You'll need at least
two hours.

After the basilica, go see *Santa Chiara,* but have your guide either take
you or tell you the whole story before you go.

A good restaurant is *Buca di San Francesco,* via Brizi 1.

Lucca

This is one of Italy's little treasures, along with Siena, Assisi, and a few
others. If you are in Pisa in the morning, have lunch in Lucca at a place called
Buca di San Antonio, via della Cervia—it's wonderful. Order *caffè affagato*
for dessert. Leave about an hour to walk around the old part of the city.

Orvieto

A boring and not recommended hotel in this town is the *Maitani,* via
Maitani 5. *La Badia,* about two miles out of town, is an excellent hotel with
an incredible restaurant.

Parma

I haven't been to Parma, but I have a hot tip about a restaurant there: *La Filoma,* via 20 Marzo 15.

Perugia

Even though we had an unpleasant experience in Perugia (meaning a lot of traffic and a noisy, crowded hotel), I can still recommend it. Beautiful old town dating from Etruscan times, now the capital of Umbria and site of a large university. *La Rosetta* is the hotel there, which we thought was just tolerable; the same goes for the restaurant at the hotel. Maybe we just hit it on the wrong night. I recently heard that the *Hotel Bella Vista,* formerly the Brufani Palace, is excellent.

Pisa

You may think it's too touristy to go see the tower leaning, and who cares, anyway? Well, go see it. There's more there than just the tower, which brave people can climb up to the top for a terrific view. Also see the *Duomo* and *Baptistry,* and do not fail to see the *cemetery,* which is the best part.

Portofino

Here is a gorgeous seaside resort on the lower Italian Riviera. If you are driving from Milan to Genoa, you can have lunch in Portofino. *Il Pitosforo* is wonderful; also recommended is *Delfino.*

Rimini

A recommended restaurant here is *Vecchia Rimini,* via Cattaneo 7/9, phone 26610.

San Gimignano

A short drive from Siena through beautiful farmland. Don't miss! Fabulous twelfth-century town virtually unchanged. Wander all around, go into the *Duomo,* the *Museum* behind it. Stay at *La Cisterna* (we had called in advance and they said they were full; we showed up around 3:00 P.M. and got a room; by 4:00 P.M. they really were full). The restaurant at the hotel, *La Terrazza,* was fabulous. Be sure you are seated in the room to the left of the kitchen with the slanted thatched roof. Order the tartuffe for desert and ask for a little pitcher of chocolate sauce to pour over it.

Siena

This wonderful city deserves a night, or maybe two. If you are going to be there during the famous horserace known as the Palio (held once in July and once in August), you'd better have very advance reservations and some sort of connection for getting you a decent seat. Best hotels are the *Park*, via di Marciano 16; the *Villa Scacciapensieri* (out of town a bit); the *Certosa di Maggiano*, strada di Certosa 82; and the *Garden*, a smaller hotel, via Custoza 2. Late word on the *Villa Scacciapensieri* is that it is an outstanding hotel with an even more outstanding restaurant. Don't miss the *Duomo*, the *Piazza del Campo*, or the *Palazzo Pubblico*. Excellent gallery, the *Pinacoteca*.

Verona

This is a lovely little town right out of a storybook. Wonderful, ancient Roman ruins. Juliet's balcony, or so they say. Nice shopping. Terrific little piazzas.

Stay at the *Hotel Due Torri* and while you're there, go look at the library on each floor and see all the main rooms downstairs. The restaurant in the hotel is very good. Other restaurants which are recommended: *Veronanticca*, via Sottoriva 10; *12 Apostoli*, corticella San Marco 3; and *Marconi*, via Fogge 4.

Don't miss the *Piazza dei Signori* in the late afternoon, about the time the fathers show up with their children to feed the pigeons. Also see the *Piazza delle Erbe*, once a forum and also where they held chariot races. See the *Arena*, the third largest amphitheater in the Roman world, dating from the first century. The *Roman Theater*, dating from Augustus, still has performances during the summer. If you are in Verona during opera season, be sure to go to one. They are held in one of the Roman ruins. Verona gets very good opera companies passing through from Milan to Venice. Also see: *Arche Scaligere, San Zeno Maggiore*, and the *Duomo*.

Viareggio

We were there in the off season and we felt as if we were walking around in a Fellini film. Quaint resort with lots of atmosphere. The *Hotel Astor et Residence* was very nice. We had a great dinner at *Margherita*, lungomare Margherita 30. Also recommended: *Tito di Molo* and *Montecatini*.

The Bay of Naples
and Vicinity

There's so much to do in the area of the Bay of Naples that you could easily spend a week there. If you haven't got a week, block out four days, or five, if possible. You can get to that part of Italy from Rome in a short time. Two hours on the train or three hours by car.

If you go by train you will arrive at the Garibaldi Station in Naples. If you aren't going to stay in Naples, but are going on to Sorrento, you'll catch a commuter train called the *Circumvesuviana*. Its like a metro and is about a three-minute walk from your train. Look for signs indicating where to go to get it. The Circumvesuviana will cost you about a dollar and stops at the little towns all along the coast. Some trains stop more than others. A taxi from Naples to Sorrento will be *very* expensive.

I've never stayed in Naples and don't plan to—I've heard nothing but terrible things about the place. The *National Museum,* however, is worth a visit; it's one of the best in Italy. Their hours are erratic, so find out in advance when they are open before you make the effort to go.

The Amalfi Drive

The Amalfi Drive isn't really in the Bay of Naples—it's on the other side of the hill, easily reached from Sorrento or Salerno, or by a nice little drive right across the middle, via Agerola. You don't want to do the drive with a hangover, a broken arm, screaming kids, or a car with a tricky clutch. You've never seen so many hairpin turns in your life. I also would not do it in a bus; too much would probably be lost in the translation. It takes at least a half a day to do the drive because you'll run into a lot of traffic from time to time, and the tour buses will drive you crazy. So why do it at all, you query? Because it's fabulous! Lunch stops are the *Belvedere Hotel* at Conca dei Marini; the dining room in the *Hotel St. Caterina;* a little pizzeria called *San Andrea,* to the left of the church in the main square in Amalfi; and the dining room in the *Caruso Belvedere* in Ravello. (Be sure you drive up to Ravello.)

If you want to spend a night on the Amalfi coast, I suggest two wonderful hotels, both in Positano: *Le Sirenuse,* in town; and *San Pietro,* just out of town. Either one will delight you.

Capri

Capri is a charming island, about an hour by ferry from Sorrento, or thirty minutes by hydrofoil, which isn't always running. You can see it in a day, or you can go stay there in one of many beautiful hotels: the *Luna, Scalinatella,* and *Quisisana.* Be sure you go see the *Blue Grotto,* even if the weather is bad. You should also take the little chairlift up to the top of the mountain for a spectacular view.

From the boat dock you can take a funicular up to the town of Capri, then get a bus up to Anacapri. There are also taxis. The boats going to the Blue Grotto leave from the main docks and you'll have no trouble finding them, as there are a lot of boatmen running around drumming up business.

Two good restaurants on Capri are *La Capannina,* via Le Botteghe 14, and *La Pigna,* via Lo Palazzo 30.

Castellammare Di Stabia

This small town, about thirty minutes from Sorrento, was and still is the site of thermal baths. There are hotels there which have spas, where you can still "take the waters." They also have tennis courts and other recreational facilities.

Paestum

Paestum is also not in the Bay of Naples, but about forty-five minutes to the south of Salerno. It's an easy day trip from Sorrento or the Amalfi coast. Actually, if you leave Sorrento early in the morning and take the autoroute to Paestum, you can return via the Amalfi Drive, thereby taking in both sites in one day. You are going to be tired when you get back to your hotel, but it's worth it. As you drive from Salerno to Paestum, you'll pass through the area where they make fresh mozzarella cheese *(bufalo),* and there are cheese stands along the way.

The Paestum area contains three extremely large and well-preserved Greek temples in the Doric order, dating from the fifth and sixth centuries B.C. There are other ruins of the ancient city as well. Across the street from the temples is a wonderful small museum in which you'll see items excavated from the area. The whole place is astounding and well worth the effort you will make to get there.

Pompeii and Ercolano (Herculaneum)

No trip to the Bay of Naples is complete without a tour of Pompeii. The Circumvesuviana train will take you there (and to Ercolano) in a few minutes from either Sorrento or Naples. Check the train schedule in your hotel. When you get to Pompeii, hire an English-speaking guide, and when you're finished with him, strike out on your own. It's quite an awesome place, and if you walk along some of the streets, you can almost hear the voices from the past. Pompeii is a good half-day trip. As for lunch, your choices are few or none in the area—just a lot of tourist-trappy places.

In my opinion, Ercolano is even better than Pompeii. It's smaller, more intimate, and for the most part better preserved. If you can, write or call ahead and request a guide by the name of Carlo Illario. Be sure you tell him I sent you. He's a wonderful guide and will go out of his way to show you as much as possible. He speaks a little English, a little French, of course Italian, and is very cute. If you don't contact him in advance, request him when you arrive. He can advise you as to where to go for lunch, although your choices in Ercolano are not much better than in Pompeii.

If you have to choose between Pompeii or Ercolano for time reasons, go to Ercolano. Ideally, you should see both; they are not the same. You could see them both in one day if you started early. However, that could be too much of a good thing in one day, so you might want to spread it out.

The National Museum in Naples contains huge numbers of items taken from these cities, as well as the surrounding villas, from the excavations which began in the eighteenth century.

Sorrento

The best place to stay is Sorrento, only an hour by the metro to Naples and less than twenty minutes to Pompeii and Ercolano (Herculaneum). Sorrento is a charming little city overlooking the bay, with some nice hotels and restaurants, plus some good shopping, if you know where to go. We have always stayed at the *Grand Hotel Excelsior Vittoria,* a former Doge's palazzo. The rooms are spacious, with great views, and the service is very good. Room 15 was gorgeous. The restaurant in the hotel, at last visit, wasn't very good. It's very pretty but the cuisine is extremely bland; they seem to cater to the tastes of the British tourists, who are there in number. There are several other good hotels in the area.

The best restaurants in Sorrento are *Parrucchiano,* corso Italia 71, and *Al Cavallino Bianco,* via Correale 11. Both are within walking distance of the Excelsior Vittoria. Actually, the town is so small that everything is within walking distance of everything else.

There's a wonderful store in Sorrento called *A. Gargiulo & Jannuzzi;* it's right in the main piazza. They specialize in arts and crafts of Italy. Their selection is large, their prices are good, they are helpful in packing for carrying or shipping, and they'll even send you a Christmas card! Another area to shop is the *Mayflower* shopping center, which is near the train station.

London

AND

Environs

London

I like London, enjoy going there, but after about four days I'm ready to move on. The British are wonderful and make me smile a lot, just listening to them talk. There are good restaurants in London, but so far I've never been knocked out by any of them. The shopping, in my opinion, doesn't hold a candle to other European cities, unless you're looking for antiques. The weather is usually miserable, although if you're lucky enough to have a nice day in London, it's spectacular. Culturally, you'll have a field day. Fabulous museums, castles, monuments, government buildings, churches, etc. —enough to keep you busy for weeks. As for the surrounding English countryside, I am sorry to say I've not been exploring yet; but it's high on my list. What I'm going to tell you here is minimal, and I strongly suggest you get your hands on any one of the million books on the market about the city.

Hotels

There is a wide range of choices. London is known for charming, small, and inexpensive hotels, about which I know nothing. The **Berkeley** (pronounced "barkly") is one of the best and is very, very nice and well located in Belgravia, near Harrods. **Inn on the Park** is considered one of the best hotels in England, owned by the Canadian Four Seasons chain. Big business clientele, 250 rooms. A couple of years ago we stayed at the **Westbury** on New Bond Street, just off Regent Street, again a very good location. I notice this hotel doesn't get high marks in other guidebooks, but we found it to be quite satisfactory, not as expensive as many of the "biggies," and they were in the process of doing a complete renovation. A lot of people like *Duke's* at St. James's Place, which is a very small but chic hotel. *Claridge's*, *The Connaught* and *Dorchester* have been highly rated for years, and I've never heard any complaints about any of them, other than that they are a bit on the stuffy side, not to mention a wee bit expensive. The *Stafford* on St. James's Place is very popular with a well-traveled friend of mine. If you're traveling with kids, or planning to be in London for any length of time and are looking for an inexpensive apartment arrangement, try the *Athenaeum* at Piccadilly. Next door to this hotel you can rent flats, complete with kitchens and all, which are very inexpensive, but the good part is that you can use all the hotel services if you want. The hotel itself is a rather large, show-biz hotel, but supposedly very good. One of the best of the small hotels is *Number Sixteen,* 16–17 Sumner Place, SW7, phone 589–5232. If you are into bed-and-breakfast (which I am not), you might like *28 Basil Street,* at moderate prices. A popular hotel with a chic crowd is *Blakes,* 33 Roland Gardens, SW7, phone 370–6701; some kitchenettes available. The *Capitol Hotel* at 22/24 Basil St., SW3, is one of the more popular of the smaller hotels, with a good restaurant. *L'Hotel* at 28 Basil St., SW3, has only twelve rooms (some have fireplaces) and is inexpensive. *7 Down Street* is smaller still with only six suites and a restaurant, and is expensive and chic. On Sloane Square you will find *11 Cadogan Gardens,* SW3, four turn-of-the-century houses made into one sixty-room hotel (no credit cards and no kids), with superb service.

Restaurants

English cuisine, on the whole, does not have the reputation of being the world's most exciting food. You can't just walk into almost any restaurant and get a good meal. Selectivity is the name of the game. Keep this list in mind when considering where to eat. (Cl. means closed.)

Bombay Brasserie, 1 Courtfield Courtfield Rd., So. Kensington, SW7 4QH, phone 370–4040.
Inexpensive. Indian cuisine, but not entirely. Delicious food and lovely room.
Boulestin, 25 Southampton St., Covent Garden, WC2, phone 836–7061.
French cuisine, luxurious surroundings, moderate prices.
Brasserie St. Quentin, 243 Brompton Rd., SW3, phone 589–8005.
French cuisine, moderate prices. Attractive, lively and popular eatery.
Cafe Royal, 68 Regent St., phone 437–9090.
Continental menu at moderate prices in a Belle Epoque setting; near Piccadilly.
Capitol Hotel, 22–24 Basil St., SW3, phone 589–5171.
Near Harrods. Small, attractive restaurant serving classical and nouvelle dishes; moderate prices.

Le Caprice, Arlington House, Arlington St., SW1, phone 629–2299. "In" and chic restaurant, moderate prices.

Carrier's, 2 Camden Passage, N1, phone 226–5353. Cl. Sun. Nouvelle and unusual French dishes in luxurious surroundings. Moderate prices.

Cecconi, 5A Burlington Gardens, W1, phone 434–1500. Cl. Sun. An old standby for solid Italian cuisine; expensive.

Chaopraya, 22 St. Christopher Pl., W1, phone 486–0777. Cl. Sun. Inexpensive Thai cuisine, for a change.

Chelsea Room, Hyatt Carlton Tower Hotel, 2 Cadogan Pl., SW1, phone 235–5411. Beautifully presented plates of fresh and light food; specialty is fish. Inexpensive.

Chez Nico, 129 Queenstown Rd., Battersea, SW8, phone 720–6960. Cl. Sun. Very popular place serving classic French dishes at moderate-to-expensive prices. Thirty minutes from downtown London.

Chuen Cheng Ku, 17–23 Wardour St., W1, phone 437–1398. Chinese cuisine, near Piccadilly, a huge restaurant with menu to match. Always full of Orientals. Inexpensive.

Claridge's Causerie, Brook St., W1, phone 629–8860. An elegant, chic, and small place to go to see and be seen at lunch.

The Compleat Angler, located in Marlowe, not far from downtown London. A wonderful country inn with restaurant to match.

Connaught Hotel Grill, 16 Carlos Pl., W1, phone 499–7070. Clubby, luxurious, expensive, a big favorite for a long time, serving French and English cuisine.

Dorchester Grill Room, Park Lane, W1, phone 629–8888. A Swiss chef doing very English dishes; very good. Moderate.

Dorchester Terrace, same address and phone as above. Expensive. A departure from the Grill Room, serving more unusual and nouvelle-type fare.

The English House, 3 Milner St., SW3, phone 584–3002. Cl. Sun. Moderate prices. A small, private house in Chelsea with lots of charm, serving classic English food.

Le Gavroche, 43 Upper Brook St., W1, phone 408–0881. Cl. Sat., Sun. One of the top French restaurants in London, very popular, expensive.

Gay Hussar, 2 Greek St., W1, phone 437–0973. Cl. Sun. Good, hearty Hungarian food, big portions, moderate prices.

Hunan, 51 Pimlico Rd., SW1, phone 730–5712. Hunan (Chinese) food, inexpensive, not fancy.

Interlude de Tabaillau, 7 Bow St., WC2, phone 379–6473. Cl. Sun. Excellent French cuisine, chic, moderately priced. One of the best.

Langan's Brasserie, Stratton St., W1, phone 493–6437. Cl. Sun. French food, show-bizzy atmosphere, moderate prices. Sit downstairs.

Ma Cuisine,   113 Walton St., SW3, phone 584–7585.
Two weeks' advance reservations are a must for one of the best French restaurants in town. Obviously very popular. Inexpensive.

Mijanou,   143 Ebury St., SW1, phone 730–4099. Cl. Sat., Sun.
French food with a twist served in a lovely restaurant at low prices.

Mr. Chow,   151 Knightsbridge, SW1, phone 589–7347.
Chinese cuisine, a chic crowd, moderate prices, a good standby.

Odin's,   27 Devonshire St., W1, phone 935–7296.
English and French haute cuisine. Big restaurant, but chic and comfortable. Moderate.

Poissonnerie,   82 Sloane Ave., SW3, phone 589–2457.
Fish and French, inexpensive, popular favorite.

Pomegranates,   94 Grosvenor Rd., SW1, phone 828–6560. Cl. Sat., Sun.
Serving an unusual and international menu. Moderate.

Le Poulbot,   45 Cheapside, EC2, phone 408–0881. Cl. Sat., Sun.
Owned by the Le Gavroche people, this elegant restaurant serves French dishes at moderate prices.

The Ritz Hotel Dining Room,   Piccadilly, W1 V9DG, phone 493–8181.
One of the prettiest and most elaborate restaurants in town, with solid French food and nouvelle cuisine at solid prices. Elegant, formal.

Rue St. Jacques,   5 Charlotte St., WP11HD, phone 370–222, in Soho.
Pretty, popular, prices are reasonable, unusual dishes.

Savoy Hotel River Room,   The Strand, WC2, phone 836–4343.
Good English cuisine at moderate-to-expensive prices.

Le Suquet,   104 Draycott Ave., SW3, phone 581–1785.
A very French restaurant specializing in fresh fish fare at moderate prices. By the same owners and with similar menu are: *La Croisette,* 168 Ifield Rd., SW8, phone 373-3964; *Le Quai St. Pierre,* 7 Stratford Rd., W8, phone 937-6388.

La Tante Claire,   68 Royal Hospital Rd., SW3, phone 352–6045. Cl. Sat., Sun.
Two weeks' advance reservations are necessary. One of London's finest restaurants, serving French and nouvelle cuisine. Expensive.

The Upper Crust in Belgravia,   9 William St., near Harrods and across the street from the Sheraton Hotel, SW1, phone 235–8444.
A cute little place for a nice lunch or light dinner, serving very English pies, casseroles, country cuisine. Inexpensive. Sit on the main floor.

Walton's,   121 Walton St., SW3, phone 504–0204.
Chic and ornate, this moderately expensive restaurant serves traditional English food.

Wheeler's,   15 Lowndes St., SW1, phone 235–2525; **Wheeler's Antoine,** 40 Charlotte St., W1, phone 636–2817; **Wheeler's,** 19 Old Compton St. in Soho.
This little chain of restaurants is famous for seafood, especially sole, served in a multitude of ways and in very large portions. Casual and fun, inexpensive.

Wilton's, 27 Bury St., SW1, phone 930–8391.
Classic British fare at moderate prices.
Zen, Chelsea Cloisters, Sloane Ave., SW3, phone 589–1781.
Open every day, moderately priced. Chinese food, good for a dimsum lunch, if you're in the mood.

If you have any connections at private clubs, try to get into the *White Elephant* on Curzon, or better yet, *Les Ambassadeurs.* For pubs, you'll find one on every street. They are especially mobbed and smoky at the lunch hour. Two rather famous and popular ones are *Ye Olde Cheshire Cheese,* 145 Fleet St., and *Dickens Inn,* St. Katherine's Way, serving different fares on different floors.

Tea Time

You can't go to London without having tea, even if you aren't hungry and don't want it. It's a tradition. There are tearooms everywhere, but some are better choices than others. The following are among the most popular.

The Basil St. Hotel, 8 Basil St., SW3 1AH, phone 581–3311.
(Near Harrods.)
Brown's Hotel, 29–34 Albemarle St., W1.
Old and comfy and English.
The Connaught Hotel, 16 Carlos Pl., W1, phone 499–7070.
The Dorchester Hotel, Park Lane, W1, phone 629–8888.
The day we went there we had been traipsing all over Windsor in the rain, had three kids with us, and were all dressed more or less like bums. They treated all of us as if we were part of the Royal Family itself, even when the kids ate everything in sight.
The Grosvenor Hotel, Park Lane, W1, phone 499–6363.
Very elegant and there's a piano.
Harrods Tearoom.
Very popular with a lot of people, but I couldn't see standing in a long line that went down the hall for at least twenty minutes, when some of the more elegant hotel rooms had immediate seating.
Richoux's in Piccadilly. Especially for chocoholics.
The Ritz Hotel, Piccadilly, W1, phone 493–8181.
St. James's Restaurant, on the fourth floor of Fortnum and Mason.
The Savoy Hotel, Strand, WC2, phone 836–4343.
Maybe one of the best.

Sightseeing

Your biggest problem will be deciding what to do first, and what to leave out if you're pressed for time. Tough decisions. Practically everything is a "must"!

Buckingham Palace and Changing of the Guard.

Drive by the palace and have a look. Skip the Changing of the Guard. A total waste of time, if you ask me.

Hampton Court.

You can reach it by a boat ride on the Thames, if you wish. Especially popular with tourists and quite spectacular.

The Law Courts and Big Ben.

You'll automatically see these as you tour around.

St. Margaret's Church.

Near Westminster Abbey and now a brass-rubbing center. You can participate if you want to; they have all the materials and will tell you how to do it.

St. Paul's Cathedral.

Should not be missed. You'll need at least an hour. Be sure you go into the crypt and up to the dome.

Soho, Piccadilly, Leicester Square, Hyde Park, Kensington Gardens, Trafalgar Square, Mayfair, Belgravia.

All neighborhoods or quarters in the city, which you will undoubtedly see while touring around. It's best to see them on foot, so don't take cabs all the time. Use the tube—it's great.

The Tower of London.

You'll need about three hours to see it all. When you arrive, look for the guides in the Beefeater costumes—they give free tours which last over an hour and are excellent. Be sure you see the Jewel House (a few interesting trinkets there), the main museum, the Bowyer Tower (for you S&M fans), and the oriental collection. There are pubs nearby for lunch at St. Katherine's Docks. Kids will really enjoy all this.

Westminster Abbey.

Allow about three hours, if you do it right. Arrange to get there in time to take the tour—you sign up at a table at the right near the back. It used to be at 2:30 P.M. but it may have changed by now.

Windsor Castle.

Easy to reach by train from Paddington Station. Try to arrive at the castle by 11:00 A.M., to see the changing-of-the-guard routine (better than at Buckingham, although different; at least you can *see* something!). The changing of the guard isn't done every day so you may want to call ahead and make sure. I strongly advise taking the guided tour (English official guides are highly trained), which you can get at a booth just next to the *Chapel*. The tour lasts about two hours and is highly informative. After the tour, do not fail to go to see the *Queen's Dollhouse* and the *Royal Apartments*. Don't let a long line discourage you—it moves quickly and is worth the wait. If you do it all, you'll need between five and six hours, so just make a day of it. In the little town there are several cafes for lunch, mostly tourist oriented, of course. For a very elegant lunch, go to *The Compleat Angler* in Marlowe (reservations necessary).

Museums

British Museum.
You'll need about three months to cover it all. Wait until you see the Greek and Egyptian antiquities! And the library! Rosetta Stone. I'll stop now before I get carried away.

The Museum of London.
Located in the banking district, not far from St. Paul's. It's a good museum to go to on your first day, as it gives a very interesting and informative presentation of the history of London. Parts of the old Roman wall are around the museum. You'll need about three hours. Good for kids.

National Gallery of London.
Quelle collection!

Percival David Foundation of Chinese Art, 53 Gordon Square, cl. Sun.
Near the University. An outstanding private collection of Chinese porcelains. Open at odd times.

Sir John Soane's Museum, 13 Lincoln Inn Fields, cl. Sun., Mon.
This is a small museum and private collection of Sir John Soane in a natural setting. A successful architect in the early 1800s, his collection includes the sarcophagus of Seti I, rare books, paintings, illuminated manuscripts, drawings, decorative arts.

Tate Gallery.
Merveilleux! Turner heaven. The restaurant in the museum is quite acceptable for lunch.

The Victoria and Albert Museum, or the "V&A".
Decorative-arts heaven. Also paintings by old masters, silver, clothes, tapestries, china, etc. Vast and important.

The Wallace Collection.
Housed in a beautiful old mansion, it contains not only decorative arts but paintings and objects. One of the world's finest private collections.

And now for something completely different:

Without giving too much away, I urge you to go to a place called *Dennis Severs House,* 18 Folgate St., Spitalfields, London E1, phone 01–247–4013. You must make an appointment to go. Dennis Severs is an American who moved to London a few years ago and bought an eighteenth-century house. He proceeded to use all his money to restore it to its original condition, without a trace of the twentieth century within. He takes you on a two-hour tour through this house, re-creating for you as you go the life and times of London in the 1700s and the intimate life of a mythical family who live in the house. Although you never see this family, you can hear them, and when you go from room to room you are aware of their presence through sounds, smells, and a feeling that they just left the room. It is spellbinding, mystical, magical. A friend of mine describes it as "the most incredible thing I've ever seen." Mr. Severs only takes small groups of around six people and only by appointment. As yet, this house remains undiscovered, so if you are in London, be among the first to experience this adventure, before the rest of the world is clammering for a reservation.

Shopping

Shopping, as I mentioned earlier, is not as good as I would like it to be. No trip to London is complete without a trip to *Harrods,* where you can get lost for days if you're not careful. It's a good place to buy just about anything, as the selection is quite large. Be sure you go to the food halls. The streets around Harrods are full of shops. *Sloane Street* is especially good. You'll find good shopping on *Old* and *New Bond Streets, S. Moulton Street, Jermyn Street,* and in the *Burlington* and *Piccadilly Arcades.* Also go to *Fortnum and Mason.*

Be aware at all times when shopping of pickpockets, purse snatchers, and camera grabbers.

Don't hold out for the duty-free shop at the airport—it's not very good and usually mobbed.

Transportation

Getting around in London is no problem. You have the cheapest and best transportation in the world—your feet. Like Rome and Paris, London is a terrific walking town, so whenever possible, go on foot. Note: be verrrry careful when crossing the streets, and if you have kids with you, hang on to them. Because of the reversed traffic flow, it's easy to get mowed down because you're looking in the wrong direction. Some of those cab drivers act as if they think they're driving in Cairo. The cabs and double-decker buses are world famous and your second best bet, along with the tube (the underground). Don't let it confuse you—just ask someone how to use it. Watch your purse and camera. If you're going out of town on an excursion, take the train. Someone at your hotel or the train station can help you get on the right train to the right place.

Heathrow Airport is gigantic and always crowded, so don't wait until the last minute to catch a plane. Getting to and from Heathrow can be done on the tube, although it's a long trip and if you have a lot of luggage, it won't be so easy. (Cheap, yes; easy, no. Quicker than a cab? No, it makes a lot of stops.) If you have to stay in a hotel by the airport for whatever reason, the Airport Sheraton isn't bad. It's easy to get from there into town on the tube.

If you go to London in the middle of summer, don't assume you'll be able to get by with sundresses and sandals. Perhaps that will be the case, but when we were there in the summer it was freezing cold and rained every day, even though each morning began bright and beautiful. Keep your bumbershoot handy, and some comfortable, close-toed walking shoes.

Two Day Trips from London

There are many excursions one can do from London, which could be the subject of an entire book alone. Here are two that I can recommend.

Bath

There's so much to see and do in Bath that you might want to spend one night, or two, but if you are short on time, you can still cover part of it in a day. Bath is located about 110 miles from London; you can get there in seventy-five minutes by train from Paddington Station, or ninety minutes by car.

The Romans built elaborate baths in the area back in the days of Claudius. These can be visited today, parts of them being under the present city. During the eighteenth century, Bath became a fashionable spa, thanks to the efforts of a man named Beau Nash. Today, the city is a jewel of eighteenth-century Georgian architecture. Be sure you see the *Royal Crescent* (thirty houses with more than a hundred Ionic columns; you can visit #1), and the *Circus* (a circle of eleven houses in three sections).

Other places of interest in Bath are the *Abbey, Parade Gardens, Pulteney Bridge* lined with shops, the *Pump Room, Royal Victoria Park,* and some of the thirteen museums in the city. The more popular of these are the *Carriage Museum,* the *Museum of Costume* (largest of its kind in the world) in the *Assembly Rooms,* and the *Holburne of Menstrie Museum.* Nearby is the *American Museum* at Claverton Manor.

In the outlying and surrounding countryside visit *Wookey Hole* and *Cheddar Caves,* any of twenty-seven stately homes, wildlife parks (such as

Longleat), old abbeys, and *Castle Combe Village.* Or take a boat ride on the Avon.

Antiques hunters will be in heaven in Bath. Go to the *Great Western Antique Center,* especially for the Wednesday market.

There are more than eighty restaurants in Bath. The best of them are: *Hole in the Wall* (maybe the best), *The Laden Table,* the *Priory Hotel,* the *Royal Crescent Hotel,* and *Popjoy's* (Beau Nash's home).

If you decide that one day is not enough and you want to spend more time, these are the top hotels:

Homewood Park, five miles out of town; a small eighteenth-century house with eight rooms.
Hunstrete House, eight miles out of town in Hunstrete, Chelwood; a country inn with good food.
The Priory Hotel, a sumptuous nineteenth-century Gothic-style country house.
The Royal Crescent Hotel, a small, luxurious eighteenth-century hotel.
Ston Easton Park

Brighton

A one-hour train ride out of Victoria Station, and about the same by car. The little seaside resort is quite quaint and there are lots of little shops and restaurants. As for the latter, try *Le Francis* in Brighton, or *Gravetye Manor* in East Grinstead, halfway between London and Brighton. Be sure you visit the *Royal Pavilion,* quite unusual and very elaborate. Oh yes, and don't forget to get your Brighton Rock.

You might also note that you're not too far from Stratford-on-Avon, the Cotswolds, and Wells (with a spectacular cathedral). It seems that this one-day trip is turning into a week's adventure!

Frankfurt
Am Main

Frankfurt Am Main

If you have to go somewhere via Frankfurt, stay there a couple of nights. Everyone will tell you not to, that it's an ugly, uninteresting city, but I think you'll enjoy yourself. You must have a good guide, however, because much of the city *is* rather uninteresting. Certainly Frankfurt does not compare to other European cities, either large or small, when it comes to being scenic, charming, old-world, or even a shopping haven. But there are things to do and see.

The two nicest hotels in Frankfurt are the *Gravenbruch Kimpenski,* halfway between the airport and town in a lovely wooded area, and the *Kronberg Castle* up in the hills. I would recommend either one, although they are two sides of the coin. The Kimpenski is a beautiful, new, sprawling, and modern hotel, very elegant and quiet. The Kronberg Castle is a real castle, built by Queen Victoria, still full of antique furnishings and goodies. We were shown three rooms, one of which, the Royal Suite, is not available for just anyone. Room 27 was gorgeous—get that one. The dining room is splendid, as was the food and service, and even if you don't stay in the castle, you must go there for lunch or dinner. At lunch you can see the surrounding forest.

We had two other outstanding meals in Frankfurt. The first was at a farmhouse-restaurant just loaded with charm and character called *Gutsf-chante-Neuhof* (pronounced *noi-hoff*). Part of the building is five hundred years old and it's located in a woods, about ten minutes from the Kimpenski. Be sure you try the fried Camembert with fried parsley and fresh cranberry compote, if available. Many seasonal dishes and German specialties. Phone: 607/3214 and 06102-3214.

The other very delightful restaurant is called **Weinhaus Brucken-keller,** located in ancient wine cellars, Schutzenstrasse 6, phone 28–42–38. Besides the wonderful food, the atmosphere was top-notch, complete with strolling musicians, interesting, ancient artifacts decorating the walls, a huge wine barrel at one end, candlelight, and flowers. Very romantic and very fun. Best chocolate sauce I've had in a long time (thick, rich, dark and fudgy). Reservations essential.

Other restaurants in Frankfurt recommended to us by our Mr. Roth (see below) are **The Table** (nouvelle cuisine), **Bistro 77** (ditto), and **Ernie's Bistro** (nouvelle/German). Not recommended is the touristy **Stubb** in the Frankfurter Hof Hotel.

By the way, you might be wondering what the Am Main (pronounced *mine*) is, attached to the end of Frankfurt. This is to distinguish the city from another Frankfurt, located in East Germany on another river. Main is the name of the river by this Frankfurt.

We had a marvelous driver/guide named Mr. Roth (pronounced *Rote*), and I recommend him highly. He really showed us what there was to see of the old and new Frankfurt (55 percent of the city was destroyed during World War II). He knew where to eat, where to shop, what to buy, etc. You can reach him through his company, Auto-Roth, 6000 Frankfurt/Main 60, Eschweger Strasse 3, West Germany, phone 06–11–47–22–16 or 47–43–42. His company also supplies cars and drivers for other cities in Germany and has a complete guest service.

The shopping in Frankfurt is good, if you know where to go. There are some nice boutiques, but in general it can't compare to Paris, Zurich, or Rome. You can find all major European brands and most designers somewhere in the city. There is one area of nothing but huge department stores, one right after the other, which go on for several blocks.

What to Buy in Germany: Mercedes, VWs, BMWs, leather items, Leica cameras, binoculars, apple wine, kirsch, Trumpf and Lindt chocolate, Adidas sporting goods, skis, sausage, Rosenthal and Meissen china and porcelain, Christmas decorations. For starters.

Like France, Germany has a tax refund for tourists, amounting to somewhere between 10 and 13 percent. You have to go through formalities as in France, but I don't know all the details. If you buy a lot, it may be worth your while to check it out.

As for museums, there isn't much to see, except the **Senckenberg Museum of Natural Science.** There's an old part of town which survived the bombings, the **Sachsenhausen** section, which is full of beer taverns specializing in apple wine. There's also a popular zoo.

There is plenty to see on day trips from Frankfurt. If you go in one direction, you can visit **Würzburg and Rothenburg**—famous, medieval towns which survived the war. On another day, in the other direction, you can visit *Heidelberg* and the *Rhein Valley*. We took the latter option and it was wonderful. Heidelberg was made famous by *The Student Prince*. It is also the site of a large university and a very large castle, now in ruins. Picturesque is the only way to describe this town and the surrounding area. Heidelberg is about an hour from Frankfurt. Another hour further on you'll come to the Rhein river and the wine-growing area of Germany. There are many large and beautiful estates on the edge of the vineyards, and as you go along the Rhein you'll eventually come to some of those famous castles. The little towns along the way are picturesque, if not totally touristy. You'll see Germany's "Statue of Liberty," a huge monument high on a hill, which you can reach by either car or cablecar.

A beautiful inn/restaurant along the Rhein is the *Hotel Krone,* 6224 Assmannshausen, Rheingau, West Germany, phone 0–67–22/20–36. The inn is closed during the winter. The food was wonderful, with a view of the Rhein, the barges, boats, and a castle on the other side.

Between Rheingau and Frankfurt you can visit *Rudesheim,* a city in the midst of the wine region devoted entirely to tourists. You can also make a stop in the very lovely city of *Wiesbaden,* known to Americans because of its large American hospital. Wiesbaden is quite pretty, with beautiful parks, good shopping and restaurants. It is the capital of the state in Germany wherein Frankfurt is located.

The autobahns in Germany are famous—excellent, with no speed limits. Therefore, you'll see some cars going very fast. Mr. Roth said that auto accidents were not numerous, but usually quite serious.

There's a certain atmosphere in Germany different than in the other European countries I've visited. Nobody has forgotten the war and everyone is nervous about the Russians. You must realize that any German (or anyone else, for that matter) under the age of fifty-five or sixty had nothing to do with the war. The military presence, and not just of the German army, is felt at all times: you rarely go anywhere without seeing servicemen, military vehicles, or convoys, usually American. The German people I met were altogether charming, gracious, and friendly. The cities and countryside are clean and neat. There seems to be an overall order and organization there, along with a certain tension. Whatever is thought or felt about the Germany of forty years ago must be balanced with a realistic and thoughtful view of the Germany of today, with its new generations, concerns, fears, and hopes for the future.

Copenhagen

Copenhagen

Copenhagen is the only city we've ever been to that we would call cute. It's just cute, that's all. You can see and do all there is in the city if you have six full days; four or five will be enough unless you want to see every single thing in every single museum.

It helps to read up a little before you go, and decide what you want to see. I looked all over for a good guidebook on Copenhagen and only found one, the *Berlitz Travel Guide: Copenhagen*. There were many guidebooks about Denmark as a whole, which you will want if you're going to go touring around there, but if you're just going to Copenhagen, this Berlitz book was very thorough without being laborious. The Berlitz book makes no suggestions as to hotels and restaurants. Fodor and Fielding and the like all have sections about the city also, which are interesting to read and compare.

We were in Copenhagen (pronounced *hay-gen*) in early May. The weather was mostly sunny and surprisingly warm (midsixties in the daytime); but if the sun went behind a cloud, or we were walking in the shade, or if the wind came up—it got cold. The evenings were extremely cold; could've used a fur coat.

Hotels

We stayed at the *Plaza Hotel* across from Tivoli Gardens. The hotel was very beautiful and elegant, but our room was awful. If you book there, insist on getting a nice-sized room with a view. The *Hotel Nyhavn,* which is recommended and touted in all the books, is certainly what you could call "quaint" and maybe you'd like it. However, it is not as centrally located as other hotels, and it is also at the end of a street I wouldn't want to walk down at night.

Restaurants

The **Baron of Beef** at the Plaza Hotel is supposedly the best place to eat in the city. It was certainly very nice. The other restaurant at the hotel, the **Flora Danica,** is also supposed to be very good and more reasonable; however, we didn't eat there. In any case you should make a point to go have a drink in the **Library Bar** of the hotel, as it is probably one of the most beautiful bars you'll ever see.

There are several places to eat in Tivoli Gardens, but the two most recommended to us were the **Divan 2** and the **Belle Terrasse.** We had dinner at the Belle Terrasse and it was wonderful. The restaurant itself was physically very charming.

For fish, the two best places to eat are both on the same street. One is **Fiskehuset** at 34 Gammel Strand; the other is **Krogs** at #38. Reservations necessary in all the restaurants for dinner.

For lunch we loved the **Ida Davidson,** Store Kongensgade 70. Real Danish food and marvelous open-faced sandwiches. A little way up the street is a bakery that is to die for, and a convenient little park across the way where you can go sit and eat the things you buy. Another good lunch place was back on **Gammel Strand,** #46. Also recommended is **Kommandanten,** Ny Adelgade 7.

As for ice cream cones, well, you have not eaten an ice cream cone until you've had one in Copenhagen. You can throw the ice cream out as it's not too exciting, but the cone is great! Look for a shop where they are making them fresh in the window. They make them on little waffle irons and roll them quickly when they're done.

Shopping

Copenhagen has the longest shopping mall in the world, or so they say. It goes on for blocks, from the Radhuset (main square) to Nyhavn Canal, with lots of side streets branching off. We figured it was all a tourist trap, so went looking for other shopping streets, but the fact is that the walking mall really *is* the main shopping area for tourists and locals alike. It is also Fur Coat Heaven. You'll see lots of gorgeous sweaters made with Icelandic wool and you can get some very good buys. (If you're planning to go to Iceland on the way home, however, wait and buy your sweaters there, as they will be cheaper.) You will also find all the Danish crystal and porcelain you ever wanted. There is a large department store there called *Illums,* sort of the Galeries Lafayette of Denmark. I found it useful for buying gifty things to take home. A few doors from the main Illums is the *Illums Bolighus Design* store. This you must see. It is full of Danish and other design items, from furniture to soap to ceramics. All is beautifully displayed.

Sightseeing

There are several museums in Copenhagen. The *Ny Carlsberg Glyptotek Museum* on Hans Christian Andersen Boulevard was marvelous, especially if you like Greek, Roman, and Etruscan art. However, the collection includes art from many other periods and is well worth a couple hours of your time, minimum. The *Mekanisk Musik Museum* could be described as "very quaint." I wouldn't list it as a must-see, but if you have kids with you, they would love it. It's all music boxes, but big ones. There's a little tour and demonstration which is ongoing.

There are three main castles to see. The one not to miss is the *Rosenborg Slot,* the castliest castle we've ever seen. You could spend two or three hours inside, going through the three floors of period rooms, jam-packed with incredible goodies. The basement is where they show off the crown jewels, and while they don't quite compare to those in England, they are still dazzling. There is another small exhibit hall just by the entrance gate. All three areas are included in your admission price. By the way, when you buy your ticket, buy the little guidebook as well, so you know what you're looking at. Be sure you walk through the gardens and see the castle from the other side of the moat where the bridge goes across. Good photo.

The *Amalienborg Slot* is where the queen now resides and I believe some of it is open at certain times for tours. Check your guidebook. There is a very fancy changing-of-the-guard which occurs here, but not daily. In your hotel you can get a little book, put out on a monthly basis, which gives times and places for everything. The *Christianborg Slot* also has the royal reception rooms, which are open for tours at specific times. Just next to the latter is the *National Museum,* which is quite large.

Tivoli should be visited twice—once in the daytime, and by all means at night. If you have to make a choice, go at night. I won't even try to describe it.

The very famous little statue called *Langelinie* is also a must-see, as it is very charming. It's a short walk from the Amalienborg Slot, and on the way you'll pass by the beautiful Gefion fountain.

Nyhavn Canal is very picturesque, but go during the day. At night they really do have drunken sailors falling by the wayside there. You can also take an hour tour of the canal from the end of Nyhavn. These run almost hourly all day. My husband did it and said it was very interesting.

I heard that if you ship things home from Copenhagen, you get a 16 percent discount on your purchases. Check this out.

No tipping in Denmark. Only a small gratuity if you feel you've been treated extra well.

If you are blond and blue eyed you will fit right in. People will automatically speak to you in Danish. Practically everyone speaks English, so if you let them know, they will immediately switch over.

If you find yourself at the airport and have forgotten to pick up a gift for someone, do not despair. The shops at the airport are some of the best I've seen. Prices are better in town, however. The airport is only twenty minutes from Tivoli.

Don't forget to adequately sample the Danish pastry in all the bakeries. It is really the greatest. And if you drink beer, you will really be in heaven.

Zurich
AND
Lucerne

Zurich

One thing you figure out right away when you're in Zurich is that there are few, if any, poor folks there. It's a very sophisticated and obviously wealthy city, and understandably so. I have a feeling most of Switzerland is the same way.

We had the good fortune to visit Zurich in late October and it was gorgeous. The forests were ablaze in fall colors. There were wild game specials on every menu—things we aren't used to seeing at home, such as hare, venison, grouse, mallard, quail, pheasant, all sorts of seasonal mushrooms, side dishes of pumpkin or chestnuts instead of peas and beans, etc. Although it didn't rain, it was hazy, foggy, and very cold; the high one day was 45 degrees. Frost on the ground in the morning; fur coats out of storage!

There are three nice hotels in Zurich: the *Baur au Lac* and the *Eden au Lac* in the city on the lake, and up in the nearby hills, the beautiful *Dolder Grand*. The Baur au Lac was lovely and very quiet. The Eden au Lac would not be as quiet since it is on one of the main streets through town. The Dolder is more of a resort, but if you decide to stay there, it's only a ten-minute drive into town. All three hotels boast excellent restaurants, especially the Eden and the Dolder.

We had one outstanding dinner and one dinner to forget in Zurich. First the good news: *Chez Max,* Seestrasse 53, 8702 Zollikon, phone 01–391–88–77. Small, romantic, musician, paintings, flowers, candles, fabulous food, expensive. (All of Zurich was expensive.)

To forget is a place called *Kronenhalle.* It's an old guildhouse and the former hangout of James Joyce. A local favorite, judging by the clientele, and crowded on a Sunday evening. There are some terrific paintings hanging on the walls (I dined with Miró), and the atmosphere is lively and warm. But the food, well, I already forgot it.

Two other restaurants recommended to us, which we did not try, are *Conti,* Dufourstrasse 1, phone 251–0666, and *Rebe 2,* Schutzengasse 5, phone 221–1065. Already mentioned were the *Dolder* and *Eden au Lac* dining rooms.

Wherever you eat, don't miss the roesti, spelled a variety of ways. This is a type of hashbrown potato with onions, and when properly done, enough to move to Switzerland for, if you could. Of course other items on Swiss menus, other than seasonal dishes, are veal dishes, liver dishes, dried beef and sausages, dark breads, raclette, cheese croquettes, fondue, regional cheeses, and chocolate. I was very disappointed in the chocolate desserts in Switzerland, not because they weren't good or well prepared, but because I'm a bittersweet type, and everything there is all milk. Also, their chocolate sauces were thin and runny—not the thick, fudgy types we're used to. By the way, streudel is pronounced *stroizel.*

About the most famous thing in Zurich is the *Bahnhofstrasse,* which means "street that goes to the train station." It's a pedestrian-only street, tree-lined and elegant to the nth degree. It's been touted as the world's best and most chic shopping street, right on up there with Fifth Avenue, rue St. Honoré, and Rodeo Drive. I would not compare it to any of those, as each is completely unique. But as far as shopping goes, it doesn't get much better! Take *lots* of money. In the fall the fur coats in the windows are something else—beautiful styles, with prices you'd love to see in the U.S. Your only problem is getting the coat through customs without paying a fortune.

The big department store in Zurich is called *Globus.* There are others along the Bahnhofstrasse and in the surrounding streets.

What does one buy in Zurich, other than fur coats? Swiss army knives, chocolate, leather and suede goods, Bally shoes, skis, music boxes, cuckoo clocks (if you must), cheese, and of course . . . watches!

There are cultural things to do when the shopping is done. The two or three large churches in the city are a bit disappointing, being northern European Protestant (they don't get too fancy). One has some Chagall stained-glass windows *(Fraumunster).* The *Rietberg Museum* has one of the best ethnographic collections in the world and is located in an old villa at Gablestrasse 15. The *Kunsthaus Ramistrasse Museum* is a fine arts museum, featuring Picasso, Munch, Van Gogh, and modern artists, plus temporary exhibits. The third major museum in town is the *Swiss National Museum,* Museumstrasse 2, with a collection of art and artifacts from prehistory to the present.

The new *Botanical Garden* at Zollikerstrasse 107 is lovely.

The Oskar Reinhart collection can be seen at the *Romerholz,* Haulden-strasse 95, in nearby Winterthur.

You can also take a boat tour around the lake. The docks are near the bridge.

The Zurich Tourist Office is located in the train station.

German is the language heard in this part of the country, but English is also widely spoken, as is French. Most signs are in German, however.

The Swiss are very friendly, but reserved. The country is picture-postcard perfect, neat as a pin, every blade of grass in place, every cow looking like a 4-H Club First Prize. It's a nice place to visit, and yes, you probably would want to live there!

Lucerne

I can't tell you all that much about Lucerne, since we did it as a day trip from Zurich. If you do it in this way, take the scenic route through the hills and small towns, via *Einsiedeln*. In that small and charming town is the headquarters of the Catholic Church in Switzerland, in the largest Catholic church in the country. It's German baroque, rather severe on the outside and an explosion of baroque on the inside.

In Lucerne there is a restaurant called the **Old Swiss House,** Lowen-platz 4, phone 041–516171. If you don't go to Lucerne for any other reason, go to eat in this place. Should you plan to arrive later than 1:00 for lunch, you'd best have a reservation. Reservations are a must for dinner. Not only is it a beautiful restaurant, the food is outstanding. Mostly Swiss dishes. The cheese croquettes in tomato sauce were incredible, as were the roesti and sausages. Someone else was eating the fondue, which looked wonderful. Every dish we saw go by we wanted. (P.S. There's a replica of the Old Swiss House in Busch Gardens, Florida, due to the fact that one of the O.S.H. daughters married one of the Busch boys.)

Up the street from the Old Swiss House is a very unusual museum called the *Glacier Gardens.* Believe it or not, the entire area was once a tropical, palm-laden beach. Then huge glaciers covered the area, leaving some very unusual "pothole" formations which we had never seen before. Next to the museum is the *Lion Monument,* a beautiful sculpture carved right out of the mountain.

You should also see the *covered bridge.* There's a large and very interesting *Transport Museum* with entire trains and planes, etc. If it's not too cold, you can take a suspension cable car ride to the top of *Mt. Pilatus.*

If it's watches you want, or music boxes, cuckoo clocks, Swiss army knives, or gift items, go to *Bucherer,* whose headquarters are in Lucerne. There are branches in other cities, but this is the big one, covering three or four floors. The other major watch store is called *Gubelins,* just down the street.

Lucerne is really pretty, located at the base of some very high, snow-covered mountains. It's basically a resort city with some gorgeous resort-type hotels all along the lake. Most of these close for the winter. I'm sure there is enough to see and do in the area to sustain a traveler for a few days, especially in warmer weather.

Belgium

Bruges

When my friends heard I was going to Belgium, they said, "Why?" My answer was that I had wanted to visit Bruges ever since I'd heard about it in an art history class about four years ago. I had also always wanted to go to Ghent and see the famous van Eyck altarpiece. Now when people ask me why I went to Belgium, I still have the same answer, but have tacked on a new word: *food!* Someone once told me that as far as the dining experience is concerned, everything that is best about Switzerland and France comes together in Belgium. I would have to agree. The food and service we had at every meal in Belgium were as good as, if not better than, any we've ever had in France (or anywhere else, for that matter).

To get from Paris to Bruges, we took the train. It was about a three and a half hour trip with a change of trains in Brussels at the Brussels Midi (south) station. The train ride was most enjoyable, especially since we sat in the first-class dining car and ate the whole way. The scenery was pleasant, although not incredibly exciting. Just north of Paris you can see a few grandiose manor houses, and the rest is mostly farmlands and small farming or industrial towns.

The best description of Bruges that I can give you is that it is a cross between Disneyland, an old Flemish painting, and Venice. Bruges is called the Venice of the North because it is laced with canals. Settlement in Bruges began between the fourth and seventh centuries, but it wasn't until the twelfth century that the town began gaining status. By the thirteenth century, Bruges (Brugge in Flemish) was one of the largest and most thriving cities in Europe, and by the fourteenth century it was a major commercial port and trade center. The canals, which led to its huge port, began to silt up, however, and Antwerp eventually replaced Bruges as a major port. The seventeenth and eighteenth centuries found the city sliding downward and falling into decay. In the early twentieth century Bruges was rediscovered and gradually became a major tourist center. A strict restoration policy by the government has returned the city to part of its former condition, and any remodeling or restoration of building facades must conform to four-teenth- and fifteenth-century design. So to walk through Bruges is like going back four hundred years in time, with quaint and charming views every-where you look.

One of the most fascinating aspects of Bruges is the architecture. The stepped gables you see on many buildings were a uniquely Flemish idea. Architectural styles span all periods from medieval to Renaissance, baroque, Gothic, Flemish-Gothic, neoclassic, rococo . . . but not modern. Most of the streets are cobbled, narrow, picturesque, and many are without cars. Canals still crisscross the city, and they are tree lined, flower bedecked, bridge covered, swan filled, and altogether charming and romantic. There are wonderful churches, Michelangelo sculpture, mind-blowing Flemish primi-tive paintings, interesting museums, cute shops, and fabulous food!

Hotels

The *Hotel Duc de Bourgogne* is supposed to be the best. Located in a restored seventeenth-century building, it faces a canal, has one of the city's best restaurants, is loaded with charm, but offers only about ten rooms. If you don't book way in advance, you can't get in.

We stayed just down the street at *Die Swaene* (Steenhouwerstkjk 1), which is in a restored fifteenth-century house, also facing a canal. It's a very small and charming place, and we were completely satisfied.

A third possibility is the *Binnenplein Bourgoensche Cruyce,* which is opposite the Duc de Bourgogne on the other side of the canal (Wollestraat 35). The restaurant in this hotel is also very good, so we were told.

Restaurants

As mentioned above, the restaurant at the *Hotel Duc de Bourgogne* is outstanding. Try to get a table with a view of the canal. Not only is the food great, the service is too, and the ambiance is the best! The desserts were not as good as the rest of the meal, and the soup was a little watery; this seemed common with all soups we had in Belgium. Dinner for two, includ-ing a 16 dollar wine, came to 70 dollars, tax and tips included.

Other ideas: Den Gouden Harynck, Groeninge 25, was also excellent. Nine tables only. Service was outstanding. Dinner for two was 70 dollars, including the wine. *Panderetjye* is the best restaurant in Bruges, according to our driver, Ian, whom I will talk about later. He says if you go there, get the "alles," which is eleven courses, sort of a *dégustation*. He hastens to add that you aren't sick when you leave, as the portions are small and the pacing is perfect. Another place highly recommended by Ian is called *L'Heure Bleu,* about five minutes out of Bruges on the road to Ghent. We drove by this beautiful house and wished we'd had time for it. *The Weinebrugge,* Koning Albertlaan 242, is also supposed to be good. Closed Thursdays. A more casual and inexpensive restaurant with very good food is *Maxmiliaan Van Oostenrijk,* 17 Wijngaardplein.

I have a feeling there are probably not too many bad places to eat in Bruges, Brussels, or anywhere in Belgium. They take food and service as seriously as the French do.

Sightseeing

We stayed two nights in Bruges, which was barely enough time. I think three nights is a better idea. Then you can really see everything, drive into the country, go into Holland (fifteen minutes away), go to the seaside (ten minutes away), see a couple of the museums, shop at leisure, and sample more of the food.

We hired a guide to show us the sights and it was a smart thing to do. Everyone speaks Flemish and French, so if you don't know either of those, you could be in trouble at times, although English is also widely spoken. There's so much rich history to the city, however, that you'll probably get a lot more out of it with a guide. Our guide's name was Mrs. DeWolf and she was excellent. It cost about 30 dollars for her services, which ended up lasting a day, although she was only supposed to give us half a day. You can write ahead to her (she speaks English) and reserve her in advance. Her address is: St. Salvatorskerkhof 21, 8000 Brugge, Belgium, and her phone is 33–51–62. The zip code is 8000 for all of Bruges, in case you write ahead for restaurant reservations.

With or without a guide, these are the sights you should see:
Start out with a *ride on the canals* in one of the many tourist boats. You'll get a nice overview of the city, plus get some beautiful photos if it's sunny (don't count on it).

Basilica of the Holy Blood,   next to the Town Hall.
Part of this very small and ancient church dates from 1150, and it is the church housing the Relic of the Holy Blood (I won't go into that; ask your guide). If you're into architecture, you'll love the interior of this church. Notice the wonderful medieval sculpture over the portals.

The Burg, a smaller square, reached via the Breidelstraat from the Grotte Markt. The Town Hall is the most outstanding building here, the oldest preserved building of its kind in the Low Countries. Next to it is the Holy Blood basilica, mentioned earlier. On the other side is the Recorder's House, in Flemish-Renaissance style.

If you walk through the archway on *Blinde Ezelstraat* and go down that street, you'll come to the Duc Bourgogne Hotel, some of the canal boat docks, and some of the loveliest views in the city.

Church of Our Lady A large beautiful church, its main attraction being a magnificent sculpture by Michelangelo, the only one to have left Italy during his lifetime. It is on the right aisle, and you can truly appreciate his genius by comparing it to other, larger marble statues nearby. You can also see in this church the *Monumental Tombs* of Maria of Burgundy and Charles the Bold; plus recent excavations of their original tombs.

The Fish Market, located between the Duc de Bourgogne Hotel and the Hotel Die Swaene. Every morning during the week, fresh fish is sold here. Some days are busier than others.

The Groeninge Museum.

This is the place to see the Flemish primitives. The collection includes outstanding works by the Flemish masters, most especially Memling, van Eyck, Bosch, Breughel, and Rogier van der Weyden.

Gruuthus Museum.

This is a beautiful old building contains a diverse collection of things from decorative arts to sculpture to coins to paintings, etc.

Jerusalemstraat and the *Jerusalem Church.*

Built according to the plans of the Church of the Holy Sepulchre in Jerusalem.

Lace making.

If you are in the market for anything lace, Bruges is the place to buy it. If you buy it in Brussels it will cost more. It's all made in Bruges. You'll see about a million lace shops, mostly tourist in nature, but if you go inside you may find someone sitting in the back, making lace in the old way. It's fascinating to watch. Measure your tables (in meters) before you leave home so you'll know what size to buy.

Market Square, the central square.

The square is surrounded by architecturally unusual buildings, both large and small. Many sidewalk cafés, the highest belfry, the Halles Building, court, post office, statues, etc. From the top of the belfry you can get a great view of the city; but you must get there by 4:30 P.M.

St. John's Hospital, also called the *Memling Museum.*

The Memling collection is housed in one of the wards. The hospital itself is very interesting, akin to the Hospices de Beaune in France. Be sure you visit the *Apothecary* before leaving.

St. John's Windmill.

From the top you get another nice view of the city.

There are other museums and monuments, squares and gardens. Get yourself a guidebook or a guide (preferably both) and enjoy this beautiful city. The church bells ring every quarter hour, and when the sun hits the canals through the trees at just the right angle, with the swans swimming and the bells ringing, you'll swear it is all a big movie set.

Audenarde, Damme, Oostkerke, and Sluice.

These are little villages (the last one being in Holland) that are five to fifteen minutes from Bruges. The countryside through which you drive or float (if you take a boat) is gorgeous.

And don't forget to get a waffle!

Ghent

If possible, get a car and drive yourself, or hire a car and driver to go from Bruges to Ghent to Brussels. The whole trip, with lunch, will take half a day, if you go slowly and stop in Ghent for an hour or so. We got very lucky in getting a wonderful driver, whom I can highly recommend. His name is *Ian Trull.* His address is 3 Fabriekstraat, Aalst, Belgium. He can also be reached through Garage Votre Confort, 13 rue Haute, Brussels, Belgium 1000. The phone there is 512–44–44 (area 02). Ian is English, has been living in Belgium for a long time, and knows all of Europe, plus Greece. His specialty is Switzerland. He knows everything about everything, including the best places to eat, and all his recommendations proved to be topnotch. He has driven movie stars, regular folks, and heads of mega-corporations, etc. Very charming fellow. Talks a lot.

The main reason to go to Ghent is to go to **St. Bevon Cathedral** (closes for lunch, so time it right) and see the famous *van Eyck* triptych, *Adoration of the Lamb.* Try to get a guide to explain it to you, as it will mean so much more. This really is something you should not miss. In the same church are other beautiful paintings and an especially unusual pulpit.

A second attraction in Ghent, which is basically a dirty, ill-kept city, is the old **guildhouses,** seen best from across the canal next to St. Michael's Bridge.

While you're there, go see the wonderful tenth-century castle. I don't even know the name of it, but it's huge and in a fabulous state of preservation. You can go inside and tour the entire thing, which takes about two hours.

Now before we get to Brussels, let's talk a minute about food. Besides the wonderful French cuisine, the Belgians have a few specialities of their own. Their famous beer is Stella Artois. Waffles, anyone? If you go into a tearoom or restaurant and order a waffle, you'll get one that is pretty much like Belgian waffles here. But if you buy one off a stand, in a napkin, you are talking waffle of a different color. They are like big, hot, sugary, soft-on-the-inside but crisp-on-the-outside cookies. Do not fail to sample one of these yummy, fattening delectables. Let us not forget Belgian endive, which they do in a variety of ways. If it's not on the menu, ask for it. They are very big on mussels *(moules)* and fresh fish, which is only a spit away in the English Channel. For all you Brussels sprouts fans (who *are* you, anyway?), you'll be in heaven. A popular regional dish is called *waterzooi* (it's actually the national dish). This is a stewlike affair in a thin cream sauce with vegetables, chicken, and/or fish. French fries are another hot item. There is a big controversy as to who invented them—the French or the Belgians. Maybe they should be called Belgian fries. *Carbonnades*, or stews made with beer, are another popular item. An asparaguslike vegetable called *jets d'houblons* (hop shoots) will appear on menus. Blood sausage *(bloedpans)*, sausages made from kidneys, pancreas, and oxtail *(choesels)*, and *hochepot* (a stew with pork and vegetables) are native dishes. A sorbet made from a beerlike liqueur called *kriek* is another specialty (also has cherries in it), although I never saw it on a menu. And for chocoholics like myself, you will reach a state of Nirvana. Belgian chocolate is some of *the* finest in the world. Their big name brands are Toison d'Or, Callebaut, Cote d'Or, Wittamers, and Godiva (which is originally a Belgian chocolate, and the candy you get in Belgium is better, they say, than what is made in the U.S.). Of course you will see other chocolate brands, and they're all good. Look for the dark and white chocolates that look like seashells. Also, have a sugared truffle. My teeth are tap-dancing thinking about them.

Brussels

Brussels is a very big, unenchanting, unquaint, dirty, commercial city. It has none of the beauty and charm of Paris, nor the antiquity and magic of Rome. It's not a place you should go for a week, or even a few days, unless you had a good reason. We went there to get a plane, but we stayed two nights to see the sights. And there are sights . . .

Grand'Place   (the central square).
It *is* magnificent. You can't stop looking at the buildings. Most of them have been cleaned, and the ones which haven't look extra dirty and black. Be sure you see it at night, too, when it is illuminated.

Hôtel de Ville and **Maison du Roi museums**   on the Grand'Place.
History of Brussels, Belgian objects d'art, and the original statue of the little boy taking a leak, which you see everywhere, unfortunately.

Musée d'Art Modern et Ancien,   rue de la Regence (also called the Royal Museum).
One of the best museums I've ever visited. Vast collection, huge museum— you'd need days to see it. We only went to see the painting collection, and didn't even see all of that. Flemish primitives, of course, plus old masters up to modern. Definitely worth a visit, or two.

Notre Dame des Victoires,   between the Place du Grand Sablon and Place du Petit Sablon.
Fifteenth-century Gothic church.

Palais de Justice.   A huge Greco-Roman monstrosity (reminds me of the Wedding Cake in Rome).
Dominates the entire city. You can walk here from the above-mentioned museum, and pass the Place du Grand Sablon on the way.

Ste. Gudule Church   (National Church of Belgium).
Two thirds of this church was closed off for repairs, because it is so old. The
interior was fascinating, and after the work is done it will be even better.
Architecturally a delight.

Of course, Brussels is full of many other museums and places of interest,
but we only had one day, and that's all I can comment on.

Hotels

The Amigo. The only good thing about this hotel is the location, about
a stone's throw from the Grand'Place. I read several articles about hotels in
Brussels, and this one was always listed as the best, or one of the best. We
found it to be badly in need of a facelift. The hallways were downright
tacky. Our room was spacious enough, but somewhere between tacky and
homey, as far as the decor. It was OK for two nights, but I wouldn't want
to have stayed there a week. Consult your travel agent for other choices.
Our driver, Ian, thinks the *Hilton* in Brussels is the best one in Europe, if
you like staying in Hilton hotels. This one and the Sheraton are the typical,
huge, tour-packed, businessman's kind of places. No character.

Shopping

Most of the shopping in Brussels is done in gigantic indoor shopping
malls, called *galeries*. They are everywhere. It's not hard to figure out why
everything is indoors, since the weather we encountered there was cold,
dreary, misty, and rainy. We went into several of these galeries: the *Galerie
de la Reine,* just off Grand'Place, and the *Galerie des Princes,* which are really
connected, are OK but not great. To be avoided altogether is the *Galerie City
2* and the surrounding walk streets—very tacky stores. *Galerie rue Neuve* is
also a pass. *Galerie Louise* was somewhat better and probably worth a trip.
Nearby is the *Galeries Toison d'Or,* which include *Galerie Duc de Bourgogne,
Marie de Bourgogne,* and *Charles Quint.* These were without doubt the
best. These are all in walking distance from the Palais de Justice and the
museum.

For antiques you have to go to the *Place du Grand Sablon.* The entire
area is riddled with antique shops. On weekends there is a big outdoor
antique market. You have to be picky, but there is a lot of interesting-
looking stuff there.

I saw some outstanding sweaters at an arts-and-crafts fair. They came
from a shop called *Marianne Reding,* Chaussée de Vleurgat 320. They were

handmade, expensive (but not unreasonably so), and if I'd had the space in my suitcase, I'd have bought one. She will make them to order, too, and ship.

Language

There is a very old war going on in Belgium between the Flemish and the French Belgians. It's a lot like the war in Quebec between the English-speaking and French-speaking. Therefore, every sign you see in Brussels, and many other cities, is written in both languages. Even if it's the same word. English is also spoken a great deal.

Restaurants

I saved the best for the last!

Where to begin? I would go back to Brussels and stay a week, just to be able to eat in more restaurants. All the stories I heard about the food were true. We did not have one single meal there, or anywhere in Belgium, that was not memorable. First I will list the places where we dined, then I will list the other places in Brussels which are considered to be the best at the moment. (Cl. = closed.)

Au Vieux St. Martin,   38 pl. du Grand Sablon.
Wonderful for lunch, serving Belgian specialities. Full of locals. Up the street in the Place du Petit Sablon is another restaurant, a little more sophisticated, which I believe belongs to the same people. Anyway it was recommended, and it's called *Au Duc d'Arenberg,* #9.

Claude Dupont,   46 av. Vital-Riethuisen.
Dinner for two was 92 dollars, including 6 dollars for wine. A small and very refined restaurant, tucked away on a hard-to-find street. Well known and highly rated. Food was terrific. Order the hot apple crêpe and the ice cream dessert.

Hostellerie Bellemolen,   1705 Affligem, Essene (a city near Aalst, about fifteen minutes out of Brussels and well worth the drive), phone 053–66–62–38.
A big lunch for three came to 80 dollars, which included a bottle of wine. This gorgeous restaurant is located in an ancient watermill which still runs. Water rushes through the restaurant and flows into a stream below. The interior is exquisite. Table settings, ditto. Food, ditto. The host and hostess are very charming. This is also an inn, so if you want to stay in an absolutely wonderful country setting, only a few minutes from downtown Brussels, this is the place.

La Villa Lorraine,   75 av. du Vivier d'Oie, 1180 Brussels. Cl. Sun.
Located in a forest. Maybe the most outstanding meal we've ever had, anywhere, anytime. Not only was the food fabulous, so was the location, the physical design, the service, the setting, the flowers, etc. Believe it or not, this is considered #2 or #3 by the Belgians. I can only dream what their #1 is like.

Couldn't possibly be better. Recommended are the duck with peppercorns and peaches, the *écrivisses,* and the chocolate soufflé with green walnut juice. Michelin: 3 stars. The same owners have two other restaurants in Brussels: *L'Ecailler du Palais Royal,* rue Bodenbrock 18, specializing in seafood, and the *Boutique du Grand Cerf,* 22 rue du Grand Cerf. The former is excellent, I hear. Don't know about the latter. Dinner for two was 130 dollars, including 30 dollars for wine.

The following I put together from various lists and articles and critiques that I read while in Brussels. The first five are the "biggies," but the rest of them are all highly rated.

1 • *Comme Chez Soi* (#1 choice of the natives), 23 pl. Rouppe, 1000 Brussels, phone 512–29–21. Cl. Sun. and Mon. Michelin: 3 stars.

2 • *The Barbizon,* 1900 Jezus-Eik, Welriekendedreef 95, Overijse, phone 657–04–62. Cl. Tues. and Wed. In a woods.

3 • *La Villa Lorraine.* Already mentioned.

4 • *La Maison du Cygne,* rue Charles Buls 2, 1000 Brussels, phone 511–82–44. Cl. Sat. and Sun.

5 • *Romeyer,* Chaussée de Groenendael 109, 1990 Hoeilaart, phone 657–05–81. Cl. Sun. and Mon. One of the best. Michelin: 3 stars.

6 • *L'Ecailler du Palais Royal.* Already mentioned.

7 • *Claude Dupont.* Already mentioned.

8 • *Bruneau,* 73 av. Broustin, 1080 Brussels, phone 427–69–78. Cl. Tues. and Wed.

9 • *La Cravache d'Or,* 10 pl. Albert Leemand, 1050 Brussels.

10 • *Moulin de Lindekemale,* 6 av. J.-F. Debecker, Woluwe-St.-Lambert. In an ancient watermill. I heard it was fabulous food, although it's a bit hard to get to.

11 • *Ravenstein,* 1 rue Ravenstein, 1000 Brussels, phone 512–77–68. Cl. Sat. lunch and Sun.

12 • *Debussy,* 2 pl. du Petit Sablon, 1000 Brussels, phone 512–80–41. Cl. Sat. lunch and Sun.

13 • *La Thailande,* av. Le Grand, 1050 Brussels, phone 640–24–62. Cl. Sun.

14 • *La Pomme Cannelle,* 6 Franklin Roosevelt. A newer restaurant serving excellent food at decent prices.

15 • *Café de Paris,* 10–14 rue de la Vierge Noive. Inexpensive, bistro-type restaurant with very good food.

For French fries (or Belgian fries, if you will), the best are supposed to be in the Place Jourdan at a stand called *Antoine's,* open every afternoon. They are called "frites" (pronounced *freet*).

For the best chocolate, go to *Mary* at 180 rue Royale. Also well known is *Wittamers* in Place du Grand Sablon, across from the restaurant Au Vieux St. Martin.

Good neighborhood bistros are *Chez Provot,* rue Victor Greyson 95, and *Bâteau à Soupe.* So says Ian.

Not-so-hot places are *Le Carlton* and *Les Arcades,* according to Ian.

Antwerp

(Anvers): although we did not get to Antwerp, we were told that it makes a nice half-day trip from Brussels. You can go there for lunch, look around the city, and be back at your hotel in time for dinner. *Liège* is a longer trip and not possible to do comfortably in a day. It is supposedly less interesting than Antwerp. If you are in Liège, however, eat at *La Ripaille,* rue de la Goffe.

Iceland

Reykjavik

Why would anyone go to Iceland?

The weather in May in Iceland was *cold*. (They don't call it Iceland for nothin'!) It was also very rainy and windy one day, very sunny and beautiful another day, but always cold. Go prepared. May is probably not the best time to go to Iceland. Better maybe in August.

There is only one way to get to Iceland if you don't have a private jet. Icelandic Airways. No first class. You land at one of two airports near Reykjavik. From the international airport you can get a bus for about 3 dollars which will take you into the other airport, where the main hotel is. A cab will be around 30 to 40 dollars.

The main hotel is called the *Loftleider* (pronounced *lay-der*). It is about five minutes from beautiful downtown Reykjavik. It's a nice, big hotel, featuring spacious rooms with views and a good restaurant and shop. There are no bellmen and there is no room service. Everyone is very nice and speaks English, just in case your Icelandic is a bit rusty.

Two useful words for you to know: "yow" and "nay."

Restaurants

There are four main gourmet-type restaurants in Reykjavik, and lots of other little places. The restaurant at the Loftleider hotel is called the *Floral Room* and it is very nice. If you want to taste all the truly unique Icelandic dishes, don't miss their daily buffet. It's sumptuous and gives you a good sampling of their cuisine. Dinner there was also good.

One of the other hotels, the Hotel Saga, has a restaurant on the top floor called the **Grill Room**. Magnificent views of the whole area. Good food. Try the fig crêpes for dessert.

The **Naust** (pronounced *Nsht*) **Restaurant** is a fish place in town. The decor is unusual—the whole restaurant looks like the inside of an old wooden ship. Fish was great—best halibut I ever ate. Also had good onion soup.

The other restaurant is in the **Hotel Holt**. We heard it was very good but did not have time to try it.

So what do you eat in Iceland? It is best known for lamb and fish. The lamb was very good, but no better than you can get in the U.S. The fish was fabulous. Absolutely the best salmon and halibut ever to cross from fork to tongue.

There is a dessert in Iceland, unique to the country, called *skyr*. It's hard to describe, but you must try it. It's a cold, creamy, sort of tart pudding on which you pour cream and sugar. Good with fruit, too. It takes about two spoonfuls to get used to it, but then you may love it, as we did.

The coffee tends to have an off taste, probably because the water all comes from underground springs which are a little sulfuric. They go heavy on the butter when they cook.

Sightseeing

There are all kinds of bus and airplane tours available for which you can sign up through your hotel. Most of them leave from the Loftleider. All tours depend on weather conditions, which can change rapidly. We took a nine-hour bus ride into the hinterlands and found it very interesting, even though the weather was atrocious. Cold. Take sunglasses, raincoat, umbrella, mittens, camera; wear walking shoes and jeans. You will tramp around gorgeous waterfalls, in and out of greenhouses, over lava beds, through geyser mists, and around hot pools. Three tea and pee stops. English guide. Worthwhile.

Shopping

Not to worry if it's too cold and you forgot your wooly hat, your wooly coat, your wooly sweater, your wooly gloves, your wooly socks or slippers. You can buy everything wooly that you ever wanted in Iceland, all handmade or knit with the famous Iceland wool. Prices are very, very good! You can get a gorgeous, hand-knit, heavy wool ski sweater for 40 or 50 dollars, or less. Knee-length hand-knit socks for 9 dollars. I've seen these same socks in catalogues and stores at home for up to 35 dollars.

They also make their own unique pottery out of lava clay. Iceland's chocolate is delicious. Then there's the usual tourist stuff—T-shirts, dolls in authentic costumes, ceramic ware, etc.

Language

Icelandic is the language and it sounds unlike most other European languages. Just about everyone speaks some English. Sign language is always good in a pinch. Pointing and smiling help. You won't have any problems.

P.S. Before you go to Iceland, get some literature from your travel agent or a library and read a little about the country.

Egypt

Egypt

There are two expressions popular in Egypt that you will hear often and use often, if you learn them. The first is: *en shah allah,* which means "God willing"; the second is: *ma'ah-lish,* meaning "it doesn't matter," "never mind," or "forget it." Traveling in Egypt is not like traveling in the U.S. or Europe or most other places. There are problems that arise, inefficiencies that overefficient Americans often don't understand, language, food, and weather that are sometimes unpleasant to deal with, etc. But if you go there with an open mind and heart and a bit of patience, you will have an experience that will be both extremely rewarding and quite unforgettable. The Egyptians and Arabs (yes, there is a definite difference) are very warm, friendly, and hospitable, and eager to assist you and make friends with you. They love the Americans and America. Going to Egypt and traveling on the Nile is something that everyone should do once in his or her life.

We took a three-week tour with the Los Angeles County Museum of Art. We have always been antitour and always done our own thing when traveling, but because of the logistics involved and the fact that we were interested in the art history aspect of the trip, we decided to try the organized tour. As it turned out, there were several people in our group (of only thirty) who had the same idea. The tour was very well organized and we saw things that many tourists never see and that we would not have seen had we tried to do it on our own. We were about five days in Cairo, then ten days on the Nile, going from El Minya to Aswan. Most tours on the Nile are three or four days and go between Luxor and Aswan. For many reasons the Nile trip before Luxor was one of the most enjoyable parts, as there were no other boats or tourists and it included some of the most striking scenery.

It is my theory that anyone going to a foreign country should learn a minimum of fifty words or phrases in that foreign language. I put that theory to a test in Egypt and learned a little Arabic before I left (four private lessons). It turned out to be the best thing I could have done. Even if you learn just twenty of the simplest words, you will be rewarded for your efforts. A few of the more useful and important words will be included at the end of this section.

It is also common sense that tells you to read up on where you are going before you go there. Having a brief idea about the Pharaonic dynasties, the hieroglyphics, and some basic knowledge about the painting and sculpture styles will add immensely to your enjoyment and understanding of what you see. As for travel guides, the best one I saw was Frommer's *Dollarwise Guide to Egypt.* There is also a nice little language book called *See and Say It in Arabic,* but be sure you get the Egyptian dialect edition. The Berlitz *Arabic for Travellers* is not good, as many of the words are not Egyptian dialect.

What To Take

The best months to go to Egypt are October through January. We were there in early October and in upper Egypt it was still around 100 degrees plus during the day. We were told that it cools down a lot in the next couple of months. It is always a good idea to take a sweater, as the evenings in Cairo can be cool. Lightweight cotton clothing was best; polyesters and blends can be hot and sticky. Jeans and pants are perfectly OK for ladies, but shorts are a little tacky, unless you're under the age of fifteen. Sundresses were also acceptable (a lot of staring). If it is hot, I recommend wearing skirts and tops, or dresses, as they are cooler than pants. A sun hat is a must. The following is a list of other items you should take.

A strong flashlight
A telephoto lens and a strong flash attachment for your camera
Binoculars
All the film you need (it's about 18 dollars a roll there)
Guidebooks, language books, etc.
Facial tissues (there were none on our boat)
Your favorite liquor, as it is extremely expensive there
Pencils and pens to give away to the children (they will ask for "stilo")
Gum and small wrapped candies to give to the children (they will ask for "bon-bons")
A Polaroid camera (they are still fascinated by it)
Pepto-Bismol tablets, enough for four to six per day, per person. Donagel or Kaopectate or other diarrhea remedies

Vibramycin or similar prescription drug that you take the minute you start getting the *touristas,* which everyone gets. If you are female and prone to yeast infections, take all that medication with you if you plan to take Vibramycin. Note: There are now other drugs on the market; ask your doctor.

Antihistamines or allergy medication (the dust makes everyone clog up)

About 25 to 50 dollars in 1-dollar bills

A small fanny pack for carrying around "stuff" if you are going to be doing a lot of sightseeing

Chapstick and suntan lotion

Extra batteries for everything

Converters and adapters

A small water bottle or canteen

Sunglasses

Tennis shoes (best for going into tombs and temples)

A can of Cutter insect repellent; use it daily to keep away the flies, etc.

Vitamins

Get a gamma-globulin shot before you go.

Cairo

If you've been to Italy and were appalled at the way they drive, you ain't seen nothin' yet. The Italians are sane compared to the people in Egypt. Two groups on our tour were involved in minor accidents in Cairo, and I was frankly glad to be alive when I finally got on the plane to come home. Be prepared.

Cairo is a fascinating city. Noisy, dirty, dusty, crowded, but completely fascinating. There are several big chain hotels along the Nile (Hilton, Meridian, Sheraton). We stayed at the *Oberoi Mena House,* which is across the street from the Pyramids in Giza, about thirty to forty-five minutes from downtown Cairo. Although it was a bit away from the center of activity, it was by far the best of the hotels. For one thing it was *quiet.* Elegant. Also, having a view of the pyramids is not hard to take. The restaurant there is lovely and supposedly one of the best in Cairo. Word of caution: don't go to Egypt looking for a gourmet holiday. Large swimming pool, pool-side dining, and away from the hectic madness of the downtown area. They were actually doing purse searches at the Hilton and Sheraton, as they were worried about bombs. Nothing like this at the Mena House.

The first thing any person must do when going to Cairo, on the very first morning, regardless of how tired you are, is go out to the pyramids between 6:00 and 6:30 A.M. and rent horses and a guide. He will take you on an unbelievable ride for one to one and a half hours, first through a little village and then out across the desert behind the pyramids. You will see them in a way unlike all the other tourists who go on buses will see them. It is important to go first thing in the morning. It is not necessary to have your hotel or anyone else arrange this for you. If you are staying at the Mena

House, just walk across the street and the stable boys will find you. If you are staying in town, take a cab out to the Mena House and walk to the stables. It will cost you about 30 dollars but is well worth it. Be sure to take your camera.

Otherwise you can see the Sphinx and pyramids the usual way—on your own in a cab, or with your tour. Try to go with a knowledgeable guide. It is possible to go into the interior of the main pyramid. There is nothing much to see there, but you should do it anyway. The sound and light show at the pyramids lasts about an hour and is lovely. Be sure you take a warm sweater and go on the night they do the English show. They don't have any shows on Friday night. You will be besieged to do the camel bit. We refused, as it seemed the ultimate in tourist trap. However, if you always wanted to ride a camel, now's your chance. You will be harassed by people trying to sell you a lot of junk. More on the shopping later. Just don't fall for it; and for heaven's sake, never pay the first price.

What to Do in Cairo, After the Pyramids

Antiquities Museum.
This museum is located behind the old Hilton. You could spend about a month there, so prepare to be a bit frustrated. It is probably best to go with a good guide if you have limited time, as he will take you to the most important items. The *Tut* rooms are the most popular and crowded. I went late one afternoon and found them empty. There are over three thousand items from Tut's tomb, as compared to eighty that toured the U.S. But the museum is crammed with incredible things other than the Tut exhibit. If you want to see *Narmer's palette,* it will cost you an extra pound (for me it was worth it). As of this writing, the mummy room has been closed permanently, as the mummies are going to be reburied.

Citadel and Mosque of Mohammed Ali.
This is the largest and most impressive of the mosques and certainly worth a visit. The view of Cairo from behind the mosque is fabulous. Look for the pyramids in the distance. There are other mosques to see, such as *Ibn Tulun,* if you have the time.

Islamic Museum.
After the Antiquities Museum this is somewhat of a letdown, especially if you have no particular interest in Islamic art. If you have the time, however, you may enjoy it.

Khan el Khalili.
The famous bazaar and shopping area and not to be missed. You could spend days wandering in and out of the streets and shops. Many of the shops are quite luxurious; others are simple stalls. No matter where you shop, be careful not to overpay. Bargaining is a must. (Some shops will not bargain; most will.)

Old Cairo.

This is the old part of the city, and fascinating to drive and walk through, to shop.

Shopping

Besides the Khan el Khalili bazaar, there are also some decent shops in the Hilton, Sheraton, and Antiquities Museum. These shops do not bargain. If you have a contact or friend in Cairo, have him or her go shopping with you. You will save a lot of money. If you go with a tour guide, he is probably getting a kickback and will only take you to the shops of friends.

I guess a few words on shopping in general are in order. First of all, the people who are hawking various bits of junk at the monuments and sights are not going to have anything genuine. Don't believe for one minute that anything they have came out of an ancient tomb. It came from their garage the night before. Never pay the asked price. Whatever they ask, offer them 50 to 75 percent less, and never pay more than 60 percent. They will start off with five pounds, and you can probably get it for two. If they won't come down, just say no thanks and walk away. They will either turn and run after you eventually and give you your price, or you will find someone else down the line who will. In many of the tourist shops you can bargain your brains out. Believe me, they will make a profit, no matter what. For example, I saw a lapis lazuli scarab I liked; the price was the equivalent of 100 dollars. I offered 50 dollars. He said it was impossible. I started to walk out. I bought it for about 45 dollars. Later I saw similar lapis scarabs for between 12 and 20 dollars. I still overpaid, and he still made a profit. Start out bargaining *very low*.

The best thing to buy in Egypt is jewelry. There is no duty on jewelry when you return to the U.S., as of this writing. Be careful how much you pay. You can really get taken, and you can also really get some fabulous deals. One of the big items is cartouche rings and pendants. I bought a gorgeous 18-karat cartouche ring from the finest jeweler in Cairo and paid 130 dollars. Others in my tour paid 150 dollars or more for the same thing, lesser quality, in tourist shops. They also have beautiful silver jewelry, ivory (be careful you get ivory and not camel bone!), semiprecious stones. The turquoise is especially beautiful.

The other hot item to buy seems to be *galabeas,* the long robes that the men wear. These will vary in price anywhere from three pounds to forty, depending on where you buy them. Luxor is the best place I found to buy galabeas. In Cairo, I found some nice ones at the Sheraton Hotel for ten pounds. Many are of very poor quality. Remember that cotton is the main crop in Egypt, so you should be able to get galabeas of the finest-quality cotton. In Luxor you can have them custom made overnight. More on this in the Luxor section.

If you travel on the Nile, you will find people trying to sell you various things each time you stop. In some cases it isn't worth it to bargain a lot (60 cents for a beautiful handmade basket is a steal). Nubian beads are a hot item in upper Egypt. They are small glass beads woven into necklaces in various colors and patterns and are quite beautiful. Never pay more than one pound for a strand, and 70 piasters is more like it. Many of the so-called mummy beads that you will see on strands are made out of spaghetti, so if you buy them (two or three pounds each), don't get them wet.

You will also see elaborately carved wooden boxes with inlay work. The asking price in most shops is between eight to twenty pounds each. I got them for three pounds each, with my Cairo friend. Don't overpay. Also check the quality of the inlay carefully.

You will also have to pay for taking pictures at times, especially in upper Egypt. If you want the picture, prepare to pay, but only a few piasters. They will let you know when they want money. The big word which you will get very tired of hearing is *bak-sheesh.* Everyone wants *baksheesh.* Literally, it means "Share the wealth." What it really means is "give me." Sometimes children will come up to you and smile and say hello, and the minute you respond, out comes the upturned palm and "baksheesh?". It gets old, very fast (you will find this in Luxor more than anywhere else). As my Cairo friends explained to me, however, most of these people are extremely poor (the illiteracy rate in Egypt is 83 percent); none of them will ever harm you. There is no robbery, rape, mugging, purse snatching, etc. You are always very safe in Egypt, and very welcome. So a little *baksheesh* here and there is a small price to pay.

Leather goods are a good item to buy in Aswan. Also in Aswan you can find fabulous buys in exotic spices, like saffron. You also can buy karkaday leaves there. This is an Egyptian drink, brewed like tea from dried flowers, then sweetened to taste and drunk hot or cold; it has a lot of vitamin C and tastes and looks like cranberry juice.

Restaurants in Cairo (Good luck!)

Mena House Hotel, a beautiful Islamic-style restaurant upstairs; nightly floor show. Some good food. Try their *umm-ali,* a wonderful, rich, pudding-type dessert.

Hilton. I had lunch in the coffee shop and had fairly decent stuffed grape-leaves. Don't know about their other dining room.

Swissair Restaurant is supposed to be one of the best restaurants in Cairo. It was nice, but we got very American fare. Maybe if you go on your own and not with a tour you will have better choices.

Arabesque is a restaurant is frequented by embassy people and seems touristy, but the food was divine. Fabulous *tahina, umm-ali,* fish, bread, brown rice.

Saqqara
and Memphis

Saqqara is about sixteen miles from Cairo and should not be missed. Here you will find the oldest man-made stone structure in the world, the **Step-Pyramid of Zoser**. Be sure you go with a guide who can tell you what you are looking at. A short distance away is **Memphis,** capital of the Old Kingdom. There is a small park there with a bathroom (of sorts) where you can eat lunch, if you brought one. Inside the building in the park is the **Colossus of Ramses II**. Behind the building are two smaller colossi, and in the area are various stone antiquities, including a smaller *sphinx*.

On the road to Saqqara you will get a fabulous view of the pyramids across the fields, so watch for it. You will also pass an area known for small rugs and carpets with bright designs on them, made by the children. I've also heard you can get good *galabeas* in this area.

It might be suggested to you to ride horses from the Cairo pyramids to the Saqqara site. This may be desirable to do early in the morning, and one way, but I can't imagine it would be a lot of fun once the sun gets up, or to make it a two-way trip. So think twice before going on such an adventure. And don't do it on a camel!

From Saqqara you can see the bent pyramid of **Dashur** in the distance. While you are there be sure you go into the mastaba tombs off to the side.

Papyrus Institute

There are several so-called Papyrus Institutes in and around Cairo. Only a couple are government approved. One of these is near the Sphinx. It is interesting to see how they make papyrus, and of course you will be given ample opportunity to make a purchase of pictures painted on papyrus. The quality and prices of these were as good as or better than any we saw elsewhere in Egypt.

A Word on Food

As I already mentioned, dining in Egypt leaves much to be desired. If you get lucky and get food that is good, try the following Egyptian dishes: *umm-ali,* a hot creamy dessert with nuts and raisins; *fool m'damas,* a bean dish similar to Mexican refried beans and very good; deep-fried *falafel* balls; *gebna* cheese, similar to Greek cheese; *baklawa; karkaday,* the cranberry-tasting drink; mint tea made with fresh mint (good if stomach is upset); Turkish coffee, medium-sweet; fresh grapeleaves; *tahina,* sesame seed sauce; various rice dishes.

Foods not to eat are: beef—it's absolutely the worst and sometimes you are getting water buffalo instead of beef; crème caramel or any custard dishes —they are all awful.

WINE AND BEER. Omar Khyam is the most popular red wine. There are also a white and a rosé, which were sometimes good, sometimes terrible. The beer in Egypt is very good.

ASEER ASUUP. This is a juice made from freshly squeezed sugar cane. It has to be drunk absolutely fresh and cold, meaning you may have to brave ice cubes.

BEWARE. You will probably get sick, no matter how careful you are. Drink only bottled water. Steer clear of ice cubes, unless you are absolutely certain they are safe. Lettuce is the worst culprit. I also don't trust the tomatoes, although a lot of people eat them. Be sure all fruits and vegetables are either cooked, or ones that can be peeled.

SPORTCOLA is the Egyptian brand cola. It's OK. Coca-Cola tastes strange there. Pepsi is the best bet.

GUAVA JUICE is very good.

Absolutely *Never* Drink Nile Water, Go Into The Nile, Or Put Any Part Of Your Body Into It Without Washing Afterward.

Examine your food for bugs. Every piece of European style bread I saw had bugs in it, and there were various and assorted critters in other foods, too. The Egyptian bread, which is like pita, is very good.

Travel Between Cairo And Luxor
The Nile will come back to haunt you.

Fayoum. This is a large oasis about two hours from Cairo.

If you are on a boat, you may have an opportunity to see the following:

Beni Hassan.
Rock-cut tombs in the mountainside of Middle Kingdom nobles. A donkey ride and hike get you there. Beautiful view of the Nile valley. Tombs are very interesting.

Tuna-el-Gebel, near the town of Malawi.
A very interesting cult center of the baboon. Underground catacombs for baboon mummies and offerings. A beautiful temple with the mummy of Isadora. An area called *El Ashmunein,* Greco-Roman; colossi of baboons.

Tell-el-Amarna.
The capital of Akhenaton and the Amarna Period. Nothing remains of this huge, elaborate city but a few stones. A short tractor ride across the desert will take you to the rock-cut tombs of the nobles; very interesting; great view of the desert and valley. Children selling baskets along the way, very cheap.

Abydos.
Cult center of Osiris; gorgeous temple. Small town of Balliana nearby is very interesting. One temple not to miss.

Dendera.
Ptolemaic temple of Hathor. You should not miss this, either.

Luxor

Luxor is Baksheesh City (I think they teach classes in it—Baksheesh 1A, Advanced Baksheeshing, or Baksheesh for Fun and Profit).

The town of Luxor itself reminds me a lot of old Tijuana. It is really dirty, and the people there will *baksheesh* you to death. The main mode of transportation is horse carriage, and you should never have to pay more than two pounds to go anywhere in the city. Luxor does have good shopping and fabulous temples.

Sightseeing

Luxor Museum.

This is a very small but very fine museum, with some quality pieces. It takes about one hour to see it.

Temple of Karnak.

One of the highlights of your trip. Go with a guide who knows what he is talking about. The sound and light show lasts one and a half hours; part of it is a walking tour, part in the bleachers. You should try to see it, as it is unique.

Temple of Luxor.

Not as big as Karnak, but also a must-see.

Valley of the Kings (Thebes), across the river.

To get there take the local ferry boats (about 50 cents). You will need a guide and driver to take you to the tombs. Not to miss are *Tut's* tomb, tomb of *Ramses*, *Seti's* tomb (closed when we were there). There is a nice rest house at the Valley of the Kings. From here you can go to *Hatshepsut's Temple.* Then to the *Valley of the Queens* to see some fabulous temples of the nobles, at the strange village of *Qurna*. Don't miss the temple of *Madinet Habu,* as the relief carvings there are some of the best. There is also a *Ramasseum* to see, and the *Colossi of Memnon.*

You should try to get to the valley by 7:00 A.M. so as to avoid the heat. You can be back in Luxor in time for lunch. Don't attempt to do it without a guide, or on a bike or a mule.

Shopping

The *souk* in Luxor is very interesting. If you walk down the street next to the New Winter Palace Hotel about two blocks, you will see the *souk* angling off to the left, between two other streets. If you take a horse carriage into the *souk,* the shopkeepers will charge you more because they have to pay off the drivers. Best to go there in the late afternoon when everything is open. Be sure you bargain. There is a small shop called the **Happy Shop** (or the Happy something). For five pounds I had a nice *galabea* made up to fit me, in fine cotton and delivered to the boat within six hours. The shopkeepers are usually honest and willing to deal. Have some small piaster notes handy for baksheeshing.

Across the street from the river is a shop called **Philip's Workshop** (there are three in a row called Philip's; look for the workshop on the right). They had pretty good jewelry and would bargain a lot, even though they said they wouldn't. You can get bone and ivory cartouches here with your name on them.

A few doors past the Winter Palace is a shop called **Chez Georges Gaddis.** A man named Joseph owns it; he also has the shops on the Sheraton boat *Aton.* He makes very fine, high-quality shirts, dresses, and *galabeas* in all styles, with your name in cartouche on them. He does custom work, usually twenty-four to forty-eight hours, and delivers to wherever you are. If you are not happy with the work, you don't have to pay. No bargaining. More expensive than in the *souk,* but high quality. The Gaddis family also owns the shop in the **Etap Hotel,** which has some very nice things, especially ladies' *galabeas* for about fifteen pounds. The Etap is a lovely hotel; a nice place to go for a cool drink.

Dining in Luxor

We ate on the boat while in Luxor. There were two places recommended to eat: one, the **Etap Hotel;** two, a restaurant called **Marhaba,** near the Temple of Luxor. A few people from our boat went to eat at these places and reported that the food was terrible at both. The big thing to eat at the Marhaba is stuffed pigeon.

From Luxor to Aswan

There are three major temples to see between these two cities.

Esna.

After Karnak, Abydos, Dendera, and Luxor, this temple is a big letdown. There isn't much of it, and what is there is not in good shape. On the way to the temple you will pass a small bazaar. Their prices are higher than Luxor. You will start to see very lightweight, gauzy *galabeas,* with flowery prints (something like flour sack print). These are very cool, but don't pay more than three pounds.

Edfu, Temple of Horus.

One of the most fabulous temples in Egypt. Fantastic state of preservation. Be sure to see this one.

Kom Ombo.

The only temple right on the banks of the Nile. A temple devoted to two gods. Very beautiful and not to be missed.

Aswan

Aswan is probably the loveliest, quietest, most European city in all of Egypt, and nothing like either Cairo or Luxor. The *souk* in Aswan is the best we saw. It goes on for blocks, is very clean, and full of the most interesting shops, sights, and smells. Try to save two to three hours to take it in. It's a couple of streets in from the river. Aswan can really be hot, so be prepared.

What To Do

Visit the *New Cataract Hotel,* seen in *Death on the Nile.*

Visit the *Oberoi Hotel* on the island (best hotel in Aswan).

Take a *felucca* ride from the New Cataract Hotel out to *Kitchener's Island* and *gardens,* the *Agha Khan Mausoleum,* and *Elephantine Island.* The mausoleum affords a great view of all of Aswan and the desert and is worth the climb.

There are some rock-cut tombs of Nobles across the river you can visit.

Go see the *Aswan High Dam,* getting a view of the first cataract on the way.

See the unfinished obelisk at the granite quarries.

There are many temples to see in the surrounding area; the temple of Philae is the best known.

Abu Simbel. The jumping off place to get to Abu Simbel is the Aswan airport. Good luck! We waited seven and a half hours in the heat while they changed a tire on the plane. Try to go as early in the morning as possible, like 6:00, to avoid the heat. When you arrive at Abu Simbel, buses will take you to the sight. Takes about an hour to see it all.

Learn a Little Arabic
(stressed syllables in italics)

Thanks to God, also the response
   for "How are you?" — El *ham*-de-lee-lah

I bought it yesterday. (Great for
   getting rid of pests) — Anna ish-*teerie* eem-*berra*.

I don't want it. (Ditto above) — Anna mish *ay-za* (if you
   are a female); Anna
   mish *aiz* (m).

This is delicious. — Da la-*zeez*.

I don't understand — Anna mish *fah*- hem-ah (f);
   Anna mish *fah*- hem (m)

beautiful — ga*meel* (m); ga*meela* (f)

tea — shy

coffee — *ah*-whah

no — la

yes — *ay*-you-wah

later — bah-ah-*den*

See you later. — *Shoo*-fak bah-ah-*den*.

water — maya

bottled water — my mah-ah-dah-*nee*-yah

That's too expensive. — Da *rhallee* k-*teer*.

I'm sorry. — Anna *aas*-fah.

OK — *qua* yas

good — *quay* as

bad — *mish* quayas

tomorrow — *bok*-rah

without ice — be-*doon* talg

goodbye — ma-a-sa-*laam*

How much (is that)? — Be-*kam* (dah)?

welcome — ah'lan wah *sah*'lan

   response to welcome — ah-lan beek

please — min fad*lik* (to woman);
   min fad*lak* (to man);
   laow sah*mat* (to man);
   laow sah*matie* (to woman)

thank you — ash*ko* rak (one to one)

thank you — *shoo*-kran; merci

What is your name? — *Iss*-mi-kay? (to female);

	Iss ma–kay? (to male)
My name is	*Ess*–me
I want	Anna aiza (f); Anna aiz (m)
bottle	ee–*zah*–zah
wine	nee–*beet*
hot	*so*–hen
cold	*bah*–red
I speak English.	Anna bat–*kah*–lem in*glee*zie.
How do you do? How are you?	Ee–*zai*–yak? (to male);
	Ee–*zai*–yik? (to female)
my husband	da *go*–zee
my wife	dee mer*ah*–tee
Where is . . . ?	Fin . . . ?
Go away.	*Em*–shee min *hen* na.
I don't have any money.	Mahn–*deesh* f'loos.
street	shar–*ree*
boat	sah–*fee*–nah
Show me.	Wah–*re*–nee.
Bring me . . .	*Hat*–lee . . .
Do you speak English?	Enta b–*tet kah*–lem
	in*glee* zie? (m);
	Enti b–*tet* kah–*lem*–mee
	in*glee* zie? (f)
you	enta (m); enti (f)
French	fran–*zah*–wee
cheap	re–*hees*
small	soo–*ray*–yar
more	*ahk*–tar
Give me . . .	Ah–*tee*–nee . . .
Do you want . . . ?	Teh–*heb*–bee . . . ?
glass (for tea, water)	koo–*bai*–yat
cup	fen*gan*
beer	beera
juice	a–*seer*
friend	sah–*dee*–ee
I want to buy . . .	Anna *aiza* ish–*teer*–ee . . .
	(f);
	Aiz ish–*teer*–ee . . .
	(m)
I will pay you only	
ten pounds.	Anna had–*fah*–lak *ash* ara
	gen*nay* bas.

the bathroom	al ha-*mam;* el kabi*nay;* el toilette
I will give you . . .	Anna ha-*deek* . . .
good morning	sah-*bah*-hel-hair
response to above	sah-*bah*-el-noor
good evening	*mahss*-el-hair
response to above	*mahss*-ah-noor
hello	hello; *mar,* ha-bah; sah-*lam*
Wait a minute.	Dee-*ee*-ah.
buffalo meat	*lah*-maht gah-*moose*
Egypt	*mees*-r (spelled Misr on buses)
Egyptian man (woman)	mees-*ree* (mees-*ree*-ya)
upper Egypt	sai-*eet*
I don't know.	Anna mish *arf*ah.
also	ka*man*
bread	aysh
butter	*zeb*-dah
salt	mahl
pepper	*fel*fel
That's all I have.	Dah *koll* el *an*-dee.
Luxor	El *oh*-sore
so-so, 50-50	Sh*wai*-ya sh*wai*-ya
perhaps, maybe	*yim*-kin
who	meen
Why?	Lay?
Why not?	Lay *la?*
I speak a little Arabic.	Anna bat-*kah*-lem *ara*bee e'*leel.*

You should also learn numbers 1 to 1000 and how to read them in Arabic, which is very easy.

Morocco

Morocco

Morocco is everything you ever thought it would be, everything you've heard, read, and seen in the movies, and much more. It is a country full of surprises and diversity. People who travel to Morocco either love it or hate it—there's never anyone in the middle. We loved it. Everything in Morocco is either wonderful or not wonderful—nothing in the middle; no middle class. The hotels and restaurants are either topnotch, first class, or really awful. Don't think you can go second class.

The one factor that could either make or break your trip is your guide. I would not advise trying to do the country on your own, not that it's not possible. It wouldn't be easy or relaxing. Driving in the cities would be almost impossible. You'll enjoy your trip much more with a car, driver, and guide. For five of us we hired a large VW van with a wonderful driver named Omar. He and our guide met us in Casablanca and stayed with us the entire week, all the way to Marrakesh. As for our guide—Allah must have been really smiling on us that day because we got a winner. Not only did he know everything and take us everywhere, he also dispensed little lessons on history, the Moslem religion, jokes, anecdotes, and folklore. He sang morning songs in French and evening chants in Arabic. He had a marvelous sense of humor, spoke four languages, was kind, loving, fun, and caring. He became a member of our little band and probably a lifelong friend. If you are fortunate enough to be able to get him, his name is Missouri Abdelouhab and can currently be reached at 36 rue des Consuls, Rabat, phone 236-49, or through Olive Branch Tours in Marrakesh. He goes by the name of Abdou.

French is the principal language in Morocco, along with Arabic and

Berber dialects. In all major hotels, most restaurants, and many shops, English is also spoken. If you have a tourist knowledge of French, you'll do fine. It doesn't hurt to pick up a few words of Arabic. Most of the Arabic I learned for Egypt was the same for Morocco.

The food is divine, but stick to the Moroccan-style restaurants for dinner. We had one Italian dinner in Marrakesh at a highly recommended restaurant and it was terrible. We had one French meal in the French restaurant at the hotel in Fez and it was boring. Our Moroccan meals were always wonderful. Individual restaurants will be discussed later. Rule Numero Uno: *never* but *never* drink the water! (No ice cubes.) Bottled water is available everywhere. Brush your teeth with it. I also wouldn't eat the lettuce or anything that couldn't be peeled. None of us got sick, but I know others who got violently ill. I won't go into detail about the various Moroccan dishes, except to say that one dish we really enjoyed, which we hadn't seen before, was a type of *tajine* (stew) with a sort of chili-tomato base, little meatballs, and eggs broken into the center of it at the last minute, which are cooked by the heat of the dish. You eat this with chunks of bread, scooping it all up with your fingers or on a fork. The dessert pastries, called gazelle horns, were also wonderful. *Bastilla* to die for. Mint tea is served everywhere and is delicious. Moroccan wines were served in all the restaurants but one, and weren't bad. Their omelets are delicious.

The most sumptuous meals in the most lavish restaurants were not expensive: about 24 dollars per person for dinner, 12 dollars for lunch, everything included. Dress in the restaurants was casual. Jackets and ties were never required anywhere, although men might feel comfortable with a sportscoat in many places. We always dressed very well for dinner, but other people were often quite casual.

The weather in Morocco could be compared to that of Southern California. A great variety of climates and temperatures. You can be skiing in the mountains above Marrakesh on one day and sitting on the beach in Agadir the next. In May the temperature ran from around 65 to 70 degrees in Casablanca, to the high seventies in Fez, lots of sun. Then in Marrakesh —cold, drizzly, foggy, and in the sixties, but then warming up with hazy sunshine to the midseventies. We never saw a desert. In order to get into the Sahara you have to go at least one day south of Marrakesh, or go to Agadir and start from there. We were always in flatlands, farmlands, rolling hills, or gorgeous mountains.

Take comfortable clothes. Unlike Egypt, you can run around in Morocco in sundresses and strappy tops without being glared at and stared at. The dress is very casual and quite Western, although the Moroccans, for the most part, wear traditional styles, and the women especially are robed and veiled. Be sure you have your most comfortable walking shoes, as the cobblestones and footpaths are not easy. Don't take any jumpsuits. They are totally nonconducive to a not-so-great bathroom situation in the country, or for shopping and trying on clothes in almost nonexistent dressing rooms.

A sweater or jacket of some kind is advisable for evenings and in the mountains. Skirts would be better for women than pants, just for convenience. A nice big purse with a strong handle which closes securely is a must. Take some collapsible suitcases to haul all your loot home. You might also want swimsuits. Many women were topless around the pool in Marrakesh. The Europeans, especially the French, run down to Marrakesh or Agadir for weekends.

As long as I brought up bathrooms—it's times like those that I wish I were a man. In the better hotels and restaurants there are no problems, but you will undoubtedly run into some situations where strong thigh muscles and a strong stomach come in handy. Take plenty of tissues, wash-and-dries, etc.

As for guidebooks, I read all of them, almost, and the best one seems to be *Fodor's North Africa*. Nagel wasn't too great and Frommer's is only for cheapie tours. The Michelin people have a green guide but it's in French. Our guide told us the *Guide Bleu* was also very good. Berlitz has a small pocket-sized book that is succinct and handy.

Take along your own pharmacy. We were advised to go on malaria pills, which we did, and two of us took Vibramycin the whole time. You will also want regular travel pharmacy stuff, like Band-Aids, antibacterial ointment, Kaopectate, etc.

Money. Take lots of money, plus your Visa and American Express cards. While the restaurants are cheap and the most beautiful rooms in the best hotels are only about 100 dollars a night, you will find lots to buy! The currency unit in Morocco is called a *dirham*. As soon as possible get your hands on *lots* of 1D coins, as you will need them to dispense constantly. The begging or *baksheesh*ing in Morocco doesn't come close to that in Egypt, but it still goes on. Sometimes people will come up to you with American coins and want you to trade them for Moroccan coins, as they can't use the American ones. If you have any francs you can use them too, since the French are all over Morocco.

Shopping

Ah, and now for the shopping! If you love to shop you will be ecstatic in Morocco. If you don't like to shop you will have a ball. If you don't think you want to buy any Moroccan rugs, you will buy some. The best shopping is in the *medinahs* (old Arab sections of town—very old! Twisty, windy, narrow streets, no cars, a maze that goes for miles with every conceivable type of shop and store and stand in the world. A feast for the eyes and all the senses. Don't try to go into the *medinahs* without a guide—you may never get out again.) Your guide will try to steer you to certain shops where he will get a kickback, but if you have a good guide, as we did, he will take you everywhere and not try to influence you to buy at any one place. Our guide showed us the best shops with the finest-quality merchandise, along with all the rest. The guides are not paid very well and part of their livelihood depends on this kickback agreement with the shopkeepers, who also depend on the guides to bring them business; so don't be angry or offended by it. It's part of their way of life. I only hope our guide got a big fat kickback, because he earned it with us.

Bargaining is the name of the game, and it is a serious game with lots of rules. The sooner you learn the ropes, the more fun you will have, and the better prices you will get. If you don't try to bargain for everything, they will think you are some kind of loony and you'll spoil their fun. Never pay the first price, ever! If they start off with 1000 dirhams, you counter with 250. They will laugh, throw up their arms, say it is impossible, carry on, etc. Then they will say to give them a better price. Then you carry on, say that's all you want to spend, say your friend bought the same thing yesterday in another store for less, etc., and you couldn't possibly pay more. So then they will say, "Give me 800." You shake your head and say, "Sorry," and start to walk away. They will say, "What is your last price?" You stop, consider, pace a little, turn the item over in your hand or look at it more thoroughly, cluck your tongue, consult your friends, and say, "Well, 280." They are aghast, say it is impossible, so you say thank you very much and walk out. Before you can get both feet out of the door they will have you by the hand, asking your absolute final offer. You say 300, they grab your hand, shake it vigorously, all smiles, and say sold! Everyone is happy. In one rug store the negotiations went on for about three hours over many cups of mint tea, and finally a delicious lunch in their sumptuous restaurant upstairs. We paid between 500 and 800 dollars for fabulous Moroccan rugs —big ones, antique killims and berbers. Opening prices were always 1500 to 2000 dollars. The price we paid included shipping and insurance, and they always took credit cards. Properly done, shopping for carpets is a ceremony not to be missed. As for other prices, for example, I bought a Moroccan dress for about 48 dollars; the opening price had been 190 dollars. I got fabulous ropy belts for 12 to 17 dollars each (they would be 80 to 100 dollars in the U.S.). *Jellabahs,* the long robes, can run from 10 dollars for cheap ones up to 50 dollars for custom-made ones with beautiful fabrics. Leather purses, all handmade, about 15 dollars each. Fabulous leather jackets, fully lined, about 60 dollars each. As for the jewelry, there isn't a lot of gold, but the antique silver stuff, the ethnic pieces, and semiprecious pieces will send you to jewelry heaven. You have to be careful, however, because a huge amount of it is fake or new. You'll see lots of amber—big chunky necklaces full of it—most of it plastic. You can get some beautiful things though, for good prices, and have a lot of fun in the process.

Don't worry too much about customs. Morocco is one of those special-status Third World countries with all kinds of trade agreements, and practically everything except clothing is considered an art or craft, or an antique.

The boutiques in the hotels are ridiculous. In one hotel shop I saw belts priced at 75 to 90 dollars which were not half as nice as the ones I'd bought in the *medinah* for about 17 dollars.

There are also *souks* in various places on certain days. These are temporary, one-day street-market affairs. If you are lucky enough to happen on one in the country, by all means stop. It's like taking a giant step backward in time, about 2000 years' worth. Be sure you see the meat market area; just hold your breath—it's unreal.

In all the markets, *medinahs, souks,* and squares you will see colorfully dressed water peddlers. They make for a nice picture, but don't drink the water!

As for the begging that goes on—well, it could be worse. The government frowns on giving money to kids, so go armed with such things as ballpoint pens, hard candies, lipsticks and nail polish for the girls (a good way to get rid of your old ones), earrings (ditto), and Polaroid pictures. You can have a lot of fun with a Polaroid camera, but be careful that you don't take pictures of large groups. A major fight will break out as to who gets the picture. Try to stick to one or two kids at a time, if possible. The adults often like a Polaroid of themselves, too. On the other hand, many people will get very upset if you take their picture; so if they start to object, don't do it. Others are happy to be part of your photo album, if you give them a few coins for their trouble. Take plenty of film—it costs a fortune to buy it there. If you have some old clothes that you were going to get rid of, take them along, wear them, then give them away. You'll end up with more room in your suitcase to bring home purchases.

You'll need to read through a couple of guidebooks and magazine articles to decide which places you want to see. If you have a good guide, he will make sure you don't miss a thing.

We didn't go to Tangiers and only saw the airport in Casablanca. We were told by everyone that Casa is not worth the effort to see, and that Tangiers is a real nightmare. Seeing is believing, however.

Rabat

The three main hotels in Rabat are the **Tour Hassan, Sofitel,** and **Hilton.** We stayed at the **Tour Hassan,** which our guide agreed was the best of the three. It was a beautiful hotel, but we had semitacky rooms. We were only there for one night so we didn't make a fuss, but if you are planning to stay longer, insist on good rooms. They have a lot of cats at the hotel and all over Morocco, for that matter, and the yowling and fighting kept us awake most of the night.

The Moroccan-style restaurant at the Tour Hassan was wonderful. The best *bastilla* I had on the whole trip.

Sightseeing Don't miss the **Chellah,** a necropolis outside the walls with ruins and storks. Also see the **Royal Palace (Mechouar), Tomb of Mohammed V,** the *Kasbah,* where you can have mint tea in a little café overlooking the whole bay; then stop in a *rug-making school* and watch them make rugs. The *medinah* doesn't hold a candle to the *medinahs* in Fez and Marrakesh, but it is still interesting and a short walk. Take in the **Ancient Gates** and **Ramparts.** There is a fine *museum* there which contains antiquities from the Roman period.

Motoring from Rabat to Meknes takes a couple of hours, and it is a very pretty drive. We were lucky enough to happen upon a *souk* on the way.

Meknes

In Meknes you should see the ruins of the **Imperial City of Moulay Ismail,** the stables, granaries, harem, reservoir, and gardens. The harem area is now a golf course (bathrooms in the clubhouse). Also see the *tomb of Moulay Ismail,* the *monumental gates* around the city, the old walls and ramparts, the *Dar Jamai Palace* and *museum.*

Volubilis

About a half-hour drive from Meknes through beautiful countryside is Volubilis, not to be missed! This is the site of the finest Roman ruins in North Africa. It's a big Roman city in ruins, spread out on a hillside overlooking a spectacular valley, with many gorgeous mosaic floors, entire streets almost intact, part of the basilica, etc. It's like a poor man's version of Pompeii, in Morocco. There's a little restaurant at the entrance which doesn't always serve food, but always drinks. We took a sumptuous picnic lunch, brought from Paris, and paid the proprietor a few coins to let us sit at his tables in a lovely garden with the ruins in the background. You could pick up picnic items in Meknes and do the same. There's also a tolerable bathroom there and a small postcard stand. You'll need about one and a half hours to see Volubilis entirely. Take your camera for sure.

Moulay Idriss

Moulay Idriss is a stone's throw from Volubilis and is extremely picturesque. It is the fourth most holy city of the Moslem world, the site where the patron saint of Morocco is buried. Until recently it was out of bounds for non-Moslems. It is very interesting to walk through the little city.

From Moulay Idriss and Volubilis to Fez is about another hour.

Fez

Fez is an absolutely beautiful city, almost equal to Marrakesh. Some people prefer Fez. We stayed at the gorgeous *Palais Jamai* and had beautiful rooms and service.

Restaurants. We ate in the French- or continental-style restaurant at the hotel and found it to be very boring. It's a shame, too, because there are many wonderful restaurants in Fez.

Dar Mnehbi.
Also recommended. We were supposed to eat there but didn't because of an accidental double booking. The owner came running over to our hotel to find out what we wanted to eat, so that he could go out and start cooking. Other books say it is good.

Dar Saada.
We did not eat here either, but our guide kept insisting it was excellent, one of the best. (Our guide was never wrong.)

L'Anmbra.
Another palace-Moroccan-style restaurant, about a fifteen-minute drive from the Palais Jamai. The food here was good, with the added attraction of a small antique shop in the back, where we managed to spend a few bucks. The items we bought there were of very good quality and ended up being some of our favorite purchases. The *bastilla* here I do not recommend because it was full of bones!

Palais de Fez.
This is a major carpet store with a beautiful little Moroccan-style restaurant upstairs. You can most enjoyably combine a lovely lunch with some heavy and satisfying carpet buying! They only serve lunch here.

Sightseeing and Shopping   *The medinah*—great shopping! As good as the one in Marrakesh. Excellent rug shops *(Palais de Fez)*. The *House of Caftans,* outside the *medinah* and by the Palais Jamai, has millions of caftans. I think you can get better prices and merchandise in Marrakesh, which had the best all-around shopping of any city.

See the many beautiful *gates (bab)*, the *medersas* (schools), *Fondouk Nejjarine* and *fountain,* the *tomb of Moulay Idriss,* the *Karaouine Mosque* (which you can't go into but can see into and walk around), the *tannery,* the view from the *Merinides Hotel.* The *new medinah* of Fez is not too exciting. Also see the *mellah* (old Jewish quarter), where there is a gold market, if you're interested.

NOTE: Friday is like Sunday here and everything closes at noon for the rest of the day, so do your sightseeing and shopping in the morning. On other days, after lunch many places are closed. So you go back to the hotel and sit around the pool and write postcards and take a bath.

About 3:00 A.M. on Friday, you will be rudely awakened by what sounds like someone being tortured and maimed. What is really happening is the *meuzzins* are calling the people to prayer (at 3:00 A.M.??!!), and they don't let up for an hour! You just have to lie there and take it. Not just one *meuzzin,* by the way, but about four of them get going at once. The hotel, alas, is situated up on a hill with a beautiful view, right in the middle of mosque land.

Driving from Fez to Marrakesh

We left the hotel in Fez at 7:15 A.M. and arrived at the hotel in Marrakesh about 6:00 P.M. We did not hurry or drive fast and made several stops along the way. The drive through the mountains was spectacular! For miles and miles and hour after hour we drove through lime-green grassy hills, forests, oceans of wildflowers in every color, little villages, and Swiss-looking towns. Along the way we stopped and went into a nomad tent, where an 86-year-old grandmother made us mint tea while we sat on her hand-woven rugs, looking out from under the flaps at a beautiful panorama. She also gave us the best bread we had on the whole trip—bread she made that morning in her extremely primitive "kitchen" (a corner of the tent). The closer the road gets to Marrakesh, the less exciting the scenery. In fact, after Beni Mellal, it's pretty boring.

Beni Mellal

This is a little town a bit more than halfway between Fez and Marrakesh, where we stopped for lunch at a hotel called *Chems* (pronounced *Shahms*). Not bad.

Marrakesh

Marrakesh! The images your mind conjures up at the sound of the word are all real. The romantic, exciting, exotic, pink city.

Hotels. The *Mamounia* is *the* place to stay in all of Morocco. I can't imagine staying anywhere else. It was sumptuous! The rooms were beautiful (ours was about 100 dollars a night, but there are less expensive rooms to be had). Beautiful gardens—be sure you walk in them at night. It's no surprise that this hotel has been world-famous for years.

Restaurants. The Moroccan restaurant at the *Mamounia* was splendid and the food was excellent. We were entertained throughout by a group of musicians and singers, ending with some belly dancing.

La Maison Arabe is also very famous and hard to get into. It's located in a beautiful home which is reached through a dark, sinister alley way in the *medinah*. A little French lady named Madame Suzy LaRochette Sebillon is the proprietress. She's from Paris and has been in Marrakesh for forty-three years. There are no menus. You are just served an absolutely perfect meal, as if you were a guest in her home, which, in fact, you are. Write ahead for reservations to La Maison Arabe, rue R'Mila, Derb Ferrane, Marrakesh. She closes from June to October.

Trattoria is a pretty Italian restaurant that was recommended to us. It was a disaster. Don't go. Pasta was OK but the rest wasn't. Well, the chocolate cake was pretty good, too.

La Taverne is closed and out of business.

Le Petit Poucet is a nice French/Moroccan place for lunch.

Bagatelle. Ditto Le Petit Poucet.

Sightseeing. The *medinah* and shopping in Marrakesh are the greatest. The main square, called *Djemaa-el-Fna,* is impossible to describe. You just have to go there, see it, hear it, feel it, try to believe it. Have coins handy to give to the people that you photograph. Hang on to your purse and your money. When you've had enough being *in* it, go to the rooftop of one of the surrounding hotels and watch it from above.

Don't miss the *Bahia Palace,* the old harem buildings, still in beautiful condition. Also go to the small but fine museum in the *Dar Si Said Palace.*

See the *Ben Youssef Medersa,* the *Koutoubia Tower,* the *dyers souk, Saadian Tombs,* the ruins of the *Al-Badi Palace,* the *mellah* (Jewish section), *Menara Pavillion* (only on a clear day). It's fun to ride the horse carriages for awhile, to see the town more slowly. You can also ride a camel if you want.

Police in Morocco. There are a lot of them. They love to stop cars on the highway and question you. They are all corrupt. If you start having any problems, and if niceness and diplomacy aren't working, ask them if they want to see a "picture of Hassan." Then slip them some dirhams.

Dope. Some members of our group acquired some hashish, or the equivalent thereof. No big deal. Just made them sleepy. Don't get caught.

UA's in Morocco seem to abound. Don't get near them. The Moroccans seem to like Americans very much, but a bad UA can spoil things for everyone.

Go now! In a recent article in *International Living* I read that the least safe countries to invest in right now are Iran, Morocco, Pakistan, Peru, and Turkey. Political stability was used as the criterion for safety. An American we met in the airport at Casa, who travels and trades on a regular basis in Morocco, said there's going to be trouble there. At no time during the week we were in Morocco did we feel any danger or apprehension. It was almost the opposite, actually. But we did feel an underlying, unspoken tension, unrest. It doesn't show on the surface, but it's there. Go to Morocco before it's too late. We rate our trip there as a 10 on a scale of 10; and hopefully you will be able to do the same.

Mexico

Mexico City

Mexico City is one of the great cities of the world. It is the most populated city in the world at this time and the population is expected to reach thirty million by the year 2000—almost incomprehensible. Mexico City is congested and noisy. The air pollution there is the worst I've ever seen. There is no place to park. Driving anywhere is not easy. The main streets are clean and well maintained, but the side streets are often unpaved and very dirty.

So why go to Mexico City? It's fun. Exciting. The architecture of the buildings is both interesting and diverse. The people are usually gracious and charming. Shopping is good. Restaurants are great. History, antiquities, museums abound. And it's close to the U.S. It is sometimes referred to as the Poor Man's Paris or Europe West; I would not go so far as to agree with either term. However, once you are there, you really do feel as if you have gone to a foreign country, and a trip there can in no way be compared to going to any of the little towns in Baja.

¿Sé habla español? No matter how bad you think your Spanish is or even if everyone is speaking English to you, speak Spanish. They *love* it.

Weather

Toward the middle of May is the beginning of the rainy season in Mexico City and it is rather tropical. It is warm, part of the day is sunny, but by the afternoon you can almost count on it to cloud up and rain, along with some thunder and lightning. If it rains, it will probably be a short shower and be over within a matter of minutes. Ditto for downpours.

Evenings are warmish, but a light sweater is advisable. Take an umbrella. The rainy season usually lasts throughout the summer.

Hotels

Where do you stay in D.F. (another name for the city, just as D.C. is for Washington)? There are two excellent hotels that I can recommend.

The *Camino Real* is located in Chapultepec Park. It is a bit too far to walk to the Zona Rosa, but great for walking or running in the park. It is an enormous hotel, very nice, and it never seems crowded. There are three pools and several restaurants. (Fouquet's is quite good.)

The *Maria Isabel Sheraton* is near the American Embassy and across the boulevard from the Zona Rosa. It is more centrally located, but it is also noisier and more crowded. Nevertheless, it is a good choice.

There is an interesting-looking hotel in the Zona Rosa called the *Geneva* which is supposed to be good. If you stayed there you would have to be sure to get a room off the street *and* away from the nightclub, or you would never get any sleep. The same is true for the other good hotel in the area, the *El Presidente*.

Restaurants

One of the biggest dilemmas when going to Mexico City is deciding where to eat. The choice of restaurants is unending and it seems that they are all good. Reservations are advised in most cases, lunches included. Perhaps I should clarify the term "lunch," used here in a broad sense. Lunch consists of cocktails, hors d'oeuvre, a couple of bottles of wine, a first course, entrée, dessert, and coffee. This usually occurs around 2:00 P.M., or later if you are Mexican. We usually went for lunch around 1:00 P.M. due to our activities. Around 9:00 P.M. you repeat the whole thing for supper. After three or four days of eating like this you wonder if you can go on; if you don't, you'll be sorry when you get home, because then it will be too late. Besides, you'll probably walk off the calories.

Les Ambassadeurs,   12 Reforma, phone 566–94–00.
This has been and continues to be one of our favorites. Elegant restaurant, continental menu, good service, medium prices. Dressy for dinner.
Anderson's,   Reforma 400.
Very popular, always lots of activity, serving regional specialties with interesting atmosphere.
Bellinghausen,   Londres 95, Zona Rosa, phone 511–10–56.
The "find" of our last trip. Eat outside on the patio, as the inside gets hot, noisy, and crowded. They don't take reservations, but if you get there by 1:00 or 1:30 P.M. you won't have trouble getting a table. The sangria there was too sweet.

They serve unusual Mexican regional dishes, if you're brave enough to try them (like fried blood and fried caterpillars!). It's very popular with the Mexicans and the day we were there we seemed to be the only Americans. Open for lunch and dinner.

Las Cazuelas, avenida San Antonio 143 E., phone 522–06–89.

Serves all kinds of delicious Mexican casserole-type dishes. Very popular with locals and you probably won't see another tourist. Open every day until midnight. Good for lunch.

Champs-Elysées, located at the corner of the Reforma and Amberes, almost across the street from the Maria Isabel Sheraton Hotel, phone 514–64–64.

Very good French cuisine.

Los Comerciales, Insurgentes Sur 2383, phone 550–69–00 and Circuito Ingenieros 39 in the Ciudad Satélite, phone 572–33–23.

A wild and crazy place with good service and food; a lot of fun.

Del Lago, Chapultepec Park, phone 515–95–85.

Timing is important if you go here. In the evening, especially on Saturday nights, don't go before 9:00 or 9:30; if you do, you come face to face with tour buses full of senior citizens. After they go home and go to bed, however, a "younger" crowd shows up. For lunch we didn't have this problem. It's actually the kind of restaurant where you can enjoy both lunch and dinner and have different experiences. During lunch you have a lovely view of the park and fountains; at night the fountains are lit and do "tricks." The food is excellent, as is the service. Reservations and ties for men are essential. The restaurant is located at the far end of Chapultepec Park and is quite a drive (don't expect to walk there), but on the way you can see the presidential quarters and other interesting sights. Expensive.

Delmonico's, Londres 87, Zona Rosa, phone 514–70–03.

Very good food. Large, spacious restaurant. Try their Aztec soup, salmon, and abalone.

Focolare, Hamburgo 87, phone 511–26–79.

A big favorite for years. Italianish. Violins or duo pianos, candlelight, plenty of romance and atmosphere.

Fonda del Recuerdo, Bahía de las Palmas 39, phone 545–72–60.

Claimed by some to have the best Mexican food in the city, Veracruz style.

Fonda del Refugio, Liverpool 166, Zona Rosa, phone 528–58–23.

For good Mexican food.

Fouquet's, at the Camino Real hotel, Mariano Escobedo 700, phone 545–69–60.

Serves excellent French food.

Hacienda De Los Morales, Vazquez De Mella No. 525, Colonia Chapultepec Morales, phone 540–32–25.

This is another hacienda like the San Angel Inn, but located in the city. It's a beautiful place with wonderful food and service. Again, don't go for dinner before 9:00 or 9:30 P.M.

Lincoln Hotel Grill, Revillagigedo 24 near Alameda Park, behind Hotel del Prado, phone 533-13-06.

A big favorite with locals; seafood, Mexican dishes, steaks. There is a newer branch in the Zona Rosa at Amberes 64; however, the former is supposed to have all the atmosphere.

Loredo, Hamburgo 29.

Specializes in seafood and Mexican dishes. Try the Carne Asada a la Tampiquena, one of the house inventions.

Majestic Hotel, Plaza de la Constitución.

Rooftop restaurant, overlooking the Zócalo. This is a good place for lunch, as you get a great view of the square. Good Aztec soup; sometimes a piano player.

Maxim's, in Hotel El Presidente Chapultepec, phone 254-00-33.

Takes after the one in Paris; a beautiful restaurant serving excellent French food; expensive.

Mesón del Perro Andaluz, Copenhague 26, Zona Rosa, phone 533-53-06.

Spanish-style food; very popular; sidewalk café.

Les Moustaches, Río Sena 88, phone 533-33-90.

French and continental dishes. The building is a renovated old home. Dress up. Entertainment.

Passy, Amberes 10, Zona Rosa.

A couple of years ago it was very good and one of our favorite places. Last time the quality had definitely slipped. It could still be good for lunch.

Prendes, 16 de Septiembre 10, phone 585-41-99.

Owned by the same people who own Bellinghausen. Seafood; good service, atmosphere. Popular with locals.

Rafaello, Londres 165, Zona Rosa.

The best Italian food in the city.

San Angel Inn, Palmas 50, San Angel, phone 548-67-46.

I think this is everyone's favorite. You shouldn't miss it. You have to take a car about thirty or forty minutes from downtown. If it's nice weather, eat out on the veranda. Saturday afternoons are the best time to go, around 2:00. Their margaritas are the best. Before lunch go to the Saturday Bazaar (mentioned later) and shop in the area. After lunch you aren't too far from the university and Xochimilco; the latter must be seen on a Sunday. Also nearby is the Frida Kahlo Museum, in Diego Rivera's house. You can stop at the Anthropological Museum or the Polyforum on the way back to your hotel.

What's Good To Eat?

Aztec soup, for starters. This is a corn and tortilla soup made in a variety of ways with many types of stocks and additions. No two places make it the same way. It's always good.

Margaritas here are different than the backyard barbecue kind we make at home. They can really hit you if you're not careful.

Mexican wines. The wines made in the country are often very good, and most are not exported. We especially liked some of the dry whites. Imported wine can be very expensive!

Holanda ice cream is pretty good.

Tortilla chips are called "totopos."

French cuisine in the better French restaurants is excellent.

Dressing in D.F.

Mexico City is a "dressy" city, like San Francisco used to be. Rarely do you see women in the better parts of town wearing jeans (the ones in jeans are usually tourists). It's too humid to wear jeans there, anyway.

They don't even wear slacks as much as dresses and skirts. Pants outfits —nice ones—are perfectly acceptable. In most good restaurants you would probably feel more comfortable in a dress, especially for dinner. The Mexicans get very dressed up to go to restaurants at night. The men are usually wearing ties and the women are wearing something very chic.

Sightseeing

The best way to see any city is to walk, so get out your good walking shoes and go prepared. However, Mexico City is very large and spread out, so you won't be able to walk everywhere without taking a cab from one place to another at times. The subway system there is dangerous and overcrowded and not recommended. It may be worth your while to hire a car and driver while you are there.

Museums

Academy of San Carlos, in the Buena Vista Palace at Puente de Alvarado 50.

An eighteenth-century architecture palace houses Mexico's collection of western European art, from the Renaissance on up (El Greco, VanDyke, Brueghel, etc.).

The Anahuacalli, located on Calle del Museo.

Built by Diego Rivera and dedicated to pre-Columbian art and artifacts. The museum, which is sort of a stone temple, also contains a re-creation of Rivera's workshop.

El Carmen Museum, avenida Revolución.

Located in a restored seventeenth-century convent, it has been compared to the Cloisters in New York City. Among other things the museum displays a number of mummies of priests and nuns. A macabre sight indeed (something kids would love, I'm sure!). Near San Angel Inn.

Chapultepec Castle and National Museum of History.

Located farther into the park in the Castillo, this belonged to the Emperor Maximilian and his wife, Carlota. Not only is the museum full of period rooms, murals, decorative arts, coaches, and carriages, it also affords a great view of the city.

Ethnographic Museum, at Guatemala and Seminario Streets.
Scale models of the ancient city, plus wax figures, costumes, etc.

Frida Kahlo Museum, Londres 247 at the corner of Allende in Coyoacán area (near San Angel Inn), located in Diego Rivera's (her husband's) home.
Exhibits are of both his and her works.

The Gil.
A museum near San Angel with Rivera cubist works, plus works by Orozco and Siqueiros.

Mexico City Museum, 30 Piño Suárez at the corner of Salvador.
A museum all about the history of the city itself, in a lovely eighteenth-century house.

Museum of Modern Art.
Yet another museum located in Chapultepec Park. The museum displays some Mexican classical painters but is mostly full of modern and contemporary works, with some temporary exhibits.

The National Arts Museum, avenida Juárez 44, opposite Alameda Park.
Just opened about two years ago in the palace of Porfirio Díaz; an architectural masterpiece (the palace, not Díaz).

National Museum of Anthropology, Chapultepec Park.
This is one of the most famous museums in the world, and probably the best one in all of Mexico. It's absolutely wonderful! I suggest taking the one-hour guided tour at first (English-speaking guide) to familiarize yourself with the museum. Then go back on your own and concentrate on what interests you. When we were there this tour began at 3:45 P.M., but arrive earlier to get a ticket. The hours may have changed. To do the museum justice would take a couple of days. In three hours you can do a run-through. Don't forget there's an entire second floor.

Palace of Fine Arts, on avenida Juárez across from Alameda Park.
This marvelous Art Deco building opened in 1934 and is the place you go to see the Ballet Folklórico. It's also an art museum with murals by Mexico's great masters, including Rivera's *Man Controlling the Universe.*

The Rufino Tamayo Museum, located in Chapultepec Park.
This contains not only Tamayo's works but the works of other outstanding artists. The wonderful restaurant Del Lago is nearby. Also in the park is the *zoo,* which, as you probably know, is where Mexico's pair of pandas live.

Siqueiros Polyforum, Insurgentes Sur and the corner of Filadelfia.
Another architecturally interesting structure, designed by the artist Siqueiros. Inside and upstairs is his masterpiece mural, said to be the largest in the world. There is a sound and light show for it, but only in Spanish, and every time we go it's at a different hour. Even if you don't speak Spanish, it's worthwhile. In the main level is an art gallery with good temporary exhibits, and on the lower

level is a really good museum shop—one of the best I've seen, for both quality and prices.

Acolman Monastery. on the way to Teotihuacán, also called St. Agostino.

Portions of the building date from Conquest times; other parts are Renaissance and Plateresque. Hopefully you'll be able to get beyond the entrance and inside, as there are some interesting murals in the cloister.

Avenida Juárez from the Reforma to the Zócalo.

A very interesting, long avenue to walk on. You'll pass many office buildings, hotels, shops, wonderful buildings, the Palace of Fine Arts, the *Iturbide Palace,* and *Alameda Park.* For more details about this area, see the next section, "What to Do on a Sunday." Across from Alameda Park in the lobby of the *Del Prado* hotel is a mural by Rivera.

Ballet Folklórico.

An extremely entertaining and "up" way to spend a couple of hours. You will never see so many beautiful young dancers expending such an enormous amount of energy all at once. It's worth it to go just to see the Palace of Fine Arts— a magnificent Deco structure with both the ceiling and the curtain on the stage by Tiffany. The ballet is only on Sunday mornings and Wednesday evenings. You can get tickets through your hotel, and sometimes the hotel will even arrange transportation.

Basilica of Our Lady of Guadalupe.

One of Mexico's most revered shrines, located on the Plaza of the Americas on Insurgentes Norte. There are two buildings, one old and one new. You definitely should not miss the *Capilla de la Pocita,* the single best example of baroque architecture in Mexico.

Bullfights.

The largest bullring in the world is in Mexico City at the *Plaza Mexico.* The bullfights are held Sundays at 4:00 P.M. You may want to arrange for a car and driver to take you there and back, as getting a cab is difficult anywhere in the city on a Sunday, but most especially after the bullfights.

The Cathedral of Mexico, in the Zócalo.

Combines Renaissance, baroque, and neoclassic architecture on the facade with an elaborate interior of many side altars and two main ones. All very baroque and ornate. Be sure you go inside and walk around.

Chapultepec Park.

Huge—you couldn't possibly walk entirely through it. Besides containing at least four museums, described earlier, it also has the zoo and the Castillo. If you go for a Sunday afternoon you'll swear that 99 percent of the entire population is there, and you could be right. There are restaurants in the park, equestrian trails, jogging trails, etc.

Cuicuilco.

Located about twelve miles from the city, this is said to be the oldest man-made structure in the Western hemisphere, constructed about four thousand years ago.

It's a conical-shaped pyramid with a succession of altars built one on top of the other. The entire area was covered by a lava flow sometime before the birth of Christ.

Fronton.

The Plaza de la República is where you'll find this, the jai alai arena. If you've never been to a jai alai game before you'll really find this interesting. It's a fast, exciting sport and the betting is a lot of fun. I don't know how legit the playing is, however.

The National Palace.

Built from stones from Montezuma's capital and temples. It looks as if you can't go in, but you can—just walk on past the guards. You don't want to fail to do this, because inside on the second level are Diego Rivera's masterpiece murals depicting the history of Mexico. There are guides around who will tell you what you're looking at and explain some of the details; it's worth it to pay them whatever they want.

Behind the National Palace.

If you wander through these streets, many of which are in disrepair or are being restored, you'll be in one of the oldest parts of Mexico. You'll see very old colonial buildings and parts of Tenochtitlán, the name for Mexico City before the Conquest.

The National Pawn Shop.

Another very old building on the square full of all sorts of goodies.

Plaza of the Three Cultures (Tlatelolco), off Insurgentes Norte.

A large square where architectural remains of pre-Conquest Mexico and Spanish colonial structures sit together with modern buildings, representing all periods of Mexico City history.

The Sagrario.

The church next to the cathedral, and at first glance it looks like it's all the same building. The Sagrario, however, is architecturally completely different, being more ultra-baroque.

San Angel and Coyoacán.

Described earlier in both the restaurant and the museum sections. This is a lovely area of the city with many large, elegant homes and mansions. The restaurant at San Angel should not be missed. The Saturday bazaar is a lot of fun. The nearby museum, plus the proximity of the university, will make it a whole day's outing. You should have a guide and driver to show you around.

Supreme Court buildings.

Inside are some large Orozco murals. Most of Orozco's works are in Guadalajara, however.

Temple Mayor Excavations.

As you face the cathedral you'll see a street leading off to the right. Go down that street about a block, and on the right you'll see the newest and largest of the excavations to be done in the city. Recently they have allowed people to go in and see them up close; however, I don't know all the details about that, as we were unable to do this when we were there. If you know anything about the pre-Conquest history of Mexico, you will find this enormously exciting.

Tenayuca.

An archaeological zone located in Puebla and not far from Mexico City, with good examples of Aztec architecture of the Chichimecan culture.

Teotihuacán.

This is the name of the pyramids located about thirty miles from the city. It takes you about two hours to get there, believe it or not. You should get a driver and/or guide to take you, as there is much to see and learn. Don't miss it! Be sure you see the Temple of the Warriors, down a dirt road and in the backyard of some farms. You should also not miss Quetzalcoatl's Temple of the Jaguars, located behind and beyond the museum. There is a good restaurant over the museum where you can go for lunch. If you hurry you can see Teotihuacán in a half day. If you take your time you can see it even better, plus take in a few things on the way, such as the monastery listed below, some markets, etc. There is also a sound and light show at the pyramids; check with your guide or hotel as to the time.

Tepozotlan.

About twenty-six miles from the city featuring possibly the most ornate ex-church you'll see all week, the *Virreynato.* It's high baroque and churrigueresque, the interior is mind-boggling, and there's a museum in the basement. Closed Mondays.

Toluca.

The principal city of the state of Puebla, located forty-six miles west of Mexico City. On Fridays they have a big market, which is quite famous and very popular. For dining, try *La Cabana Suiza* or *Nautilus.*

Xochimilco.

All that remains of the vast lake and canal system that used to *be* Mexico City back in Aztec times. Some will tell you it's a waste of time, tacky, a tourist thing, etc. Well, maybe it's partly that. It's a lot of fun. Go there on Sunday afternoon after lunch, hire a boat, and cruise along through the canals. Musicians come by, people sing. Entire families of Mexicans are having an elaborate picnic on the next boat. People are selling flowers and things to eat (don't eat!). You'll have a great time. Back at the docks there's an open-air market where we got great buys on baskets and clothes.

The Zócalo.

The large, main square in the old section of town. You must not miss this. It's also called Plaza de la Constitución. There you will find the *Cathedral,* the *Sagrario* (church next door to the cathedral), the *National Palace,* the most recent excavations of the former *Aztec city,* and many old and interesting buildings. Many of these buildings were built with stones taken from the temples torn down by the Spanish. Don't fail to go into both churches and into the National Palace, described below.

Zona Rosa.

Sort of the Beverly Hills of Mexico City. There you will find the chic shops, good restaurants, charming walk streets, and lots of activity. It's very noisy at night, so if you want to stay in one of the hotels there, be aware. It's very busy at all times of the day and, of course, quite touristy.

What to Do on a Sunday

Get up early and go to the 9:30 A.M. performance of the Ballet Folklórico at the Palace of Fine Arts. Don't believe anyone who tells you it's impossible to get tickets (it usually means you'll have to pay more to get them). We've never been when there haven't been lots of empty seats. If necessary, go to the ticket window yourself. Get to the theater by 9:15. The show is over around 11:30.

Exit the theater, turn to the left, and walk down the avenida Cinco de Mayo. Cross the street and about a half block down is Sanborn's House of Tiles. Go in and look in the main dining room. You can shop a little in the gift shop if you want, but then go back out the way you came in and continue on Cinco de Mayo toward the Zócalo. Cross the street, and on the corner is the Bar Opera, with a charming, ornate interior that deserves a look-see. Also see the Iturbide Palace on avenida Madero, an eighteenth-century building of baroque/Renaissance/Mexican architecture.

When you get to the Zócalo, go into the main cathedral. Walk around and look at all the chapels and altars; listen to part of the service, if you want. Then go outside and next door and into the other church, which is not connected but looks as if it is. The interior will be vastly different from the cathedral. (The second church is called the Sagrario.) Now go back into the square, go to the corner, turn left, walk about two blocks, and on the right you will see the new excavations where they are uncovering an Aztec temple, the Temple Mayor. It's very interesting, and if you return on a weekday you can watch them working. Parts of the excavation are now open to the public.

Go back to the square and go into the National Palace—a large, formal-looking building on your left with guards at the entrance. It looks as if you can't go in, but you can. See if you can get an English-speaking guide to explain the Rivera murals on the second level. Go see them anyway, with or without a guide. Leave the National Palace the way you came in and walk to the far end of the square, so you can get a longshot view of the cathedral and church (see how they sag?). Exit the square by walking up avenida 16 de Septiembre. About two doors off the square is the Gran Hotel—go inside and look at the lobby; look up. Continue on avenida 16 de Septiembre to San Juan de Letran. Turn right and walk back to the Palace of Fine Arts, where you saw the ballet. You can probably get a cab here or across the street at Alameda Park. If worse comes to worst, walk up Juárez to the hotels on the street and try to get a cab at one of them.

Take the cab (if you get one) to the Zona Rosa and arrive at the Bellinghausen restaurant around 1:00 P.M. Get a nice table out on the patio and enjoy lunch. No reservations taken.

After lunch do one of the following: walk around Chapultepec Park, taking in a museum or the zoo; go out to Xochimilco (arrive no later than 4:00 P.M. if possible); or go to the bullfights, if there are any. Depending on how you spend the evening, this will be a very full day.

Other Guidebooks

I want you to have some other books along with you when you go to Mexico City. One of the best books I've used can be bought in Mexico at most hotel bookstalls. It's called *Travelers Guide to Mexico* and costs about 12 dollars, depending on the peso. It's quite complete and you'll use it a lot. Another good book for easy reference is called *Guide to the Best of Everything in Mexico City,* by Rudi Robins. You can supposedly get this book by writing to Ammex Asociados, S.A., Lago Silverio No. 224, Mexico 17, D.F. Write in advance, however, and find out how much it is. (I bought mine while there.) You should also have a map of the city, which you can pick up when you get there from a bookstore or a street vendor.

As for art, history, and culture, please-please-please know something about them before you go. The history of Mexico is one of the most fascinating and heartbreaking you'll ever learn. Their art from pre-Conquest times to the present is diverse and extremely interesting. You will appreciate and understand this wonderful country so much more if you have even a vague idea of what the people have gone through, throughout the ages. Two very good novels you could read in advance are *Aztec,* by Gary Jennings, and *The Luck of Huemac,* by Daniel Peters. Although they are novels, they are based on historical fact and you will find them spellbinding in many ways.

Shopping

Shopping in Mexico City—or anywhere in Mexico, for that matter —is always a lot of fun. The peso has been fluctuating and devaluating so much in the past two years that it's impossible to quote any prices right now. Things that cost 25 dollars two years ago now cost anywhere from 8 to 14 dollars. Bargaining is definitely acceptable in many cases, such as at street stands and stalls, markets, and in some privately owned shops. Some shopkeepers will not bargain with you no matter what, and you can certainly respect that. The large department stores and government stores will also not bargain. If you buy something at a market or stand, you can save a lot because they won't charge you sales tax, which is something like 10 percent. Compare prices and shop around a little before you buy such items as jewelry or clothing. It helps to know what's available and for how much. Be careful when buying silver—make sure it's of a high quality. There's a lot of junk on the silver market there. On the other hand, for silver jewelry you won't beat the quality or the prices in Mexico, if you are clever and careful.

Prices in hotel shops are usually 25 to 40 percent higher than elsewhere, for the same merchandise.

If a hired guide takes you to a particular shop, undoubtedly he's getting a kickback. Don't feel pressured to buy if you don't want to, and remember, you're probably paying a higher price because of this kickback.

The *Zona Rosa,* as I mentioned before, is where you'll find all the most chic boutiques. Many of them sell knock-offs of European names and merchandise, so be careful. You may not really be buying what you think you're buying. That doesn't mean, though, that the article won't be of high quality and worth the money. This is particularly true when it comes to shoes. The leatherwork and shoes in Mexico are, in many cases, top quality, and they are great buys. I've picked up some great all-leather shoes for about 15 dollars, but not in the *Zona Rosa.*

The *flea market,* on Sundays only, is a lot of fun. It's quite large and very crowded, so watch your wallet and purse. After the first two or three aisles it gets to be a bit repetitious, but I think it's worth going for an hour or so, if you like that sort of thing.

Already mentioned is the *Saturday bazaar* and a flea market at Plaza San Jacinto in the San Angel neighborhood. The bazaar features very high-quality Mexican arts and crafts with prices to match, but it's a good one to go to. Some great jewelry. Just outside the bazaar building and to the rear you'll see a local open-air market selling all sorts of Mexican things. Across the street from that, in a lovely old building, are a couple of fabulous gift and antique shops. Out in the square will be paintings done by local artists. Naturally, when you are through with all of this, you will go for a wonderful lunch at the San Angel Inn, where you have made reservations for about 2:00.

The best shops for buying really good Mexican arts and crafts are the shop in the basement of the *Polyforum Siqueiros* and a shop called *Museo Nactional de Artes e Industrias Populares,* avenida Juárez 44. Good shopping with the locals is along *avenida Juárez* and the streets near the Zócalo.

Fonart is the name given to smaller government price-controlled stores in various locations around the city. There is one on avenida Juárez across from Alameda Park.

The *Mercado Central* is up off the New Reforma and is the largest government-controlled market in the city. If you are looking for the standard Mexican-type arts and crafts, jewelry, clothing, leather, etc., this is probably the best place to buy them, as the prices are fixed by the government and supposedly fair. One advantage is that the place is enormous and you can get everything under one roof. Prices were about the same as we got after bargaining with street vendors. One disadvantage here, and in many stores, is that you have to pay a 10 percent sales tax, which you do not have to pay to street vendors. The types of items you find at this market can be found everywhere in the city for various prices and qualities.

Sanborn's is a chain of drugstore/department stores with good prices and good gift items, if you get stuck at the last minute.

Tane is considered to be the best place to buy silver, for quality. It's also the most expensive; but some of their pieces are works of art.

The *Travelers Guide to Mexico,* mentioned earlier, has a very good section on specific shops.

Remember, you have to go through customs when you get back home.

If you buy some large baskets that you think you will carry home with you on the plane, you'll be in for a surprise when you get to the gate and they take them away from you. They stow them somewhere on the plane and you get them back when you pick up your luggage at home. So far we've never lost one, but I wouldn't pack breakable items inside them.

Getting the Revenge on the Revenge

So much has been written about getting the Aztec Two-Step, or Montezuma's Revenge, or whatever you want to call it, that I hate even to bring it up. However, few are the people I know who return from anywhere in Mexico untouched. I must admit that conditions seem to have improved over the last couple of years, but then I've got a system now, so maybe it all is working together. Here is my system for avoiding "it":

1. Wash your hands with soap as often as possible, especially before eating.

2. Don't put your hands in your mouth or up your nose.

3. Take two Pepto-Bismol tablets before each meal; if that's too much, take a couple at night and a couple in the morning.

4. Don't drink anything except bottled water; this means no ice cubes, which you probably won't be able to avoid.

5. Don't eat anything that cannot be peeled. Lettuce is OUT. Tomatoes are questionable. You'll have to go by the quality of the restaurant you're in, and how brave you are.

6. If you are really worried, get a prescription from your doctor for

Vibramycin or something similar. Start taking it two days before your trip and take one pill a day while you're there. Recently there's been talk about the medication's side effects and that maybe it's not such a good idea after all, but I can swear that it has saved me more than once (not only in Mexico, but in North Africa). There are side effects, such as yeast infection and sensitivity to sun.

7. Take along some Donagel, Kaopectate, or a similar prescription.

I know several people who are afraid to travel in Mexico; most of their fears are based on what they read in newspapers or hear from someone else. I've traveled often in Mexico and I can only say my experiences, without exception, have been wonderful. I feel no less comfortable there than in any other country. Mexico has its problems, which could get worse before they get better, and common sense along with ordinary travel precautions is necessary. I, for one, can't wait to go back.

The Yucatan

The Yucatán is a large and fascinating area in Mexico about which I can impart a few tips.

Take your passport. Bug spray. Camera. Flashlight (for some ruins). Electric current and outlets are the same there as here. Take tissues! Take your time.

The weather in November in the interior was perfect—warm and breezy. Without the breeze it would have been uncomfortably hot and very humid. I hear that when it rains there, it *rains*—so always take an umbrella. The bug situation wasn't too bad, although we did have a few exemplary mosquitos. Take some bug repellent and something for the bites you do get. As for poisonous snakes and spiders—didn't see any of the critters, but they're there. We did see a vulture, but no jaguars.

The origin of the name Yucatán is a bit strange. When the Spanish arrived in the area back in the early sixteenth century, they approached the natives on shore and in Spanish asked them the name of the area. The Mayans, of course knowing no Spanish, responded in Mayan with something like "Yeceten," which meant, "We don't understand you." The Spanish— you guessed it—believed that was the name of the territory.

Getting to the Yucatán isn't all that difficult. You have to fly one of the Mexican airlines, and it's a good idea to pack a nice lunch, as the food on board is inedible. No liquor served on any of our flights, except beer.

Cancún

("Pot of Gold" in Mayan)

The drive from Chichén Itzá to Cancún will take you almost three hours, and it's the longest, straightest road you'll ever ride. I think it turned twice. There's not much to see, except a few more Mayan villages and some great Spanish colonial churches, especially in Valladolid—a cathedral and a church. If you leave Chichén after lunch, you'll get to Cancún in time to see the sun go down into that turquoise Caribbean.

Hotels   One hotel I can definitely *not* recommend at Cancún is the *Fiesta Americana.* When we arrived there, exhausted from our trip, they didn't have one room left. We had booked about three months in advance *and* had sent deposits *and* had our vouchers with us *and* our travel agent had reconfirmed by phone two days prior to our arrival *and* they still gave away our four rooms. However, they were able to call around and get us into another hotel about a half mile away called the *Krystal,* which was very nice. Half the hotels in Cancún face the Caribbean and the rest face the Gulf of Mexico. The Gulf-facing hotels seemed to have calmer beaches and probably better chances to snorkel. The water everywhere is that incredible turquoise blue, and very warm.

Almost all the hotels were built about the same time and probably there won't be a major difference between any of them. New hotels are going up for as far as you can see. A friend of mine stayed at the *Sheraton* there and said it was really terrible.

Weather   Our weather in November was iffy. We were getting the tail-end of a tornado that was somewhere else, so there was a lot of wind, some torrential-type rains during the night, a few squalls during the day which sent everyone running for cover (but they only lasted about five minutes). Despite the rain and wind, it was hot and humid and the rays were strong, so be careful in the sun. Because of the heavy surf, the snorkeling wasn't good, and we weren't able to muster the energy to go to snorkeling beaches.

Restaurants   In Cancún restaurants abound, but you have to be choosy. *Carlos and Charlie's* is the big favorite, but I absolutely would not go back. If you want to relive your freshman frat days or something, or if you are deaf, or stoned, or both, you might enjoy it. Actually the food was pretty good, but the atmosphere and noise level were intolerable. Our best meal was at *Fonda del Angel* at 85 avenida Cobá in Cancún; really fabulous Mexican food. Go with a big appetite. The best Mexican restaurant there is called *Perico's* (everyone agreed on this), but it was closed for remodeling when we were there. We had another good meal at a tacky bayside place near the Hyatt called *Gypsy's;* good local fish, but take it easy with the margaritas—verrrrry potent. They have what they call a black sauce that they put on the fish and it's great. Other restaurants recommended by either friends or hotel people were **Chocos and Tere, Carrillos, Chac Mool, and Bogart's.**

Shopping can best be accomplished at the Mauna Loa Commercial Center. Half the stores are nice. My favorite store is called Georgia's. There was also a good jewelry store in the center, but it was always closed when we went there. Remember—the Mexicans are on siesta time, which means that the shops shut down for three or four hours per day, but they all don't shut down at the same time. Some were shut from 12:00 to 4:00, some from 2:00 to 6:00, some from 4:00 to 6:00. Very frustrating. There is also a large Mexican "market" at the center, which consists of about fifty stalls, modernized, selling all sorts of arts and crafts. Typical Tijuana-type stuff, but if you're looking for inexpensive gifts, it's a good place to go. We got some great buys on some beautiful silver jewelry in one of these stands, but you have to be careful, shop around, compare prices, and, above all, *bargain.* My friend bought a shawl for 20 dollars which was marked 80 dollars. It's probably worth $7.95.

Pesos When we were in the Yucatán the banks and hotels were giving seventy pesos per dollar. Don't go for it. Let it be known to a waiter or bellboy that you want to change some dollars and they'll quickly find a "friend" who will sell you black market pesos. We got one hundred pesos per dollar on the black market. Oddly enough, we got our best exchange right at the L.A. airport while waiting in line to check in. Some Mexican came up and sold us one hundred ten pesos per dollar. I heard of someone else getting one hundred twenty the same way. If you run out of pesos, they're real happy to take your dollars. In fact, they almost prefer it. Take a lot of one-dollar bills.

Sightseeing

As for Cancún in general—it's simply a big tourist resort built for Americans; 99 percent of all the tourists come from the United States, many of those from Texas. There's nothing exotic about Cancún, so don't go expecting some charming little Mexican seaside resort. However, there are some really exciting things to see not far from Cancún.

Akumal.
A diving and water sports resort just a short drive from Tulum. It's known for its palm trees, snorkeling, and museum. The hotel there is not very good, so I hear. You can do Cobá, Tulum Xwl-ha, and Akumal in one day, if you leave very early in the morning. Arrange to take a picnic lunch.

Cobá.
About thirty miles inland from Tulum and probably a two-hour drive from Cancún. Go with a guide. Cobá may turn out to be the largest and most important of all the Mayan sites, but for now it is largely unexcavated. There are paths to follow and some excavations to see, and it must be very exciting indeed. Also, it is really in the jungle. There's a Villa Arqueológica there, if you need a hotel.

Cozumel.
A large island where many people go and stay. There are day trips there from Cancún via airplane (seven minutes) or hydrofoil.

Isla Mujeres.
A smaller and closer island, about forty-five minutes by boat, where there is a popular snorkeling beach called El Garrafón. A path at the entrance will lead you to the remains of a Mayan ruin. There is a very good article on Isla Mujeres, mentioning hotels, restaurants, other beaches, etc., in the November 1982 issue of *Travel & Leisure*.

Ruinas del Rey.
These are ruins near the road on the way to the Cancún airport.

Tulum.
This seaside ruin is about a one-and-a-half-hour drive from Cancún, and very different from Chichén Itzá. Dramatic views.

Xcaret.
A privately owned ranch forty miles from Cancún, with a restaurant, ruins, a grotto, good swimming, good snorkeling.

Xel-ha.
A large natural aquarium famous for snorkeling, but I've been told the snorkeling is a bust for anyone with the least bit of experience.

Entertainment

The *Krystal* hotel offers a floor show twice nightly of Mayan traditional dances. The early performance is a dinner show which you probably could skip, but the 10:00 P.M. show has no extras. The costumes and dancing are very interesting and the whole thing lasts about forty-five minutes. If you are into Mayan culture or history, you would enjoy this.

I read somewhere that the *El Presidente* hotel has performances of the famous Mayan flying pole dancers. I didn't check into it, but it would really be something to see if they still do it.

Chichén Itzá

The main reason anyone goes to Mérida is probably to get to Chichén Itzá or Uxmal.

The drive from Mérida to Chichén is about two hours, or slightly more if you stop on the way at *Izamal,* which is well worth the short detour. Izamal is a truly wonderful old town, inhabited continuously for over one thousand years. The entire city is painted yellow-gold, and the Mayans are there. In fact, you have to drive through many small Mayan villages on the way, and you get a glimpse of how the ancient Mayans lived, since the architecture of the houses has not changed: sapling-pole walls and thatched roofs, packed mud floor, little furniture. Notice the distinct Mayan facial features on many of the people; you'll see their ancestors in Mayan reliefs and paintings. Anyway, back to Izamal. This was the earliest of the Spanish colonial towns, established around 1520 or so. The church there is the main attraction. It was built by a Franciscan named Landa, to whom goes the dubious distinction of having destroyed all but eight or nine of thousands of Mayan books, wiping out very effectively all written knowledge of their amazing civilization. Anyway, if you can get over your rage about that, the *Church of San Francisco* is worthy of a few minutes of your time. It has the largest courtyard (peristyle) in Mexico. The interior has a later baroque altar. If you look off into the distance across the main plaza, you can see remnants of an ancient pyramid. In fact, the church itself is built on the platform of one of the pyramids, which explains why it is elevated. Of course by now you know that all the churches you see are built from the stones of the ancient temples and pyramids, which the Spanish couldn't wait to rip down.

Now on to Chichén Itzá. Along the road between Izamal and Chichén you'll see more Mayan villages, and lots of jungle-covered mounds. These mounds are all unexcavated Mayan temples and tombs.

There are two *hotels* at Chichén Itzá. We stayed at the **Hotel Maya-land,** which was charming and completely comfortable. It's on American plan, so when you go into the dining room they just serve you whatever it is they've cooked that day. The food was OK—not good, not bad. The hotel was pretty quiet, except for a few cars on the road at night. Get a bungalow or request a room off the road. In the morning you are awakened by the chirping of a grillion birds. You'll see birds, including parrots, like you've never seen before. If you are at the hotel at dusk, go stand in the

main entryway and look through the round-arched doorway to the silhou-
ette of the observatory—a sight right off a postcard!

The other hotel is owned by Club Med, although it is not a Club Med.
It's called the **Villa Arqueológica.** We had lunch there and it is a lovely
hotel. A friend of mine stayed there and said it was very nice. During our
lunch, however, it was invaded by about two hundred noisy, rowdy, Club
Med people that had been bussed over for the day from Cancún. The food
at the Villa was also OK. There's not much you can do about the food in
the area, since there aren't any restaurants except in the small town a couple
of miles away, which would be iffy, at best.

I would recommend spending the night at Chichén, rather than taking
a one-day bus tour from Mérida or Cancún. It was very pleasant to start out
at 8:30 A.M. to see the ruins, while it was still cool and before the dozens
of buses arrived.

As for the ruins, be sure you have a good guide and allow about four
hours. There is much to see, much to know. If you're half as smart as you
think you are, you'll read up on the subject before you go. Four hours will
just cover the basics.

Mérida

Mérida is a very charming, very old Spanish colonial town, founded
in 1542 by the Spanish on ruins of the Mayan city of Tehox. The architecture
is wonderful. As for *hotels,* I can only tell you where *not* to stay—*Hotel Casa
Del Balam.* The noise level was deafening and no one slept for one minute.
Our guide, Pedro, suggested that the best hotel there is now the *Holiday Inn*
in the Montejo district. A "Passport" newsletter article suggests that the *Hotel
Panamericana* is best. Indeed we did drive by this hotel and it looked
promising.

Our *restaurant* experience in Mérida was not exciting, since we had
breakfast at the hotel and lunch at a terrible place called *Surf and Turf* (don't
go). Articles I have read suggest *Alberto's Continental,* corner 64th and 57th
Streets; *Portico del Peregrino,* 501 57th Street; *Château Valentin,* Calle 58-A
499-D; *Las Palomas,* 55th and 56th Streets.

Three hours is enough time to see the high spots of Mérida, since it
is a very small town. You should walk all around the *Zócalo* and look at
the varied architecture. Don't miss the front of the *house of the Montejo.* Also
drive up and down *Paseo de Montejo* and see all the fabulous homes. In the
most spectacular home is the *Museum of Archaeology and History,* definitely
to see.

Farther up the street is the *Monumento de la Patria.* If you want a lot
of local flavor, go to the *mercado* and walk around, although you probably

won't find anything you want to buy. Panama hats are the big item; also things made from sisal.

Before I continue, a note on the water. I was told by people both at home and in the Yucatán that the water there is safe to drink. They always say that in Mexico City too, but I never believe them. We drank only bottled water.

The local specialties in food sound good. There's a sauce called *pibil* which they put on everything. Another local item is *paunucho*—fried tortillas, beans, turkey, and onions. Then there's *puchero*—a dish of meat and green vegetables. *Papa-dzul* are tortillas filled with pumpkin seeds and tomato sauce. Turkey is a big number, and you'll see a lot of them if you go driving through the villages. Beef is OK if cooked right, which it usually isn't. The local beer is called Montejo, named for the conquistador who settled the area way back when.

Uxmal

Alas, we did not have time for Uxmal, but a friend of mine went and said it was indeed fabulous. It is earlier than Chichén, which is Toltec and classic. Uxmal is classic Maya. There are three hotels at Uxmal: *Hotel Hacienda Uxmal* (recommended in *Gourmet* magazine), *Hotel Misión Uxmal,* and *Villa Arqueólogica.*

Other ruins are all around, such as Kabah, Dzibilchaltun, Labna, Sayil, and Xlapak. From Uxmal you can also head for Palenque, although our guide suggested it's better to fly there. There's also a large sisal factory somewhere between Mérida and Chichén where you can get a short tour which I hear is very good. They were having lunch when we got there.

Final Thoughts

To really see the Yucatán and have time to relax a little, too, would require ten days to two weeks. In a week you could also cover a lot of ground. Six days was just not enough. If you are interested in taking in the archeological sites in any depth, be sure to allow yourself adequate time.

The Mexicans in the Yucatán are very gracious. Never did we feel we were being ripped off. In fact, it was almost the opposite. The bill for eight at dinner—and we all ate and drank profusely—came to anywhere from 48 to 60 dollars each night. Cab fares were about a dollar to go up and down the strip at Cancún. Everything was incredibly cheap. The people were eager to please, friendly, and practically everyone speaks perfect English. If you can speak Spanish, do it. They love it. Even lousy Spanish. There are many really Ugly Americans there, so try to avoid them when you see them. Many of the Yucatecans are descendants of the Mayans. They speak Mayan, wear the ancient dresses, and have the distinctive Mayan ethnic facial features. Often you feel almost as if you've stepped back in time. The jungle is endless —low, flat, humid. The beaches are gorgeous: white sand, turquoise waters. Weather, as in any tropical climate, is unpredictable. You know it rains a lot—how else that thick jungle?

NOTE: This section was written before the major earthquake struck Mexico.

Cabo San Lucas

If you've got four days with nowhere to go, this is the place, especially if you like to fish. We stayed at the *Hotel Cabo San Lucas,* which is one of the older ones, and it was terrific. If you take kids, or go with another couple or group, get one of the beach-front houses instead of a regular hotel room. The food, when we were there, was outstanding, but I've heard reports to the contrary, at times. It depends on who's in the kitchen, I suppose. The fresh fish can't be beat.

If you go fishing, be sure you keep what you catch and have the hotel cook it for you for dinner. See about having the rest frozen, then packed in dry ice to take home with you. We made the mistake of giving away eight huge mahi-mahi (dorado). The fishing was fabulous. You can arrange for a boat through the hotel or just walk down to the dock. Have the hotel pack you a lunch.

Friends stayed at the *Palmilla,* another old hotel, and hated it; they said the help was very surly. The *Twin Dolphin* hotel is supposed to be very nice. There are new ones springing up all the time.

There's not much to do in the little town of San Lucas—you can see it all in about an hour or so. Other than the beach and fishing, there's not a lot going on in the area. That means you have to relax.

Cabo butts up to the edge of a vast desert-type region, and for that reason you will encounter several crawly critters and mysterious-looking things, both flying and on the ground. Don't run around barefoot—there are scorpions. Shake out clothes thoroughly before getting dressed. Take verrrrry casual clothes—there's nothing too fancy here.

You can fly directly into Cabo San Lucas.

Ixtapa-Zihuatanejo

Of all the resorts I've been to in Mexico, this one is the big winner. Cancún was OK, mainly because of the archaeological zones, and I would go back there just to see more of those. For just a terrific beach resort—it's Ixtapa.

Ixtapa (pronounced *Eees-tapa*) is south of Puerto Vallarta and north of Acapulco, closer to the latter. There are some direct flights from Los Angeles on Western Airlines, but not every day. The flight takes around three hours. You land at a little airport that is about a ten-minute drive from a small town called Zihuatanejo. That town, in turn, is inland and about a ten-minute drive from a beach resort area called Ixtapa. There is one long main beach and one smaller one in a cove all its own. It is in the smaller one that you find the **Camino Real** hotel.

We went to Ixtapa over Memorial Day weekend, arriving on the heels of a major storm—outskirts of a hurricane. Luckily it didn't rain more than a few hours after our arrival, but it had been a big enough storm to take away our beach and cause havoc with roads and sewer systems in the area. Fortunately, these types of storms are unusual (you can tell by looking at the bone dry hillsides). Once it cleared up it was intensely hot, the humidity wasn't bad, and the ocean temperature was over 80 degrees.

Hotels

The **Camino Real** is the only place I would stay, for several reasons. First, it is in its own private cove—no other hotels in sight and no room to build any. You really feel as if you are totally isolated and away from the rest of the world. Second, architecturally the hotel is fantastic. It's a type of Mayan-stepped design, scaling a hillside. Physically, the hotel is magnificent from all angles. The public pool area is one of the most beautiful I've ever seen. Tropical plants, fragrant flowers, lots of birds, fantastic vistas, and a big white sand beach (although it had been washed away by the storm when we were there).

All the other hotels are located on the next beach over, the one called Ixtapa. There are about six hotels there now, with more going up. Reminds you of Cancún or Acapulco. Some of the hotels you may have heard of before—the *Aristos, El Presidente, Hilton, Sheraton;* others had names new to me. The beach there is wonderful. But it's like living in Hotel Land if you stay there.

We had a fantastic suite (#1836–7–8) at the Camino Real with private swimming pools, Jacuzzi, huge rooms, and panoramic views. There are only a few of these rooms, so if you want them, reserve well in advance. All rooms have private patios, views, and a hammock.

Restaurants

This is not a major dining mecca. Every hotel has two or three restaurants, but you know how hotel food is. At the Camino Real there were three rooms: the *Esfera,* the most elegant; the *Solarium,* by the pool and open 6:00 A.M. to 6:00 P.M.; and the *Azulejos,* sort of a sophisticated coffee shop. The food in the *Esfera* was very mediocre and the service was impossible (more on service later). The buffet breakfast in the *Azulejos* wasn't bad and you can also order from the menu. Excellent pastries and fruit displays. The *Solarium* served pool-side fare, plus breakfast. The Mexican food in all the restaurants was the best I've had in Mexico. Once we figured that out, that's all we ate.

The popular chain, *Carlos and Charlie's,* has a place at one end of Ixtapa. After the one in Cancún, I swore I'd never go to another one. But we went. Now I *know* I'll never go to another one! What a bad place! Kept us waiting for one and a half hours, meanwhile slipping through their "friends." Once we finally got a table (about 10:00 P.M.), the food we got was just so-so. Definitely *not* worth it all. A walk on the magnificent moonlit beach afterward helped calm our nerves.

As for the other hotel restaurants, we were told that *The Reef* at the Krystal hotel was the best of the lot. We ate there, and it was OK, not great but not too bad. The big problem there was noise coming from the lobby bar, which competed with a nice pianist in the restaurant.

One thing we did not do, which would probably have been the best thing, was to go into Zihuatanejo, wander along the beach front, and just pick a little place that looked good and get some fresh grilled fish. Well, next time . . .

There are several restaurants in Zihuatanejo, but you'd have to consult some local hotel people to find out which ones are good.

An exceptional restaurant is **Villa de la Selva,** phone 42096, on the road above the Camino Real hotel (Paseo de la Roca). Great views and fresh fish; especially nice at sundown. Reservations essential. Open 6:00 P.M. to 1:00 A.M.

A word about the *service:* it's *awful.* Everywhere. You must go down there with that in mind. They don't know the meaning of the word. Everything takes forever. You have to ask for things over and over. The orders get all mixed up. You can't be in a hurry. They don't do it maliciously, they just don't know any better. At least they're friendly. At the Camino Real hotel, it took us almost one hour to check out. So don't wait until the last minute to do this, if you are running for a plane. If you are going to use a credit card, give it to them when you arrive and tell them to check it out at that time, not when you are ready to leave.

Same is true for cabs: at check-out time, there are none. At dinner time, there are none. They have a serious cab shortage. You might have to wait a half an hour to get one. Other times, there are cabs everywhere. If you have an 8:30 dinner reservation, you should start heading to the cab stand about 8:10, even if you only want a short ride.

Shopping

All the hotels have shops, of course. The one at the **Sheraton** was better than some of the others, because they carry a line of sports clothes and sweats called Aca Joe, which is really nice.

Across the street from the hotels on Ixtapa beach is a shopping zone called **Centro Comercial.** It's a small shopping complex with several stores, some of them very nice. The two we liked best were **Mandarina** and **Roberto's.** Mandarina is a big, crazy place full of jewelry and clothes and all kinds of stuff; some of it is really good. Saw some Mexican labels there that I'd seen in Mexico City, but the prices here were about half. Wonderful costume jewelry and great prices! Roberto's is a very nice jewelry store, not schlocky, and they make all their own stuff. Prices were a bit higher than we saw in Zihuatanejo, but then so was the quality. The lady who runs the Mandarina told us they are very fair with their prices at Roberto's.

In **Zihuatanejo** there is an area which you can tell was designed just for the tourists—all cobblestone walk streets, lots of pleasant little shops, a couple of banks, and the waterfront at one end. You can wheel and deal there, but some of the prices in the nicer stores were way out of line. On the way to this area, you will pass a market which is for the people who live there. While you may not buy anything there, it's interesting to walk through it.

Money

It was hard to get our hands on pesos over the weekend. They didn't even have any at the hotel, and the banks were closed. The shops could not give change for large bills. It's a good idea to go down there with a lot of small U.S. dollar bills (ones, fives, tens, and twenties, but nothing larger). You can use your dollars as easily as you can use pesos. All the shopkeepers would convert on the spot and give you the going rate (which was 1.49 pesos per dollar). We didn't see any black market traders as we did in Cancún.

Golf and Tennis

All the hotels had tennis courts, and there's a big golf course in the middle of everything. Our friend Bob played on it one morning and says it's the only golf course he's ever seen where you can lose your ball on the fairway. In other words, it's not in great condition. Someone else I was talking to later said they saw alligators in the ponds when they were playing there. Still another friend, on a different weekend, said it was super golfing. You take your chances!

Other Sports and Things to do

In your hotel you can find out about all kinds of activities: deep-sea fishing, snorkeling, trips to outer beaches and to Ixtapa Island, game hunting, archaeological zones, day trips to Mexico City and Acapulco, parachute flying, water-skiing, etc.

Nightlife

Discos are a big number in Mexico. Almost every hotel has its own, starting anywhere from 9:00 P.M. to midnight.

At the Camino Real, on Saturday nights, they have a big Mexican Fiesta. People from the other hotels come to this. You can get your tickets in the main lobby starting Friday afternoon. They have live entertainment (music and dancers), and a huge Mexican buffet. It is beautifully presented and the food is fantastic. They serve margaritas, tequila, and piña coladas in the hallway before it all starts, but once you get inside, you can't get the margaritas, although you can still get everything else. So if you want to continue drinking them with your meal, you'll have to go all the way to the lobby bar, buy them, and carry them into the party. Better to start with something else and you will avoid the problem.

Clothing

Casual casual casual. Hot hot hot. Women get dressed up for dinner, but in a casual way. Forget sportscoats and fancy dresses. Too hot for anything but cottons. During the day—shorts, sundresses, and bathing suits.

Rio de Janeiro

Rio de Janeiro

Hedonism. That's what you think of when you're in Rio. Rio is sexy, sultry, and samba. It's beaches, bikinis, and bodies. Even on the hottest days there's energy, a continuous pulsating rhythm under the sun. Rio is the French Riviera, Mexico City, Africa, Portugal, and South America all shaken up together and spread out among beaches, bays, mountains, and valleys. The girls from Ipanema go walking side by side with the body builders from Copacabana, the tourists from everywhere, the *favela* dwellers from the suburbs, and the masses of suntanned families who all seem to be interested only in finding a spot on the already crowded sand. There's only one thing to do in Rio—enjoy.

In January it was hot, I mean really hot—between 100 and 106 degrees during the day, cooling off to around 80 degrees at night. Only a nice breeze kept it from being unbearable. Along with the heat there is the humidity —the city sits on the Tropic of Capricorn. The weather, along with the almost total carefree attitude and abandon, means everyone dresses casually. I doubt if the Cariocas (residents of Rio) even know what a necktie is unless one happens to be the groom in a wedding, and even then . . . Bikinis, mostly skimpy in nature, are *the* thing to wear during the day, during the evening, at the beach, in town, shopping, walking. Of course, as a tourist you'll be more comfortable in very lightweight, extremely casual clothes. For the daytime, sundresses, shorts, T-shirts. (Note: Men are not allowed in some churches without long pants.) In the evening, more sundresses, casual outfits, never a jacket for men and never, never a tie. Stick to cottons so your clothes won't stick to you. Air conditioning is hard to find outside hotels, better restaurants, and a few boutiques. As for the weather during the rest of the year, it must be very mild; our guide said no one ever wears wool unless he is going into the mountains.

There are two main beaches in Rio—*Copacabana* and *Ipanema/Leblon.* The two best hotels are on Copacabana—the *Rio Palace* at the juncture of the two beaches, and the *Meridien* at the Sugarloaf end of Copacabana. We stayed at the Rio Palace, a lovely hotel with fabulous views, good service, efficient personnel, and the best location. There are hotels on Ipanema, but they are not as highly rated: your best hotel bet is the *Cesar Park.* If you don't want to be exactly in Rio, try the *InterContinental Hotel* in *Barra,* just across the street from a lovely beach and a five-minute drive into Ipanema. A double at the Rio Palace runs around 150 dollars, and an executive suite is around 350 dollars per night. One added feature at the Rio Palace is the presence of safes in each room, which eliminates the need to use a hotel safe-deposit box. Believe me, in Rio you must use one or the other.

Well, since I brought up the need for safe-deposit boxes, I guess I will elaborate. Rule Numero Uno is never, but never, wear jewelry on the street. No, not even your wristwatch. It doesn't matter if your watch only cost 5 dollars, it's still an invitation to get robbed. Keep your watch in the safe, or in your pocket or purse, if you must carry one. Keep your money and traveler's checks spread around—pocket, wallet, money belt, compact, tissue packet, etc. Lock your passport in the safe. If you leave your camera in the room, lock it in the safe; also your travel clock and anything that would be the least bit tempting. You'll hear all the stories. Unfortunately, it is a fact of life—theft is a huge problem and big business.

The authorities are far more concerned about where you park your car than about having your money or jewelry stolen. They can't control it, don't try, and don't seem to care. We wore only simple stud earrings, and some inexpensive, locally made beads that we bought for $1.50 from a street stand. That goes for at night, also. Only when we ate in the hotel did we put on anything more. Our guide was walking into our hotel to pick us up on the second morning, and someone tried to rip her bracelets off her arm right in front of the hotel. This is common. It happens, and it will happen to you if you don't obey the rules. Everyone will tell you not to wear any jewelry; actually, they don't tell you not to, they *beg* you.

As for getting around in Rio, which is a very big, complicated city, getting a guide and car is your best bet. We had a marvelous guide named Consuelo Soto Cabral. She works out of the office of Antur Turismo, rua Buenos Aires 100A, phone 224–9191 or 224–9060. Consuelo's address is rua Professor Eurico Rabelo 215, Casa 2, Maracana, CEP 20271, Rio de Janeiro, Brasil; her phone is 248–3129. You can contact her at either address, and I can highly recommend her. She was very organized, knew everything there was to know, recommended good restaurants, and had a lot of energy, plus a good sense of humor. Be sure you tell her I sent you!

You'll probably hear or read a lot about the terrible driving in Rio. Well, it isn't the greatest; but if you've been to Cairo or even Italy, you won't be too shocked. Just be careful crossing the street, and tell cab drivers you're not in a hurry.

Brazilian money is called "cruzeiros," and there are two exchanges: the "official" and the "unofficial," better known as black market. The difference between the two is 40 to 50 percent. This also means don't change your money at hotels, banks, or exchange bureaus. Your guide or practically anyone can take care of getting you the black market exchange with no problem. Everyone does it. Shops will give you the black market rate. Don't use credit cards—you'll end up paying almost double. Take traveler's checks and good ol' dollars, the latter being easier to trade. Of course, it is a bit risky to travel around with a lot of cash, but don't put it all in one place. Keep it locked up, using it little by little. Cruzeiros are worthless outside Brazil, so don't cash more dollars than you think you will need, as you'll end up being stuck with Brazilian money. Traveler's checks work almost as well. When we were in Brazil, the "official" exchange was 900-something. Our guide was getting us 1250 cruzeiros per dollar. H. Stern Jewelry Co. gave us 1330, and some boutiques gave us 1450; so you see, there's no standard. You'll find your money goes a long way in Brazil, because everything is very inexpensive. More about that later in the shopping and restaurant sections.

P.S. Save about 6 dollars per person to get out—there's an airport departure tax. Also, it's very handy to take along about 25 dollars in one-dollar bills; these are very good for tipping.

Language

Fala portugues? I thought not. What do you do about communicating when in Brazil? Portuguese is what they speak, but it isn't the same Portuguese that you may have learned to go to Portugal. That Portuguese will work just fine, however, so if you know a little, brush up on it. If you don't know any at all, learn some. If you know Spanish and/or Italian, you're in luck. You'll be understood if you speak Spanish, and you'll be able to recognize a lot of words if you speak Spanish or Italian. The big problem for me in learning Portuguese was the pronunciation. Like French, very few words are pronounced the way they are spelled, and there are lots of nasals and shshing going on all the time. If you pick up some cassettes teaching Portuguese for travelers and spend a little time with them, you'll get an ear for the language and be able to speak a few words. At the end of this chapter I will list some that will come in handy. English is spoken in all the better hotels and restaurants, although sometimes with such a thick accent that it is hard to understand. In some shops no one speaks English, so you get by with Spanish, smiles, and gesticulations. Noooooo problem! Just stick a few "shshs" on where there's an "s" and you'll almost have it.

Restaurants

Now, let's get serious: food. Dining in Rio is inexpensive, fun, and the food is great. Here's a list of places I can recommend.

Antonino's, avenida Epitacio Pessoa 1244, Leblon, phone 267–6791 or 287–6549.
This is a very nice continental-style restaurant, attractive decor, good food, good service. The continental food had a slight Brazilian flair. Dinners came to around 43 dollars each, everything included, which we thought was a bit high for food that was good, but not great.

Café Un, Deux, Trois, in Leblon, phone 239–0198 or 239–5789.
Excellent restaurant with music and dancing on the side, for those interested. Serves very late. The grilled salmon was memorable. Dinners were about 29 dollars each.

Castelo da Logoa, avenida Epitacio Pessoa 1560, phone 287–3514.
This is where we had feijoada, the Brazilian national dish. On Saturday afternoon when all the locals are eating *feijoada,* so did we. This is basically a black bean and rice dish, upon which you pile various kinds of meats and condiments: beef, pork ribs, pig's ears and pig's tails, beef tails, sausage, chicken—whatever. You don't have to eat the pig's ears if you don't want to. It's served with some sort of cooked greens, plus cold vegetables, tomatoes, palmito, etc. Very unusual and quite tasty, but a bit heavy, so go easy. Total cost for five people for lunch was 38 dollars. That included drinks, wonderful desserts (try the chocolate mousse), tip, and all we could eat. Before you leave the restaurant walk into the adjoining Chiko's Bar and look at the beautiful display of bottles and mirrors.

Mariu's Churrascaria, avenida Atlantica 290, Copacabana Beach.
Reservations essential. OK, so what is a churrascaria? It's a barbecue that should not be missed. At Mariu's they serve *rodizio,* where the barbecued meats are brought to your table. Other churrascarias are buffet style. Waiters come to your table with huge skewers full of various types of delicious barbecued meats, and they slice off all you want. At Mariu's they had beef, *cupim* (hump of the bull —delicious!), chicken, sausages, turkey wrapped in bacon, lamb chops (center cut), pork ribs, pork roast, and ham. They just keep coming around and piling up your plate, and it's all fabulous! In addition, they bring side dishes and pile them on the table, and when the dish is empty, they bring another one: french-fried potatoes, french-fried manioc, fried bananas, rice, sliced tomatoes, lettuce leaves, asparagus, fried corn fritters, palmito (palm hearts), french-fried onions, raw marinated onions, and bread. We ate until we could eat no more,

and the entire tab, with liquor and tip, was about 12 dollars each. There are many other churrascarias in Rio which are also very good; ask your guide. Mariu's was terrific!

Pre Catalan,   Rio Palace Hotel, phone 521–3232.
The French chef Lenôtre got the act together in the kitchen here and the food is excellent. The decor is lovely, and you are serenaded throughout dinner by a harpist, albeit a quite exuberant one in our case. Good service. Dinners came to around 20 dollars each. The chief rival to the Pre Catalan is the *St. Honoré* in the Meridien Hotel, but at the time we were in Rio, the word was that the Pre Catalan was better. All this can change, of course, depending on the chef.

Also recommended are:

AlbaMar, Praça 15 de Novembro; for seafood and a view of the harbor.
Antiquarius, 19 rua Aristides Espinola, Leblon, phone 294–1049.
Four Seasons, rua Redfern, Leblon.
Jardim, 225 rua Republica de Peru; *churrascaria.*
Ouro Verde, avenida Atlantica 1456, phone 542–1887; continental.
Roane, in the Lagoa area; popular and very "in" place; good food.
Le Streghe, in Ipanema.

Last but not least, if you happen to be shopping in the Rio Sul shopping center, go up to the second floor and look for the *Vienna Delicatessen.* A great place for lunch. Fabulous selection of salads, meats, hot dishes, pizzas, sandwiches, empanadas and croquettes, ice creams, etc. A real feast for not much money.

Brazilian food is very salty, so don't put any salt on anything until you've sampled the food. You get sort of used to it after a while, but at first your taste buds do a backflip. Chocolate in Brazil is fabulous—the rich, dark kind. Anything we had made with chocolate was always excellent. Ice creams are wonderful. The breads and butter for the most part were on the boring side. For lunch get freshly made empanadas, croquettes, and little meat pies at a lunch place—they're delicious and not too heavy. No diet soft drinks available. Wonderful fresh fruit juices. *Cafezinho* is the Brazilian equivalent of espresso—rich and delicious. *Farofa* is manioc meal, served in various ways depending on the dish. *Chopp* (pronounced *shope*) is the local beer. *Molho* (pronounced *mole-yo*) means sauce. A *caipirinha* is a delicious cocktail made from *cachaca* and lime, something like a margarita. *Cachaca* is a type of liquor native to Brazil. You can substitute vodka for it, but it isn't as powerful as you'll read that it is. The beef in Brazil, other than at the churrascaria, is so-so, on the tough side, not up to U.S. standards in that respect, and many notches below Argentine beef. Shrimp *(camaroa)* are excellent. Drink only bottled water: *agua mineral (com gaz,* pronounced *gash,* for carbonated; or *sem gaz* for natural).

One nice feature in Brazilian restaurants is that the minute you sit down, they start bringing out all sorts of little dishes of goodies to eat, like hors d'oeuvre. You can wear shorts to restaurants for lunch if it's hot; ties are never required; jackets only at the most lah-de-dah places (but no hard and fast rules). Vanilla is called crème. If you want something cold, it's *gelado,* which doesn't necessarily mean it has ice in it. *Gelado* also means ice cream. If you want ice, it's *com gelo;* without ice, it's *sem gelo.*

Nightlife

Nightlife in Rio takes on many forms, since music is an integral and unavoidable part of the city. You never seem to be able to get away from the samba music, no matter where you go. It can be quite infectious and you may notice parts of your body involuntarily beginning to move with the beat. Too much of it, however, can wear on your nerves. In January everyone is getting ready for Carnival, and you can arrange to go see some of the samba schools rehearsing. Consult your guide or hotel about this. There is a giant samba show presented at an amphitheater on the first level of *Sugarloaf.* Don't go—it's touristy, they oversell the room so many people are left to stand throughout a three-hour show, and those sitting behind the standing people can see absolutely nothing. The show starts out with a bang but quickly deteriorates into a typical tourist shtick with people being dragged out of the audience to show what klutzy samba they can do. The only good thing about going to this particular show is seeing the lights of Rio by night, but you can go up to Sugarloaf and see that without having to see the show.

A really knockout floor show featuring not only samba but all types of Brazilian music and dance is called the *Plataforma.* This is a two-and-a-half-hour show, very lively, and you've never seen costumes like this in your life. Be sure you get a table near the stage or runway, so if you're shooting high-speed film you'll be able to get good pictures. Plataforma is located at 32 rua Adalberto Ferreira, Leblon, phone 274–4942, 274–4652, 274–4022.

A nightclub that was recommended to us (which we did not go to, however) is *Asa Branca* on Rua Mem de Sá, downtown. It's where you go to hear *gafieira* music, typical of Brazil. It's not recommended for dinner, only as an after-dinner place at which to listen to music and dance. There are many other such boîtes throughout the city, which your guide or hotel can recommend to you. The *Oba Oba,* which shows up in several guide-books, was not recommended to us by the locals.

As soon as you hit town, have your guide start working on getting you to a *macumba* ceremony, or service, or whatever they call it. I won't go into what *macumba* is, as it's very complicated and I really don't know enough to talk about it accurately. It is the spiritist religion which over 80 percent of Brazilians believe in, combining both white magic and black magic, having originated in Africa and come to Brazil with the slaves. All I can tell you is, seeing is believing. There's no way to describe what goes on; it's absolutely fascinating. Perhaps you will be able to participate—there's nothing to be afraid of, and it's an experience you'll long remember. These ceremonies start around 9:00 P.M. and last two hours or more; however, you can leave when you want to. Believe me, it's worth the effort to go. Be sure someone explains it all to you in advance so you know what you're seeing.

Sightseeing

As for sightseeing, there's a lot to see. If you have four whole days you may be able to get in the highpoints, with enough time to shop and go to the beach. If you have a guide (the best idea), he or she will automatically take you to the main points of interest. You don't want to miss going to the top of *Sugarloaf* and *Corcovado.* You don't want to go too early in the morning to either place, because of haze and smog, which tends to clear out by late afternoon. It's best to go late in the day, just before sunset. On the way to or from Corcovado you'll probably drive through the *Tijuca* forest to see the waterfall, small but nice. You'll also pass through *Barra de Tijuca,* the newest beach development with lovely homes and new hotels, plus a very beautiful beach.

A quick aside to Corcovado: when you start climbing up the steps, on the first landing you'll see two souvenir shops. We found better Rio T-shirts at these shops than anywhere else. At the base of the steps where the parking lot is located there is a snack bar where they make wonderful fresh-squeezed juices of all kinds; very refreshing after the climb up to the top.

You'll also want to see the downtown area, where the *National Cathedral* is located. Unfortunately, it was closed every time we tried to go and we were never able to get inside. You can't miss it—it's very Mayan-looking. You'll also see the old aqueduct, various monuments, the square Praça Floriana with the *Municipal Theater* and the *Opera House,* which everyone compares to the one in Paris (there's no comparison), and several churches. One church that stands out from all the others is *São Bento,* and don't miss it. Men are required to wear long pants, so take some along in the car if you're wearing shorts. There are many museums in the city, but we were basically short of time to see them and were told they weren't all that exciting, anyway. The one exception we made, which became a running joke throughout the week, was to go to the *Carmen Miranda Museum.* I think we're the only whackos who'd been there in a month. Then there are those beaches, beautiful to look at, crowded to be on during the heat of the day, and famous. If you do much reading at all before you go, you'll learn that most of the waters are extremely polluted. If you go to the beach take only your towel; anything else could be swiped. People do wear other types of bathing suits besides bikinis, and not everyone is tall and tan and young and lovely. In fact, it's quite the opposite.

A half-day excursion you may want to make out of town will take you to *Petrópolis,* where one of the palaces of the Portuguese kings is located. The drive is interesting, as you see some of the suburbs, some *favelas* (shanty towns), some mountains, and the colonial mountain town of Petrópolis, which is quite lovely. The palace is beautiful and furnished as it was when the king was in residence. There are roadside cafés along the way where you can stop for lunch. There's a chocolate "factory" in Petrópolis, Patrone, which you can skip. And there's a funny little house where a fella by the name of Alberto Santos-Dumont lived. He was a pioneer in aviation and the Brazilians are very proud of him. He was the first man to fly a controlled airplane and he did this controlled flight around the Eiffel Tower. Cartier designed a wristwatch and named it after him—the Santos watch, which is still a very popular style.

Shopping

Now that I've taken care of culture, more or less, let's go shopping. On Sundays there is an open-air market called the *Hippie Market,* held at one of the parks, but it isn't a hippie thing at all. It's a giant market crammed with arts and crafts, tons of color and music. It's especially good for buying costume jewelry and some leather goods, and you'll see everything from expensive paintings to dresses for babies. Don't miss it.

On Saturday afternoons, at another park, there is an antiques market. This was somewhat of a bust, maybe because we got there late. If you enjoy antique-ing, however, you may want to see this too, but get there when it starts. We were told that most of the people selling the antiques had a lot of money and only did this as a hobby, so they weren't interested in bargaining and prices are too high. A couple of things I was interested in did seem to be overpriced.

The thing to buy in Brazil, which I'm sure you already know, is gems. They are famous for them, especially emeralds and topaz. *The* place to buy those gems is *H. Stern.* I researched this thoroughly and not one single person would recommend wholeheartedly anyplace else. They are known around the world, with stores located in cities in other parts of the world; they stand behind their merchandise and guarantee it 100 percent. If there's ever any problem with what you buy you can go back to them and they will take care of it. Now in Rio, there are several H. Stern shops, especially in or near the hotels. Go and look, but don't buy until you go to the main store, 113 rua Garcia d'Avila. If you call them up they will send a car for you and give you red carpet treatment. This is a first-class operation, believe me. I did some comparison shopping at some other jewelry stores that appear in most guidebooks, and nowhere did I get treatment as I did at H. Stern. In fact, after Stern's, the others seemed almost sleazy. Anyway, when you get to Rio call up Izabela London at the main store, phone 259–7442. She really knows her business and has been with Stern's for thirty years. She was charming, helpful, and forthright. You'll be in good hands with her. The best part is: all the gems and jewelry you'll buy are duty-free, at least at the time of this writing. Anyway, double-check to be sure, if you make a purchase. They give you full documentation and certificates for everything you buy, plus a card for customs officials about the duty-free-ness (I made that word up).

The other thing to buy in Rio besides wonderful jewelry is leather goods. However, if you are going to Buenos Aires on the same trip, save your leather buying for that city, where it is better. That doesn't mean you should pass up something you really love in Rio, or something that you feel is a good buy. You'll notice that everything is remarkably inexpensive.

Clothing is wonderful in Rio, providing you are going home to a warm climate and not blizzard conditions. You'll see very inexpensive and chic fashions, all for summer and resort wear. To give you an example: sandals made of leather and fabric, 10 dollars. Cotton and linen dresses and two-piece outfits, 30 dollars. Leather belts of high quality and style, 15 dollars. Cotton blouses, 6 dollars. The best area for clothes shopping turned out to be on a street called *Visconde de Piraja* in Ipanema. There's a park there called Praça Nossa Señora da Paiz, and if you walk on Piraja to the right and left of this park for a couple of blocks, going into all the galerias, you'll find plenty of boutiques. Our favorite was in a galeria located directly across the street from the park on the first floor, called *Bagagerie Studio*. A great store for costume jewelry, belts, and bags is *Rosa Benedetti,* located just off Visconde de Piraja (check the exact address in a phone book). The *Rio Sul Shopping Center* is like most indoor shopping malls, with a few interesting stores and many lesser-quality stores and department stores serving the local populace. The shopping arcade at the Rio Palace Hotel is just so-so; the lower level has mostly antique stores. The hotel shop by the swimming pool sells tote bags which say Rio Palace. If you want a Rio Palace T-shirt, call up Housekeeping and they'll deliver one to your door. (As I mentioned before, the best selection of T-shirts was at the first landing on the steps going up to Corcovado.) There were some nice ones also in the Rio Palace arcade.

A very pleasant shop for women's wear is *Maria Bonita's,* Rua Vinicius de Morais.

While shopping keep a tight grip on your purse. Carry some money or traveler's checks in your wallet, but not all. We found it very convenient to wear a money belt and stash money in other areas of our purses. Take a calculator along with you; it helps in making conversions.

One nice little touch, which occurred in some shops, was that they'll give you some small gift when you buy something, a token of their appreciation. It's usually not anything you'd buy for yourself, but it's a wonderful gesture.

Guidebooks

Rio is hard to describe—it's unlike anywhere else I've ever been. There's a feeling in the air there that can't be put into words. I happened to find a book by Douglas Botting called *Rio de Janeiro* (Time-Life Books, The Great Cities), which gets about as close as one can get to giving you a real insight into Rio. If you can find the book (look at Crown Books, for starters), read it before you go. I found Fodor's *South America* to be OK for general descriptions but thought Stephen Birnbaum's *South America* was better. The more you read before you go, the better your experience will be.

If you're planning to go elsewhere in South America on the same trip with Rio, go to Rio last. After Rio, anywhere else will be anticlimactic.

Some Useful Vocabulary

hello, good day	bom dia
good afternoon	boa tarde
good evening	boa noite
good night	boa noite
please	por favor
sometimes the more formal	faca favor
thank you	obrigado (if you are a man);
	obrigada (if you are a woman);
	shortened to "brigad"
you're welcome	de nada; shortened to "d'nad"
market, store, fair	feira
with	com
without	sem
toilet	sanitario, toilette
goodbye	ciao
more formal	adeus
what?	o que?

where?	onde?
how much?	quanto?
How much is this?	Quanto custa isto?
I would like . . .	queria, gostaria
beer	cerveja
water	agua
tea	cha
coffee	cafe
wine	vinho
hot	quente
cold	frio
you	voce
I	eu
I don't understand.	Nao compreendo.
of course	claro
Do you speak English?	Fala ingles?
I don't speak Portuguese well.	Nao falo bem portugues.
the bill	a conta
See you later.	Ate vista.

NOTE: The Berlitz *Portuguese for Travellers* is good for basics, but you need to listen to a cassette for pronunciation.

Buenos Aires
AND
Iguazu Falls

Buenos Aires

Going from Rio to Buenos Aires is like going from Disneyland to a library. If you're planning to do both cities in one trip, go to B.A. first. You could not find two more totally opposite cities if you tried. Everything that Rio is, B.A. is not. You need no more than three days in B.A. to see all there is to see, plus do some shopping. There isn't all that much to see there, but that would give you time to visit some of the suburbs.

Buenos Aires is often called the "Paris of South America" and indeed, there are some similarities: the wide boulevards, many monuments and parks, tree-lined streets, cobblestones, and an abundance of nineteenth-century French architecture, some of it quite grandiose. Unlike Paris, however, the prevailing mood in B.A. is somewhat sober, serious, businesslike, even to the point of being dour. Parts of Buenos Aires remind you of Barcelona or Madrid (having never been to Spain, I am quoting my friend, Glenn). There are a couple of sayings: Porteños (citizens of B.A.) are a bunch of Italians who can speak Spanish and would love to be English; someone else said that they are very embarrassed and annoyed at having to be located in South America, and if they could they'd move the whole city to Europe. As a tourist you will not receive anything but gracious attention. If there are any anti-American sentiments there we never saw or felt them. One thing we did notice, both in B.A. and in Rio, is the out-and-out rivalry between these two cities. The Porteños and Cariocas can't wait to put each other down.

In January the weather was almost perfect, except for one blast-furnace day. Otherwise, temperatures were in the high seventies and low eighties, going to high sixties at night. The air, as a matter of fact, is very bueno. B.A. sits on the Río de la Plata, which at this point is really an estuary and so wide that you can't see across it. It's extremely muddy and brown and discourages one from drinking the water there. In one respect B.A. is something like L.A. in that there is a downtown area with high-rise buildings but most of the city is a sprawling suburb that goes on for miles. If possible, get a guide and driver to take you around. You'll see more, learn more, and enjoy it more.

Because of the predominately sober mood in the city you'll feel comfortable dressed in more serious clothes than you'd wear in Rio. This doesn't mean that you have to get all decked out to go shopping or sightseeing, but people don't run around in beachwear, either. At night you'll definitely want to be dressed up for dinner, meaning jackets and ties for the men. Most of the restaurants are very European in atmosphere.

Crime in B.A. is not a problem and you can feel free to wear jewelry on the street. It's still a good idea to keep valuables locked in the hotel safe and not to carry all your money, checks, and passport in one place.

Argentine currency is in a constant state of flux. There used to be old pesos and new pesos mixed up together. Now there is something called an Austral. Best to check on currency denominations before you leave. There is the "official exchange," which you don't want to get, and the "unofficial exchange," which you do want to get. Your guide or someone at the hotel can get you the black market rate, so don't use the hotel cashier, the bank, or credit cards. Traveler's checks are best. At the time we were in B.A. we were getting thirty pesos per dollar.

There are two good hotels in Buenos Aires, the **Plaza** and **Hotel Claridge.** We stayed at the Plaza, which was very nice, very European, and centrally located. Our only complaint was that the rooms are furnished rather cheerlessly or garishly, depending on which one you are in. Suites run about 275 dollars per night, while singles are around 120 dollars.

Spanish is what they speak, although you'll find many people who speak English as there is a large English sector. There seems to be little if any remaining hostility toward Englishmen. There are some pronunciation changes, however. For example, a double "l" in B.A. is pronounced like a "j," so "amarillo" becomes "amarijo," and "ella" becomes "eja," and "parillada" becomes "parijada," and so on. Another difference I noticed is that in some cases a "y" is pronounced like a "z," so "ayer" sounds like "azer," etc. In any case, if you speak Spanish you'll get along fine, but at first these differences may throw you. "Yo" is pronounced "jo." Goodbye is "ciao."

Dining in Buenos Aires is something you should look forward to— excellent food, beautiful restaurants, old-world charm and service. Porteños eat late; they usually don't arrive at a restaurant for dinner before 9:00 or 9:30. A couple of evenings when we had to eat early (8:00), we were the only ones in the place for the first hour. There is no automatic service percentage put on the bills, so you have to figure the tip yourself. The food is basically continental, but with a South American twist. Is the beef as wonderful as they say? *Yes.* You'll be confused as to what the cuts of beef are, since they are not the same as in the U.S. "Bife de lomo" is top sirloin; "bife de chorizo" is a New York cut, which they translate as a T-bone, but it really isn't; "matambrito" is flank steak; and "babi beef" or "baby beef " is prime rib cut. As for the size—HUGE. They don't know what a small steak is. They also serve "papas fritas provençales," which are french fries seasoned with garlic and parsley—you can't stop eating them. A "clerico" is like our white sangria, and a "sangria" is red wine, lemon, and sugar. Butter is "manteca," and chocolate is fabulous, no matter how you get it. They do have Tab in Argentina, so you can cut calories in one way, at least. The ice cream is wonderful.

Restaurants

La Cabaña, Entre Ríos 436.
Considered the best place to go for steaks. Well, I wouldn't argue with that. Mine was outstanding. Even though I ordered a small portion there was enough to feed three people. They have many super potato side dishes. 14 dollars each.

Look, Costanera Norte, phone 783–1375.
Good for lunch, nice view of the city. The restaurant sits at river's edge and is called a "carrito," meaning it evolved from little barbecue stands that used to dot the river banks; you'll still see a few. There are several *carritos* in the area, but we were told this one was the best. Very large menu, everything from steaks to pizza; all delicious. About 18 dollars each for lunch.

La Payanca, corner of Marcelo T. Alvear and Suipacha streets.
A good place for lunch if you're shopping on Florida Street, just a couple of blocks away. Go upstairs to eat, as it is a bit calmer. Try to get there around 12:30 P.M., because by 1:00 the place is jammed. All the customers are locals. We were the only tourists in the place. It's a funky, old, small, noisy, crowded hangout, and the food was very cheap—total of 10 dollars for four, and we ate a lot.

Refugio del Viejo Conde, Cervino 4453, phone 773–6907.
This also is a beautiful restaurant with good service. When you arrive you are seated in the bar for cocktails. Shortly thereafter you are shown to a small room off the bar, where every dish available that night is displayed, so you can actually see what it is you're going to eat. On one table is a row of eight huge chafing dishes, each with a different "cazuela" inside. They are also noted for their game dishes. Dinner came to less than 30 dollars each.

El Repecho de San Telmo, Carlos Calvo 242, phone 362–5473, 46–9570.
This is one of the most charming, beautiful restaurants we've ever dined in; white-gloved service on antique silver and fine china; beautiful presentation of

food; many extra touches; fabulous food. Dinner came to about 15 dollars each.

Also recommended are: **Hostal del Lago,** Palermo Park, phone 76–87–60; **Claridge Grill** in the Claridge Hotel, Tucuman 535, phone 32–40–01; **El Hueso Perdido** in Olivos.

A couple of guidebooks recommended going over to the old Italian neighborhood called La Boca for a nice, homey Italian meal. Our guide told us there are no good restaurants there, all the food is awful, and what's there is very touristy. So much for that idea.

Now for a treat you'll never forget. Go out to the suburb called Martinez to an ice cream store called **Gelateria via Flaminia** on avenida del Libertador. Get an ice cream cone "cucurucho" style—meaning dipped in chocolate; but this, folks, is no ordinary chocolate-dipped cone. It ends up about eighteen inches high because of the special way they pack the cone. Not only is it spectacular to look at, the ice cream and chocolate sauce are tops. You'll pass through Martinez on your way to Tigre if you happen to be doing some sightseeing in that direction. It's worth a special trip just to go to this ice cream store. Another ice cream store in B.A. itself also makes cucurucho-style cones, but not as high. It's called **Postres Helados,** located at the corner of Ayacucho and Presidente Quintana in the Recoleta area, which happens to be a beautiful neighborhood. This latter ice-creameria is one of the most popular in the city. Read more about the Recoleta district in the sightseeing section.

Sightseeing

As I said before, there's not a heck of a lot to see in B.A. except the various quarters of the city itself, the suburbs, the river. If you have a guide, he or she will undoubtedly make sure you see every monument, park, and major building in the city. That takes a couple of hours.

Some of the areas you should be sure to see are **La Boca,** the Italian area, known for a little street called Caminito and several very old wooden buildings; **La Recoleta,** a very beautiful, tree-lined neighborhood with nice shops and restaurants, a good ice cream store, park, and the Recoleta cemetery, where you can go visit Evita; the suburbs of **San Isidro, Olivos, Martinez, Tigre, Luján** (don't miss the cathedral but skip the zoo). The major museum in B.A. is the **Nacional de Bellas Artes,** containing fine arts from all periods and countries. Don't miss the older quarter called **San Telmo,** full of antique shops, with an antique fair every Sunday in the park.

Shopping

There are several main shopping streets in Buenos Aires and we tried to see them all. I found the shopping to be generally disappointing for everything except leather and skin goods. The clothing styles are very uninteresting, nonchic, and somewhat Mexican-looking (lots of ruffles). We never did see a cashmere sweater and the fur coats we saw, for the most part, were kind of ugly with scrappy-looking furs. Leather, on the other hand, is a different story; also snake, lizard, croc, and alligator. Be careful when buying any of the latter that you'll be allowed to take it back into the U.S. —some of it you can't. Every leather store and shoe store will stick a stamp on whatever you buy to assure you that their product is "wildlife approved" and permissible in the U.S. That's pure nonsense—they only want you to buy. Crocodile is definitely not allowed; some alligator is; snake and lizard should be, although one of us got hassled in U.S. customs over a pair of lizard shoes. Prices are comparable to U.S. prices in some cases; in other cases you'll pay much less in B.A.

We had the best luck shopping on *Florida Street,* especially when we got into the galerias. We found good shoes at Francopuggi, Galeria del Sol; also at Celine and Nordo, both on Florida. Lopez has several stores and carries clothing and purses. *Avenida Santa Fe* is the other main shopping street, but after walking about five blocks we gave it up—nothing unusual, exceptional, or even interesting. *Alvear Street* is very chic and the shops look great as you drive by, but going on foot and really looking was another story —again, not much. There were nice shops in the *Recoleta area* on Avenida Ayacucho and Avenida Presidente Quintana. The big find in the whole city was right in our hotel on the first floor—a purse store called *Cesare Mauro.* The selection and quality were outstanding, the prices fantastic. They also carried Gucci bracelets lined in skins of different colors, at very reasonable prices. Maybe they aren't really Gucci, but who's gonna know? Ah, yes, that reminds me: you'll see all sorts of European labels in B.A., such as Gucci, Celine, Pierre Cardin, Dior, Missoni, Charles Jordan, and Harrods. You'll get very excited because the prices are so low. Secret: what you get is not what you see. They are all copies, made in Argentina, but I defy anyone to tell them from the real McCoy without using a microscope. It is possible that they are copied with the blessing of the original company, or possibly are subsidiaries; who knows? Anyway, they're well made, beautiful, and the price is right. For antiques go to *San Telmo* around Dorrego Square on Defense and Humberto streets.

Nightlife

Tango, anyone? What samba is to Rio, so is tango to Buenos Aires. You absolutely must not fail to go to a tango show. You'll think you're in an old movie or something. The best one is *El Viejo Almacen;* it costs about 13 dollars per person, which includes two drinks. There are two shows— one at 10:30 P.M. and one at 1:00 A.M. I suggest going to the earlier show. It's mostly music with some dancing, and it's just wonderful!

You may notice that the mamas of Buenos Aires tend to dress their children like twins, even when they're not. Several times we saw a family with two or three daughters of various ages, all dressed alike. For what reason, I don't know. The children there are really beautiful—you'll see such faces!—but they are very ill-mannered. It seems their parents let them do whatever they want to do, which is somewhat of a surprise considering the sedateness of the city. They must get all their joie de vivre out while they're young because they don't seem to have much of it later.

Be sure you save about 6 dollars each to take to the airport, for the departure tax. It takes several extra minutes (in our case, about twenty) to take care of this tax business, so don't arrive at the airport at the last minute. We flew Aerolineas Argentinas, first class, and it was excellent. Although the food was beautifully presented and prepared, it was lacking somewhat in flavor. You can't have everything, can you?

As long as you're in the area, meaning south South America, plan to spend a day and a night at Iguazú Falls, if possible (see next section). If you can't stay overnight you can see the falls in one day by flying there and back from either Rio or B.A. You should make the effort; it's well worth it.

Buenos Aires is not one of the world's most exciting or exotic places, but it is interesting to go to once, being one of South America's largest and most important cities. We enjoyed our visit there very much.

Iguazu Falls

No trip to Buenos Aires or Rio or anywhere else in that part of the world should exclude a trip to Iguazú Falls, located on the border of Argentina, Brazil, and Paraguay. You can fly there in about seventy-five minutes from either Buenos Aires or Rio. The trip can be done over and back in one day, but for a better experience plan to spend one night there.

Iguazú Falls are among the largest in the world, rivaling Niagara. They are located in the heart of a dense jungle full of exotic plants and wildlife. Besides the falls you'll see many species of butterflies, the kind you usually only see pinned to a board in a museum. You may also see giant lizards (we saw a baby one that was the size of a cat), and all sorts of weird insectos. There is a nice little airport, two main towns, and several hotels and motels.

One of the principal hotels is on the Argentinian side, but the best one is on the Brazilian side, a stone's throw from the major part of the falls called *Devil's Throat*. That hotel is the *Hotel das Cataratas* and is government owned. It's a large, pink and white, colonial-style hotel with pool and transportation to the falls (across the street). If I had to do it again I would without question stay at this hotel for one night. There are many relatively new, large, and beautiful motels along the road as well.

Be sure you have your passport with you when you visit Iguazú to avoid any hassle at the airport or crossing the border, which is the river. For best results arrange to have a car and driver meet you at the airport and show you around.

Many of the roads and walkways over the falls were washed out in 1983 by severe flooding, but it is still possible to see all of the falls from every angle. If you have to make a choice between the Brazilian side and the Argentinian side, see the Brazilian. The best thing, of course, is to see both sides because each is different.

Wear comfortable walking shoes, which will get wet, and cool clothes, which will also get wet. It's very hot, muggy, and jungly, but we didn't encounter any pesky bugs looking to make lunch out of us. Take lots of film.

For a great lunch stop go to *Rafain Churrascaria,* Avenida das Cataratas, just outside the town of Foz do Iguazú ("foz" means where the two rivers come together), near the Hotel Bourbon. A huge place, semi open-air, with a giant buffet barbecue Brazilian-style, live music, a big dessert buffet, and plenty cheap. Three of us ate for 12 dollars total.

You can also go visit the ruins of a very old monastery and you can take a helicopter ride over the falls. But you'll only have time to do everything if you stay overnight or if you arrive very early and leave very late. No matter how you go, GO.

P.S. There's a wonderful chocolate store just outside the entrance to the park on the Brazilian side. The shop is called *Chocolate Caseiro das Cataratas,* and if you're a chocoholic, you'll go nuts. They also have delicious juices.

Peru

Peru

Most of what I want to say about Peru I cannot put into words, because a great part of the trip was a very spiritual encounter, or "religious experience" as people like to call it. This is nothing new to anyone who has been to Peru or done any amount of reading on the subject. I have been drawn to Peru for a number of years without really understanding why until now. To put it in the simplest terms possible, there are a lot of very strong vibrations there, which emanate from the land and the people. Three of us went together, and we all felt it, and none of us can verbalize what we felt. Consequently this account will be mostly in an informational format dealing with logistics and advice. Just let me say that when you go to Peru, leave yourself open for anything that comes your way.

Unfortunately, Peru is one of the struggling Third World South American countries that has more problems than it can possibly deal with. The poverty level there is very high and seems almost insurmountable. Aside from that, it is a country of great contrasts, great architecture, spectacular scenery, colorful and friendly people, fabulous handicrafts, beautiful restaurants, Incas, mysticism, mysteries, and magic. (Please finish reading before you pack your suitcase.)

Your trip to Peru, if you are going on a tourist basis, should be arranged according to when you go to Machu Picchu, rather than when you are going to be in Lima, regarding weather. Lima is on the coast in the desert region and the last time it rained there was in 1970. For four months (their spring, our fall) it is shrouded in fog and mists, with partial sun sometimes. You won't be spending much time there anyway, and it's far more important to have good weather in the mountains or jungle. Consult the Machu Picchu section as to the best times to go there.

As for what to put into your suitcase, you don't have to pack your best suit or fanciest dress. Even the most lavish restaurants in Lima did not require a tie or even a jacket, although men would probably feel more comfortable with the latter. At the same time, you would not want to wear jeans and T-shirts; something of a casual but sophisticated nature is best. Comfortable walking shoes with rubber soles are a must, with hiking or tennis shoes imperative for the mountains and ruins. (More specific information about these areas is found in the following sections.) They don't have decaf coffee in Peru, and the coffee they have is *very* strong, so you might want to take your own instant decaf if that is what you are used to. Don't pack a lot of heavy sweaters or jackets, because you can buy all the warmest woolen items you want when you get there. Take pants or slacks that have deep front pockets (I'll explain in a minute). Ladies should carry handbags made of a very sturdy material that cannot be slashed, with a short double handle that fits over the shoulder and close to the armpit. A money belt is essential. Take binoculars, a lot of film, about 30 dollars in one-dollar bills, antidiarrhea medication, a lot of tissues and wash-and-dries, a couple of collapsible extra suitcases with appropriate luggage tags and straps, locks for all your baggage, converters and adapters (electrical current is 220–240), an umbrella, and guidebooks.

Now, to clarify the pants with the deep front pockets. Thievery is rampant and perfected to a high art in Peru. When you consider the incredible poverty and unemployment problems they have, and the fact that the government either can't or won't do much about it, it's no small wonder that these people are forced to crime in order to survive. Never carry anything of value in your purse. Divide all money between your two front pockets and a money belt, not letting any of it bulge out. Do not put anything in a back pocket. Do not let your purse or camera dangle carelessly from your shoulder or around your neck. Leave your passport and whatever money and traveler's checks you don't need for daily excursions locked in your hotel safe. Lock your suitcases when you leave them in your hotel room. Be constantly aware of people crowding around you, trying to get you to look or move in some direction. When walking in a crowd, keep your belongings under a tight grip, and if possible, stay close to a wall. If someone squirts mustard or something on you "by accident," watch out. Many thieves work in teams of two or three and are very innocent-looking, well-dressed people in their thirties. Others are street kids who move like lightning. I'm not telling you all this to scare you, but you must be aware. We did not have any misfortunes in this area, but we were always on guard. I have heard unhappy stories from others.

The best guidebooks I could find stateside were Fodor's and Birnbaum's *South America* books; Birnbaum's had an extra section just on Lima. Hiram

Bingham's *Lost City of the Incas* is required reading for Machu Picchu. Once you arrive in Peru you can find other guidebooks in bookstores and hotels which deal more specifically with various areas. The October 1979 issue of *Gourmet* magazine has a good article on Lima.

Spanish is the most commonly spoken language in Peru, and certainly a traveler's knowledge of the language would be most useful. If you have a guide with you, he can do the translating for you. In better restaurants and hotels you will always find someone who speaks English. When you go into the mountains and small villages, most of the natives speak the ancient Inca language called Quechua, and maybe Spanish as well.

As for the food—well, it's very good. We never had what could be considered a bad meal or even one that was disappointing. There are many regional dishes that you've never heard of, and some of the vocabulary is different than you find in other parts of the Spanish-speaking world. There is a short list of some items below. A drink called a "pisco sour" is very popular and delicious. It tastes something like a margarita. Another pisco drink which tastes something like a vodka collins is a "chilcano de pisco." A delicious and very unusual afterdinner drink (because it is so rich) is called an "algarrobina," made from a syrupy liqueur of carob. Stick to bottled water (although we drank pisco sours all week with no ill effects and they're made with crushed ice). The two best bottled waters we found were Selva Alegre and Milagro; all are carbonated. Potatoes and corn are used frequently. Some of the corn is very different than the American type, and very good. The chicken and beef were good. Fresh seafood and shellfish abound and were always delicious. The bread is not exciting but the butter is wonderful. Ice creams are grainy but tasty. There is a lot of fresh fruit, but be sure to stick to those that can be peeled. Stay away from most raw vegetables. Avoid eating anything from a food stand or in a questionable restaurant. Generally speaking, if you stick to the good hotels and eating establishments, you don't have to worry too much. So what else is new?

Here's a list of some of the local foods.

ahi: a local chili pepper.
a lo macho: a dish served with shellfish sauce.
anticucha: a shish kebab; usually a first course.
cherimoya: a sort of apple.
chicha: a corn liqueur, popular with the natives, as it was for the ancient Incas. Usually bootlegged.
chicharrón: refers to something that is deep-fried, and specifically to deep-fried pork. In the U.S. we know this as deep-fried pork rinds.
choclo: corn on the cob.
choros: mussels.

chupa: a hearty, Peruvian soup.

coca tea: a tea made from cocaine leaves; a pick-me-up.

conchitas: scallops.

corvina: sea bass, the main local fish.

criolla: refers to Peruano-style dishes; Creole.

cuy: roasted guinea pig, a common dish (I hear it's good).

gaseosa: a soft drink (no diet drinks available).

leche frita: flan (fried milk?).

lomo: beef steak; the cuts seemed to vary.

palta: avocado.

pan con ajo: garlic bread, and very good.

picarones: pumpkin doughnuts, fried, with maple syrup; churros.

If you attend a folklorico show or even hear some Peruano music in a restaurant, you may be approached by the musicians to buy a cassette of their music. These are of the homemade variety and cost about 4 or 5 dollars. We bought two such tapes and when we got home and listened to them we were not disappointed. Peruvian music is unusual, lively, and a bit other-worldly, just like the whole country.

Lima

Lima is the largest city in Peru, the capital of the country, and not the most exciting part of Peru. Still, there is enough to see and do there to warrant two or three days. The city center is quite dirty and polluted, but the suburbs of Miraflores and San Isidro are lovely, neat, and clean: it's like comparing downtown L.A. to Brentwood. The traffic is heavy but not gridlocked. Weather during the foggy months is gloomy. The people are relatively friendly and not pushy. Some begging but not much.

Hotels

There are three good hotels in Lima. The best one is the *Lima Sheraton;* it's very big but well run, with an efficient staff; nicely decorated. We safely left some of our luggage with them when we went to Cuzco. The second choice for the downtown area is the *Gran Hotel Bolívar* on Plaza San Martín. It's an older hotel, smaller, with a European flavor. If you want to be away from the city center, stay in the suburb of Miraflores at the *Hotel César.* When I go back to Peru (you'll notice I didn't say "if") I'll stay at the Sheraton again.

Restaurants

The only problem with restaurants in Lima is deciding which ones to go to. Most are open for lunch and dinner. The most we spent at any restaurant was 50 dollars for three people, which included everything (and we can eat and drink a lot!).

Carlin, La Paz 646, phone 45–88–43

is of a more modern decor, small and pretty, located in Miraflores about a block from the Hotel César in the El Suche shopping lane.

Los Condes de San Isidro, Paz Soldan 290, phone 22–25–57

is in an old Spanish colonial mansion. Very good food, lots of atmosphere, piano. Ask to see the private chapel.

La Granja Azul, Carretera Central, phone 35–07–77

is a twenty-minute drive out of town (14 km.). Their specialty is barbecued chicken; their sauce is made from the algarrobina liqueur, mentioned earlier. It's said this is the best barbecued chicken you'll ever eat.

José Antonio, Monteagudo 200, phone 61–99–23

serves good local food; in San Isidro.

El Pabellón de Caza, Alonso de Molino 1100, Monterrico, phone 35–25–62

is a gorgeous restaurant next to the Gold Museum. The decor is very "Amazon," and the garden contains all kinds of lush, tropical plants and flowers, plus large, beautiful parrots and other birds that roam freely. Their specialty is local lobster.

La Rosa Náutica, in Miraflores

is a new and very beautiful Victorian-style restaurant at the end of the pier, full of lush hanging plants and views of the surf and coastline. The food was excellent. Their specialty is seafood, mainly *corvina*. Good ceviche. Piano.

Tambo de Oro, Belen 1066, phone 31–00–46

is a short walk from the Sheraton and another restaurant in a Spanish colonial mansion, but this one is much more spectacular than Los Condes. It's very baroque. The dining area is in the inner courtyard, which has been covered. There is a small section of shops at the back of the restaurant selling native handicrafts. We found some things there we hadn't seen elsewhere, some of better quality. The market stays open until about 9:45 P.M.

Las Trece Monedas, Jirón Ancash 536, phone 27–65–47

is yet another restaurant located in a former Spanish mansion. They serve *criolla*-style food.

Shopping

My advice is to save most of your shopping for Cuzco. The majority of the handicrafts come from there to begin with, and you'll find a much larger selection and lower prices. However, if you must shop in Lima, we found the following to be the best and the *only* places:

Avenida de la Marina. Artesanías del Peru 669 and 665, an Indian market on both sides of the street near the airport.

Very good selection of handicrafts at very low prices. It could be the runner-up to Cuzco, and a good bet if you didn't finish your shopping there.

Miraflores. El Suche and **El Alamo** shopping arcades, located on avenida La Paz a block from the Hotel César.
Also along La Paz and on some of the side streets are a few antique stores.
San Isidro. Artesanías del Peru, avenida Jorge Masadre 610.
This is a very large store which has a sample of just about every handicraft available in Peru. Prices were OK. Selection of sweaters did not come close to what we found in Cuzco. For other items, however, they had a better selection.
Tambo de Oro restaurant.
The handicraft shops in the patio, already mentioned.

There are other isolated galleries and shops we missed that are probably very good. We did not find the jewelry to be particularly outstanding anywhere. Lots of antique silver items, or so they would have you believe. Buyer beware when it comes to antiques and Incan artifacts (remember it's a serious crime to take antiquities out of the country). The big items to buy are: woolen goods made from alpaca, including sweaters *(chompas),* vests *(chalecos),* blankets, hats, socks, leg warmers, mittens, ponchos, shawls, jackets, mufflers, etc. Wall hangings of all types and qualities; some could double as rugs. Fabric bags and purses. Alpaca slippers, coats, rugs, etc., of the fuzzy, furry type. Silver and Indian jewelry of a lesser quality. T-shirts—the best selection we saw was in El Suche and El Alamo in Miraflores, and at the train depot at Machu Picchu. Little wooden boxes that open to expose charming scenes of teensy figures. The usual assortment of trinkets, knicknacks, and junk.

Final note: the shopping on the downtown streets of Unión (a pedestrian mall) and La Colmena, both next to the Gran Hotel Bolívar, was terrible. Don't even bother. And don't expect to find anything high-fashion in Lima; I don't think it exists, with the exception of a small number of items in the most expensive boutiques, which are few and far between.

As for prices, see the Cuzco section on shopping.

The Peruvian unit of money is called a "sol" (for one), or "soles" (pronounced something like *solace;* for more than one).

Sightseeing

The reason you may need three days for Lima is because of the vast amount of things to see there. If you like museums and churches, you will have more than your fill.

Churches

The Cathedral, on the Plaza de Armas
looks more intriguing from the outside than it is on the inside. Its chief attraction is that it contains the remains of Francisco Pizarro. There is a small museum in the cathedral, too.

La Merced, Jirón de la Unión 621
has a very elaborate facade and interior.

San Francisco, Jirón Ancash 300
has a marvelous interior of red and white patchwork. In the cloister you will find magnificent old Spanish tiles lining all the walls. The ceilings are also very beautiful but in a state of decay. They are doing a lot of restoration on this church at the moment. In the church are lavish side altars, and don't miss the catacombs with their eerie display of bones and tunnels. A flash camera is a must.

San Pedro Jirón Ucayali 300
dates from 1750 and contains very lavish rococo-style side altars. Down the street is the *Torre Tagle Palace,* dating from 1735. It is now a foreign affairs office and you can't go in, but it's worthwhile to take a look at the very beautiful facade.

Santo Domingo Jirón Camaná 170, Plazuela Santo Domingo
is a good example of Spanish colonial architecture.

Museums

There are several museums in Lima, and the first three listed below should not be missed.

The Amano Museum, calle Retiro 160, phone 41-29-09
is a very small, private museum in Miraflores, and you must have an appointment to visit. You will be given a one-hour tour (in Spanish) of this small jewel, containing some of the most outstanding examples of Peruvian antiquities. Most notable are the pots and weavings. Definitely worthwhile, even if you don't understand Spanish.

The Gold Museum, avenida Alonso de Molina 1100, Monterrico
private collection owned by Miguel Mujica Gallo, needs another two hours really to be seen well. The two main collections here are antique arms and costumes (including the sword of Pizarro and the uniform of San Martín), and over 12,000 pieces of ancient Indian gold. The latter are truly amazing to see.

Museum of Anthropology and Archaeology, Plaza Bolívar in Pueblo Libre.
We did not go to this museum, because we had been to the one in Cuzco. You should go to one or the other. The one in Cuzco is smaller and supposedly better organized.

The Museum of the Inquisition, Jirón Junín 548
is located in the Holy Office of the Inquisition in the Plaza Bolívar. The Congreso building is also on this square. See the wooden ceiling in the main hall before taking a macabre journey through the torture rooms, complete with life-sized mock-ups of some poor torture victims. It's a little corny but drives home the horrors of the Inquisition.

Museo Larco Herrera, avenida Bolívar 1515
contains over 40,000 *huacos,* or ancient pots, but these are not just ordinary pots! You have to see them to believe them. Be sure you go to the room of

pornographic pots next to the gift shop. Besides the *huacos,* the museum has a wonderful display of all types of ancient artifacts and tapestries, plus a very fine collection of mummies. The museum was once a private home, and the building and grounds are quite beautiful. You could really spend a minimum of two hours here, just to run through. This is a private collection.

Tour Service

We used a company called Lima Tours for everything in Peru and I can highly recommend them. They were excellent in every respect, highly efficient, and made our trip much easier by taking care of all the "business" (airline tickets, transportation, hotel checking in and out, restaurant reservations, tour guides). With the exception of one sort of unfriendly but not unpleasant guide, we were blessed with excellent guides and drivers everywhere we went. Their address is 1040 Belen, Lima, phone 5114–276624 or 276720.

Other Sights in Peru

Besides the places described later in the chapter, you might also consider seeing the following:

Arequipa. Peru's second largest city, located south of Nasca and called the "White City" because all the buildings are made from a white volcanic stone. It is said to be truly beautiful.

Iquitos. North of Lima and Peru's gateway to the Amazon. Excursions of all types and lengths into the jungle and down the Amazon depart from this city.

The "lines" at Nasca. These are the fabulous and huge lines and pictures, numbering in the hundreds, in the desert south of Lima. You can do a day trip to and from Lima, or you can go overnight there. Our guide said the accommodations are simple but clean and adequate. You should fly over the area.

A minimum of two weeks for Peru is necessary to cover the basics. But there's so much more to this country than what you see on the surface. Don't forget to watch the skies, too.

Cuzco

When you go to Cuzco you're going to get high, whether you plan to or not. The elevation there is 11,000 feet and higher when you go exploring. The first thing that happens when you arrive at your hotel is they make you sit down in the lobby for about thirty minutes and drink coca tea, made from you-know-what. Then they suggest that you take a three-hour nap before going out, moving slowly at all times. This is all very sound advice. If you aren't careful you can get *sorroche,* or altitude sickness, which is not fun and can definitely ruin your trip. We relaxed for about an hour and a half and that was all I could stand. We never had any altitude adaptation problems at all, aside from a minor headache and running out of breath on the first day.

Cuzco is another world. Half the city is built on the foundations of Inca walls (you can't miss them); a great many buildings are seventeenth- and eighteenth-century Spanish colonial style; the rest is adobe. Local Indians and peasants abound in the streets with their colorful native costumes, some with llamas. Every street is an experience and a view. There are tons of shops selling Peruvian handicrafts at unbelievably low prices. The air is clear, and the surrounding mountains are full of Inca ruins, terraces, small villages, steep gorges, snow-capped peaks, and fertile valleys.

There are three or four nice hotels in Cuzco, the best one being the **Libertador,** which is where we stayed. The hotel was formerly a large Spanish townhouse and much of the original colonial building remains. The inner courtyard is especially charming. The personnel are very pleasant and the food in the dining room is quite good. Try to get a room that faces the inner courtyard (17 and 18 were good).

As for restaurants, you don't have a lot to choose from. There are several places on the Plaza de Armas: *Roma, Chef Victor, El Tumi,* and *Paititi.* These are all mediocre. Just off the Plaza de Armas is a small restaurant upstairs called **El Mesón de Espaderos.** Their specialty is grilled foods, and what we had was quite good. There were no other Americans there (we consider this a plus). The garlic bread was fabulous. You can also get grilled guinea pig if you want to try something new (this is a very common food in Peru, going way back to Inca times). Dinner for three came to 20 dollars.

The two best dinners we had in Cuzco were dinner at our own hotel (Libertador) and dinner at **El Truco.** There was entertainment at both places which was very good. At El Truco be sure you ask for the regular menu and not the tourist menu. Their evening program of entertainment began at 8:30.

You can dress very casually in Cuzco, and no restaurant is what could be called fancy. Rubber-soled shoes are a must; all the streets are cobbled and can be slippery as ice and difficult to walk on. During the day (in September) it was warm and sunny, even hot, but at night it got pretty chilly. You don't need high-heeled shoes, dresses, sportscoats, or ties.

The main square, **Plaza de Armas,** is one of the most gorgeous central squares I've seen in any city in the world, and that includes anything in Paris or Italy. There are three large Spanish colonial churches on the plaza and all the color you could ever want. You'll find the local peasants selling just about everything; shopping really is best between 8:00 and 11:00 P.M. If you want to take a picture of a lady with a llama, be prepared to pay the mama. Very adorable, very dirty, and very poor kids will approach you selling all kinds of stuff that you really don't want and can't use. Buy something anyway. You can often barter for a photograph by buying whatever it is they're selling, which usually costs less than a dollar. American one-dollar bills, by the way, are very useful here. Be sure you visit the Plaza de Armas in the evening, after dark but before 8:00 P.M., to see the church illuminated. It looks like Christmas.

The **Basilica Cathedral** on the Plaza de Armas dates to 1560 and you should go inside. It contains the largest silver altar in Peru and some fabulous gold baroque side altars.

The **Church of San Blas** contains a very famous and elaborately carved wood pulpit which you should not miss. The church also has one of those enormous rococo main altars.

La Merced Church is a definite to see, for two reasons. First, the cloisters are among the most spectacular I've viewed anywhere in the world. Second, the museum of the church has a very famous ornament called the *Monstrance,* made of gold and containing hundreds of diamonds, pearls, and other precious stones. It's quite marvelous. You have to pass through the cloisters to get to the museum.

The *Archaeological Museum of Cuzco,* which belongs to the university, is small but very good, especially interesting after you've been to Machu Picchu.

There is a stone in the wall of the Palace of Inca Roca called the *12-Angled Stone,* which everyone goes and looks at. It really is an amazing example of the incredible stone technology that the Incas possessed. If you go to Machu Picchu (or maybe I should say *when* you go, because no one goes to Cuzco only) you will see a 36-angled stone!

Cori Cancha, or the Temple of the Sun, is embedded in the Church of Santo Domingo, and dates circa 1200–1400. It's a fantastic architectural comingling of two cultures. Excavations continue to uncover more and more of the ancient Inca structure, which was maybe the most important one in Cuzco in its day.

For sightseeing in the city you really don't need a guide, and almost everything is within walking distance of everything else. For touring the surrounding countryside, you must have a driver and guide. I can highly recommend Lima Tours for such a purpose; their address is in the Machu Picchu section. Our guide's name was Benny and he was excellent.

You really need a minimum of three days in Cuzco: two for the city and one for the countryside. Four or five days would be better if you like wandering around quaint towns and taking in local color without being rushed.

The areas you should visit outside the city are:

Sacsahuaman. A large fortress on the hill above the city, affording great views of the area. Ten minutes from town.

Tambomachay. At an elevation of almost 12,000 feet, this is an ancient Inca sacred fountain. Ten minutes from Sacsahuaman.

Kenko. Between the above two are caves, used by the Incas for burial purposes, housing mummies.

The *Urubamba Valley,* Sacred Valley of the Incas, at 10,000 feet. The drive to the valley affords magnificent views of the countryside and Andes peaks, most notably Mt. Veronica at 19,000 feet and Mt. Chicon at 18,000 feet. The little square in the city of Urubamba is probably very typical of most of the small towns in Peru. In the area known as *Yucay* (formerly a favorite place of the Incas) is a lovely restaurant in an old Spanish colonial hacienda called the *Alhambra.* Reservations in advance on weekends. Be sure you ask to see the private museum and the cockfight arena. The proprietor is very proud to show them off.

Perhaps the most spectacular ruins in the area are at *Ollantaytambo,* at 9500 feet. This is a huge fort and town in excellent condition. The little town there has managed to keep intact most of the former Incan town, and to walk through its streets is quite an experience. You can take pictures of the townspeople if you are discreet.

Pisac is at the other end of the valley and is where the famous Sunday market is held. It's another small but charming town. If you have the energy, there are more fantastic Incan ruins at the top of the mountain above the city. It's a fifty-minute walk up the mountain, however.

Throughout your driving tour of these areas you will be amazed at the endless terraces, built by the Incas and pre-Incas. They go from valley floor to mountaintop and never end. It is impossible not to be in total awe of the people who built them.

Back in Cuzco, you may be approached by someone selling you a ticket to a folklórico show in a local theater. The ticket is only about 6 dollars and the show is legitimate, but it is incredibly amateurish and much too long and basically boring. You're better off going to El Truco, which has very professional groups. There are two such presentations in the city; the one we had the misfortune to see was at the Teatro Machu Picchu.

As for shopping, you'll find plenty to buy. Be sure to take a couple of collapsible suitcases with you, or you can buy wonderful fabric bags on the spot for 5 to 10 dollars. The best ones we saw were in the shop directly across from the Libertador hotel. You can bargain with the people if you want, but when you know that the average yearly income in Peru is less than 1000 dollars, and when you observe the way most of these people live, it seems pretty silly to overdo the bargaining bit. A dollar or two might mean nothing to you, but to them it can feed their whole family for a day. The alpaca and wool items are fabulous. We bought beautiful sweaters and jackets for between 8 and 20 dollars; large alpaca blankets of fine quality for 15 to 50 dollars. Small pots for 1 to 5 dollars. Antique weavings for 40 to 90 dollars. Wall hangings, ponchos, T-shirts, Indian jewelry (not good), alpaca slippers, musical instruments, all kinds of trinkets and goodies—a real feast for a shopper on any budget. It's *very* hard to spend a lot of money shopping in Peru.

Take along some packaged cookies and candies to give to the kids there, especially the ones you see out in the country. You would also have fun with a Polaroid camera.

I cannot think of one negative thing to say about Cuzco. It is one of the most charming, quaint, and easy-to-love little towns I've ever seen. It was very hard to say goodbye.

Machu Picchu

No, Dorothy, this is not Kansas, nor is it Tibet, but this *is* Shangri-La: this is Machu Picchu!

To say that Machu Picchu (pronounced *mah-choo peek-choo*) is awesome, astounding, and breathtaking is an understatement. There are not enough clichés going around to describe the emotional and visual impact one has when experiencing this "lost city of the Incas." Of all the ancient ruins I've seen thus far, I have to put this one way up on the list.

The best time to go to Machu Picchu is, of course, during the dry season, which is between April and September (the latter month being considered the off season.) The worst months to go are November and December because of rain, January, February, and March because of rain and tourists, and July and August because of tourists. From April to June it can be clear, but cold. We were there in September and the weather was gorgeous: very warm and sunny in the daytime and cool but not too cold at night. One would be very sorry to be at Machu Picchu in the rain; this would preclude doing any hiking or just quiet, contemplative sitting in the ruins, which is the best way to experience their magic and majesty and whatever else.

Machu Picchu (known to the Incas as Vilcapampa) extends across a terraced plateau between three mountains: Machu Picchu, which is above the small, government-owned hotel, and Huayna Picchu and Wawa Picchu on the other side. The elevation there is about 8000 feet and the surrounding Andes are as high as 19,000 feet. This is what you call scenery.

It is imperative that you spend the night at the hotel at the site. Your itinerary in Peru should be arranged around which night you can get into the hotel, as it is very small and reservations can be hard to get. We were there on a Sunday night and the hotel was half empty, this due to the fact that most tourists prefer to stay in Cuzco and visit the Sunday Indian market in Pisac. Contrary to what we'd heard, we found the hotel to be very nice, simple, clean, with edible food, fabulous views, and a well-stocked bar. The electricity, and therefore the water, go off every day between 3:00 and 5:30 P.M. and again between 11:00 P.M. and 6:00 A.M. However, we were there at the very end of the dry season and water was getting scarce, so perhaps that was the reason. It was not an inconvenience in any case.

I strongly suggest taking a guide with you on the train from Cuzco who can explain things that you see along the way and who can give you a detailed tour of the ruins. We had an excellent and charming guide named Benigno Rivas S. (Benny) from Lima Tours (avenida El Sol 567, phone 2809; or Box 531, Cuzco, Peru). If you do not have your own guide, be sure to have a decent guidebook with you. The most popular one seems to be *A Walking Tour of Machu Picchu,* available at bookstores in the U.S. and Peru. Another must for reading, either before or after your trip, is Hiram Bingham's *Lost City of the Incas.*

To get to Machu Picchu you must take the little train which runs daily from Cuzco. The trip takes four hours each way and it's a beautiful ride. It's horrifying to think of going up and back (actually it's down and back) in the same day: eight hours on a not very comfortable train in order to spend two hours in one of the world's most stupendous archaeological areas. If you stay at the hotel you can be extremely leisurely about exploring the ruins. After the train leaves to go back to Cuzco with all the tourists on board, you are left with a small handful of other hotel guests and you can visit the ruins almost in solitude. The following morning be sure to get up to see the sun rise from behind the Andes peaks and bathe Machu Picchu in glorious early-morning light. After breakfast you'll have plenty of time to take a long hike, either to the top of Huayna Picchu or up the old Inca road to Puerta del Sol. Both hikes take about two hours. The former is the more strenuous and difficult, as you will see just by looking at the trail.

You need to have advance reservations for the train. Either you or your guide should arrive at the train station early to make sure you get seats on the left side of the train going to Machu Picchu, and on the right side going back to Cuzco. There are rudimentary bathrooms on the train and they sell packaged snacks and various drinks on board. Many people take their own food along. The train makes one three-minute stop at Ollantaytambo. When the train arrives at the M.P. station you must be prepared to push, shove, and run to the bus line, while either your guide or someone in your party runs to the ticket line. There are not enough buses to transport all the people on the train up to the ruins, and if you do not get on the first set of buses you could wait as long as an hour to get up the mountain. Once you arrive at the hotel area you will find a snack bar or you can have lunch at the hotel.

When you return to the train station to go back to Cuzco, you will find a nice Indian market selling all the same items you find in Cuzco, which is where all the stuff comes from.

It is best to leave most of your luggage at your hotel in Cuzco and take only a carry-on bag on the train. If you go during the warm, dry months, you'll need shorts, jeans, T-shirts, and a warm sweater for evening, plus a waterproof windbreaker in case it does rain a little. Hiking or tennis shoes and socks are a must. Also take plenty of film, binoculars, insect repellent, bug spray and insect bite medication, sunscreen, a hat, and tissues. Machu Picchu is located at the beginning of the Amazon jungle, so you have to be prepared for no-see-ums, which take teensy little bites that itch for days. Because of the high altitude and totally unpolluted air the sun is very intense. There are four kinds of poisonous snakes in the area which keep to the bushes, meaning you should keep out of the bushes. They do have antivenin there in case of emergency. Condors used to be numerous but have taken to less populated areas. If you have a clear, moonless night, be prepared for a display of stars such as you have never seen. Maybe even a UFO.

To spend twenty-four hours at Machu Picchu seemed barely enough time. The longer we were there the more spiritually and emotionally involved we became. It is an experience of intense wonder, peace, and awe.

New York City

New York City

This section is not for people who live in New York or who go to New York frequently. It is for people who have never been there or who only go once every other year, more or less. I am by no means an expert on this city and what I present here are but a few tips, which I hope will help make your visit a little easier and more enjoyable.

I recommend getting the Michelin green guide *New York City,* as it presents a lot of little details and business that I can't be bothered with. Another good source is Gault-Millau, *Guide New York.* For restaurants outside of the ones I mention, write for a handy little booklet called *Zagat New York City Restaurant Survey,* 55 Central Park West, New York, N.Y. 10023, and include 5 dollars. This book gives quick, concise, and beautifully organized critiques of a giant number of restaurants. If you want something more formal and elegant you can get Mimi Sheraton's *Guide to New York Restaurants* (Times Books). Her book is much more thorough and descriptive than the Zagat book, but it doesn't pack as easily. For an outstanding book on what to see there's a beautiful hard-cover volume called *New York Open to the Public,* by Cheri Fein, which you could research from, but again —it's a little big for packing. A good book for shopping, especially, is Garry Frank's *Where To: Find It, Buy It, Eat It in New York.* There are many others on the market.

So much for the competition. Now, what does one wear when one goes off to the Big A? Well, that will depend on the weather, so what you should do the day before you leave is call the New York City Weather Bureau and find out what's going on there, meteorologically speaking. That number is 212–976–1212. Remember, you want to blend in when you get there, so stay away from some of your chic Hawaiiana outfits or Southern California beachwear. People in New York dress (a) rather well, or (b) rather poorly. There doesn't seem to be much in the middle. As a tourist you want to look nice, blend in, and be comfortable. Shoes for walking are of utmost importance. Take your jogging duds, if that's what you do, because jogging in Central Park is *the* thing to do. Umbrella. Nonpickpocket purse. Raincoat, unless it's the dead of summer and 95 degrees in the shade. When it's humid (they say *yoo-mid*), it's very very. If you plan to go to the better restaurants, dress with a little style. At night the chicness in people tends to come out. As for theater, people tend to be more casual. For a matinee you can wear almost anything. Even in the evening, people don't seem to get as dressed up as they do for theater elsewhere.

Hotels

My list of hotels will not be for budget-minded people. I really don't know where the inexpensive hotels are, or which of them are any good. For that information get your hands on a travel agent or some friend who knows. Actually the Gault-Millau book that I mentioned above has a pretty good list.

The *Carlyle,* 35 E. 76th Street at Madison Avenue, is the current pick as the best hotel in the city, according to what I've been reading. Also up on the list is the *Pierre,* Fifth Avenue at 61st Street, which is indeed wonderful, but costs an arm, leg, and eyebrow. Next door is the *Sherry Netherland,* 781 Fifth Avenue at 59th Street, where we have always had beautiful rooms and suites for much less than at their neighbor. The *Plaza,* which is the most famous hotel in New York, is not the most popular, nor can I recommend it, based on several disgruntled former clients. It's fun to go there for tea in the Palm Court, however. Down the street on Central Park South is the newly renovated *Ritz-Carlton,* which is excellent. In the same block are the *Park Lane* (not so hot), and the *Essex House* (mixed reviews). The *Drake,* 30 W. 54th Street, was a disaster when we stayed there, but they were renovating and I should hope it's better now. Several friends have stayed at the very beautiful *Palace,* 455 Madison Avenue (formerly the Vuillard House), and loved it. The only reason we've never stayed there is that it's too far from the park for my husband, the Jogger. A rather new hotel is the *Parker-Meridien* of the French chain. It has a swimming pool and terrible phone service, but otherwise people seem to like it. The *St. Regis-Sheraton,* 2 E. 55th Street at Fifth Avenue, has a great location and I hear tell it's a nice, relatively small hotel. Then there are the *Waldorf Towers,* 100 E. 50th Street, which many people like. (Not to be confused with the *Waldorf-Astoria,* where you can get a good cake, but I can't comment on the rooms.) Anyway, that's enough of a list to get you started. Ask around.

Food

I have to say "Food" instead of "Dining Out" or "Restaurants" because in New York there's more to eating than dining out in a restaurant. What I mean is, there's lots of good-to-great food to be had from little cafés, street vendors, and food emporiums. I will begin with finer dining, however, and give you a run-down of where we've eaten. Believe me, there are a zillion restaurants in New York, so this is not a complete list. I doubt if one exists.

Italian

Cent'Anni, 50 Carmine Street, phone 989–9494.
I ran into a lady who lived most of her life in Florence, and she told me that next to Da Silvano, this place has the best Italian cuisine in New York. We'll see.

Da Silvano, 260 Sixth Avenue between Houston and Bleecker Streets, phone 982–0090.
One of the best Italian meals we've had this side of Roma, and in New York, which is famous for great Italian restaurants. The duck here is simple and outstanding. The pastas are fabulous. Charming restaurant, sidewalk dining when weather permits, good people watching, casual. Florentine specialties. For dessert go two blocks away to Steve's on Sixth between 10th and 11th.

Elio's, 1621 Second Avenue, phone 772–2242.
Gets mixed reviews; love-hate relationships.

Giordano, 409 W. 39th Street, phone 947–9811.
Used to be better.

Grotta Azzurra, 387 Broome Street, phone 226–9283.
Fun, good food.

Il Monello, 1460 Second Avenue, phone 535–9310.
Same owners as Il Nido, which is better.

Il Nido, 251 E. 53rd Street between Second and Third avenues, phone 753–8450.
Another excellent and lovely Italian restaurant. Sophisticated service, beautiful room.

Lello, 65 E. 54th Street, phone 751–1555.
Small, intimate setting; very good food. Romantic if you go late.

Lusardi's, Second Avenue at 78th Street, phone 249–2020.
Big favorite on the Italian restaurant list. Nouvellish.

Nanni's,　146 E. 46th Street, phone 599–9684.
Very good and popular.
Parioli Romanissimo,　1466 First Avenue, phone 288–2391.
Rave reviews by everyone who eats there.
Patsy's,　236 W. 56th Street, phone 247–3491.
Mixed reviews. I know two guys who go directly to Patsy's from the airport before going to their hotel.
Pietro's,　201 E. 45th Street, phone 599–7920.
A favorite of my New Yawk friends, Mawge and Bawb, who took us there for our first meal in the city; was very good. Small and crowded, however. The entire kitchen could fit into your bathtub.
Rao V,　455 E. 144th Street in East Harlem, phone 534–9625.
Everyone says it's the safest place in town, being *very* Sicilian, if you get the picture. Supposed to have terrific food.
Trastevere,　309 E. 83rd Street, phone 734–6343.
Dinky, with charm; Italian cuisine; quite good. Get the veal with fresh tomato.

Other top Italian places in town are: *Quilted Giraffe,* 955 Second Avenue, phone 753–5355; *Primavera,* 1570 First Avenue, phone 861–8608; *Tre Scalini,* 230 E. 58th Street, phone 688–6888; *Tre Amici,* 1294 Third Avenue, phone 535–3416.

French

Café des Artistes,　1 W. 67th St, phone 877–3500.
Close to Lincoln Center. French bistro fare, a celebrity hangout, good for pre- or post-theater. Open every day. Medium-expensive.
Le Cirque,　58 E. 65th Street, phone 794–9292.
Double ditto.
Chanterelle,　89 Grand Street, in SoHo, phone 966–6960.
One of the top French restaurants in the city.
La Côte Basque,　5 E. 55th Street, phone 688–6525.
Excellent.
Le Cygne,　55 E. 54th Street, phone 759–5941.
Ditto, ditto, and ditto.
La Fondue,　43 W. 55th Street, phone 581–0820.
Also good for late-night dining; fun menu; more than fondue.
La Grenouille,　3 E. 52nd Street, phone 752–1495.
Outstanding food, decor, and service. And prices.
Lutèce,　249 E. 50th Street, phone 752–2225.
Ditto.
Le Perigord,　405 E. 52nd Street, phone 755–6244; and **Le Perigord Park,**　575 Park Avenue, phone 752–0050.
The latter seems to get better marks than the former, but both are good.

For French-type lunches: *Les Pleiades,* 20 E. 76th Street, phone 535–7230; *La Mangeoire,* 1008 Second Avenue, phone 759–7086; *Truffles,* 696 Madison Avenue, phone 838–3725 (also Italian dishes; great French toast and dark raisin bread).

Chinese

From French to Chinese . . . I only have five Chinese restaurants to talk about. The first two are highly recommended; the third and fourth are medium recommended, the fifth is not recommended.

Auntie Yuan, 1191A First Avenue, phone 722–4040.
Next to Maxwell's Plum. New, chic decor, outstanding food. Get the duck salad and the duck skins in spring rolls.
Pearl's, 38 W. 48th Street, phone 586–1060.
A lot of people think or used to think that this was the only place to get good Chinese food in New York. We thought it was mediocre; service was poor; people were almost rude. There are better ones around.
Peking Duck West, 199 Amsterdam, phone 799–5457, **Peking Duck House,** 22 Mott St, phone 227–1810, **Beijing Duck House,** 144 East 52nd Street, phone 759–8260.
Same owner for all three. For Peking Duck, of course, and no advance orders necessary.
Shun Lee Palace, 155 E. 55th Street, phone 371–8844.
Nice decor, outstanding Chinese food. Good service. Has a cousin, *Shun Lee West,* at 43 W. 65th Street, phone 595-8895, near Lincoln Center.
Tse Yang, 51st Steet next to Helmsley Palace.
Not recommended.

American

You might be getting the idea that there are no good ol' American restaurants in the Apple. Yes, there are! Here are a few of them.

Carolina, 355 W. 46th Street, between 8th and 9th avenues, phone 245–0058.
Featuring Southern-style cuisine and a lot of ambiance.
Christ Cella, 160 E. 46th Street, phone 697–2479.
A lot of people love this place. It's pronounced something like *Grizellas* or *Krisellas,* and not the way it looks or should be pronounced.
The Coach House, 110 Waverly Place, phone 777–0303, near Washington Square.
Elegant and popular steakhouse with Southern flair. Food is usually excellent.
Four Seasons, 99 E. 52nd Street, phone 754–9494.
One of New York's best restaurants in every respect.

The Palm,   837 Second Avenue, phone 687–2953.
Huge portions, huge prices, but terrific steaks, lamb chops, lobster, potatoes, etc.
Papa to the one in L.A. and elsewhere.
River Café,   1 Water Street, phone 522–5200.
Great views of the city. Everyone loves it.
Texarkana,   64 W. 10th Street, phone 254–5800.
As you might expect, Texas-style food. Every time we suggest going here
someone wrinkles his or her nose, talks us out of it, or takes us somewhere else.
Still, there are those who say it's good. Maybe one day we'll find out.
Wally's,   224 W. 49th Street, phone 582–0460, in the theater district.
Terrific steaks and chops, homemade potato chips, etc.

Delis

Delicatessens are everywhere in New York, but there are those that are better
than others. Several of them are in the theater district, which is lucky for
you if you want a quick pretheater snack or a posttheater nosh. No elegant
or fine dining, however; it's strictly deli.

Carnegie Deli,   854 Seventh Avenue at 55th Street.
Open late.
Kaplan's Deli,   71 W. 47th Street, near Sixth Avenue.
Convenient if you're buying jewelry or going to the theater for a matinee.
Katz's,   205 E. Houston Street.
Ratner's,   138 Delancy Street, between Norfolk and Suffolk.
Open late.
Second Avenue Deli,   156 Second Avenue.
Stage Deli,   834 Seventh Avenue, between 53rd and 54th Streets.
Open late.
Star's Deli,   593 Lexington Avenue near 52nd Street.
Open late.
Wolf's Deli,   101 W. 57th Street at Sixth Avenue (also known as Ave-
nue of the Americas).
Open late. The best of them.

Et cetera

Continuing the list are restaurants not to be pigeonholed with the ones
already mentioned. They're all a little special in their own way.

Grand Central Oyster Bar,   at Grand Central Station, downstairs.
Closed weekends.
Major seafood.
The Helmsley Palace,   455 Madison Avenue at 50th Street, phone
888–7000.

The mansion was built in 1882 and the public rooms are opulent. A great place to go for lunch (Trianon Room), tea (Gold Room), or cocktails (The Hunt Room). If you're in the bar walk across the hall to the stairway and go up and see the Library. Before you leave go see the Grand Ballroom (Versailles Room). Even if you never eat in the place you should go and *see* it. You can also stay there in the adjacent hotel.

Madame Romaine de Lyon, 32 E. 61st Street, phone 758–2422.
For lunch only, with over five hundred types of omelets. I have to give credit to any place that can come up with that many ways to cook an egg. If you go there get something besides a cheese omelet, just so all the creativity doesn't go to waste.

Maxwell's Plum, 1181 First Avenue.
Not a place you go to eat, exactly. It's a wild and crazy place; wild in the decor and crazy in the people. Fun, however. You could go for dessert. Good at least once. The one in San Francisco can't compare.

Jim McMullen, 1341 Third Avenue at 76th Street, phone 861–4700.
A real hangout, pickup place on a very high level; celebrity-viewing restaurant. Interesting people-watching. Menu is also interesting, but we found the food to be otherwise. Also, the service wasn't too swift. Still, there are many who won't leave New York without going here first.

One Fifth Avenue, of the same address, phone 260–3434.
The little place where the girlfriends gathered in the film *An Unmarried Woman*. The interior is decorated with parts of an old British cruise ship called the S.S. *Caronia*. It's a very popular place, always crowded; food is good and it's fun.

The Palm Court, in the Plaza Hotel.
A must for brunch, lunch, tea, or late dining. It's elegant, romantic, old-fashioned, corny, and fun, all at once.

The Russian Tea Room, 150 W. 57th Street almost at Sixth Avenue, phone 265–0947.
One of the city's most popular places to see and be seen. You are almost guaranteed a movie star at lunch. Open very late for après-theater. Expensive, but fun. Food is usually pretty good.

Serendipity, 255 E. 60th Street between Second and Third Avenues.
The best hot fudge sundae in the world and universe. This is the expert speaking. They also have all sorts of coffee drinks and ice cream things, gigantic hamburgers, etc. The decor is funky and so is the crowd. It's a lot of fun.

Sign of the Dove, 1110 Third Avenue at 65th Street, phone 861–8080.
Gorgeous to look at, but the food has never had high marks. Go for a drink.

Tavern on the Green, Central Park West (67th Street) in Central Park, phone 873–3200.
Again, no one ever raves about the food here, which isn't all that terrible. It is one of the prettiest restaurants you'll ever see, especially if there's snow on the ground, especially at holiday time. It's worth a trip there at least once; go for lunch.

Windows on the World, at the World Trade Center, phone 938–1111. Really three restaurants at the top of this amazing skyscraper. It's a must for everyone to do at least once. The *Cellar in the Sky* and *The Restaurant* are the main ones, with *L'Hors d'Oeuvrerie* just for "snacks," tea, or cocktails. Reservations in advance are necessary. Elegant, sumptuous dining, not cheap, with a nice little view. P.S. If the weather is not clear, don't go.

The following is a list of restaurants open late enough to go to after the theater—that is, serving until at least midnight. I won't go into any details and unless I've talked about one before, I can't say personally how good they are. You'll have to take your chances, but at least you've got a list here to start with.

French:

Au Tunnel, 250 W. 47th Street.
La Bonne Soupe, 48 W. 55th Street.
Café des Artistes, 1 W. 67th Street.
L'Escargot, 47 W. 55th Street.
La Fondue, 43 W. 55th Street.
Tucano, 33 E. 60th Street.
Le Vert Galant, 109 W. 46th Street.

Italian

Forlini's, 93 Baxter Street.
Giambelli 50th, 46 E. 50th Street.
Giordano, 409 W. 39th Street.
Il Menestrello, 14 E. 52nd Street between Madison and Fifth Avenues.
Il Monello, 1460 Second Avenue at 76th Street.
Johnnie's, 135 W. 45th Street
Piccolo Mondo, 1269 First Avenue at 69th Street.

Delis

Carnegie Deli, 854 Seventh Avenue at 55th Street.
Celebrity Deli, 700 Eighth Avenue at 45th Street.
Frankie and Johnnie, 269 W. 45th Street.
Stage Deli, 834 Seventh Avenue at 53rd Street.
Star's Deli, 593 Lexington Avenue at 52nd Street.
Wolf's Deli, 101 W. 57th Street at 6th Avenue.

Others:

Brasserie, 100 E. 53rd Street in the Seagram Building (open 24 hours).

Centre Court, near Lincoln Center.

Chin Ya (Japanese), Woodward Hotel, 210 W. 55th Street.

The Edwardian Room, Plaza Hotel.

Palm Court, Plaza Hotel.

Pier 52, 163 W. 52nd Street.

P.J. Clarke's, 915 Third Avenue at 55th Street.

Rumpelmayer's, St. Moritz Hotel, 50 Central Park South (59th Street).

The Russian Tea Room, 150 W. 57th Street near Sixth Avenue.

Serendipity, 255 E. 60th Street between Second and Third Avenues.

Sign of the Dove, 65th Street at Third Avenue.

Tony Roma's, 400 E. 57th Street.

Wally's, 224 W. 49th Street.

Bits, bites, and pieces: here comes a list of everything that's left that I can't fit anywhere else. Most of this info has been gathered firsthand or contributed by New Yorkers.

American *Stanhope Hotel,* across the street from the Metropolitan Museum, is a good place to go for lunch or tea if you've been museuming.

The *best pizza* in New York is a toss-up between *Ray's Famous* and *John's*. *Ray's Famous* is in two locations (11th Street and Sixth Avenue in the Village, and 72nd Street and Columbus.) *John's* is at 278 Bleecker Street in the Village. I also like *Charlie's Corner* on Lexington Avenue, about two blocks from Bloomingdale's. For the uninitiated: it's not necessary to order an entire pizza. The thing to do is to get just a big slice. Don't confuse *Ray's Original* with just *Ray's*. Another good pizza is *Mariella's* at 57th Street and Eighth Avenue.

Steve's Ice Cream on Sixth Avenue between 10th and 11th Streets in the Village doesn't necessarily have the best ice cream, although it's good. What they have is a gimmick called "add-ins," meaning someone mixes in any one of a number of toppings before you are served your scoop.

The *Papaya King* stand at the corner of Third Avenue and 86th Street serves the best hot dog, according to Willy. Down the street one block on 86th Street is a place called *Filet Mignon,* which serves the best Philadelphia Steak and Cheese Sandwich (with onions, please).

The above-mentioned Willy also recommends *Yono Schimmel* on Houston Street near Orchard Street for the best blintzes.

On Madison Avenue (1006 at 78th Street) there's a teensy bakery called *G. and M. Pastries*—to die over.

Up the street between 82nd and 83rd streets (still on Madison Avenue) is another bakery called **Buttercake Squares.** Just the name makes you want to go, right?

At the **Haagen-Dazs** store on Third Avenue near 70th Street, they make ice cream sandwiches with David's Cookies. Next to Mrs. Fields, David's are the best.

Food Emporiums

There isn't much of anything like this on the West Coast, but in New York and Europe they are quite popular. Some of them are very big; some are more neighborhoody and small. They're a lot of fun to go into and look, and some even have a place to sit and eat. Otherwise, it's take-out and gourmet foods shopping.

Balducci's, on 10th Street and Sixth Avenue in the Village, is now very popular.

Dean and DeLuca, at 121 Prince Street, is a big take-out favorite.

Food, on Prince Street, is also good for a quick lunch.

Food Emporium, here and there.

Neuman and Bogdonoff, 79th Street and Third Avenue.

William Poll, 74th Street and Lexington Avenue.

Zabar's, on Broadway at 80th Street, might be the most famous and the most fun. Something for everyone.

Getting Around

For a first-timer in New York it can be very confusing. Everyone is saying "Upper East Side," "down in the Village," "the West Side," "SoHo," and you're saying "so what?" You don't know the "lower Eighties" from Timbuktu. Best thing to do is orient yourself a.s.a.p. Here goes a crash course in where's where.

Bear in mind that New York City is located on a long island (not *the* Long Island, however) called Manhattan, which basically runs north and south in length. Being the island that it is, it is surrounded by water, in the form of rivers called the Hudson on the west side, and the East on the east side. More or less a bit to the north of the center of the island is Central Park. The city is divided by this park as to east and west. Everything to the east of the Park and Fifth Avenue is called the East Side, and everything to the west of Fifth Avenue is called the West Side. At the northern end in the middle of the island is Harlem. At the southern end is Battery Park with a view of the Statue of Liberty. New Jersey is across the Hudson River (west), and Queens and Brooklyn are across the East River, but don't worry about any of those places for now.

The north end is called "upper," the south end is called "lower," and somewhere in the middle is called "midtown."

The streets running north and south are avenues. The streets running east and west are streets. They mostly have numbers, but some have names and some have both (i.e., Sixth Avenue = Avenue of the Americas; and Seventh Avenue = Fashion Avenue). Note: New Yorkers refer to them by the number.

Then there are areas like "the Village," which means Greenwich Village, which is around N.Y.U. And SoHo, which means "south of Houston" (pronounced *house*). And Chinatown, and Wall Street, etc.

Now the test. If someone says to you "I live in the upper Eighties on the East Side," you know that this person lives between 80th and 89th Streets to the east of Central Park. It's helpful to know that the high numbers are at the north end running to low numbers at the south end.

Now that you know where you're going, how do you get there? The easiest way is to walk, which is always the best way unless you have to go too far, it's raining too hard, you're too lazy or tired, or your left leg is in a cast. After walking, cabs are best. We'll skip over hired limos. They aren't all that expensive. The bus system is very good, but you have to know where you're going to get off and must have the correct fare. At the bottom of your choices is the subway system, unless you are a sumo wrestler or have suicidal tendencies. A lot of New Yorkers will tell you it isn't so bad, but for someone like me who is used to the nice, clean, safe Paris or London metros, it's awful.

Sightseeing

Museums

American Museum of Natural History and Hayden Planetarium,
Central Park West between 77th and 81st Streets.
Huge building containing a fascinating collection. You can take a decent tour which lasts about an hour and departs from the main floor foyer. It's a good idea to take the tour, as you can get a quick overview. Especially interesting were the dinosaur bones on the fourth floor and the gems on the first floor. This would be a good place for kids of all ages.

B. G. Cantor Sculpture Center, One World Trade Center, 105th floor.
An outstanding collection of Rodin sculpture. By appointment only; phone 938-5136.

The Cloisters, Fort Tryon Park.
Closed Mondays. You'll need to take a long cab ride to this museum, but it is well worth your time and expense. An outstanding museum in a monastery atmosphere, housing a fabulous collection of medieval art.

Cooper-Hewitt Museum of Decorative Arts and Design, 2 E. 91st Street at Fifth Avenue.

Closed Mondays. A division of the Smithsonian Institution; the collections, both permanent and temporary, are housed in the old Carnegie Mansion.

Fraunces Tavern, second floor, corner of Broad and Pearl Streets, in the financial district.

Closed weekends. Dating from George Washington days, this is one of New York's oldest and most historical buildings. The collection is very small, containing items from the Revolution and the likes of George himself. The restaurant downstairs is said to be the oldest in New York. You can also visit Wall Street, the World Trade Center, and the Statue of Liberty and Battery Park while you're in the area, which makes for a rather complete day of sightseeing.

The Frick Collection, 1 East 70th Street at Fifth Avenue.

Closed Mondays. The former mansion of Henry Clay Frick, housing his amazing art collection. Has been described as a gem, a jewel, a treasure—take your pick.

Guggenheim Museum, 1071 Fifth Avenue between 88th and 89th Streets.

Closed Mondays. The collection is twentieth-century art; the building is round, by Frank Lloyd Wright.

Metropolitan Museum of Art, Fifth Avenue at 82nd Street.

Closed Mondays. One of the country's major museums; should not be missed. Always has some fabulous temporary exhibition. The permanent collection is outstanding. Note: for lunch or tea, the *American Stanhope Hotel* across the street is convenient, and good. If you have a museum membership to some other museum in the country, check to see if you have a reciprocal agreement with the Met; then you can get in free.

Museum of Holography, 11 Mercer Street, west of Broadway.
Closed Mondays and Tuesdays.

Museum of Modern Art, 53rd Street between Fifth and Sixth Avenues.

Closed Wednesdays. Another spectacular museum, and one not to miss.

Pierpont Morgan Library, 29 E. 36th Street, off Madison Avenue.

Closed Mondays. Permanent and temporary exhibitions in the exquisite library. Paintings, manuscripts, books, small sculptures, furniture, etc. A small gem which doesn't take too long to see.

Storm King, about one and a half hours from the city,
is not really a museum but a giant outdoor sculpture garden covering several acres, with monumental sculpture. You would have to hire a car and/or driver to go there if you do not have your own car. It is quite something and an excellent way to spend a day getting out of the city. Directions as to how to get there are as follows. Go over the George Washington Bridge to the end of Palisades Parkway at the Bear Mt. traffic circle. Follow 9 W north for ten miles. Get off at Cornwall, route 307. Turn left onto route 307 west and go one mile. Bear to the right to route 32 north. Cross a bridge and go left to Orr Mill

Road. Go one and a half miles and turn left on Old Pleasant Hill Road. The Storm King Art Center entrance and parking will be on the left side in a quarter mile.

Whitney Museum of American Art, 945 Madison Avenue at 75th Street.

Closed Mondays. Rich collection of American art, usually with a good contemporary exhibition.

There are many other smaller museums of interest in New York and the surrounding areas, which most tourists never have time for. In your hotel room you'll probably find copies of books and magazines with more details and suggestions.

Places of Interest

For an overview of Manhattan, a friend of mine, who lives there recommends taking the *Circle Line Boat Tour,* which you find at Pier 83 at the foot of W. 43rd Street. He says you get a wonderful perspective of the island and city. For flightseeing contact *Island Helicopter Tours,* located at 34th Street and the East River, phone 895–5372 or 683–4575.

Broadway and Times Square.
The heart of the theater district, this is what you could call touristy, seedy, or exciting, depending on the time of day you are there. If you go to any Broadway plays (I know you will) you will automatically be in the area. During the day it's not as colorful as it is at night, when all the lights go on. Watch your purse.

Central Park.
Nice to walk in during the day but not at night. If you aren't too embarrassed, take one of the horse carriages through the park, although at the moment there is a movement afoot to keep them out. The park is huge, so you won't cover it all at once. The zoo is closed for the moment to be renovated, which it sadly needs.

Fifth Avenue.
From Central Park to the Empire State Building is the most famous section of Fifth Avenue and maybe all of New York City. You will, of course, go by all the well-known shops, boutiques, and department stores; *Rockefeller Center* and the *Channel Gardens* (the lower level is either an iceskating rink or a café, depending on the time of year); *St. Patrick's Cathedral;* the *New York Public Library;* and the *Empire State Building.*

Side trips off Fifth Avenue, by a block or two, will lead you to *Radio City Music Hall* on 50th Street; *Grand Central Station* on 42nd Street; *"diamond row"* on 47th Street (don't go on weekends); the *Pierpont Morgan Library* on 36th Street; *MOMA,* or the *Museum of Modern Art,* on 54th Street.

Greenwich Village, or "the Village," around N.Y.U. and Washington Square.

Good for people-watching, atmosphere, little shops, and restaurants. Watch your purse.

The Intrepid.

The aircraft carrier is now open to the public at Pier 86 at 46th Street daily from 10:00 A.M. to 7:00 P.M.

Lincoln Center, corner of Broadway and Columbus Avenue.

Six buildings for music, dance, and theater. Guided tours leave daily from Avery Fisher Hall.

SoHo, south of Houston Street around Broadway and Canal Street.

Currently the artists' and gallery area of New York, especially for what's currently "in."

The South Street Seaport.

A recently renovated, eleven-block historic area which features the Fulton Market, restaurants, shops, museums, interesting old buildings, old ships—much to see and do, much walking.

Statue of Liberty.

The statue can be seen from various points on the southern end of Manhattan, along Battery Park or from the World Trade Center towers. You may think you want to take the ferry out to the statue for a close-up view. Forget it! It'll shoot the better part of a morning and once you get out there, there's nothing to do except wait for the next ferry to take you back. It takes about fifteen minutes to walk around the statue and go inside, where there's nothing much to see. If you want to climb to the top, it's hot, narrow, usually crowded with screaming school kids, and again, there's not much to see. I do *not* recommend seeing the statue by this ferry system. If you just must get an up-close view, take the helicopter, as described above. (The statue is undergoing renovation at this writing and is surrounded by huge scaffolding.)

The United Nations Building, on the East River around 46th Street. Guided tours daily.

Everyone should go once.

Wall Street.

Don't bother going to the financial district unless it's during the week, and during trading hours. It's a small district, covering only a few blocks, but is very interesting during the daytime with all the hustle and bustle. You can go into the Stock Exchange Building and observe the activity on the floor from a viewing platform above. There are also many exhibits which explain how the Exchange works.

Note: Wall Street, the Statue of Liberty, The World Trade Center, and Fraunces Tavern can all be done at the same time, as they are all right next to each other. Don't miss the charming little *Trinity Church.* The Michelin guide is very good for walking tours of the area.

World Trade Center.

Wait until you have a clear day to see this. In one of the towers you can take an elevator to the top, where there is an excellent observation area. Be sure you go out onto the roof. The lines are often very long to get into the elevator, but they move quickly, so don't be discouraged.

Obviously, there's more to see in New York than what I've just mentioned. I've just covered the basics, which is more than enough for the average tourist on limited time. As with any big city, even if you live there, you never get around to seeing it all.

Shopping

If you're a millionaire or even a hundred-thousand-aire, you'll be in Shoppers' Heaven. If you don't fit into the above categories, fear not: some of the best bargain shopping is in New York and I'll get to that later. Even if you don't want to buy anything (are you sick?), you'll have a great time window shopping.

Fifth Avenue is the place to start for shopping, window or serious. Begin at 59th Street by the Plaza Hotel and head downtown. Most of the best boutiques are between there and Saks Fifth Avenue. *Henri Bendel* on 57th Street between Fifth and Sixth Avenues is a big favorite. It's small, chic, and fun. A couple of doors past Bendel's (going toward Sixth Avenue) is a large shop carrying discount evening clothes.

Back on Fifth Avenue you'll see *Tiffany's,* which does not serve breakfast, but does serve up some great window displays. Don't miss *Steuben*— go in and browse, especially in the back room. The *Trump Tower* could take hours by itself; it's quite spectacular and if you need a refreshment stop, there's a little cafe downstairs.

At 47th Street hang a right and walk over to Sixth Avenue (Avenue of the Americas). This is the "Diamond" area, as you will clearly see. Don't go on weekends (it's all closed down).

Fifth Avenue is wonderful on Saturday mornings when the pace is slower and people are out strolling. Sundays are also good, especially in nice weather or on a holiday, but most of the stores are closed.

Madison Avenue between 87th and 50th Streets is also pretty good— in fact, *very* good. You'll find everything from wonderful little bakeries and food emporiums to fabulous antique stores and great boutiques. For you bargain hunters there's a terrific little purse shop called *Rosette Handbags* at 1188 Madison Avenue between 86th and 87th Streets. It's small and stuffed, but you'll find good pickins. If you want costume jewelry and fakes go to **Mariko,** 845 Madison Avenue between 69th and 70th Streets. For wonderful pastries try *G. and M. Pastries* at 1006 Madison Avenue at 78th Street, or *Buttercake Squares* farther up on the same side of the street. For discount shoes try 1186 Madison, between 86th and 87th Streets. One block down is *Bolton's* for discount clothes.

Seventh Avenue (Fashion Avenue) and the Garment District. Unless you have a connection or a specific address in mind, don't waste your time here. There are very few houses which will sell to the public. There is a good one, however, called **Stan Rose,** which is a few floors up in one of the buildings. They have a great selection of designer items at a discount and can usually order whatever you want if you have the proper information and have tried the garment on elsewhere for size. The address is 491 Seventh Avenue. Another OK place for bargain shopping is *S&W* at two locations on Seventh Avenue, around 26th and 27th Streets.

Nearby on Broadway and 34th Street is *Macy's.*

Bloomingdale's is great fun, sort of the Galeries Lafayette of New York City. It's on Lexington Avenue between 59th and 60th Streets. You could use a guide there. Everyone loves Bloomies, but it's so big and so confusing I hardly ever buy anything there. *Lexington Avenue* has a lot of shops, but in general it's not as good as Madison Avenue. *Third Avenue* also has a lot of shops. *Park Avenue* has a few.

Next to MOMA is a small and interesting gallery called *Margot Gallery* at 26 W. 54th Street, beside the Dorset Hotel. The collection is mostly ethnic art and crafts; good for gift items, as well.

For the best bargain shopping in the U.S.A. you must go to *Orchard Street.* I know a few women who have plenty of bucks and they go frequently. It's a real experience. Don't go on a Saturday or Jewish holiday. Sundays are their big day. They are open the rest of the week from around 9:30 A.M. to 6:30–ish. Take a cab to the corner of Orchard and Houston Streets. Don't wear your very best clothes or lots of jewelry. Take cash, credit cards, checkbook, etc.

You'll notice when you get out of the cab that this isn't Fifth Avenue anymore. In fact, you may be put off by what you see. One cab driver begged me not to get out and said he'd drive me back uptown for free. Don't let any of that nonsense bother you. This is a great adventure.

Clutching your handbag firmly in your hand, head straight for *M. Friedlich's* at #196. You have to ring the bell to get in. On the first floor you'll find a great selection of sportswear and sweaters. Be sure you go downstairs for the designer stuff. Sometimes the people who work there are real nice. Sometimes they are not. Ignore that. You should also not wear your undies that have the holes in them, as there are no dressing rooms. Everyone crowds in one little space around two dinky mirrors. That's OK though, because you get lots of opinions. You'll hit or miss on Orchard

Street. I always manage to hit. You will save 40 to 60 percent. For example: I just bought a pair of Calvin Klein wool trousers at Friedlich's and paid 120 dollars. That same day I went over to Saks and saw the *exact* same trousers for 290 dollars. See what I mean? And it's not last year's stuff; it's all current.

If you have any money left after Friedlich's (which is the best, by the way), go a couple doors down to *A. Altman,* #182. They're good for silk blouses, running 60 to 80 dollars. Gorgeous stuff!

At #150 is *Arivel Fashions,* which had a pretty good selection.

For purses and bags there's nowhere on earth like *Fine and Klein,* #119. Upstairs and main floor. The selection is enormous. Prices are not bargain-cheap but are reasonable. Upstairs immediately next door is a terrific designer shoe store, *Sole of Italy.*

Once you get to Delancey Street, the best of the Orchard Street shopping is over, so you can get a cab.

There are many, many stores on Orchard and you can sort of tell from the outside which ones are better. Most of the boutiques have either an upstairs or a downstairs with higher-quality merchandise. One thing is for sure—it's a fun place to go shopping and if you hit it right, you can save a lot of money. It isn't a tourist place either, as most of the other shoppers you'll run into are New Yorkesses. There are men's stores there too, selling everything from designer jeans to expensive Italian suits.

There's no place like New York City. It's exhausting and energizing all at once, and always exciting. I love that song Sinatra has made famous, "New York, New York": "My little town blues are melting away" is what happens every time I go there. "I want to be a part of it, New York, New York . . . . . ."

Washington, D.C.

Washington, D.C.

If you haven't been to Washington, D.C., *go*. There's so much to do and see and so many good restaurants you could easily spend ten days. I was there for four days and can comment on the following.

Hotels

I stayed at the Ritz Carlton Hotel (formerly the Fairfax) 2100 Massachusetts Avenue NW, phone 293–2100, in the Dupont Circle area. The location was a bit away from the center of things, but by no more than ten minutes. The hotel itself is beautiful: small, tastefully and expensively decorated, with a good bar and restaurant. Our room was very small, but nice. Another very posh hotel in the city is the *Henley Park* at 926 Massachusetts Avenue. New and very large is the *Marriott* on 14th Street, with rooms running from moderate to expensive, four restaurants, and opening onto a four-tiered mall with fifty shops and restaurants. Three other good choices are *The Madison,* 15th and M Streets NW, phone 862–1600; the *Four Seasons,* 2800 Pennsylvania Avenue NW, phone 342–0444; and the *Sheraton-Carlton,* 923 16th Street NW, phone 638–2626.

Restaurants

The American Café, 1211 Wisconsin Avenue, NW, in Georgetown, 547–8200,
is a small, casual, nice place for lunch, with wonderful huge croissants and sandwiches. A branch can be found at 227 Massachusetts Avenue NE.

Au Pied de Cochon, also 1335 Wisconsin, NW, in Georgetown, stole its name and a few other things from the one in Paris, but the comparison ends there. Food is so-so. Crowded and noisy.

The Bread Oven, 1220 19th Street, NW, phone 466–4264, is a pastry shop, bakery, and restaurant à la brasserie, popular for eat-in or take-out breakfast, lunch, and dinner; inexpensive.

Cantina d'Italia, 1214A 18th Street, NW, phone 659–1830, serves pretty good northern Italian food with lots of hokey atmosphere. Dinner for four with two bottles of wine was 150 dollars.

Chez Grand-Mère, 3057 M Street, NW, in Georgetown, phone 337–2436, is an inexpensive little bistro serving good home cooking in a cozy atmosphere.

Clyde's, 3236 M Street, NW, in Georgetown, phone 333–9180, is very casual, very popular, cheap, serving good ol' American food.

Dominique's, 1900 Pennsylvania Avenue, NW, phone 452-1126, is a fun place with French food, a clubby atmosphere, moderate prices. A kind of crazy après-theater hangout. Crowded, lively.

Germaine's, 2400 Wisconsin Avenue, NW, in upper Georgetown, phone 965–1185, is modern and chic with an Asian flair, serving above-average pan-Asian cuisine. Very popular. Dinner for three with wine was 100 dollars.

Jean-Louis, in the Watergate Hotel, 2650 Virginia Avenue, phone 298–4488, has nouvelle French cuisine on the expensive side; good for a Sunday brunch, too.

The Jockey Club, 2100 Madison Avenue, NW, in the Fairfax Hotel, phone 296–8000, has excellent continental cuisine in a beautiful restaurant. Expensive.

Lafitte, in the Hampshire Hotel, 1310 New Hampshire Avenue, NW, phone 466–7978, serves excellent Cajun and Creole style lunches and dinners. Open daily.

Lion d'Or, 1150 Connecticut Avenue, NW, phone 296–7972, is a long-time popular restaurant. French food, moderate prices. Closed Sunday.

Maison Blanche, 1725 F Street, NW, phone 842–0700, is a large place, popular, serving classic and nouvelle dishes.

Marrakesh, 617 New York Avenue, NW, phone 393–9393, serves tummy-filling seven-course Moroccan meals. Open daily.

Mel Krupin's, 1120 Connecticut Avenue, NW, phone 331–7000, is a popular hangout for Washington bigwigs, especially at lunch. You never know who you'll see. American food, moderate prices.

Old Ebbit Grill, 1427 F Street, NW, phone 347–5560 is a good bet for lunch if you're visiting the Treasury Building or the White House.

The Palm, 1225 19th Street, NW, phone 293–9091, is a branch of The Palm of New York and Los Angeles. Steak, gigantic lobsters, huge lamb chops, potato dishes, big portions of everything. Noisy, fun, expensive. Closed Sunday

Le Pavillon, 1050 Connecticut Avenue at L Street, NW, phone 833–3846,

is one of the best, serving nouvelle French fare in a pretty room. Expensive. Closed Sunday.

Potomac, in Washington Harbour between 30th Street and Rock Creek Park in Georgetown,

promises to be open by the fall of 1985. Same owner as Maxwell's Plum and Tavern on the Green in New York.

1789, 1226 36th Street, NW, in Georgetown, phone 965–1789,

is on the quiet, intimate side. French food, moderate prices.

Sichuan Garden, 1220 19th Street, NW, phone 296–4550,

has creative Chinese food at moderate to expensive prices.

Suzanne's Café, 1600–12 21st Street at the Phillip's Collection, phone 387–2151.

Best bet for lunch if you're visiting the museum. Closed Monday.

Tiberio, 1915 K Street, NW, phone 452–1915,

is an Italian eatery which has been around for a long time. Moderate.

209 1/2, Pennsylvania Avenue, SE, phone 544–6352,

is an expensive, sophisticated, and small restaurant with an ever-changing menu of internationally inspired and nouvelle American dishes. Reservations.

Val de Loire, 915 15th Street, NW, phone 737–4445,

is on the romantic side, with nouvelle and classic French dishes at moderate prices.

Viet Château, 2637 Connecticut Avenue, NW, phone 232–6464,

is very inexpensive, nothing fancy, with very good Vietnamese cuisine.

Vincenzo, 1606 20th Street, NW, phone 667–0047,

specializes in Italian food and seafood. Moderate prices, unpretentious.

Woodward and Lothrop Department Store, 7th floor.

If you are touring around the White House, the Treasury Building, or the National Portrait Gallery and the National Collection of Fine Arts, and you are wondering where to go for lunch, this is a good bet. Large, pretty rooms, two restaurants, a bar, big and diverse menu, good food and service, cheap.

Guidebooks

It is essential to have some sort of guidebook in Washington because there is so much to see and do, and only so many hours. The very best guidebook that I found, which isn't a guidebook, was an article in the November 1979 *Travel & Leisure* magazine. It tells everything you ever wanted to know about Washington.

As much in advance as possible before you go to D.C., write your local senator or congressman and ask for V.I.P. tickets for the White House tour.

Also ask for gallery passes for the Senate and House of Representatives, so you can go and listen. Also ask for any other information that might prove useful. You also need special passes to go on the F.B.I. tour or you have to stand in line. The F.B.I. and White House passes are for specific dates and times, so you must know exactly when you want them.

If you have any problems when you get to D.C., go see your senator or congressman. Many of them have offices in the Russell Building (across from the Capitol Building).

As soon as you get to your hotel get your hands on a good street map and a metro map. Learn to use the metro. The system is good and cheaper than a cab. The cabs in D.C. are quite cheap, as they operate on a zone basis. Be careful, however; you can still get ripped off.

Museums

Most are free. Washington, D.C., is Museum Heaven. I managed to get to nine of them, only missing one major museum. Here goes:

The Corcoran Gallery, 17th Street and New York Avenue, NW (the one I missed), across from the White House.
Has a comprehensive collection of American art, plus temporary exhibitions which are strong on contemporary.

Dumbarton Oaks, 1703 32nd Street, NW, corner of Q Street, north end of Georgetown.
Entrance to the sixteen acres of formal gardens is on Q Street, while the entrance to the beautiful house and library is on 32nd Street. The house and galleries contain an impressive collection of Byzantine art, rare books, and pre-Columbian art. The gardens are enormous and have overhanging trellises full of wisteria, flowerbeds bursting with tulips, large lawns, small orchards, etc. A lovely place to go on a warm, sunny afternoon, after a nice lunch in Georgetown.

The Hirshhorn, Mall, Independence Avenue and 8th Street.
They call it the "doughnut" because of its shape. A most impressive museum with a marvelous collection of paintings and sculpture. Don't miss this one either.

Museum of History and Technology, Mall.
Whenever you hear of something "going to the Smithsonian," this is where it goes. Don't go to this museum unless you've had a big breakfast, a good night's sleep and are wearing your walking shoes. It is enormous and the collection is beyond description. There is one of everything ever made in this place, from the inaugural ballgowns of all the First Ladies from Martha on up, to Billy Jean's tennis skirt, to an entire post office moved from the midwest. It is endless.

National Air and Space Museum, Mall, Jefferson Drive and Independence Avenue.
If you ask twenty people what they liked best or remember most about D.C., nineteen of them will tell you the Air and Space Museum. Try not to go on

the weekend. It is truly amazing. Be sure to see one of the films. Cafeteria on the upper level is not so bad if you're starving or staggering.

National Gallery and PEI (East) Wing, 6th Street and Constitution Avenue.

Two separate buildings across the street from each other are connected by an underground passage. Don't miss either one. Fabulous!

National Portrait Gallery and National Collection of Fine Arts, G and 8th Streets.

These two museums are side by side in a very impressive classical building. The portrait gallery is interesting and the upper floor is really beautiful. The National Collection is strong in some areas, but generally is a sorry second to the National Gallery.

The Phillips Collection, 1600–12 21st Street, NW, at Q Street, a short block from the Fairfax Hotel and the Dupont Circle metro station.

The Phillips Collection is housed in a beautiful 1897 brownstone, to which a new wing was added in 1960 to allow for expansion of the exhibits. The collection was founded in 1918 by Duncan Phillips. It was the first museum of modern art in the U.S. The collection now contains more than two thousand works of art. Artists range from Giorgione to Rothko. Not all paintings are exhibited at the same time. Those in storage are frequently exchanged for those on display, so that the exhibits change from time to time. Have lunch at Suzanne's Café, at the museum

The Renwick Gallery, part of the Smithsonian Institution, Pennsylvania Avenue at 17th Street, NW, across the street from the White House and a couple of blocks from the Corcoran.

The building that houses the Renwick Gallery is of interest in itself. It was designed in 1859 as the Corcoran Gallery to house the private collection of a wealthy merchant and banker. In 1897 that collection was moved to the present Corcoran Gallery. The building is described as French Second Empire style. Two rooms in the building are furnished in the styles of the 1860s and 1870s. Nine separate areas have changing exhibits of this country's examples of design, crafts, and decorative arts. There are usually five separate exhibits being shown at one time.

There are still other museums in Washington (not many), but these are the most important.

Government Buildings (all free)

Arlington National Cemetery.

Be sure you see the changing of the guard at the Tomb of the Unknown Soldier. This is done on the hour or half hour up until 7:00 P.M., and is very impressive. Stand at the far right-hand side to see the inspection procedure. While you're at the cemetery you can see the graves of the Kennedys.

Bureau of Engraving and Printing.

Friends who went here said it was definitely not worth the long wait in line.

Capitol Building.

There are guided tours of this building, for which you can wait in line a long time; or you can mosey around on your own. The tours begin in the Rotunda, last forty minutes, between the hours of 9 A.M. to 3:45 P.M. After your tour, stroll around on your own and go see what you missed. The tours do *not* cover everything. Be sure you see the old, now unused Senate room on the main floor. If the Senate or House is in session you can get into the galleries and listen, as long as you have a pass from your senator or representative.

F.B.I.

Conducted tours on a regular basis. I heard the tours were just so-so, not mind-boggling. You can get V.I.P. passes to this, also, or go wait in line.

Iwo Jima Monument.

One of the most impressive things you will see. On the way to the Arlington Cemetery. Don't miss it.

Jefferson Memorial.

Library of Congress.

This is a very beautiful, ornate, Italian-style building with much to see. Catch the slide show before you tour around so you know what's going on. Conducted tours at regular intervals.

Lincoln Memorial.

You can walk from here to the Washington Monument.

NASA Office, 400 Maryland Avenue, room 6035.

You can go to this office and order photographs of where you live, shot from space.

National Archives.

Here you can see the original Declaration of Independence, Bill of Rights, and Constitution, plus numerous other well-displayed documents and a very good photo exhibit.

Supreme Court.

There are short lectures given inside the courtroom every half hour or so when court is not in session. When court is in session you can wait in line to get in. There is a three-minute line and an as-long-as-you-want line. The three-minute line moves much faster, obviously. Once again, if people are lined up outside on the steps, just say you want to go inside to look around, and once inside get in the indoor line and save some time. No one pays any attention. No cameras indoors. Security check like in airports.

Treasury Building.

We couldn't get in because it was closed, but heard that the presentation for the general public was worth seeing (not on Mondays).

Washington Monument.

White House.

Write in advance of your visit to your senator or congressman and get the V.I.P. pass. The tour is at 8:15 A.M. and is conducted. Otherwise, you have to wait in endless lines for hours to get a walk-through. The V.I.P. tour takes about 45 minutes. Non-V.I.P tours are from 10–12 P.M. and start at the East Gate.

What Else To Do

Go over to **Georgetown** and have a nice lunch and walk around the town. Then walk up and down a few side streets and look at the beautiful houses. You can also visit the university. We walked from Georgetown to the Fairfax Hotel along P Street. It took about forty minutes and was a very nice walk.

Go to one of the theaters in **Kennedy Center** and see a play, ballet, opera, etc. There are two bars and restaurants on the upper floor, but you need a reservation just to stick your head in the door. Don't bother.

Everyone warns you not to walk around at night. I would take that advice, after getting a couple of blocks off Pennsylvania Avenue and the main drag in the middle of the day.

Shopping

Shopping in D.C. is not all that exciting. Your best bets are *Georgetown Park,* an elegant center with lots of boutiques at Wisconsin Avenue and M Street, and *Washington Square* on Connecticut Avenue.

Outskirts

If you have the time and a car there is a lot to do outside of Washington.

Annapolis, thirty miles from D.C., about forty minutes by car on Route 50.

Gettysburg, Pennsylvania, one and a half hours north of D.C., the site of the turning point of the Civil War. Tour the battleground.

Harper's Ferry, West Virginia, a National Historical Park one and a half hours north of Washington. This is a famous Civil War town and the site of John Brown's raid and capture. Many restored buildings and shops.

Monticello, Jefferson's home in Virginia, three hours away.

Mt. Vernon, Virginia. George Washington's home on the Potomac River. Take the Washington Boat Line Cruise to get there (phone 554–8000).

Williamsburg, Virginia, about a three-hour drive each way. If you decide to go, call and make sure they're going to be open, and that the buildings inside are going to be open.

Santa Fe

AND

Beyond

Santa Fe

Santa Fe is one of our favorite places. It's a charming little high-desert town (7000-foot altitude) in the mountains, surrounded by the dramatic northern New Mexico countryside. All is rich in history, various cultures, and art. Santa Fe is famous for its many fine art galleries, which can take hours or even days to see. The food ranges from terrible to terrific, so you have to know where to go. The architecture is wonderful; you'll see many honest-to-gosh Indians; and the air is clean. The sky goes on forever and the weather can be dramatic.

It's an easy trip to Santa Fe. First you fly to Albuquerque. From there you can rent a car and drive about sixty miles by freeway up to Santa Fe. There is a small airport at Santa Fe for small planes, which would be the most convenient way to go, if you can arrange it.

We have been there twice on the Labor Day weekend, which is a good time to go. The weather has been perfect both times. Santa Fe has a major arts and crafts fair twice a year and this is one of the weekends it is held. So, in addition to the many wonderful art galleries, you also get the main plaza crammed with artists from all over the southwest selling their wares. Some of the merchandise is typical artsy-craftsy stuff, but you'll also find some very fine things. Another exciting time to go to Santa Fe would be during their annual big Fiesta, held mid-September. According to the locals, the only time not to go to Santa Fe is from January through March, as the weather can get miserable.

Hotels

There are many places to stay in Santa Fe. Our favorite so far is *La Posada,* an old, quaint hotel about two blocks from the main plaza. The rooms are individual *casitas* in pueblo architecture and Indian decor, and they are quiet. *La Fonda* is smack in the middle of town and seems to be extremely touristy and noisy. I have heard that *The Inn at Loretto* is a nice hotel, but it is very large and in the middle of town. There is one place you must absolutely *not* stay and it's called *Bishops Lodge,* about three miles north of downtown. It's the worst, most poorly run, most insulting hotel we have ever stayed in anywhere in the world, with terrible food. About six miles from downtown is a resort called *Rancho Encantado.* We went out there and looked the place over and would definitely try it out next time. The location and main building were beautiful. People who have stayed there (either in the older bungalows or newer condos) have reported liking it very much.

Restaurants

As I mentioned before, you can eat really well or get poisoned, so be choosy about where you go. The best meal we had, without question, was at *El Nido,* which is a ten-minute drive from the plaza. (Go out Washington Street, which becomes Bishops Lodge Road, which will take you to El Nido.) Casual and excellent. The second-best place we've eaten is the well-known *Pink Adobe.* Their top item is the steak—one of the best steaks we've tasted. They're also known for their Chicken Marengo and a pork dish called Napoleon something-or-other. We had some of their Mexican dishes, which were hot and spicy (that's an understatement) and found out later that the Mexican dishes are *not* among their specialties. Their apple pie is to die for. The *Plaza Ore House* is supposed to have the best rack of lamb in town, but they were out of it the night we went. What we did order there was tasty, but a bit mediocre. If you do eat there, skip the desserts and go across the street to Haagen-Dazs.

Tomasita's, located in the old railroad terminal, is the local favorite for Mexican cuisine. It was very good, but be aware that New Mexican–style Mexican food is different from California-Mex. The former is more peasanty, heavier, and spicier than the latter. They really go in for chili sauces. Tomasita's has something called a Golden Margarita, which really gets you going. Order *sopaipillas* as an hors d'oeuvre, and a side order of the flour tortillas. The desserts were forgettable, except for an unusual Mexican custard. *La Plazuela* in the La Fonda Hotel is another one to pass. We had a lousy breakfast there. Just outside La Fonda is a small but very popular pastry shop called the *French Pastry Shop*. Also recommended for pastries and desserts is *Palace Swiss Bakery,* on Guadalupe. The *Guadalupe Cafe* was touted as having the best Mex food in town two years ago, but locals now say it has gone downhill. Friends ate in *The Bull Ring* and said it was lower-mediocre; the locals said don't go there. The locals highly recommend two places for lunch—*The Shed* and *Josie's*. *The Compound* is the big lah-di-dah place in town, but the locals said it was overrated, overpriced, and the food was not all that great. No one would recommend *Ernie's* and we were advised against *The Palace*. The *Periscope* was highly recommended for lunch, and they have dinner on Saturday nights. Don't bother going to the Sunday brunch at *Bishops Lodge*. *Le Mirage* got an OK from the locals and it looked very charming from the outside; typical French menu. *La Tertulia* was definitely *not* recommended by everyone we spoke to. *Rancho de Chimayo* is about thirty miles out of town and is a charming old hacienda-type place with lots of atmosphere. We found it to be highly touristy and the food was mediocre. However, if you're out driving around the countryside, it would be OK, especially if you have kids. They had good margaritas, *mariachis,* etc. If you're doing the galleries on Canyon Road, there are a couple of little places to get lunch along the way. You should get reservations for all the restaurants. Tomasita's doesn't take any so you have to wait, but we found that a little bribery hurried up the wait time by half. Most restaurants accept casual attire but it's a good idea to check. We noticed that people did dress nicely for the better places, even when casual attire was permitted.

Sightseeing

Santa Fe has such a rich and varied history that a little reading up on the subject before you go would be a good idea. In the town itself are many interesting and important buildings from a historical and an architectural point of view. Not to be missed are: *Governors Palace and Museum, Sena Plaza, St. Francis Cathedral, Oldest House, Chapel of San Angel, San Miguel Mission, Loretto Chapel* with staircase, *Museum of Fine Arts, Cristo Rey Church* (top of Canyon Road).

Then there are the galleries. There are many good ones around the plaza, but Canyon Road is also a must. Start out at the bottom on Paseo de Peralta near Canyon, at the *Fenn Gallery*. If Mr. Fenn ever gets tired of this business he can just change the sign outside to "Museum," because that's what this place is. It's probably the most fabulous art gallery I've ever been in. Not only does he have wonderful treasures spanning all ages and

cultures around the world, but the building itself is a must to see. You might
hint around that you'd love to view the private apartments behind the
gallery—they just may give you a tour.

I won't give a blow-by-blow description of all the galleries up Canyon
Road, but I will mention a couple that we especially liked. Of course, it's
all a question of taste. The **Laura McAdoo Galleries** are very nice. **The
Southwest Spanish Craftsmen, Inc.** (#922) had a lot of wonderful things,
but the house itself is the main interest here, dating from the early 1700s.
Way up at the top of the street, past a long block with no galleries, is **Shop
of the Frightened Owl** (#1117), another beautiful house with lots of
European antiques and some very wonderful Indian jewelry. Just beyond
that is **Roger H. Rodgers,** a local artist of some repute who works in many
media and has many interesting creations. Past Roger and around the corner
is the **Cristo Rey Church,** which is worth a visit. It's the largest adobe
structure in the U.S., with an important altarpiece inside. You might have
to go through a side door. There are so many galleries with such a variety
of arts and crafts that it would be impossible to describe them all. Give
Canyon Road a good two or three hours if you want to see it all. Get your
hands on the map of Canyon Road, available in hotels and galleries.

Every day the Indians come into the plaza and set up shop, usually
consisting of a blanket on the ground, under the porch of the Governors
Palace. If you're in the market for Indian crafts and jewelry you will want
to check this out.

Beyond Santa Fe

You could easily spend a week in Santa Fe and go somewhere different
every day, for there is so much to see and do. I will list below some trips
we did, and some we didn't.

Abiquiu.
This is where Georgia O'Keeffe lives. It is a beautiful area with the Ghost Ranch
Museum, a dam, and an echo amphitheater.
Albuquerque.
We have not spent too much time in this town because there doesn't seem to
be any reason to be there, other than the airport. If you find yourself with some
time on your hands there, meander over to Old Town and walk around. It's
something to do.
Carlsbad Caverns.
I know Carlsbad Caverns are nowhere near Santa Fe, but they *are* in New
Mexico, so I thought I'd throw them in. These are really worth the trip. They're
closer to El Paso than to Albuquerque. You'll probably want to stay overnight
there in one of your more "chic" desert motels, so that you can take the ranger

hike and attend the bat flight. The latter, by the way, is a must, even if you aren't a bat lover.

Cliff dwellings.

I have already mentioned Puye, unusual and small, and run by the Indians. Well worth a visit. Even if you go to Puye, Bandelier is a must because it is much bigger and entirely different. From Santa Fe you can take a five-hour trip and see all of Bandelier, with a stop at San Idelfonso Pueblo and Shidoni Foundry (see below). At Bandelier get the self-guiding trail guide and follow it as you go. This is something that kids will love. Bandelier is a National Park.

Ghost towns.

There are a couple hundred so-called ghost towns, or old mining towns, in New Mexico. You can easily go through three of them when you drive from Santa Fe to Albuquerque. This drive will take less than two hours. When you leave Santa Fe take St. Francis Drive south until you get to Interstate 25, then go toward Albuquerque. Soon you will see the signs for Madrid on Highway 14. You will cut out across the desert, past the penitentiary, and soon will be in a very scenic mountain area. Cerrillos will be the first ghost town (not too ghostly or interesting), then Madrid, then Golden. It's worth a stop at Madrid to take a look around. Proceed southward on 14 and you will eventually see the signs to Albuquerque. It's a beautiful drive, better than the freeway and not too long. When we did it we saw four huge tarantulas crossing the highway. They are amazing creatures and if you see one you may want to pull over and watch it for a while. (What other guidebook do you know of that tells you to look for tarantulas on the road?)

Pueblos.

There are so many Indian pueblos in the area that you couldn't see them all, nor would you want to, since many of them are nothing more than tacky towns. The two nicest have been talked about already. What you *do* want to do, however, is find out if any of these pueblos is having a festival or a dance and if so, go see it. They are supposed to be quite something, especially for the kids. Very authentic, with costumes and ancient music, etc.

The *Acoma Pueblo* is said to be well worth the trip, but it is a 250-mile round trip from Santa Fe. If you are staying in Albuquerque you could go from there.

Shidoni Foundry and Gallery.

This could be listed along with the other galleries, but it is so special and such a surprise that it's going to get its own paragraph. If you go out Bishops Lodge Road (an extension of Washington Street), you will eventually get to the Shidoni Foundry, which is generally open all day. Here you will encounter an amazing sculpture garden (everything's for sale) with sculptures impossible to describe—everything from the sedate to the bizarre. Twice a week the public is allowed to watch them pour, so find out at your hotel when that is, if you are interested.

Taos.

Taos would be number *one* on your priority list of day trips. Plan for the whole day. Leave Santa Fe no later than 9:00 A.M. Get a map and follow the road up to Pojoaque, where you should go left, following the signs to San Ildefonso Pueblo. This is where the black-on-black pottery was made famous by the Indian artist Maria. It is still made in this pueblo, which is supposedly one of the nicest and best of the pueblos to visit. After you see the pueblo continue on toward Puye Cliff Dwellings. This will take you about one and a half hours to see if you decide to climb through them, which you should. Then head up Highway 68 toward Taos, where you should arrive in time for lunch. I don't have any restaurants to recommend for this purpose, but there are many around the main plaza. On Kit Carson Drive you can visit ol' Kit's home. Also on the street is the Carlson and Black Gallery, which is very good. The main plaza is in the opposite direction.

On the way out of town heading north, just next to the Taos Inn, is the Clay and Fiber Gallery, worthy of a stop. Now you'll want to get to Taos Pueblo—the biggest, the best, and truly wonderful. Spend some time here and wander around and see it all. When you leave the pueblo, continue north on Highway 3 to route 64 west, where you'll go left. Shortly thereafter you'll come to the Rio Grande Gorge, another sight you don't want to miss. As you head back into town look for signs to the Millicent Rogers Museum, supposedly having one of the finest collections of southwest arts in the country. By now it is late afternoon or later, and you've got to get back to Santa Fe. Take the scenic route, if you have the energy and time, along Highway 76 through Penasco, Truchas, Chimayo, etc. If you get to Rancho Chimayo by dinnertime you may want to stop and eat. In order to do all of the above in one day, you will have to move along. You may want to take the scenic route (the high road through the mountains) when you go up to Taos, and the freeway when you go down. You could also skip the San Ildefonso Pueblo and the Puye Cliff Dwellings and see them another time, as they are not far from Santa Fe. It all depends on how much time you want to give to Taos and whether or not it's daylight savings time.

Books you can obtain in Santa Fe, which you may find useful, are: *Day Trips You Can Take Around the Santa Fe and Taos Areas;* The New Mexico North Guidebook *Santa Fe, Taos, Chama* (a fat pamphlet available free at hotels); *Taos Pueblo: A Walk Through Time,* by John Bodine; *Ghost Towns and How to Get to Them,* by Betty Woods. You can also pick up a little book called *Travel Tips: Santa Fe,* free at hotels. *Enjoy Santa Fe More,* by J. and J. Cartwright, is a good general book. An interesting background novel by Willa Cather is *Death Comes to the Archbishop.*

Did I mention hiking, horseback riding, skiing, fishing, the famous Santa Fe Opera, Ruidoso horseraces, hot-air balloon festivals . . .?

The only problem with going to New Mexico is you probably won't have enough time to do everything you want to do. So whatever time you've allotted, add a few days. You won't be sorry.

New Orleans

New Orleans

New Orleans is, as they say, a nice place to visit but you probably wouldn't want to live there.

It's shoddy/quaint, not too clean, interesting from a historical standpoint. The French Quarter, which isn't too French, is something like Tijuana, if you ask me. The weather when we were there in May was oppressively hot, humid, wilting, and debilitating. Take an umbrella for sure. We have never seen so many UA's in one spot at one time. There's a place not too far from downtown N.O. called Fat City and I believe that everyone for whom that city was named must have been in N.O. the weekend we were there. It almost became an obscene joke.

It sounds as if we didn't like New Orleans. Not true—we did. It's a real fun place to go for a four-day weekend, especially if you like to eat and shop for antiques. Just don't go with romantic visions of a charming little town on the Mississippi.

Hotels

We stayed high up in the *New Orleans Hilton.* Our suite was beautiful but let's face it, a Hilton is a Hilton. There are old homes-converted-to-hotels there which are probably nice, but be sure you get one that's in a quiet location. Being anywhere near or on Bourbon Street would eliminate any sleeping you might want to do. You also want someplace that is air-conditioned. Friends recently tried the Cornstalk Fence Hotel and checked out immediately—it was *very* tacky.

Restaurants

The most important subject when in N.O. Of course the town is famous for what's to eat, and we sure did our share. Here's a run-down of the places where we stuffed ourselves. For oysters, the most popular bars are *Felix's,* 739 Iberville; *Acme,* across the street; and the *Desire Room* of the Royal Sonesta Hotel, 300 Bourbon Street. At the latter we also got excellent gumbo, potato skins, fried fish. These three places, by the way, are not fancy, and that's an understatement. One of our best meals was at *LeRuth's,* 636 Franklin, in Gretna, about a twenty-minute drive from the Vieux Carré. Fabulous duckling, among other things. Everything was good!

Brennan's, 417 rue Royale.
The place to go for brunch, which was wonderful, although the service was terrible.

Café du Monde, 800 Decatur.
This is where everyone flocks for the N.O. doughnuts (beignets) and café au lait. I guess you have to do it once. The beignets were tasty but a bit on the heavy side and not like the beignets I've had in Paris. Coffee was good.

Caribbean Room, Pontchartrain Hotel, 2031 St. Charles Avenue.
Very good lunch; the desserts were fabulous. Pretty room.

Commander's Palace, Washington Avenue and Colosseum, in the Garden District.
This is one place where we did *not* eat, much to our dismay (we just ran out of time). It's owned by the Brennan people and I have heard that it is excellent. One friend told me it was the best meal in town. Others say it's so-so.

LeRuth's, 636 Franklin, in Gretna.
About a twenty minute drive, from the Vieux Carré. We had one of our best meals there. Fabulous duckling, among other things. Everything was good.

Pascal's Manale, 1838 Napoleon Avenue, in the Garden District, almost.
This is a wild and crazy place, a real local hangout, noisy and crowded, so be sure you have reservations. The food is sort of a cross between Italian and Creole and it's verrrrry good.

Popeye Chicken, all over the place.
This is N.O.'s answer to Kentucky Fried Chicken and it's real tasty! Spicy.

Winston's, in the N.O. Hilton.
A pretentious, lah-de-dah restaurant with, well, nouvelle-continental-English-Creole food (?). The food was good but the number they do there is a bit much.

Recommended places we didn't get to: the latest "in" restaurant in the city is *K. Paul's Louisiana Kitchen.* It's very small, they don't take reservations, and you have to line up on the street and wait for a table. Paul Prud'homme, the chef, is the current guru of Cajun cuisine. *Galatoire's* is also popular. The *Court of the Two Sisters,* 613 rue Royale, is recommended for lunch. *Arnaud's* is getting good again. *Jonathan's* provides rather expensive nouvelle-Orleans dishes and is popular with the natives. P.S. For oyster lovers, the happy-hour oyster bar in the *Hilton Hotel* dishes them out for 15 cents each up to 6:00 P.M. (then they go to 35 cents each).

Shopping

Shopping is another reason to go to N.O. The shopping along *Bourbon Street* will get you nowhere unless you like tourist junk. Over on *Royale* and some of the other streets you'll find lots of gorgeous antique stores. Most are expensive and many have a combination of really nice antiques and new fakes. You can wheel and deal a little, too. There are two or three perfume shops that carry their own brands, which are not sold anywhere else. One of these is called *Hove* and another is *Caro* (both on rue Royale). The perfumes I bought are very nice and not expensive.

Sightseeing

Before you go to New Orleans write to the Greater New Orleans Tourist and Convention Commission, 334 rue Royale, N.O., La. 70130, and ask them to send you a visitor's guide.

For openers, there are N.O.'s many little streets which you must wander in, including the main squares. Also a few old homes that give tours, the two best being the *Beauregard Keyes House*, 1113 Chartres Street, and the *Gallier House,* rue Royale. Forget the *Voodoo Museum.* There are some museums around, like the *Cabildo* (Louisiana Purchase signed here). If you have a car, drive down St. Charles Avenue into the *Garden District,* then cruise through some of the side streets to see beautiful old houses. Part of this area is now a historical monument. If you've been to Europe, the so-called *French Market* will be a major disappointment for you, and I really can't recommend even bothering with it. Along the street on the way to the market are some deli-type grocery stores selling a big sandwich called a "muffaletto." There are all kinds of sightseeing excursions offered by the locals, including horse carriage rides through the Vieux Carré. Our driver was less than brilliant and not too informative, pointing out the Chart House restaurant and a fried chicken store. You can also take boat rides on the Mississippi, which are half-day or all-day affairs.

A very nice half-day trip by car is to drive out into the bayou to look at antebellum mansions, or *plantations.* We left the city around 11:30 A.M. and got back to the hotel around 5:00 P.M., during which time we visited three antebellum mansions. The *Destrehan Plantation,* 9999 River Road, is the oldest remaining mansion and still has some slave houses on the property. However, when we were there it was only halfway restored and not as good as the next two. **San Francisco Plantation House,** Highway 44, was the most beautifully decorated. Across the river (by ferry) and about forty-four miles from N.O. is the spectacular **Oak Alley Plantation,** which is really worth the drive. There are guided tours at all of them. P.S. Pralines, which I generally consider inedible, were being sold at Oak Alley and had been made locally by a neighbor. They were fabulous and tasted nothing like those sold by the thousands in the tourist shops. One of the Mississippi River cruise boats stops at Oak Alley.

Dress in N.O. is super casual and only a couple of restaurants get picky about ties for dinner; take one anyway. In the better restaurants people were very well dressed, but not to the extent of being "semiformal." Men definitely need jackets.

Then there's always the jazz . . .

By the way, if you think you can practice your French in New Orleans you'll be sadly disappointed. Not one word of the language did I hear. Moreover, the gross mispronunciation of French names and words in the city will frustrate any aficionado of the French language.

Alaska

Alaska

Going to Alaska is almost like going to a foreign country. In fact, you have a tendency to call it a country instead of a state. You also wonder why the Russians ever gave it up. It's a vast territory and much of your time is eaten up just getting from A to B. We were there for only five days, a very short time for such a very big state, so obviously we covered only a small portion of it. I'll tell you our experience in the event you are thinking about going there, and maybe it will be of some help to you.

Tourism in Alaska is the second biggest industry, after fishing. People generally go to Alaska in one of two ways: by group tour, which may include a cruise, or on their own. We did it the latter way, which was more to our liking. All arrangements had been made in advance by us and our travel agent, and other than one small foul-up, we had no problems. In most cases the people traveling on their own were families, backpackers and campers, and people like ourselves, who enjoy doing their own thing. The tour groups that we saw were made up of an older crowd.

Going on one of the cruises offered by various shipping lines is very popular; I know several people who have done it; their opinions vary in degree from "nice," to "OK," to "wish we'd done it on our own." The cruise ships carry a *lot* of passengers, and when they come into the little Alaskan towns (which is all there are), suddenly the town is crammed with three hundred people at once, all scrambling into the one main street and the shops.

The area that the ships cruise—from Seattle to Juneau and into Glacier Bay—is certainly beautiful, and a cruise would be most relaxing, to be sure. However, that area is not representative of all of Alaska, so if you are interested in getting a broader view of what the state is like, you might want to consider taking extra time after the cruise, or doing it another way altogether. The terrain doesn't change much and four days of the same thing could be a bit much.

We went to Alaska in August, the height of the summer and the height of the tourist season. In Glacier Bay the temperature was in the forties and fifties most of the time. In Juneau, midfifties to sixties. In Denali, fifties to sixties. In Fairbanks, high sixties and low seventies and muggy. Lots of clouds and usually a lot of rain, although we didn't get much. Some very cold winds in Denali. In other words, be prepared for all kinds of weather, but mostly cold. Warm gloves and a ski cap are not out of line. Be sure you take binoculars and a telephoto lens, if you have one. The overall dress code in Alaska is casual, verrrrrry casual. Jeans, tennis shoes, flannel shirts, boots, etc. Leave your cocktail dresses at home.

Juneau, the capital of the state, can be reached only by boat or plane. There are no roads going into or out of this town. It's very small and quite charming. The "downtown" consists of about two or three blocks of shops and little cafés, and is real touristy. The "famous" **Red Dog Saloon** is strictly for tourists, we were told. We stayed at the **Cape Fox Sheffield House,** 51 W. Egan Drive, phone 907–586–6900, and the suites we had were very nice. One thing you quickly realize when going to Alaska is, it isn't the Ritz. From the motel you can walk all over town. If you go into every single shop you can cover the whole place in less than two hours.

The *Alaska State Museum* in Juneau is definitely worth the trip. Another attraction in the town is the **Wickersham House.** It's a big house which belonged to a judge. Now his niece gives guided tours of the memorabilia therein and ends by making everyone a flaming sourdough waffle. Sounds charming, right? Well, maybe it is. A couple of Alaskans suggested it was on the corny side and the waffles are one-bite sized. Take your chances on that one.

The big attraction in Juneau, in my opinion, is the **Mendenhall Glacier.** You can't miss seeing it as you fly in—it dominates the area. You absolutely must drive up and see it from the front. Even more important is to book yourself on a Flightseeing tour over it. You can't really appreciate or understand these glaciers until you fly over them. You can arrange for a Flightsee right at the airport. Of course the weather will determine whether or not it's possible to go, but by all means, try to make it work. It's an experience you won't soon forget. Another thing: on your way to or from the glacier on the road, stop off at **Steep Creek,** and go see the salmon spawning. This would be during the summer months, of course. Steep Creek is only about a hundred yards from the parking lot at the Mendenhall Glacier. You can see the salmon right next to the road or take one of the trails leading up the mountain for about five minutes, and you will get even a better view. You can usually find the spot, as other cars will be stopped along the road.

Sitka, a little village south of Juneau (about thirty minutes by plane), is gorgeous.

Glacier Bay was far and away the highlight of our little trip. You don't want to miss this. Most people who see Glacier Bay do so on a big cruise ship, as it's usually a part of the itinerary. There is one disadvantage, and a big one, in seeing it that way. Those ships are big and are not able to get too close to shore or go into some of the narrow inlets. You also miss much land and shore wildlife.

If you are not on a cruise ship you will get to Glacier Bay by flying from Juneau (about twenty minutes) or some other place to *Gustavus.* This is not one of your major airports, by the way. From Gustavus a bus will pick you up and drive you along a mostly dirt road to Glacier Lodge (takes about thirty minutes). Now you have two choices: to stay at the lodge and do an eight-hour cruise up and back in one day, or to go on the *Glacier Bay Explorer* (a boat) and spend the night way up in the bay. I heartily recommend the latter. The way this boat is built (very similar to the boat we rode on the Nile), it can pull right up to within a few feet of the shoreline and go way up the tiny inlets. In one place the boat was actually almost beached next to a glacier, allowing us to get off and walk around. The boat itself is spic and span, everyone has his own stateroom with private bathroom, the food is very good (lots of fresh fish and all you can eat), there is a state naturalist on board the whole time, and the experience is downright fantastic.

The boat leaves the lodge every day at 2:30 P.M. and returns the next morning around 9:30. It sails all day until about 10:00 or 11:00 P.M. Along the way you see all kinds of wildlife, which the naturalist points out to you and talks about. The highlight is going into one of the inlets among the ice floes, many of which are bejewelled with seal pups and their mothers, and parking about a half mile from one of the active glaciers. Then for about two hours you watch the "show." The glaciers "calve"—that is, huge chunks of them (the size of houses sometimes) break off and crash into the water, making sounds like cannons or explosions and causing huge swells in the bay. If you're lucky you'll see this happen about once every two to five minutes. The noise is unbelievable. It's something you will never see at home and an experience you will never get out of your head.

Glacier Bay Lodge is quite pretty. The lodge and the *Explorer* are operated by the same people. Those who stay at the lodge can take advantage of local fishing and hiking. There is a beautiful rain forest all around the lodge, and park naturalists are always on hand to do nature walks and provide lectures and film presentations.

Fairbanks is one town I won't rush back to: don't go out of your way to get there. You may end up there for a night because it is a jumping-off place for somewhere else. The main attraction is the university and its museum. As for motels, your pickings are slim. I can best point out one place *not* to stay and that is the **Capt. Bartlett Inn.** It's right on up there on my list of terribles. Just take my word for it—don't go! An acceptable motel is *Traveler's Inn,* 813 Noble Street. We had a decent room for about 100 dollars a night. (By the way, everything in Alaska is expensive.)

Two restaurants I can highly recommend are **The Pumphouse** and **The Ranch Dinner House,** 2223 S. Cushman. The Pumphouse is about a fifteen-minute drive out of town and is located in an old pumping station on the Chena River. It's very popular, so you may have to wait for a table, but the bar is interesting and lively. The food was good, the atmosphere fun. Worth the effort to drive out there. The Ranch Dinner House is probably what Fairbanksians would call "elegant," but you can wear jeans. The food was also good. Bear in mind that it's probably difficult to find "great" food in Alaska, if not impossible. All that wonderful fresh fish you think you're eating isn't fresh at all. We were told by a waiter that it's a state law in Alaska that all fish has to be partially frozen for handling and processing. I also heard the same story in Hawaii and California. The only way you can be assured of getting fresh fish is to catch it yourself and have it cooked the same day.

A number of other restaurants in Fairbanks that the locals said are pretty good are the **Bear and Seal** at the Traveler's Inn (it looked very nice, as far as decor goes), **Club 11, Ivory Jack's,** and **Clinkerdagger's.** A cab driver told us the best pizza was at **Mafia Mike's.**

Denali, formerly Mt. McKinley National Park, can be reached via paved highway, small private plane, or train from either Fairbanks (two and a half hours) or Anchorage (three and a half hours). The train ride from Juneau doesn't get too interesting until the last half hour, when you start into the mountains. Denali is quite beautiful, certainly worth a night or two, but if you've done a lot of traveling in the Rockies, especially Yellowstone, you may not find it very exciting. The best place to stay there is the very beautiful and new **McKinley Chalet.** The **Mt. McKinley Park Station Hotel,** located next to the railroad station, is big, but many of the rooms are in old converted railroad cars. It's also very busy there with lots and lots of buses and people all over the place. The Chalet is much quieter and much nicer.

The only way to get into the national park itself is by guided tour, unless you are camping. You can't drive there yourself in your own car. This is disappointing until you realize the absolute chaos which goes on in places like Yellowstone. You can take a conducted bus tour, which lasts seven hours and which goes deep into the park. It's quite tedious. They give you a so-called box lunch which is full of junk food and mush fruit, so you may want to take along something more substantial of your own. If you're lucky you may get a glimpse of Mt. McKinley (highest mountain in North America), but most of the time it's hiding behind clouds. You will probably see moose, reindeer (caribou), dall sheep, and grizzly bears. Once again, if you've been to Yellowstone this could all be a big letdown for you. On the other hand, as long as you're there you may as well go for it and see it, because you may not get there again.

There are lots of other things to do in Denali besides taking this nature-viewing bus tour. If you like backpacking and hiking, you'll be in heaven. You can also go horseback riding. The fishing there is iffy because many of the rivers are glacier-fed (they look milky and silty) and the fish don't hang around. A real fun thing to do is to go on one of the organized float trips. You can do the four-hour or the two-hour trip. Our boatman said the best rapids are on the two-hour trip. They provide all the gear to keep you dry and they do all the work, so you just have fun and get wet anyway.

Ketchikan and Yes Bay

From my friend DeeDee come the following comments:

"Ketchikan is probably like all of Alaska's seaport cities—uneventful. We were there for twenty-four hours and saw almost everything. Ketchikan is Alaska's first city and has the largest pulp mill and the largest collection of totem poles in the world. We visited the *Totem Heritage Center,* which was rather disappointing. Near the center is a lovely park and a nature trail which leads to the *Deer Mountain Salmon Hatchery,* very interesting. The town is small, and the museum, which is housed in the public library, was closed in the middle of the week. *Creek Street* is charming, with an interesting gallery of Eskimo sculpture and art.

"*Yes Bay Lodge* is fifty miles northwest of Ketchikan, hidden in a beautiful inlet. Art Hack and family own and run the lodge. A private seaplane picks you up at the Ketchikan airport and takes you for a twenty-minute flight over gorgeous Alaskan terrain. We were met at the dock by the Hacks and guides. We were immediately fed a great lunch and shown to rooms which were comfortable, but nothing posh.

"Each couple was assigned a fishing boat and private guide for the entire stay. The guides were very qualified, around twenty years old, and knowledgeable with regard to fishing, boat mechanics, Alaskan waters, plant and animal life, etc.

"Our meals were served family-style and at regular hours. There were picnics and barbecues when weather permitted. Each day we had fresh-baked breads, rolls, cookies, cakes, etc. They would try their best to make whatever you requested and a menu for the day was always posted.

"Rain gear was provided (boots, overalls, jackets, hats). I would recommend bringing a couple pairs of warm, waterproof gloves. Otherwise, we wore jeans, turtlenecks, T-shirts, sweatshirts, and lightweight parkas—things that could be layered.

"The day began at 8:00 A.M. with breakfast, followed by fishing, then lunch, then more fishing, then cocktails and dinner, then evening fishing, then bed. We caught king salmon, pink salmon, silver salmon, halibut, and cod (someone in our group caught an 82-pound halibut!). Our guides baited our hooks, taught us how to catch the various types of fish, unhooked the fish after we reeled it in, weighed all the fish back on shore, and then either smoked them, filleted them, or cut them into steaks, and packaged them. When we left, all our fish were packed into freezer boxes and sent on the plane home at no extra cost. Someone described the whole experience as the Gucci of the fishing set!

"One day we were lucky enough to take the seaplane with two guides to An An (a river), where the salmon were spawning. We hiked about a mile in this beautiful rain forest to a bear watch. On the trail we saw golden eagles, bald eagles, and bear tracks. We arrived at the bear watch—but no bears. We decided to fish downstream. As we were unpacking, a six-hundred-pound bear started feeding on salmon, not ten feet away from us! We waited until he moved downstream and continued fishing with him for the rest of the day.

"The trip was most relaxing. There are no phones—only a maritime radio—and no TV. There is a huge fireplace and cozy bar at the lodge. The cost to stay at the lodge with meals, boats, guides, and fishing gear came to about $300 per person per day. The only thing which would have made the trip perfect would have been to see the sun!"

Other Alaskan Sights

What about Anchorage? Katmai National Park? Cordova? Above the Arctic Circle (Nome, Kotzebue, Barrow, and Prudhoe Bay)? What about Kodiak? And the Aleutians? The Kenai area? Skagway and Wrangell? Valdez? Prince William Sound? Deserts, volcanoes, polar bears, Eskimos, and igloos? Dogsleds? Whales? Didn't I tell you we only had five days? Transportation is unpredictable due to weather. Distances are great. To see everything Alaska has to offer would take months, I'm sure, and way more than five days. You could probably do a real good run-through in two weeks. You wouldn't be able to drive everywhere. There are few roads and many of them lead to nowhere. There are many good and complete guidebooks on Alaska available in your bookstore. *Fodor's Alaska* is quite good, I think, for the basics.

Just so you'll know that Alaska has a similar effect on other people, I'll end this section with a quote from a letter written by my Uncle Charlie back in 1977, when he had the good fortune of spending four months there:

"Many new and rewarding Alaska insights we experienced during four months of ministry and four weeks on campgrounds there . . . true adventure, like discovering another country instead of another state. We traveled 6000 miles by plane, seaplane, Alaskan Railroad, bus, and car, but on no ferries.

"Spectacular were the many ranges of high mountains, ice fields, winding glaciers, icebergs, and 20,320-foot Mt. McKinley. A small plane flight, at 10,000 feet near McKinley, was very special. Many meandering rivers carry gray glacier silt into wide valleys.

"We became acquainted with native Indian, Eskimo, and Aleut fishermen who used fishwheels, fishnets, and crab pots. Salmon, king-pink-silver, along with halibut and king crab, were caught and processed at canneries in fishing communities with picturesque boat harbors.

"Beautiful forests are abundant in southeastern Alaska on the many islands. Alaska has thousands of lakes. More northerly forests are affected by the tundra, permafrost, and muskeg. Spruce and birch are most common. We picked blueberries, raspberries, salmonberries, and cranberries. Cabbages grow very large. Flowering fireweed, Alaska cotton, nasturtiums, daisies, roses, and large mushrooms were colorful. There are vast expanses of soggy marshes.

"Hunting season was open for moose, bear, bison, and goat, and trapping for fox and wolf and smaller animals. We saw alive only moose, beaver, seal, whale, ducks, and geese. At the dogsled capital, Tok, there were kennels of huskies, Siberian and Alaskan, and interbreeds with wolf.

"Alaska University at Fairbanks displays a 5,220-pound raw copper nugget and a 3-foot-by-4-foot block of jade. Traces of gold are still panned. From intricate crafts to totem poles were ivory, soapstone, jade and wood carvings, paintings and fine basketwork.

"There are many old structures and churches, such as Russian Orthodox, and old log houses. Anchorage is a large, up-to-date city. The site of the proposed new capital at Willows is still an undeveloped area. Juneau has some new state buildings.

"The Northern Lights favored us with unusual displays several nights. The big dipper was exceptionally bright. We saw a sundog and double rainbows. June and July had eighteen hours of daylight, with sun on the mountain peaks at 10:30 P.M. Weather was mostly cool, mild and rainy."

If you've toyed with the idea of traveling to and through Alaska, stop playing your games and start planning for it for next summer. You won't be disappointed.

The Hawaiian Islands

The Hawaiian Islands

The saying "You've seen one, you've seen them all" does not apply to the Hawaiian Islands. Each island is different from each of the others. Each island can boast a variety of scenery and climate, depending on which side of it you happen to be. There's a lot to like about the islands and a lot to be disappointed about. I'll take them one by one.

Oahu

Most people who go to Hawaii for the first time plop themselves down in Waikiki and think they've arrived, seeing there are some palm trees in the area and fancy rum drinks at the bar. Waikiki, in my opinion, is one of the disaster areas of the world. I'd almost rather stay home. I suppose everyone should see Waikiki and Honolulu once; but once is enough, and four days or fewer will do it.

There's only one place to stay in Honolulu, and fortunately it isn't in Waikiki, but close enough to it. I'm speaking about the *Kahala Hilton,* ten minutes away by cab or shuttle bus. The Kahala is one of the most gorgeous hotels I know of, with lovely rooms and great service. It boasts one of Honolulu's finest restaurants, the *Maile Room,* and has one of Hawaii's best jewelry stores, Bernard Hurtig. There is a large porpoise pool complete with performing porpoises, warm-water penguins, giant tortoise, colorful tropical fish, etc. You can get a room in the tower or a room around the lagoon, which is where we always stay, as it has easy access to the beach and pool. Our favorite room is suite 1130–1130A—very spacious and luxurious. The beach at the Kahala leaves much to be desired, as does the ocean swimming.

If you have kids, though, it's the greatest. There's a good masseuse at the hotel named Mrs. Bourlin; you can make appointments through the Beauty Shop (she's also in the phone book). It's just too bad that the Kahala can't be picked up and set down somewhere on a different island.

There is one good thing about Honolulu and Waikiki—the restaurants. You can get some pretty good food there. The *Maile Room* at the Kahala Hilton is very good, especially when they have a special buffet and you have kids. Our favorite is **The Third Floor** at the Hawaiian Regent Hotel; the food is usually good, but the atmosphere and the little extras are what we really enjoy. *Michel's* at the Colony Surf Hotel serves French-type food in a lovely semi-open-air room. **Bagwell's 2424** at the Hyatt Regency Waikiki Hotel is on the stuffy side, but the food is good; I especially like the coffee service and the waiters' costumes. *Hy's* is physically a beautiful restaurant, but we found the food mediocre and service poor. Good for cocktails in the library bar. Also recommended is **Chez Michel**, not the same as *Michel's*. For Chinese food try **Yen King** (formerly the Winter Garden) in the Kahala Mall. You can walk there from the Kahala Hilton Hotel. **Wo Fat** is another popular Chinese restaurant, 115 N. Hotel Street, a rather seedy neighborhood. We were not impressed with the restaurant at all and wouldn't go back. Several friends love the **Willows,** 901 Hausten Street, but we haven't tried it. For fish, beat a path to **John Dominis** in the harbor area. Ask to sit in the Banquette Room. Wonderful ceviche! And for a wonderful and authentic Japanese dining experience, go to the **Tea House,** 87 Laimi Road off Pali Highway, phone 595–2885 and 538–9184. Reservations essential and in advance. Once you make a reservation, don't cancel or no-show, as each meal is specially prepared.

Dress for all restaurants in Hawaii is casual; at night some men might feel more comfortable with a jacket. I don't think many restaurants, if any, require ties; you can always ask when you make your reservation. No shorts, please. It's a good idea to have a lightweight sweater or jacket along, as many places get carried away with air conditioning. Even though it's a balmy 80 degrees outside, you can be deep-freezed inside.

Sightseeing is pretty good on all the islands, including Oahu. You can start by taking a drive around the island. The **North Shore** is quite beautiful with wild surf, huge waves at the right time of year, shark warnings on the beaches, dense forests, and beautiful beaches. The big drawback to this side of the island is the wind, which never seems to stop blowing. Also, the swimming can be very dangerous. The best hotel there is the **Turtle Bay Hilton** (originally the Kuilima).

Next you can, and should, go see **Pearl Harbor.** There are two ways to do this. The first, which you do *not* want to do, is to take a commercial tour; this will cost you a few bucks and you'll see a lot less than the second way. The second way is to go with the U.S. Navy, which is free. Call up and make a reservation and find out what time the tours go. You enter by the Halawa Gate off Nimitz Road. You'll get a first-rate tour, and I guarantee you you'll be impressed. Bring your camera.

Now, you can take a day and drive up to the *Polynesian Cultural Center,* run by the LDS Church. On the way you'll pass by *Koko Head,* a beautiful swimming beach called *Hananuma Bay,* and the *Blow Hole,* among other things. I don't advise eating at the P.C.C. as the food was ghastly when we were there. It will take you the better part of the day to do the trip, but I thought it was very interesting, well done, informative, fun, etc. Kids will like it.

There are several other trips and tours you can do around the island and in the city: *Sea Life Park,* the *Iolani Palace, Waikiki Aquarium, Punchbowl Memorial Cemetery, Chinatown, Paradise Park, The U. of Hawaii, Queen Emma Museum,* and the *Kawaiahao Church.*

Shopping turns out to be very touristy, naturally. Save some time to sit on the "beach," or what's left of it. Be careful no one steps on you.

Maui

Maui seems to be everyone's favorite island, and for good reason. It's big, diverse, beautiful. Once again, be careful where you stay. There's a good area and a not-so-good area.

I'll start with the latter. *Do not* go to Kaanapali/Lahaina. Ten years ago it was beautiful: three hotels, miles of gorgeous beaches, a quaint little village called Lahaina, and up toward Napili there were a few apartments and condominiums. During the past ten years a few people have decided to make Kaanapali into Waikiki-on-Maui, and they've done a real good job. Now it's wall-to-wall hotels (big ones), and where there isn't a hotel, there's a condo, or a shopping center, or a fast-food joint, or a parking lot. The hotels are crammed with bus tours and you can hardly stumble through the lobby for the suitcases and tour directors. The pool areas are mobbed. The restaurants are terrible. If you miss the traffic jams back home, this is where you can go to find them. It's heartbreaking to see what has been allowed to happen there.

About ten miles up the road from Kaanapali is the *Kapalua Bay Hotel,* originally a Rockefeller resort. Our experience there was a disaster and we checked out and moved to another hotel on a different island. That was a while back, however, and the hotel has now changed hands, so perhaps some improvements will be forthcoming. My main complaints about the hotel are the location and the weather. It's on a windy point. It seems to get more rain than the rest of the island (although I don't have exact statistics). When we were there, there was *no* beach due to a very high tide. I have friends, however, who like this hotel very much because of the golfing facilities in the area.

So, where *will* you stay when you go to Maui? At the **Wailea Beach Hotel,** about three miles from Kihei. If that hotel is booked, stay at the **InterContinental,** which is the only other hotel in the area. You can't see one hotel from the other. There are no traffic jams in Wailea. No tour buses (or at least so few as to be unnoticeable). No gigantic shopping centers. No fast-food restaurants. No mess, no clutter, no noise. The Wailea Beach Hotel is quiet, beautiful, has good food, good service, and one of the most gorgeous views on all the islands. You can stay in the tower building or in a beachfront room (100s and 200s). About a quarter of a mile away is a small, quiet shopping complex, where you'll never see more than twenty people at once.

Restaurants in the Wailea/Kihei area abound. A couple are very above-average (by Hawaii standards) and a couple are very bad, by any standard.

Ambrosia,   Wailea Shopping Village,
is one of the worst. They had the nerve to serve one of us eggplant parmesan without eggplant. When the waiter was asked where the eggplant was, he replied that they'd run out, and had substituted carrots instead (but of course, no one said that up front). Two entire meals were spilled on the floor while being served. We couldn't get ice cream because they'd forgotten to put it in the freezer and it melted. Need I go on?

Chuck's Steak House,   in Kihei,
is the ubiquitous steakhouse with salad bar and noisy bar and no surprises.

The Fairway,   Wailea Golf Course Clubhouse, phone 879–4060,
is open and airy and sort of pretty, but the food is forgettable. They got the orders all mixed up; service was slow.

La Familia Restaurant,   2511 S. Kihei Road, phone 879–8824,
serves mediocre Mexican food for people who don't know Mexican food. Good margaritas, and after two of them, who cares?

Gaspare's,   1993 S. Kihei Road, phone 879–8881,
serves tolerable pizza and other Italian dishes.

Hong Kong Restaurant,   760 S. Kihei Road,
is a Chinese restaurant which you can skip. Couldn't get anything on the menu, not even a glass of water.

Island Fish House,   1945 S. Kihei Road, phone 879–7771,
is the best fish restaurant in Kihei. Small menu, but everything is fresh and well prepared; service is good. Try the combination fish plate to sample the local specialties.

Kiawe Broiler,   InterContinental Hotel,
is a casual broiler/grill with pretty good food.

Kihei Prime Rib House,   Kai Nani Village, phone 879–1954,
is often good, sometimes not so good. Salad bar is better than most, drinks from

the bar are very good; service tries hard. Up and down in all areas, however. Look in the portholes of the model ship in glass for a surprise.

Kihei Seas, 2439 S. Kihei Road, phone 879–5600, is upstairs in a small shopping mall, quite large, with a popular piano bar. Large, 44-item salad bar; dinners were passable.

Le Grand Ice Cream, Rainbow Mall, Kihei, is a good place to go for dessert if you're at any of the restaurants in the area. They make Danish-style waffle cones on griddles right before your eyes, and you can fill these with their unusual homemade ice creams.

Mama's Fish House, Hana Highway, Route 36, one and a half miles past the town of Paia, phone 579–9672, a twenty-minute drive from Wailea.
The *best* fish on the island. Very casual. Worth the trip.

Maui Onion is the pool-side café at the Wailea Beach Hotel. They have the best onion rings in the whole world, plus excellent sandwiches, milkshakes, smoothies, chips, salads.

The Maui Outrigger, 2980 S. Kihei Road, is probably the worst dining experience we've ever had. The Outrigger is to the restaurant business what the black plague is to a tea party. We waited almost one and a half hours for our dinners; my husband finally stormed the kitchen to tell the cook that we were leaving, and to forget serving us our meal. The cook said he hadn't started cooking our food yet, so it didn't matter. Then we got a bill for the food which we'd never seen, and when we said we weren't paying it, the man in charge said he'd call the police. Meanwhile there was a singer with a terrible voice, singing several decibel points above the acceptable pain level. The salad bar had several empty bowls, and no one made any attempt to replenish them. If there was any liquor in my mai-tai, it was a minuscule amount. The restaurant was busy when we arrived (on time), but almost empty when we finally had the sense to leave. We ended up at Le Grand Ice Cream for hot fudge sundaes.

Ming Yuen is a Chinese/Hawaiian restaurant, very near the Kahului Airport.
All the locals say it's the best restaurant in the area. About a twenty-minute drive from Wailea.

Ocean Terrace Restaurant, 2960 S. Kihei Road, phone 879–2607, is small, OK, nothing to write home about.

La Perouse, at the InterContinental Hotel, is one of the two nicest restaurants in the area. Exquisite room, nice and often unusual menu, good service, and the food is usually quite good. More elegant than the average, so don't go in your beachwear. Jackets are requested, but not imperative, for men. Expensive.

Polli's Mexican Restaurant, 101 N. Kihei Road.
We were told by just about everyone not to go. We didn't.

Raffles, at the Wailea Beach Hotel, is your best bet for a really nice meal; very good food, beautiful decor. Dress

up a little. Expensive. They have an outstanding Sunday brunch, but be sure
you reserve well in advance.

Robaire's,   61 S. Kihei Road, phone 879–2707,
is a funky little almost-French place with nice people and French food, which
was tasty. A nice switch from the usual Hawaii-type places.

Set Point Restaurant,   Wailea Tennis Center, phone 879–3244.
Go for lunch, not dinner. Nothing special.

Wailea Steak House,   100 Wailea Ike Drive, on the road to the tennis
courts, phone 879–2875.
An OK steakhouse, no salad bar, good drinks, Caesar Salad and hot mushrooms.

If you venture over to the Lahaina side of the island (which I don't
recommend), the best place to eat is the *Swan Court* at the Hyatt Regency
Hotel; rather elegant with good food. For lunch you might try *Longhi's*
in Lahaina, which is very popular, but I thought it was mediocre. Everyone
likes the Chinese restaurant in the Lahaina Shopping Center (but no one ever
seems to know the name of it, including me!).

Shopping in Wailea is rather limited. There are some nice shops in the
Wailea Shopping Center. At the InterContinental Hotel there is a marvelous
jewelry store; their merchandise seems to be several cuts above everywhere
else. There's a little market in the Wailea Shopping Center where you can
stock up on stuff for the fridge in your room, which is a lot cheaper than
getting the goods through the hotel. Kihei has a couple of small shopping
centers.

Sightseeing on Maui can take you a few days if you want to see
everything. The drive to *Hana* is an all-day affair over a twisting road, but
so far I've never heard anyone say it wasn't worth it. The *Hotel Hana Maui*
(808–248–8211) has a very good reputation and is said to be the ultimate
in quiet. It has recently changed hands and as of this writing I don't know
what changes will take place. The *Iao Needle* is easy to get to, and interesting. If you drive out past the Kapalua Bay Hotel you'll arrive at some
pineapple fields, and on good days you can watch some spectacular surfing.
One thing you really should do, even though it's easier said than done, is
go up to Haleakala Crater at sunrise. I know, I know—you have to get up
at 3:00 or 4:00 A.M. and drive for over an hour, and when you get there it's
frrrreeeezing cold, but it's a sight worth seeing, and you're only required to
do it once in your life. If you don't feel like driving yourself, call Roberts
Tours, or one of the other tour companies, and take their guided tour. You'll
return to your hotel by 9:30 A.M. and then you can go back to sleep. Be sure
you see the silversword plants while you're at the crater; they're very rare.
And wear all the clothes you have—you'll freeze.

Molokini is a little crater off the coast of Wailea and they claim it has
the best snorkeling and diving in the islands. There are commercial tours you

can take out to the crater; they provide you with all the equipment, instructions, cutesy camp-counselor types to help you with everything, group singing, whale watching, lunch, and beer-drinking contests on the way back. Too much for your money! As for the snorkeling—well, ho hum and yawn. Maybe we're spoiled, but if you've ever been to the Caribbean or the South Pacific, you can skip this. The best snorkeling we've seen in Hawaii was on the back side of Lanai at Manele, and about the only way you can get there is on a private boat.

If you're in the islands in January, February, or March, keep your eyes peeled for whales. They're everywhere; huge, beautiful, and thrilling to see.

If you plan to rent a car anywhere in the islands during holidays, reserve it well in advance. It's nearly impossible to get one at the last minute.

Kahului Airport leaves much to be desired. It's always jammed and confusion reigns. Don't arrive at the last minute for a flight. If you're going to fly directly home, you'll have to go through a ridiculous agricultural inspection, which takes extra time. You have to open *every* bag, so don't put your chains and locks on until after you've gone through this hassle. I understand the reasoning behind this inspection, but it's so cursory as to be practically useless. The runway at Kahului isn't long enough to accommodate 747s, but supposedly there are plans afoot to extend it in the future. American Airlines is currently flying in DC-10's. United also has direct service to Maui from the mainland. The American Airlines flights, service, and planes are, at the moment, superior to United's. Our United flight was canceled; this was on New Year's Day and we had to go stand-by from Maui to Honolulu, then stand-by again to get back to the mainland, with no help or apologies from the United people. We've heard many stories about other canceled flights and long delays due to planes with "equipment failure."

It always cracks me up to see people hauling boxes of pineapples onto the plane. I guess if you live in North Dakota or Minneapolis it's worth the effort, but if you live on the West Coast, don't bother. You can get the same pineapples at home for the same amount of money, or less. Same goes for macadamia nuts—they aren't any cheaper in Hawaii. What you can get more easily in the islands, however, are chocolate-covered macadamia nuts, and other confections made with this oh-so-delish and fattening little nut. Pick these up at the airport in Honolulu, which has some pretty good shops.

Kauai

A lot of people love this island, but we don't go there because they have more rain on Kauai than on the other islands. It's a good idea to go once, however, and make up your own mind. It's gorgeous! Half of it approaches what Tahiti looks like (I said approaches); part of it looks like a little Grand Canyon. *Poipu Beach* is a popular area for hotels. *Hanalei Bay* is beautiful. The *Waimea* drive is very worthwhile, and if you go all the way to the top to *Kalalau Lookout,* make sure it's on a clear day or you'll be wasting your time. You can take a boat tour up the *Wailua River* to the *Fern Grotto;* it's touristy, but fun if you're in the mood. Be sure you stop and see or go sit on *Lumahai Beach,* which is that picture-postcard-perfect beach you see in the film *South Pacific.* For hotels and restaurants you'll have to ask somebody else; it's been too long since we've been there to give you any tips. Good luck with the weather.

Molokai

This island has only been opened to tourism in the past few years, and opened slowly. It's a wonderful island, however, and I can recommend going there. The *Sheraton Hotel* is beautiful and the beaches around it are just spectacular. The food, when we were there, left something to be desired; all that can change with a new chef. I've heard the burro ride down to the Kalaupapa Peninsula is a wonderful experience. (This is where you'll find the former leper colony and Father Damien's church.) If you are sailing or if you can hire a helicopter, be sure you see the "back" side of the island —sheer cliffs plunging into the sea, with waterfalls everywhere, deep and beautiful valleys, exciting shoreline. I'm referring to the north side of the island from Halawa Bay to Ilio Point. It's one of the most breathtaking sights I've seen. I have a feeling tourism in Molokai will grow substantially in the future, so if you want to enjoy it peacefully, go now. So far it's "undiscovered."

Hawaii, The Big island

It's a toss-up as to which island I like better: Maui or Hawaii. It's not a fair contest because we're talking apples and oranges. Hawaii has a lot to offer and should be on your itinerary.

You can fly directly to Hilo from the mainland, which is convenient. You don't want to stay in Hilo, however, because there's not much to do there and it's usually raining. You can rent or hire a car and go either north or south to the other side of the island.

If you go the south route you'll come to the *Kalapana* and *Kaimu Black Sand Beaches,* worthy of a detour because they're quite beautiful. Don't get tempted to run off into the jungle, as there are some very big spiders in there. There's nothing to do at this beach except take a look and take some pictures, and then you can be on your way. Next you'll come to *Volcanoes National Park,* where Kilauea erupts from time to time. You can spend a good two hours in the park exploring the roads and trails, and visiting the Visitor Center, eating lunch, and learning something about volcanoes. Good for kids of all ages.

Heading into the Kona Coast you'll pass the City of Refuge and that is worth the time to stop and take the little tour; about an hour. Then you'll pass Kealakekua, known for the "Little Grass Shack"—for all you hula fans.

Now you'll be in Kona, where there are several hotels, a small town, and a shopping area. You can spend about twenty minutes there because it isn't all that exciting. The *Kona Surf* in Keauhou is pleasant, has a nice pool area (especially for kids), and a good surfing beach next door. However, it's always full of bus tours so we stopped going there. The *Kona Hilton* is also good.

Past Kona you'll head up through the volcano fields once again and you'll come to the three best hotels on the island: *Kona Village, Mauna Lani,* and *Mauna Kea.* The *Mauna Lani* just opened, so I haven't had a chance to get there; friends who have been there say it's nice, not great; beach is OK but not great; food is OK but not great. Another recent hotel guest told me it's fabulous. Well, it's a new hotel, so we'll give it time. The *Mauna Kea* has been famous and popular for years and used to be first-rate in all respects: for golf, for tennis, for beach, for service, for rooms, for class. One drawback (and this goes for all three of these hotels) is it's isolated, and your restaurant selection is limited to what the hotel has to offer. The *Kona Village* is a whole different experience than the other two. It's very isolated; until a few years ago you could only get there by boat. Each room is a separate bungalow done in the style of a south-seas hut, simply furnished, but comfortable. No phones in the rooms, no TV, no radio. No shopping center, no *New York Times.* It's summer camp for adults. A black sand beach. Big barbecues every day for lunch. A different menu every night for dinner. Old movies shown on the lawn in the evening. A luau once a week. A natural pond full of wildlife. Birds, birds, birds. Petroglyphs near the pond. Colorful parrots, one of which has been there since before the hotel was built. Casual, relaxing, comfortable, hang-loose, let-go. Tennis courts. If you want to play golf they'll take you to the Mauna Kea. A small airstrip for small planes. I really like this hotel.

One of the best things about Hawaii's Kona coast is the weather. It probably has the best all-around weather of all the islands. You'll notice when you're there the very desertlike appearance on one side of the island. The hotels are plush and beautifully landscaped.

On top of the island is *Kamuela,* the center of the cattle ranch area of Hawaii. Only by flying over Parker Ranch can you get an idea of how vast it is.

Back over on the Hilo side you can go visit *Akaka Falls* and *Laupahoe-*

hoe Beach; they're on the way to wherever you're going and only take a few minutes to see. There are also macadamia nut farms in that area which give tours, if you are so inclined.

If you've never read James Michener's *Hawaii,* you've denied yourself not only a terrific novel, but the opportunity to learn about the history of the islands through this great story.

I've heard more than a few people pooh-pooh Hawaii who've never been there. How good can it be, they say? Isn't it like the South Pacific? No, it sure isn't like the South Pacific! I wish it were. Hawaii, with all its faults, is a pretty good place to go, especially if you live on the West Coast, as it's very close. Maybe you won't get the world's greatest food there and maybe some of the overbuilding will dismay you, but you can get away from all of that, find some good fresh fish and fruit, and walk on some fairly exotic beaches. It's impossible to get away from tourist centers, since the entire state is devoted to tourism. Just be careful which of those tourist areas you go to, as the quality of your experience will depend on it. Pack lightly, take your most casual, carefree clothes, watch out for the hot sun, go for the rum drinks at sundown, and lie back.

Tahiti

AND

Fiji

Tahiti

Comparing Tahiti and Hawaii, Tahiti is diamond, Hawaii is glass. If you've been to Hawaii and think you've seen the South Pacific, you're quite deceived. Hawaii is mid-Pacific, and there's a big difference. Tahiti, like Fiji, is a true South Seas tropical paradise. Tahiti and Fiji are quite different from one another, as well.

If you're going to Tahiti for the first time, try to take at least two weeks, maybe longer; this will give you time to see the main islands and relax in the process. If you've only got a week, your choice is simple: go directly to Bora-Bora.

Each of the Tahitian Society Islands is beautiful with something to offer. Save Bora-Bora for the last, because none of the others can compare.

The island of *Tahiti* is where you begin, staying somewhere around *Papeete.* This, the largest port, is interesting for about two hours. Then you can rent a car, or hire a guide and driver (better) to drive you around the island. Outside Papeete it gets quite beautiful. Don't miss the *Gauguin Museum* on your tour. When I was there they didn't own one single original Gauguin, yet it was still an interesting and very beautiful museum. I had an opportunity to speak with the curator of the museum awhile back and he informed me that they were actively trying to acquire some originals. There is a lovely restaurant by the museum for lunch. For lunch or dinner, don't miss the *Belvedere* above Papeete.

The island of *Moorea* is everyone's next stop. You can fly from Papeete in five minutes, or you can take a one-hour boat ride, which can be very rough, depending on the seas. When you get to Moorea stay at the *Bali Hai Hotel.* If they offer a picnic trip for the day, take it; they take you to another part of the island for snorkeling and lunch. Rent a little jeep and drive around this island, too. **Cook's Bay** is gorgeous, as is the drive up to the lookout above it. The **Club Med** is at one end of the island. The setting is quite nice. We're not the Club Med types, but if you are, you may enjoy it. The accommodations are quite primitive, and when we were there as guests for dinner, the food was inedible.

Raiatea, another island, also has a nice **Bali Hai Hotel,** situated next to Tahiti's second largest port. Again you will want to rent a jeep and take a drive around the island. Some of Tahiti's largest and most famous ancient temples are on this island. You might also enjoy the one-day river cruise, which includes a snorkeling stop. Wherever it was they took us, it was without question the most outstanding and breathtaking snorkeling we've ever experienced anywhere in the world.

The island of **Huahine** has a lovely **Bali Hai Hotel** with excellent snorkeling just off the beach, especially in the late afternoon. The hotel will offer motorized outrigger canoe excursions to remote *motus* and beaches for picnics and snorkeling. Be sure you go.

Bora-Bora is the gem. The **Hotel Bora-Bora** is fantastic. Reserve an overwater bungalow (this is also true for most hotels on all the islands). Ours was called "Black Fish" and we had regular manta ray visitors at all times, which are harmless. Rent a bike and go for a ride down the road. The natives are very friendly. The snorkeling and beaches are unreal. You'll definitely think you've died and gone to heaven, but there you are—alive in paradise!

A few tips

Take a lot of bug spray, bug-bite ointment, insect repellent. Most of the hotels provide it but take your own, just to be sure. Don't leave your suitcase open; you'll find it has turned into a bug motel by the next morning. Don't plan for your hair dryer always to work. Sometimes, no matter what you do, you can't get the system of converters and transformers to work. Take only the most casual clothes—no jackets and ties for men, no stockings for women. You'll need practically no clothes at all, in fact. Other than bathing suits, everyone buys and wears a *pareu,* which is a large piece of cloth that can be tied up in about a hundred ways. Anyone will be happy to show you how. French and Polynesian are the official languages, but you'll have no trouble with English. Take lots of film, plus an underwater camera. Also, take your own flippers, snorkel, and mask. Most of the hotels will provide them, but they are obviously not going to be in very good shape. Be careful of the sun, especially the first couple of days—it's very intense. Don't expect incredible food; it's good, but not great. Stick to fresh fish. Be sure you eat the grapefruit (*pamplemousse*); it's green and delicious. Don't take your

Hawaiiana outfits—you'll stand out like a big mosquito bite. If any hotel offers a reef-walking excursion, take it. For this you will need old tennis shoes (take some along, anyway). The Tahitian children in the villages will get a kick out of Polaroid pictures, small candies, and balloons. Glass-bottom boat trips are definitely worthwhile, even if you've been on one before in Hawaii or somewhere else. Take in a Tahitian revue, especially on the outer islands—the smaller, more native, and less commercial, the better. Drink only bottled water. Take medication for diarrhea, although the opposite problem can easily arise. Kick up the sand in front of you as you wade into the water, if you aren't wearing flippers—this will shoo away any stonefish in your path. Don't try to get friendly with any water snakes. Get away from the hotels and into the little villages and see the people. Hinano beer, the Tahitian label, is delicious. The most important piece of advice I can give you is—get to Tahiti as soon as you can.

Fiji

Fiji is a beautiful South Seas paradise type of place, very different from Tahiti. The Fijians are very dark-skinned. The men are big, muscular, strong, and gorgeous; the women are fat. They have beautiful eyes and beautiful children. Their hair is kinky black.

The weather is typically tropical. Rainy months are November to April; the dry season is May to October. We were there in November and encountered two days of rain out of ten, which isn't bad. The rest of the time it was *hot* and *humid*. In the sun, which is piercing (watch out), it's about 95 degrees during the day. At night it's in the seventies and very pleasant. Water temperature runs between 78 and 90 degrees. You need only lightweight clothing, lots of beach wear, sandals, and snorkel equipment, if you have it (or you can rent it there).

Food in Fiji is not so hot. The service isn't the greatest. But everyone smiles. Good things to eat there are peas, bacon, coffee, cheese, fish, apples, and a drink called lemon squash. Things not so good to eat are duckling, chicken, steak, hamburgers, and hot chocolate (hot chocolate?). The hot dogs are weird. Pineapple and papaya are different than in Hawaii. Curries are good (they should be, as Fiji is overrun with Indians). Chinese food is so-so.

A few Fijian words you'll want to know, of course:

isaleigh *(ee-sah-lay)*	farewell (it's also the name of their most famous song)
ni sa bula *(nee-sah-boola)*	hello
ni sa yadra	good morning

ni sa moce *(mo-kay)*	goodbye
vinaka	thank you
papa	papaya
walu	good local whitefish
meke	traditional Fijian songs and dances
sulu	Fijian men's skirt
mana	magic
bure *(brrr-ray)*	house or hut

The electricity is 240 volts. The outlets are different than any we've ever encountered, and none of our adapters or converters worked. Some hotels can provide transformers. In general, trying to get your hair dry is not easy. You can buy adapters there in some stores, but you have to hunt.

Accommodations

On the main island near Nadi (pronounced *nandi*) is the newest and nicest hotel, called the **Regent of Fiji,** with 300 rooms. From the hotel you can take all sorts of day trips to the nearby outer islands. Nadi is about ten minutes away from the hotel and good for shopping. You'll find a number of duty-free shops with good buys on tape recorders, radios, computers, cameras, watches, beautiful beachwear, and all at low prices. I would suggest staying two nights at the Regent.

The **Fijian** is also on the main island and is another large resort with 320 rooms. It's older than the Regent and located in a different terrain. They offer reef-walking nature trips at low tide, which means you'll need some old tennis shoes. The food at the Fijian was better than at the Regent. Neither spot has good snorkeling.

Plantation is a small resort on a small island. I would not recommend staying there. The bay doesn't catch the breeze, so it is hotter and more humid there than at some of the other resorts. There are also more bugs, and at low tide it didn't smell very good. It would be OK for a day trip.

Mana Island Resort. Go! It's a real South Seas paradise which comes closer to the splendor of Bora-Bora than anywhere else in Fiji that we saw. Fantastic snorkeling off the north beach, about fifty yards out in midbay. Request rooms *(bures)* #1, 2, 3, 4, or 5 on the north beach. The rooms are not fancy but they have the basics. You can really relax here. The food was OK but nothing to write home about. Be sure your room isn't near the dining room or you will not get a lot of sleep.

Castaways seems to be the most popular resort there. The island it's on is only 38 acres in size, whereas Mana is about 350 acres. We didn't stay at Castaways because we couldn't get in. A pilot told us it was very well run and well organized, which was why it was so popular. Small.

Beachcomber and **Treasure Island** are two other tiny islands with resort areas on them, probably similar to Castaways and Mana.

At all hotels you can go water-skiing, coral viewing by boat, fishing, sailing, etc., or get day trips to other islands. They all have frequent barbecues, *lovos* (similar to luaus), and *mekes,* which are presentations of the island songs and dances, not to miss.

Getting around between islands can be done by ferry, small boats, or seaplane taxis (Turtle Airways). The last is fastest and best for sightseeing —and the most expensive, of course.

On Saturday at 1:00 P.M. all the shops close down until Monday morning.

Fiji is nine hours direct by jet from Los Angeles; about twelve hours if you have to stop in Honolulu or Tahiti. We flew Pan Am one way and Air New Zealand one way. The Air New Zealand flight was superior; it is one of the best airlines we've flown.

Hong Kong

Hong Kong

I always wondered if Hong Kong would live up to its reputation once I finally got there to see it for myself. Not only did it live up to it, it surpassed it. Hong Kong is a beautiful city, always picturesque, clean, efficient, fun, exotic. There's a lot to see and a lot to buy, so allow yourself several days on a first visit. We were there for four days, which wasn't long enough; seven would have been more like it.

The residents of Hong Kong, most of whom are Chinese, are now living in a sort of never-never land between what Hong Kong is, or was, and what it may become in the next ten years. What will ultimately occur in 1997, no one knows for sure. Many businesses are leaving; many have already relocated elsewhere. Others are sticking it out, being optimistic; we'll see how long this attitude can last. For now, however, it's a great place to visit, and it will be very interesting to go to H.K. around the year 2000 and see what changes have taken place.

As for language, English is widely spoken, but you'll find that in some cases, you could use a little Chinese (the main dialect is Cantonese). If you stick to the main hotels, shopping arcades, and restaurants around the hotels, there is always someone who can speak at least a little English. More than a few times, however, we found ourselves in restaurants where little or no English was spoken, but we got by just fine by pointing and gesturing. We also had our guide with us to help out in a couple of cases. Take my advice —don't chicken out and only eat at tourist restaurants: borrrrring! You'll probably get good food, to be sure, but you'll be missing the experience of eating with the locals and eating the foods they do. Hotel cuisine is always watered down for tourists. Be adventuresome. It wouldn't hurt you to pick up a few words of Cantonese, which I will conveniently provide for you at the end of this chapter.

Dress is very casual, but men should have a jacket and tie for an occasional dressy restaurant. If you plan to visit any temples, don't plan to wear shorts. In the hot season, women will be most comfortable in skirts or dresses, or very lightweight slacks. Most Chinese restaurants are very casual. As it can be cool in the evenings, and you can run into energetic air-conditioning units, take a light sweater or jacket. It's not always tropical and balmy there, so consult your international weather guide to find out just what the weather will be when you are going. Always plan for rain. Take comfortable walking shoes.

Hong Kong is divided into two basic areas: Hong Kong Island and Kowloon, which is on the mainland. It's a seven-minute ferry ride between the two, or fifteen minutes by car via the underwater tunnel. Most of the hotels are located on the Kowloon side, in the district called Tsimshatsui. There are hotels on the H.K. side also, the main area there being called Central. The most popular beaches are on the island. New Territories (extending to the Chinese border) is on the Kowloon side. Whichever side you stay on, you'll probably find yourself shuttling back and forth.

For sightseeing your best bet is to hire a guide, who can whisk you around to all the main spots and give you all the running commentary that you want. There are around four hundred highly trained and licensed guides in H.K.; the exams they have to go through to get their license are mind-boggling, so you can bet they all know their stuff. We had an excellent guide, named Rose Marie Tang, whose address is 63 Ma Tau Chung Road, ground floor, Kowloon, H.K. (phone 5–290131). If you can't reach her, try Plan Travel Ltd., Canton House, 1st floor, 54–56 Queen's Road, Central, H.K. (phone 5–229158 or 240133). A car can be provided with the guide (we had a Mercedes limo). In two half days she showed us many of the main sights, although we barely covered the basics. We could have used a couple more days to see everything, but there's always next time.

Hotels

We stayed at two hotels, just for variety.

The **Regent Hotel,** located on Kowloon, is the newest and probably biggest of the hotels in that area. It sits right out over the bay, affording incredible views from every window. We had suite 1400, which was beautiful and very large. The service was outstanding. However, we hated the lobby. It's a giant lobby crammed with Americans; noisy, crowded, totally uncharming. We avoided the lobby as much as we could, but it was still annoying to have to walk through it. I would go back to the Regent because of the service and the view (you could spend the whole day just sitting at your window, watching the activity in the harbor). If you don't stay at the Regent, you should go over there and have a drink in the main bar. They also have the best and newest shopping mall there.

The *Peninsula Hotel* has received such a mishmosh of reviews that we really didn't know what to expect. We'd heard it was run-down and stuffy; it isn't. It's wonderful. Very old-world, very charming. Incredible service. We stayed in the Marco Polo Suite, which is said to be the most outstanding hotel suite in Southeast Asia, and one of the finest in the world. I would not dispute either point. It's huge: two oversized bedrooms with nice (but not large) marble bathrooms, a very big sunken living room, a sunken dining room with round table to seat ten, a complete kitchen, a spacious entry and sitting area. At all times there were one or two servants in the room, even when we were out for the day. They do everything from answering the phone or the door to serving you coffee in the morning. The view from the room is OK but does not compare to the views from the Regent. Unfortunately, they are about to build a high-rise building right in front of the hotel, which will further obstruct the already-obstructed view. Now I realize not everyone is going to run to stay in the Marco Polo Suite, so you'll want to know what a regular room is like. I did not see a regular room, but I've spoken to several people lately who have stayed at the Peninsula and loved it. There are also smaller suites on the sixth floor. Go for tea in the lobby, if nothing else.

If your travel agent puts you in the *Hyatt Regency,* fire the agent and switch hotels. It is without question one of the worst hotels I've ever seen, including the shopping arcade and the restaurants. We heard it is in bankruptcy, which could explain a lot, but even so, you don't want to stay there.

Restaurants

As I already stated, you'll do very well to avoid hotel restaurants and get out into the regular H.K. places, where the locals eat. It's almost impossible to get a bad meal in Hong Kong. Don't let the appearance of the restaurants fool you. They are not fancy or elegant. Most of them are huge rooms, decorated in a variety of ways that you would never consider, and jammed with big groups of Chinese happily stuffing themselves. Don't worry about making a mess; it's the custom there. If you watch the Chinese, you'll notice they are messy eaters, and their tables are always a disaster area when they're done. Yours will be too, but that's OK. A lot of places don't give you napkins to use during the meal. Every place gives you a wet towel at the beginning and again at the end of your meal. You just have to have greasy fingers the rest of the time. You'll get several plate changes during the meal, so don't worry about keeping your little plate clean. There are never any knives, always chopsticks and a spoon (sometimes two spoons: a long-handled silver one for dishing things up, and a little ceramic one for eating soup and rice). You always get tea.

You'll have superior fun if you go for dimsum at lunch (in Chinese it's "dianxin"). If you don't know about dimsum, let me explain. Ladies go around the restaurant, up and down the aisles, pushing carts. Each cart has something different on it: dumplings, wontons, barbecued duck, various soups, all kinds of desserts, *sui mai,* noodles, fruit, various rice dishes—the list is endless because each dimsum place probably has over two hundred different dishes. So when the lady comes by with her little cart, you say yes or no (point, if she doesn't speak English, which she probably doesn't) and she gives you a little plateful. There are usually three items to a plate. After about eight plates, you begin to fill up, but all these little carts keep coming by and everything looks delicious, and since everything *is* delicious you have a tendency to eat even more. For all of that, you'll probably get a bill for between 5 and 10 dollars per couple, including tip and whatever drinks you've ordered. If you don't get your fill from dimsum, most of these places also have a huge menu, from which you can order even more.

Crystal Jade, 71–77 Peking Road, 2nd floor, Kowloon, one block from the Peninsula Hotel, phone 3–673288, 3–694902–5.
Lunch, dinner. The director is a charming fellow named Vincent Yip. Fresh fish in tanks as you enter, which you can eat for lunch. They serve dimsum after 2:00 P.M., which was good. By then, however, we'd already consumed enormous amounts of items off the menu. Recommended are hot and sour soup, sautéed greens, deep-fried stuffed scallops, deep-fried water chestnut fruit (a dessert), and green wrasse fish. Casual, medium priced, and one of the best meals we had in two weeks.

Fu Tao Restaurant, 39 Ma Tau Wai Road, Hung Hom district, up-stairs.
This is an experience you will never forget. We found it quite by accident, while shopping in the "garment district." I am not exaggerating—this restaurant is the size of two football fields, side by side. You keep thinking there's a mirror there, but it's all one gigantic room. There must be seats for over 2000 people, arranged in round tables for ten. You sit at a table with other people and eat dimsum. They must have over 300 types of dimsum. No one speaks English. You just have to point. We ate ourselves sick and the bill came to under 5 dollars, for two, total. We were the only Americans in there, and maybe the only ones who'd *ever* been in there, judging from the polite and curious stares. Great fun!

Hugo's, Hyatt Regency Hotel, Nathan Road, phone 3–662321.
The decor is somewhere between airport Sheraton and a prison. There is a loud, obnoxious-sounding quartet of strolling musicians who annoy you throughout

your meal (we had Mexican music for forty-five minutes). The food, for the most part, is ordinary-to-bad (terrible steak, terrible soufflés, terrible prawns). Even the long-stemmed rose that they present to each lady has no fragrance. On the plus side: the service is very good, they try hard. The soups are cooked at table, the salads are tossed at table. Good bread, good lobster, outstanding mangosteen sorbet served between courses. Altogether, however, a very unsatisfying dinner.

Lo Fau Shan district fishmarket restaurants.

And now for something completely different. You'll need someone to take you here, as it's about an hour's drive from downtown Kowloon, and hard to find. Also, no one speaks any English, and no tourists go there. You must go in the morning to experience this fabulous, small, fishing village fishmarket and auction. Wear rubber-soled shoes and jeans or slacks. For lunch, choose any fish or shellfish from any one of a hundred tanks, take it into the nearest restaurant, and they will cook it for you, charging you a cooking fee. I can't explain this properly—you just have to try it. We had marvelous shrimp, flowering greens with oyster sauce, corn on the cob, and meat crabs.

Orchid Garden, 37 Hankow Road (two blocks from the Peninsula Hotel), Kowloon.

Excellent dimsum lunch. Make reservations, if possible, or show up and wait for a table.

Peking Garden, Star House, 3rd floor, Kowloon.

Outstanding food. Inexpensive. Reservations necessary. Advance order the Peking duck, beggar's chicken, and sizzling fish with sweet and sour sauce. Also get shrimp in spring onion, walnut chicken, and don't miss the fried shredded *conpoy* (scallops) with chili, maybe one of the most wonderful things I ever ate. Arrive by 8:30 P.M. so you can see the noodle show (a man takes a big glob of dough and turns it into thin spaghetti, simply by tossing it around in the air and banging it on the table). Also open for lunch.

La Plume, Regent Hotel, Salisbury Road, phone 721-1211.

Nouvelle cuisine with a Chinese flair. Very dressy, very elegant, very wonderful. You should not miss this one. Coat and tie for the men. Reserve in advance. The food and service are outstanding. The soufflés are not memorable. Save this one for your last night.

Sze Chuen Lau, 486 Lockhart Road, Causeway Bay, Wanchai district, phone 5-7902571; and 67 Granville Road, Tsimshatsui, Kowloon, phone 3-7236390.

This is a Szechuan (Chinese "sichuan") restaurant, popular with Americans. Good dishes are sizzling shrimp, kumquat beef with orange, and fried noodles with sizzling beef. Casual; medium priced. Reservations necessary.

Tai Pak floating restaurant, Aberdeen.

I've read and reread that you should avoid, at all costs, any of the floating restaurants in Aberdeen. Our guide concurred, but added that the Chinese like to go to Tai Pak for fresh seafood. If you do not go with a group, and know where to sit and what to order, apparently this is good. We didn't try it. The other floating restaurants there are huge, garish, and touristy, serving mediocre food, at best.

The following restaurants are also recommended (derived from word-of-mouth and lots of reading).:

American Restaurant, 151 Wanchai Road, H.K., phone 572–8122. Peking duck.

The American Restaurant, 20–23 Lockhart Road, Wanchai district.

The Cleveland Restaurant, 6 Cleveland Street, Causeway Bay, phone 5–763876.
Authentic Szechuan restaurant.

Crystal Palace, 16 Cameron Road, Kowloon, phone 366–5784.
Mongolian hotpot, Peking duck.

Fung Lum, 20–22 Leighton Road, Kowloon, phone 576–6389.
Get melon soup, stuffed crab claw.

Gaddi's, Peninsula Hotel, Salisbury Road, phone 366–6251.
Word is that it is still good, but not as good as it used to be. Still worth going to, although the dining room is like a banquet hall and not too intimate.

Jade Garden, Star House, 4th floor; and other locations.
Unusual decor, in that it is very Western, but serving good Cantonese food. Peking duck.

The Lobby, of the Peninsula Hotel.
A must for tea, from 4:00 to 6:00 or 6:30.

Luk Yu Tea House, 24–26 Stanley, H.K., phone 5447231.
For dimsum.

ManWah, Mandarin Hotel, 5 Connaught Road, phone 522–0111.
Very elegant, but they serve Americanized Chinese food.

Maxim's Palace, Convention Center, Causeway Bay, phone 5–760288.
For dimsum.

Peak Tower Restaurant, Victoria Peak.
This is a revolving restaurant, usually the kiss of death, but in this case I hear it's pretty good and a nice place for lunch if you're touring around.

Siam Bird's Nest, 55 Paterson Street, H.K.
Chiu Chow style (a regional cuisine, a little on the sweet side). Try the thin noodles cooked into a crisp pancake, the assorted hors d'oeuvre, and sautéed chicken with baby corn.

Unicorn, 11 Kingston Bay, H.K., phone 779117.
Cantonese (Guangdung).

The Verandah, Peninsula Hotel.
For a buffet lunch.

Yung Kee, 32–34 Wellington Street.
Used to be one of the biggies, but lately it's been getting thumbs down from everyone I've talked to.

Unless you order plain, steamed rice, you'll probably be served Yang-chow fried rice, which is delicious (has egg, some vegetables, and either shrimp, pork, chicken, or all three). Soy sauce is not slopped all over everything. Ingredients are extremely fresh. You don't have to worry about the water in Hong Kong. Great jasmine tea. You can also get such items as jellyfish with beef filet, sliced octopus with wasabi sauce, chili squid in bird's nest, duck's webfeet in cayenne sauce (we actually tried duck's webfeet and wished we hadn't), preserved small octopus, preserved duck's tongues, fish lips in sauce, snake steak, etc. I am quoting from a menu I brought home. They eat everything that moves in the Orient, so you can have a field day if you're getting bored with the usual crisped duck bills.

Sightseeing

The problem with going to Hong Kong is dividing up your time between sightseeing and shopping. This is always a problem for me, but it gets worse in H.K., because H.K. is nothing but one big wall-to-wall shopping center. Anyway, there is a lot to see there, which is why you should plan to spend about a week, if it's your first visit. Of course, if you don't plan to shop (impossible), you won't have any problems. We only scratched the surface of the sightseeing department. As I said, we had a car, driver, and guide, which sped things up and made things easier and more fun. You could probably do most of these things on your own in a taxi, or even on the public transportation, but you better have a lot of time and patience.

In one afternoon, you can drive around and see all of the following.

Aberdeen, where everyone lives on big junks, parked side by side. When you get to the main wharf, you can take a thirty-minute junk ride around the "neighborhood," which I highly recommend (don't forget your camera). You will go by the floating restaurants, discussed earlier. It's especially colorful at dusk, when all the lights go on, but then you'll have trouble taking pictures.

Causeway Bay and Repulse Bay, both beach resorts, and very pretty.

Victoria Peak, with a commanding view of the whole area. There is a trail that you can take around the peak, which takes about forty-five minutes. You can also eat lunch there at the Peak Tower restaurant. If it's cloudy, don't go, as you will see nothing but a lot of fog.

On another afternoon, or better yet, in a morning, you can visit:

New Territories, The area between Kowloon and the Chinese border. Unless you have something specific in mind to see, just driving around New Territories is not thrilling; it's one big suburb. But if you have a guide, you can see Buddhist temples, the Lo Fau Shan fishing village (already mentioned in the restaurant section and highly recommended), and the lookout at the Chinese border at Lok Ma Chau. The lookout has lost some of its attraction, since you can go to China whenever you want now. As for the Lo Fau Shan fishing village, you'll never see anything like this. Be very careful taking pictures, as the people are touchy about it and may come after you with a fishing knife. You can take general photos of the area, but don't stick your camera in anyone's nose. The ladies wearing the hats with the black curtain are Hakka, and are especially nonfond of photos. For best results, do the fishing village in the morning, so you can see the auction, the activity, and have lunch there. On your way to the village you'll pass Peking duck farms—they're big, fat, white, American farmyard-looking ducks.

Other sights to see:

Fung Ping Shan Museum.
Macao, the Portuguese island, a fifty-five-minute hydrofoil ride from Hong Kong.
Take your passport. My husband went and said it was very interesting, different from H.K., with some very old churches and buildings, of course Portuguese/European style. Can be done in a half day.
Man Mo Buddhist Temple, on Hollywood Road.
The oldest and most famous one in H.K.
Ocean Park, (an amusement park) and **Marineland** (aquarium and performing dolphins, penguins, etc.).
Po Lin Monastery and **Tung Chung Fort.**
Space Museum, the bubble building between the Regent and Peninsula hotels, Kowloon.
Tiger Balm Gardens. Unusual; now restored; interesting for about ten minutes; fun for kids.

Places to skip, according to our guide, are the Sung Dynasty Village (tourist trap) and the Lai Chi Kok Park (for kids only).

The outer islands are also interesting. Cheung Chau can be seen as a day trip, since it is quite small. Lantao is very big, however, and would require an overnighter, or even a few days. Many H.K.'ers go there for vacation.

Shopping

Of course I saved the best for the last. When I said that H.K. was a wall-to-wall shopping center, I wasn't kidding. The problem is, they give you too much for your money. There are *so* many shops and malls and arcades, *so* many streets, *so* much to look at and choose from, it's dizzifying. If you have a vague idea of where to go, or at least where to start, it helps.

What about tailor-made clothes? I'm sure you've already heard and read that you can no longer get well-made, top-quality tailoring done in H.K. Nothing could be further from the truth. The secret is, you have to know where to go, you have to give them enough time (four days minimum), and you have to know what you want and be specific. If you are planning to have clothes tailor made, follow these rules: go first thing on the first day and get things started. Take along a suit or shirt so they can copy it (for men), or at least use it as a guide. For ladies, take whatever outfit you want copied, or take a picture, a photo, a drawing, or a pattern. Don't go empty-handed and empty-headed. If you are worried about finding just the right fabric, take your own (this applies to women only, as men won't have any trouble). For example, I wanted to have a couple of dresses made up in expensive French jacquard silk, so I spent a couple of days shopping at home and took it with me, so I would have exactly what I wanted. As it turned out, the tailors we used had tons of silk fabrics to choose from, and contrary to what you might hear, there are some fabulous Chinese silks available of very high quality, including jacquards (although still not as good as European ones). Once you get going with the tailor, make sure you see him every day for a fitting, and keep telling him exactly how you want things done. (With the tailors I am going to recommend, you won't have any problems.) Take high-heeled shoes to your fittings. Be specific about buttons, pleats, belts, etc. If you aren't going to be in town long enough for the garments to be finished, arrange to have them sent to you.

What does all this cost? My husband had gorgeous suits made for between 250 and 350 dollars, depending on the quality of the fabric (the H.K. tailors have the finest English wools and oriental silks available in an astounding range of weights and colors). He also had slacks and jackets made up for even less. I had nine items of clothing made, all silk and wool, and the total cost, including shipping, was 900 dollars. For example, I had a Valentino two-piece silk dress copied for 200 dollars, which included the fabric. The two dresses that I had made up with my own fabric were 100 dollars each. I had a Valentino wool gabardine pantsuit copied for 250 dollars, beautifully tailored, fully lined. Silk blouses (copies of a Valentino and one I took with me) ran between 60 and 85 dollars. My girlfriend had a two-piece wool and leather pants outfit copied from *Vogue* magazine, for 250 dollars. You can't afford *not* to do this!

The tailors: for men, go to **Ying Tai, Ltd.,** mezzanine level of the Peninsula Hotel; Charlie Chang is the owner. For men's shirts, go to **Ascot Chang,** also in the Peninsula hotel. For ladies, go to **Elegante Tailor,** 8–10 Hankow Road, 2nd floor, one block from the Peninsula Hotel. I've also heard that George Chen and Betty Clemo, both in the Peninsula Hotel, are good, for men's and women's suits. P.S. Ascot Chang is also in other locations and travels to the U.S.

If you want to have custom-made shoes, there's a place in the Peninsula Hotel which makes them. You have to give them at least two days and take care with fittings.

As for jewelry, you have to be very careful. We didn't end up buying any jewelry in H.K. (we sort of ran out of steam), but you can get fantastic stuff, if you know where to go and what to look for. Most jewelry stores in the better hotels are probably your best bet. For pearls, I have two recommendations, based on friends who are satisfied customers: *Trio Pearl Co.*, Peninsula Hotel, and *Amerex International,* 7th floor, Takshing House (this may be in the Hung Hom district). If you buy pearls, don't have them strung and you won't have to pay as much duty on them when you get home. If you have them strung, leave the clasp off, and mail yourself the clasp; again, less duty to pay. Unset stones are less costly, customs-wise, than set pieces. If you find a piece of jewelry and you love the setting, have the jewel removed and carry it with you, and mail yourself the setting. Be extremely careful everywhere when buying jade.

What about bargaining? Except in exclusive hotel shops, bargaining is totally acceptable. Everyone is ready to wheel and deal, and you'll see why when you see the kind of competition there is.

Bargain Shopping

I managed to find the H.K. equivalent of the garment district in New York City. These stores are mostly in the Hung Hom district, which is a ten-minute cab ride from downtown Kowloon. You have to pick through a lot of stuff, but there are real bargains to be had (like silk blouses anywhere from 10 to 35 dollars, silk camisoles for 5 dollars, silk dresses for 30 to 80 dollars, etc.) Here's a list of the places I found, in one half day (there are others which I did not have time to look for).

Kaiser Estates, Hung Hom district, Man Yue Street, Phases II and III (meaning buildings).

Bargain Hunter, around the corner and down the street at 10 Man Lok Street, Phase III.
More sportswear, Dior, Sir for Her, etc. I bought a knit dress for 12 dollars.

If you shop in this area, be sure you go for lunch at *Fu Tao Restaurant,* 39 Ma Tau Wai Road, just around the corner.

Other bargain basements that I did not get to (yet):

Bloomwear, room 808, Tak Shing House, 20 Des Voeux Road, Central, H.K.
Ca Va, Ltd., 17th floor of Star House, room 1726.
Camberly Enterprises, on the corner, Phase II.
Very nice store, very good buys: Ann Klein pants 50 dollars, A.K. jackets 75 dollars, A.K. blouses 25 to 30 dollars. Denise Dalban two-piece silk dress, 77 dollars, D.D. silk blouses 28 to 40 dollars.

Four Seasons, 2nd floor, Phase II.

Very inexpensive, crowded racks of dresses, blouses, slacks, lingerie, etc. A couple of really low-priced sale racks. The problem was that most everything was size 10 or 12 (I wear 4 or 6).

Leather Concepts, 11th floor, Union Hing Yip Building, 20 Hing Yip Street.

Lerida Fashions, below Four Seasons.

Lower-quality items, less selection. Beene Bag shirts 5 dollars, silk camisoles 5 to 8 dollars, Liz Claiborne silk dresses 41 dollars.

Lim Ying Ying, 10th floor, H.K. Chinese Bank, 65 Des Voeux Road, Central H.K.

Oriental Pacific, 7th floor, Shui Hing House, 23–25 Nathan Road.

For sweaters.

Vica Moda, across the street at 30 Man Yue Street (Summit Building); also at Shop No. 1-B, Bank of East Asia Building, 2nd floor; 10 Des Voeux Road, Central H.K.; and Shop LG22 in Tsimshatsui Center. Mody Road, Kowloon.

This was the best of the bunch, as far as selection. Silk blouses for 30 to 50 dollars, silk dresses for 35 to 80 dollars. Also a lot of cotton items.

Wintex, Pedder Building, 12 Pedder Street, room 404.

There are a few street markets and night markets where good bargains are also to be found. *Stanley Market* goes every day, but is best on Sundays for local color. I got some gorgeous all-silk, lined kimonos here for about 15 dollars. They also had a lot of leather goods, knock-offs, and copies of most known sportswear lines (maybe they were even the real thing), and one shop in particular had major buys on silk dresses and blouses, with labels like I. Magnin and Liz Claiborne (20 dollars for the blouses; 40 dollars for the dresses). Hang on to your purse and shop carefully.

The other market, which we did not get to, is called the *Poor Man's Nightclub* at the Macao Ferry wharf. It's open every day from 8:00 A.M. to midnight, but is best at night. A lot of junk, but good people-watching and picking.

Every day from 9:00 A.M. to noon is what they call the *Jade Market,* on Canton Street in Kowloon. Good for picking up cheap little gift items, but not good for major jade. Just for fun.

A real bargain place is *Welfare Handicrafts,* a dumpy-looking little store between the Peninsula Hotel and Star House. All the items are made by handicapped people, and they are dirt cheap. Great place for buying all-silk lingerie bags, little silk boxes, and bags of every size and shape and color, stationery, some children's items, other artsy-craftsy stuff. Good workmanship.

All over H.K. you will see *Chinese Arts and Crafts* stores. Don't bother with any of them except the one in Star House. It's ten times bigger than all the rest and has a hundred times more selection. You should look here before shopping anywhere else. It's great for gift items, wood carvings, furniture, silks, silk clothing, doodads, embroidery, kimonos, etc. A mind-boggling selection; very inexpensive. Also jewelry, antiques, pottery. You name it, they got it. No bargaining.

For local, side-street shopping, try the area around the corner of **Nathan Road and Humphrey Avenue,** Tsimshatsui East district. The equivalent on the H.K. side is Hollywood Road and the surrounding streets, starting with the Man Mo Temple. There is a street called Ladder Street, but all the hilly stepped streets are called ladder streets, or cat streets. Be careful taking pictures. Go to Jervois Street, Wing Sing Street, Wing On Street, Central district, H.K.

Silk kimonos and embroidered blouses are in every third store (the other two stores carrying jewelry and electronics). We found a good selection of the kind of kimonos we were looking for (plain silk, no embroidered dragons on the back) in the Sheraton Hotel arcade at **Wong's Arts Co.,** 2nd floor. Floor-length, all silk, fully lined, and beautiful kimonos were 30 dollars; shorter ones were 20 dollars, and cotton ones ran 7 to 10 dollars. For another 2 dollars, they will ship them to you, or you can write to them later if you want more. Ask for the Four-Season Flower kimonos. They make great gifts.

Ocean Terminal is the largest shopping center in the city, located at Star Ferry Terminal, next to the Hong Kong Hotel in Kowloon. It's very nice and looks new. You can find just about any kind of shop in there that you want, including a See's Candy store. As for chic, European-style clothes, however, I didn't see any, which doesn't mean they aren't there somewhere.

Star House is next to Ocean Terminal, but is not really a shopping arcade, although there are a few shops on the first two levels, most of which were not too good. There are some shops on the upper levels, but you have to know where to go. There are two excellent restaurants in Star House (Peking Garden and Jade Garden), and the Chinese Arts and Crafts store. Otherwise, it's mostly offices and empty store space.

The **Lane Crawford Department Store** on Queen's Road, Central H.K., is supposedly the Harrods of Hong Kong.

The Landmark in Central district, H.K., is a vertical mall with over eighty boutiques and restaurants.

Charlotte Horstmann and Gerald Godfrey, 104 Waglan Gallery in Ocean Terminal, is good for antiques and unusual items.

Swire House, Central district, H.K., is another shopping complex with more chic boutiques.

As for the shopping arcades or malls, they are all over the place. Obviously, I didn't get to all of them, but it became apparent after a very short time that the best ones are located in and under the best hotels, meaning the Peninsula and the Regent. At the Regent Hotel you'll find the **Regent Arcade** and the **New World Center,** an immense complex on six floors with a jillion shops. The better shops were on the upper floors and near the hotel. The **Peninsula Hotel shops,** located on the lower, main, and mezzanine levels, were by far the best in all respects. The **Sheraton Hotel** arcade, with the exception of the kimono store already mentioned, was a bore. The **Hyatt Regency Hotel** arcade was pure schmutz. On the Hong Kong side is the **Mandarin Hotel** arcade, which I did not see, but I hear it's OK.

Last, but not least, is a little stand in the Star Ferry Terminal, almost where you board the ferry. They had Cabbage Patch dolls, Chinese style, for about 25 dollars, that were adorable. They also had the best selection of T-shirts we saw.

Guidebooks

About the best overall guidebook I read was Fodor's *Southeast Asia, 1984,* especially the first 122 pages. He gives you a really good overview of all aspects of the culture of the area, including history. His general comments about Hong Kong were pretty good. I also used a little book by Carol Clewlow called *Hong Kong, Macau and Canton* (Lonely Planet Publications, Australia). The pocket-sized Berlitz book, *Hong Kong,* is very handy for quick reference. I relied most heavily on magazine articles, however, especially those from *Travel & Leisure* and *Gourmet.*

Bits and Pieces

The bathroom situation in Hong Kong was not the best. The "Oriental style" toilet is a hole in the floor, or a trough in the floor with running water. Toilet paper was almost nonexistent, so stock up on tissues. In hotels and better restaurants the bathrooms were Western-style, often with an attendant who requires a small tip. (Still, take your own paper along.) Take wash-and-dries, too.

There is an airport departure tax of 100 Hong Kong dollars, so don't go to the airport totally broke. The airport is about fifteen minutes from the Peninsula Hotel. The X-ray machines at the airport are not film-safe; so don't bury your camera and films in the bottom of the bag, because you'll have to remove them to go through security.

It's easiest and least economical to change money at your hotel. Banks are extremely cautious and it takes a long time, but you get a better rate (though only slightly). It took my friend and me forty-five minutes to change traveler's checks at a bank, because of the suspicion and scrutiny. We started to feel as if we'd done something wrong. This is very typical, we found out. Many small shops don't want to take big bills; they think they're fake. Most better stores take credit cards.

However much money you're planning to take with you for shopping, double it. If you don't have a large, collapsible suitcase to take with you, plan on buying a cheap one there, to get yourself home with all your loot. If possible, ship bigger items (from reputable stores, it's safe).

Go to your local airport before leaving home and register anything that has a serial number: cameras, lenses, watches, tape recorders, anything you plan to take with you. This will save you hassles at customs when you return. If you take good jewelry with you (always a mistake), take receipts or jeweler's appraisals with you, or you may get stuck for it when you re-enter the country. Keep a few receipts to show the customs people—they love to see receipts. Be careful if you buy alligator or crocodile—some species are endangered and you won't be able to bring in the goods. Ivory, at the moment, is no problem. Arts and crafts items and antiques are exempt. For the antiques, you must have some sort of certificate.

Survival Cantonese

Chinese is a tonal language, so it is nearly impossible to get the pronunciation correct without hearing it spoken. One word can mean five different things, depending on the tone in which it is spoken. I'll give you the words, but you're on your own with the true pronunciation.

good morning	jo sahn
good afternoon	nnnng-on
good evening	mang-on (something like *"hang on"*)
please	mmm-goi
thank you	mmm-goi
thank you (for a gift)	doh-jeh
yes	hai
no	mmm-hai
good	ho
bad	mmm-ho
delicious, very good	ho ho
How much?	gay doh cheen
bottoms up	yam seng
goodbye	joy geen
too expensive	tie g'wy
It doesn't matter, not to worry	mmm-gahn yo

Have you had your rice yet?	Nay sik jo fan may ah? (a way of greeting someone)
the bill	my dahn
tea	chah
water	soy
ice water	tung soy kah bing
go	hoi
stop	ting

Thailand

Bangkok

The Thais call Thailand Muang Thai, meaning Land of the Free, because Thailand is the only country in Southeast Asia never to be occupied by a Western power. Bangkok is known as Krung Thep, meaning City of the Angels. This, the capital and largest city, has a population of over five million, out of a total of the fifty million people who live in Thailand. Over 90 percent are Buddhists. Therefore, there are around 300 wats, or Buddhist monasteries, in the city of Bangkok alone. The Thai Buddhist wat is totally different from the Chinese Buddhist temple, and it is very interesting to compare the two architectural styles, including the manifestation of Buddha himself. Basic to any traveler going to Thailand should be some knowledge about this religion, as well as about Hinduism, Confucianism, Taoism, and animism. All Thai houses and many businesses have a spirit house somewhere on the property—small copies of a Buddhist wat on which offerings are placed at various times to protect the home and its occupants. Saffron-robed monks are to be seen everywhere, adding what seems to be an ascetic grace to what is otherwise often a dreary city. The Thais themselves could not be more endearing; they are gracious, quiet, smiling, and charming. They will go out of their way for you, and seem to like Americans very much.

If you are planning a trip to Thailand, allow yourself at least a week. Four and a half days are sufficient to see Bangkok, unless you want to do the all-day trip to Ayutthaya (pronounced *Ay-you-tee-ya*), the former capital. You will also want to allot two days and nights to Chiang Mai, plus another night if you want to go to Chiang Rai. The beach resorts, such as Pattaya, could take another day or two.

The best time to go to Thailand is in November, as this is when the weather is driest and mildest. We were there in mid-May. Fortunately, we did not experience any rain (just a few drops now and then), but the temperature was over 100 degrees every day, with a relative humidity of what seemed to be 100 also. At night it cooled down to about 90 degrees. Very uncomfortable. The monsoon season begins in June and lasts a few weeks. Apparently during the worst part of the rains, the streets are completely flooded and life comes almost to a standstill. Always take an umbrella.

Bangkok is not the exotic, dazzling capital of Siam that you might envision. Truthfully, it is a very large, sprawling, smoggy, dirty, trash filled, often malodorous, overpopulated, traffic congested, polluted city. Most of the buildings desperately need to be cleaned, torn down, or painted. It is a frustrating daily fact of life to wait fifteen minutes or more just to get through an intersection, only to turn the corner and find yourself waiting the same amount of time for the next intersection. The traffic flow, coupled with too many cars and too many little three-wheeled taxis, causes traffic jams worse than I've seen anywhere, including in Cairo and Mexico City. The Thais drive like maniacs on top of it, so my advice is, hire a driver to take you where you want to go, and forget about ever driving yourself; you won't live to tell about it (plus that, all the traffic is reverse direction).

Now that I've painted a rather dismal picture of Bangkok, you're wondering why anyone should go there. Well, there is something about the place which is infectious. I can't put my finger on it; you just have to be there. For starters, the people, the food, and the temple architecture are all not to be beat anywhere in the world. It's a way of life and a culture that you must experience, not just read about. It's a real full-blooded Third World country, struggling to make a go of it—one of my favorite kinds of places.

As for packing your suitcase: no shorts, please—not for women, not for men. Shorts are highly frowned upon, and if you want to go see any of the wats, you won't get in with shorts on. One of the wats (the Grand Palace) does not even want women to wear slacks. Women are safest and coolest wearing skirts and casual dresses; men should plan on lightweight slacks and shirts. Only one restaurant required a jacket and tie for men; otherwise, all the restaurants were very casual. Take comfortable walking shoes, hopefully ones that will stand up in the rain. Sandals are ideal for the hot months. If you go during the hot months, plan on wearing a different outfit every day; so either pack enough clothes or plan to have some laundry done. By the end of the day, what you are wearing looks like it's been through the wringer.

Outside the hotels and nearby shops, you'll find that most people do not speak English. If you are glued to a guide the whole time, you won't have to worry. Since that will probably not be the case, it's a good idea to know a few words of Thai. The language looks complicated but really isn't, and they love it when you speak a few words. At the end of this chapter I will give you a few of the most necessary words. Thai, like Chinese, is a tonal language, but not as tonal, so it's easier to get the pronunciation down.

If you go around in a taxi, be sure you have the address written down in Thai (your hotel can do this for you), plus your return address. Decide on the taxi fare before you get in. We were advised not to ride the *tuk-tuks* (three-wheeled taxis) as the drivers are reckless and they tip over frequently.

If you can do it, hire a driver and guide. We had a wonderful guide named La-Ong Bhumsukho, known to us as Ong. Her address is 27 Soi Khonghiran, Ram Indra Road, Bangkapi, Bangkok. If you cannot contact her directly, she works for the agency Boonvanit, 420/9–10 Siam Square Soi 1, Bangkok 10500 (phone 2527892, 2510526–7 or 2520151). The director's name is Bessie Samargachan. Ong spoke English very well, knew a lot of facts, took us everywhere we wanted to go; we took her to restaurants, and she had a charming personality.

Hotels

The **Oriental** is far and away the top hotel, miles ahead of any competition, if for no other reason than their location, right on the Chao Phraya river (pronounced *Chow-pee-yah*). The hotel has been around for a long time, but the building is entirely new, and gorgeous. Most rooms command a view of the river and city. The service was outstanding, as good as any we had in Hong Kong. On the day we arrived, we sent out two huge bags of laundry and dry cleaning at about 1:00 P.M. When we returned to the hotel at 5:00 P.M., not only was the laundry all finished, it was hung up or put away. That's just one example.

We stayed in the Oriental Suite, known as the finest hotel suite in Thailand, and one of the two best in Southeast Asia (the other one being the Marco Polo Suite at the Peninsula Hotel in Hong Kong). The Oriental Suite is very large, about 1500 square feet, with a panoramic view. It's beautifully done in modern decor. I don't think I can say which of the two suites is better: they are both marvelous in every respect.

The Royal Orchid is another large hotel built a short distance away from the Oriental, and right on the river. We did not see this hotel, but its location is also excellent. Ask your travel agent. All the other hotels in the city were not located along the river, and tended to be in the busy city sections.

Restaurants

As I mentioned, one of the reasons to go to Thailand is for the food: wonderful, wonderful, and more wonderful. Keep away from the hotel coffee shops. It's very curious, but all the guides we had seemed to assume that we would not be interested in eating anywhere but in our hotel, and they would eagerly start steering toward the hotel around lunchtime. We refused to eat in the hotel and would only eat in the local places where the Thais eat. The guides said that most Americans prefer hotel food, as they feel it is "safe." It's also boring and unadventuresome.

Thai food is basically spicy. We started out with mildly spiced food, but at the end of the week we were eating everything that came our way, no matter how many chilis. The flavors are wonderful, the vegetables are only the freshest, the sauces are inexplicable. So many dishes, so little time.

When you enter the restaurant and are seated, you are given a wet towel; you get another one at the end of the meal, and sometimes one in the middle of it. The Thais use forks and spoons, not chopsticks (only for noodles). There are never any knives. Order bottled water, called Nam Polaris.

Bangkok Snake House,
wherever that is, serves up snake in a variety of ways. Let me know . . .
   Bankeo Ruenkwan,   212 Soi 12 Sukhumvit Road, phone 251–8229, 2513281.
A beautiful restaurant, excellent food. Order the Tom Yam soup for sure.
   Chandr Phen (Chicken House),   phone 2863549 or 2860933.
Popular with locals for lunch, when the specialty is barbecued chicken. Also good spring rolls. For 5 baht extra you can sit in the air-conditioned room, where they gave us too much cold air for the money (we would've been happy with 3 baht's worth).
   Chit Pochana,   1082 Paholyothin Road, phone 279–5000; and Soi 20 Sukhumvit Road, phone 391–8346. Other locations are at the airport and in Singapore.
This is a large and very popular restaurant serving excellent Thai cuisine. They have a huge buffet on the lower level, which you might want to check out before ordering. Try their Thai noodles, and chicken wrapped in pandan *(toey)* leaves.
   D'Jit Pochana Oriental,   across the river from the Oriental Hotel, also known as *Sala Rim Nam,* phone 2349920–9,
is run by the same people as Chit Pochana in conjunction with the Oriental Hotel. This is a large and beautiful room, where you are seated at low tables (leg space underneath). The menu is fixed, and you are served about eight courses. I thought the food was excellent; my husband didn't. Along with the dinner you get a one-hour floor show of classical Thai song and dance. The

dancers and costumes are fabulous. It's designed for tourists, naturally, but if you want a culture show, this one is probably the best in the city. Dress is casual, transportation is provided from the Oriental Hotel, and the cost was about 20 dollars apiece.

Normandie Grill, Oriental Hotel.

This is a very elegant and formal restaurant at the top of the old hotel, serving continental cuisine. If you have been traveling in the Orient for a while and need a break from the food, you might enjoy this restaurant. The food was very good, as was the service and decor; exceptional place settings and view. Coat and tie for men were requested. Expensive. Try the local bass *(plakapong)* en croûte.

Oriental Hotel Terrace

has a huge barbecue every evening, with more choices than you could ever eat. The food was delicious and the setting could not be better. For dessert, try the teeny little pastries that look like tacos.

Rose Garden, Sala Inn-Chan, km. 32, Petkasem Road, Sampran, Amphoe Sam Pharn, phone 01–311171.

This restaurant is in a large, rose-garden setting, as the name implies. The dining room overlooks a rapidly moving river. The food is very good, although not as good as other meals we had. Try the Thai stuffed omelet and the coconut ice cream. You would only go to this place if you were out sightseeing in the area, or if you wanted to go to the Thai Village and Culture Retreat, which is also on the property (idea similar to the Polynesian Cultural Center in Hawaii).

Scala, Siam Square, phone 251–2863, behind the theater.

Outstanding Chinese food and the best Peking duck we had. Also delicious shrimp toast, and beef with black bean sauce.

Restaurants not recommended, according to Ong, are: Baan Thai, Soi 32 Sukhumvit Road (touristy and mediocre food); Sarn Daeng, Kaeng Thai Rama, Yong Lee, and Royal India. The Rice Barge also sounds iffy—looks extremely touristy.

There are a few things you must eat while in Thailand. They have a delicious hot and sour soup called *Tom Yam,* which comes in a variety of ways with different meats. Noodles are made in many ways; they were always delicious. The fruit is fabulous and some of it is very unusual. Be sure you get fresh mangosteen, fresh lichee, rose apples, durian, and pomelo (a type of grapefruit). These are all seasonal. The papaya there is red, and the pineapple is different. Local fish and shellfish are great. Fried rice usually comes Yangchow style and is wonderful. Most of the ice cream is home-made. Be sure you try the chicken wrapped in *toey* leaves, served everywhere.

Sightseeing

You will spend most of your time in Bangkok sightseeing, as the shopping isn't all that great (more on this later), especially if you're going to go to Hong Kong on the same trip. There is a lot to see in the city; getting from one place to another is time-consuming because of the traffic. Do not wear shorts if you are going to temples (do not wear shorts, period). Take lots of film. Wear comfortable shoes, preferably ones that are not too complicated to take off and put on, which is what you have to do at the temples (monasteries, wats).

The Ancient City (Muang Boran) is about forty-five minutes from Bangkok and is really a large, outdoor museum on two hundred acres. This is not a real ancient city, but one reproducing famous buildings and temples from Thailand's history. Many of them are lifesize, others are three-quarter-sized. There are over sixty monuments here, plus statues, villages, *klongs,* etc.

Ayutthaya, the ancient city, can be visited on a package tour, which goes partly by boat, partly by bus. The boat, a large and beautiful one, leaves in front of the Oriental Hotel every day at 8:00 A.M. (Mondays and Fridays excluded). Along the way you see Wat Arun, the Royal Barge Shed, Bang Pa-In summer palace, and lots of *klong* scenery. Takes all day.

Bang Pa-In is about one hour out of town and was the former summer palace of the king. It's a large complex with several buildings, the main one being the residence. When you go inside you are treated to sumptuous rooms and furnishings; no shoes, no pictures, no shorts. This palace is also included in the day trip to Ayutthaya.

Crocodile Farm, near the Ancient City, has thousands of crocs waiting to be sacrificed in the name of shoes, belts, and bags. Daily feedings at 11:00 A.M. and 3:00 P.M.

The Damneon Saduak Floating Market at Rachburi is something you must not miss. It's a two-hour drive out of Bangkok, and well worth it. This is a floating market in a small village, far away from tourist-town and totally authentic. Seeing is believing. Take a lot of film. There is a floating market in Bangkok, but we were told it's mainly for the tourists now.

The Grand Palace, the former seat of the court of Siam, is an absolute must. If you miss this, you should've stayed home. I cannot begin to describe it. All I'll tell you is—it's incredible, dazzling, and awe-inspiring. Try to go on a sunny day. Also, try to go at night, when it is illuminated. The main chapel, called *Wat Phrakaeo,* is the personal chapel of the king and the house of the *Emerald Buddha,* which really isn't emerald but a solid piece of jasper about two feet high. We were not able to go inside the wat, since we were there on a major celebration day (Buddha's birthday, also his death day, and we were lucky to be able to witness the ceremonies going on). We could see the Buddha through the door; it sits very high up, and even had we gone inside, we probably wouldn't have been able to see it too well. Another thing you must see at the Grand Palace is the gigantic mural of the Ramayana; also the model of the Angor Wat. You'll need about one and a half hours to take in all there is to see here. Bring a lot of film.

The National Museum is the largest museum in Southeast Asia and was originally a palace (1780s). There are some guided tours in English.

PhraMen Grounds Weekend Market, near the Grand Palace, should not be missed. If you aren't the only tourists there, I'll be surprised. This huge outdoor market is for the locals, and they sell everything from plastic laundry baskets to Chinese pottery to fish stomachs on hooks. The market continues across the street in a large building, which is even more interesting. You'll see things you've never seen before and I can't tell you what they are, because I never saw them before, either, and don't know what they're called. Hang on to your purse.

Pratunam Market, on Petchburi Road is the weekday version of the PhraMen market.

The Rose Garden Country Resort can be seen along with the last two places. There's a nice restaurant, already mentioned, and a culture show in a village setting, which includes elephant rides, Thai boxing, music and dances, and crafts demonstrations. If you aren't going to go to Chiang Mai, you might enjoy this.

The Snake Farm is at the Pasteur Institute, Rama IV Road. There are two giant pits, home of several nasty-looking snakes, many of them cobras. Every day at 11:00 A.M. some very brave (or very foolish) men come out and milk the snakes for the venom. They also force-feed some of them. The whole thing takes about fifteen minutes and is very interesting. Makes you think twice about tromping through any jungles.

Standing Buddha is at Wat Indra. It's quite impressive to see, very high and very gold.

Thai Boxing, different from international boxing, can be seen almost any night at one of two arenas: Ratchadamnoen or Lumphini stadium. It's called Muay Thai. You can also see it on TV, but being there is better. Sit ringside and bet with the locals.

Jim Thompson's House/Museum, 6 Soi Kasemsan 2, open weekdays from 9:00 to 4:30.

Jim Thompson was an American who settled in Bangkok after the Second World War and was responsible for the revitalization of the silk industry there. He mysteriously disappeared in 1967 while visiting Malaysia. His house, now a museum, is really six traditional teak Thai houses put together. He collected these houses from around the country. The house is full of priceless antiques, and there are guided forty-five-minute tours in English.

Wat Arun (also called Wat Chaeng and Temple of Dawn) is seen from the river, and is part of the boat excursion to Ayutthaya. Nearby you can also see the *Royal Barge Shed.*

Wat Benchamaborpit, the best example of pure Thai architecture, is made of white Carrara marble and has a large collection of bronze Buddha statues; a good place to see Buddha in his many positions and attitudes.

Wat Nakhon Pathom and the Phra Pathom Cheddi can be seen on the way back from the floating market (which ends at noon or so). This Cheddi is the largest, highest, and oldest in the country, in Indian style. About 90 miles from Bangkok.

Wat Po, (also called Grand Wat Jetupon, or Wat of the Reclining Buddha,) is near the Grand Palace. This is a very interesting wat, its chief attraction being the 150-foot-long reclining Buddha, all covered in gold leaf. Be sure you see the bottom of the feet. Outside in the courtyard you can indulge in such tourist activities as having yourself draped with a large snake, or having your picture taken with lovely Thai ladies in classical costume (all for a fee, of course).

Wat Sraket, the Golden Mount is the wat you can climb, affording sweeping views of the city. It also contains a very large bronze Buddha.

Wat Trimitr contains the incredible solid *gold Buddha,* all five and a half tons of it, dating from the fourteenth century (they think). Just outside the wat are people selling birds in little cages. You buy the birds and set them free, but first you make a wish. You'll see this done in various places in the city, and it's not always birds; sometimes it's frogs or snakes or eels.

Shopping

I was expecting big things in the shopping department in Bangkok and was disappointed. To be sure, you can buy all the Thai silk you ever wanted. Thai silk is not like European or Chinese silk. It's very shiny and irridescent. When properly done up, the effect can be stunning, but you have to ask yourself, "Will I really wear this when I get home?" As for jewelry, you certainly have a wide variety to pick from, but you must be very careful. Fakes abound, or so we were told. If you like rubies, this is the place. There are also a lot of sapphires around; many of them are beautiful, but I'm not sure about the quality. They were a good deal cheaper than the sapphires we saw in Rio. Buyer beware, as usual.

Bargaining is accepted and expected, but not in hotel shops or department stores. Use your judgment.

If you are going to go to Chiang Mai, save your arts and crafts buying for there, since that is the center for such things. On the other hand, if you really see something you love, buy it. You never know if you will see it later somewhere else. If you spend just a couple of hours shopping around you can get a real good idea of what's available and what prices are. A knowledge of Thai numbers wouldn't hurt.

Central Department Store, Silom Road.

Don't bother.

Julie, 1279 New Road, about four minutes by foot from the Oriental Hotel.

This is a tailor shop for women, and we were lured in by attractive blouses hanging in the window. We ended up having pants outfits made, which took less than twenty-four hours, cost less than 70 dollars for the two pieces, and which were delivered to our hotel. They have very good styles, the workmanship was excellent, and there were a lot of fabrics to choose from.

Jim Thompson Thai Silk Co., 9 Surawong Road, phone 234–4900, open 9:00 to 6:30 daily, except Sunday.

By far the best place to buy silks off the bolt, clothing, gift items, pillowcases, placemats, purses, ties, etc., made out of Thai silk. Fine quality of silk and much to choose from. Upstairs is where you'll find the clothes, plus a big case full of marvelous ethnic jewelry, which is expensive. Some of the clothes here are really nice, and in styles you would wear when you got home. Prices are reasonable, but not cheap, although the little silk boxes and gift items were quite inexpensive.

Lin Oriental Gems, 14/7 Oriental Avenue, near the hotel.

This jewelry store had above-average-looking jewelry, they were willing to negotiate, and I think they are probably reliable. I bought a fabulous 18-karat gold dragon ring, with diamonds, emeralds, and rubies, for 500 dollars. The same ring down the street was going for a thousand. I probably could've gotten the ring for even less if I hadn't been so tired. They take all major credit cards.

Oriental Hotel Arcade and Plaza (one block away at 30/1 Oriental Avenue) is the most elegant shopping you'll find. We were disappointed in the shops in the plaza; most of them had clothes that were overpriced or unstylish. A few antique stores, some artsy-craftsy stuff, but generally, nothing to write home about. In the Oriental Hotel Arcade is a Fauchon Store, which sells fabulous pastries and chocolates.

Royal Lapidary Co., 253 Rachawithi Road,

is a government price-controlled shop with fixed prices. They have a huge selection of all kinds of jewelry, with every imaginable stone, and are reliable. Upstairs they have Thai silks, clothes, gift items (a lot of schlock, actually). If you're going to buy jewelry, this place might be a good bet.

Siam Bootery,

I was told, has a great selection of shoes and boots. We passed it but did not have time to go in.

Star of Siam and Design Thai, another store known for Thai silks and clothes, could not compare to Jim Thompson. Cheaper, however.

I was advised not to go to the government Narayana-Phand store.

Don't worry about paying duty on things you buy in Thailand. Because it's a developing Third World country, most of what you buy there is duty-free when you get back to the U.S. This goes for all arts and crafts items, and jewelry. So have a ball.

Guidebooks

Finding good guidebooks for Thailand was not easy. The best I found is Fodor's *Southeast Asia, 1984.* Another handy little book is *Thailand: A Travel Survival Kit,* by Joe Cummings (Lonely Planet Publications; Australia). Lots of information. Also check past and present travel and Gourmet Magazines for articles.

Reminders

Save 40 baht apiece for departure tax.

The airport is about forty-five minutes from downtown Bangkok. Don't cut your travel time short, because you could be sitting at one of those twenty-minute intersections while your plane is taking off. Some of the X-ray equipment at the airport is not film-safe, so don't bury your camera and film; you may have to dig it out to go through security.

Take mosquito repellent and bite medication. Get cholera shots before you go, despite what your travel agent tells you. Take malaria pills.

Don't drink tap water in Thailand. Almost all the raw sewage (for centuries) is dumped right into the *klongs* and rivers, as you will see (and smell) when you get there.

Chiang Mai

A sharp contrast to the hustle-bustle of the Bangkok metropolis is the second largest city in Thailand, Chiang Mai. Located about five hundred miles to the north, Chiang Mai (sometimes spelled Chiengmai) is in a mountainous area and is relatively clean, calm, and quiet. Sixty thousand people reside in the city, with a total of one million in the surrounding countryside. The area is chiefly agricultural, but Chiang Mai is known for its beautiful women, resortlike atmosphere, and as the center of the arts and crafts industry of Thailand. Two nights spent in this lovely town are enough to see all there is to see. The easiest way to get there is the fifty-five-minute flight from Bangkok.

Hotel

The best hotel in town is the **Chiang Mai Orchid,** 100–102 Huey Kaew Road, phone 053–22–2099, and the best room there is the Presidential Suite, room 1004. It's a small, pretty hotel, with good service.

Guide

It's almost essential to have a guide in Chiang Mai, as things are very spread out. You can contract a guide and driver through the Boonvanit Agency (see Bangkok section), or through Experience Tours, 108 Nantaram Road, Chiang Mai (phone 232975).

Restaurants

The cuisine in Chiang Mai is much the same as in Bangkok, with the addition of a few spices and "northern Thai dishes." We had one of our best meals on the whole trip at the first restaurant mentioned below.

Nang Nual, 27/2–5 Koaklang Road. Recommended for seafood, although the guide said it wasn't nearly as good as the New Krua Thai.

New Krua Thai, an open-air and very large restaurant, obviously very popular with the Thais, and very nontouristy. Almost no English spoken, but no problems. Their fresh grilled seafood was fabulous (try the char-grilled *krapong* and the giant prawns—really giant). Also outstanding were the Tom Yam soup, maybe the best we had; the rice in pineapple shell; the chicken wrapped in pandan *(toey)* leaves and grilled. A most memorable and pleasurable evening.

Scala Palace, 2 M 5 Wangsingkam Road, a bit out of town. Another nontouristy place where we had a great lunch. Excellent Tom Yam soup, Chinese sausages, and beef salad.

Other good restaurants in town, but not as good as the above, are *Aroon Ri* and *Thanarm.*

A couple of the hotels offer what is called a *khantoke,* which is a floor show of regional tribal songs and dances. This is supposed to be completely different from the classical-type shows you see in Bangkok. You are served a northern-Thai style dinner in period rooms. We did not have time for this, but it was recommended by both our Chiang Mai guide and our Bangkok guide.

Sightseeing

There is plenty to see in Chiang Mai and the surrounding countryside, which is why I advise staying two nights.

Chiang Dao, about thirty-five miles out of town, is where you go for a demonstration of how they work elephants. This is set up strictly for tourists, but you can imagine how impossible it would be for tourists to go to where the elephants actually work. You have to get there by 10:00 A.M. or earlier to see them bathing. The demonstration lasts about twenty minutes, and then you have the option of hanging around and taking rides on the elephants. As you enter the compound, you can buy bananas and feed them to the elephants.

Arts and Crafts Industries. These are very spread out and very numerous. It might sound touristy and uninteresting. The former is true; the latter isn't. In some cases you really visit the factory where they are making a particular type of thing, and it's an eye-opener to see just how much labor and skill go into some of the items you see at every gift stand. We visited a silkworm farm and saw the little worms doing their thing, then various people processing the silk. There were two shops on the premises, one of them containing some outstanding hand-sewn quilted pillow covers and quilts. We paid about 5 dollars each for the pillowcases, which are exquisite. I've only seen these once before, at home, and they were asking about 80 dollars each for them. They are made by little old ladies, and apparently it's a dying art, as the young girls aren't interested. This was the U. Piankusol Farm on Sankampaeng Road, I think.

Another very interesting stop was at a lacquerware factory. Those little painted lacquer boxes that you see everywhere take hours of painstaking work. The shop was crammed with hundreds of different sizes and shapes of lacquer boxes and figures, at extremely low prices. They make wonderful gifts. There are three lacquerware places, all on Sankampaeng Road.

A third industry is teakwood carving, which we almost skipped. Glad we didn't. This is the place for you to buy furniture—fabulous, hand-carved teak furniture; every size and shape. Chiangmai Treasure, 99/4 Chiangmai-Sankampaeng Road; Sudalak Carving, km. 6, 97/9 Sankampaeng Road. Look for the large, beautiful teak and white building.

The celadon pottery place was not as interesting as the others, but we got some great pots for about 10 dollars, all neatly wrapped for packing.

The umbrella factory was one we really resisted, but we said, as long as we're here, why not? Turned out to be quite interesting and a very big place. Not only did we see all phases of umbrella making but watched several people painting them in beautiful Chinese and Thai designs. In the shop you can buy every conceivable type and size of umbrella and fan at very reasonable prices. Go to Umbrella Village, Borsang Intersection.

All this running around to the crafts industries will take you between two and three hours, depending on how much negotiating you end up doing in the shops. You can also visit nielloware factories, jade-carving places, and silver factories.

Doi Prathat Suthep Temple is the big monastery you see up on the mountainside. It's about a thirty-minute drive from the downtown area, and well worth the trip. When you get there you'll see the Naga (dragon) stairway, which leads up to the monastery. Good views from the top.

Phu Ping (also Bhu Bing) Winter Palace is a few miles beyond the Doi Prathat Suthep Temple. You can visit the grounds on Fridays, Saturdays, and Sundays, unless the king is there. You can't go inside the palace, but the grounds are beautiful—magnificent gardens full of every kind of flower, especially roses.

Wat Pla Sing (or *Phra Singh*) was built in 1345 and is well worth a visit. It's doubly interesting because of the new wat built right next to it;

you can get a very good idea of Thai temple architecture then and now. The interior of the old wat is beautiful, with frescoes covering the walls.

Wat Suan Dork has one of the country's largest bronze Buddhas.

Shopping

The Night Market should not be missed. It's at Chang Klan Road between Tapae and Loi Kroh Roads, and includes the Chiang Mai Plaza, which is where most of the stalls are. Don't worry if it rains—it's all covered. Be sure to bargain for everything. We bought some fabulous Chiang Mai cotton shirts for about 7 dollars each (label Slot Shop). Cotton kimonos were also about 7 dollars, but I forgot to bargain so they probably could have been bought for around 5 dollars. Lots of stuff, lots to see, lots to buy, very low prices. Great fun, too.

Club 124 in the Chiang Mai Orchid Hotel is a small shop on the lower level which sells very stylish and wonderful cotton clothes for women. A two-piece dress ran about 40 dollars. We could have bought a lot here, but his clothes are so popular that the owner can't keep the shop stocked properly. He sends a lot to various stores in Bangkok.

Across the street from the Chiang Mai Orchid Hotel are two nice shops: Shinawatra Trading and S. Shinawatra Thaisilk.

Crafts Industries, already mentioned.

Chiang Rai

An overnight trip from Chiang Mai is to Chiang Rai, 130 miles away. Our guide suggested this was a very pleasurable trip, going one way by boat, the other by plane. There is a good hotel in Chiang Rai, called Wiang Inn, the scenery is nice, and you can visit the Golden Triangle, which is the borders of Thailand, Burma, and Laos. At the time of this writing, however, it is unsafe to go to this area due to border skirmishes and drug traffickers who attack tourists. Besides the Golden Triangle, you can visit remote hill tribes and what's more, more wats.

A Course In Instant Thai

Thai is a fun language. It's tonal. It's not complicated. For one thing, the verbs are generally not conjugated, so the verb "to go," which is "by," means "I go, we go, you go," etc. For future tenses, you put the word "jah" at the beginning of the sentence, and the sentence becomes future. If you are a woman speaking, you add "kah" at the end of every sentence. If a man speaks, he adds the word "krahp" at the end of a sentence.

hello, goodbye, how are you?	sah-wah-dee-kah (if a woman speaks); sah-wah-dee-krahp (if a man speaks)
What is your name?	Koon chuh ah-ry?
My name is . . .	Dee chan chuh . . . (woman); pome chuh. . . . (man)
to go	by
I would like (+ noun) . . .	Yaak dy . . .
thank you	khop khun (kah, krahp)
thank you very much	khop khun mahk (kah, krahp)
Can I have . . . ?	Kaw . . . ?
ice	nahm kang
with	sigh
without	my sigh
the check, bill	sheck, bin, bill
bottled water	nahm polaris
coffee	gah-faa
I don't understand	My kow jy
Do you understand?	Kow, jy my?
I understand	Dee chan kow jy, kah (woman); Pome kow jy, krahp (man)
How much?	Rah-kah-tau-ry?
How much is this?	Nee rah-kah-tau-ry?
How much is that?	Nun rah-kah-tau-ry?
hotel	wrong ramm
Can you speak English?	Koon poot pasaah angrit, dy my? (kah, krahp)
I speak a little Thai	Dee chan poot pasah Thai nit-noy (woman) Pome poot pasah Thai nit-noy (man)
I (masculine)	pome
I (feminine)	dee chan
You	koon
Mr., Mrs., Miss	koon
a little bit	nit noy
Speak slower, please	Poot cha cha noi, see (kah, krahp)
I like	Chawp
I don't want it	My ow
room key	g'oon jaah
airport	s'nahm bin (Don Muang is the airport in Bangkok.)

Thailand	Muang Thai
Bangkok	Krung Thep
food, rice	kow
too expensive	pang mahk, pang pie
doctor	maw
hurry up	ray-o, ray-o kow
Do you have?	(object) mee my?
street	tah-nun
how?	yang rye?
How do I get to the hotel?	
	By wrong-ramm yang rye?
restaurant	rahn-a-hahn
hot	rawn
cold	yen, now
tea	chah
excuse me	kah-thot
canal	klong
I don't have	My mee
come	maa
How much is it to go to the Oriental Hotel?	Bye wrong rramm Oriental rah-kah tau ry? (kah, krahp)
market	tah-laht
wine	wine
I don't speak Thai.	Dee chan (pome) poot pasaah Thai, my dy (kah, krahp).
Do you speak French?	Koon poot pasaah farangseht, dy my (kah, krahp)?
foreigner	f-wrong
I am an American	Dee chan (pome) ben cone American (kah, krahp).
delicious	aroy mahk
Don't worry, it's OK.	My ben ry.
bathroom	hong nahm (water room)
room	hong
water	nahm
Chao Phya (Phraya)	chow pee-yah
Where is . . . ?	(object) you nye? You tee nye?
Where is the bathroom?	Hong nahm you nye?
right	kwah
left	sigh

yes	chai
no	my, my chai
OK	kah
please	gah-roo-nah
taxi	taxi
telephone	tora-sap

NUMBERS:

1	nung	19	sip gow	101	nung roi nung
2	song	20	yee sip	110	nung roi sip
3	sam	21	yee sip-et	167	nung roi ho sip jet
4	see	22	yee sip song	200	song roy
5	hah	30	sam sip	300	sam roy
6	ho	31	sam sip-et	460	see roy ho sip
7	jet	32	sam sip song	542	hah roy seé sip song
8	bat as in baseball	33	sam sip sam	900	gow roy
9	gow	40	see sip	1000	nung pahn
10	sip	45	see sip hah	1400	nung pahn see roy
11	sip-et	50	hah sip	5000	hah pahn
12	sip song	58	hah sip bat	10,000	nung mung
13	sip sam	60	ho sip	20,000	song mung
14	sip see	69	ho sip gow	40,000	see mung
15	sip hah	70	jet sip		
16	sip ho	80	bat sip		
17	sip jet	90	gow sip		
18	sip bat	100	nung roi		

P.S. Some Thai Superstitions

If you use an umbrella indoors, you will go bald.

If you do not eat everything on your plate, including all the rice, you will marry someone who is pock-marked.

If, when you leave your home, a step breaks under your foot, you are going to die.

If your mother dreams she lost a tooth on the night before you leave home, you will die.

If you give someone a handkerchief, he will soon have need of using it.

If you eat in a lazy fashion, in your next life you will be a snake.

If a son looks like his mother, or a daughter looks like her father, he or she will have a happy life. If the opposite is true, the life will be unhappy.

It is rude to point your toe at another person. It is very rude to pat children on the head, as the head is considered the temple of the body.

Singapore

Singapore

About the most exciting thing I can say for Singapore is that it's the only place in Southeast Asia where you can find Haagen-Dazs ice cream and Mrs. Fields cookies. I guess that's going a bit too far, but compared to the other countries I've been to, Singapore is something of a yawner. If you are short on time, my advice is—skip it. If you have a lot of time and are curious about the city, plan for two days, tops. You can see all there is to see in that time.

You don't have to wonder what the weather is going to be: it's always about the same. That means it's very humid, balmy, hot, sticky, with the possibility of rain on any day. Daytime temperatures in May ran about 85 to 95 degrees; evenings cooled down to about 80 degrees. High humidity.

Packing, therefore, is easy: take cool cottons and forget about stockings. You are not allowed in temples with shorts on. Restaurants tend to be on the casual side, although I'm sure there are one or two that prefer men to wear jacket and tie.

Everyone speaks English. The other language is Malay, but unless you're wandering around in the countryside, you won't have anything to worry about.

Seventy-six percent of the Singaporeans are Chinese. The country lies eighty-five miles north of the Equator. The water is OK to drink. The laws are very strict: if you get caught throwing anything on the ground, there is a big fine. Ditto for jaywalking, having a third baby, and getting caught with dope (for which the penalty is automatically death, no questions asked).

Everything is so strict there you begin to wonder if the government hasn't gone too far; a little more moderation in some cases might be a good idea, but since I don't know what it was like before, I really can't make any big judgments. The government is intent on sterilizing the city. Every neighborhood that is old and charming, or has any character at all, is being systematically torn down and replaced with large, high-rise buildings. I guess if you live there, you might think this is a boon, but for a tourist, it is a bore.

There are some people who really like Singapore, so you can consider this the opposite point of view. I found it mildly interesting, but would have preferred to have spent the time there in Thailand or Hong Kong instead.

There are two guidebooks I used for Singapore. The first, and best, has already been mentioned in the previous chapters: Fodor's *Southeast Asia, 1984*. The other is the pocket-sized Berlitz *Singapore*. I also gleaned much information from magazine articles and travel sections of newspapers.

We had an excellent guide named *John Samuel*, 4-B Jalan Mahmudiah, Johor Bahru, Johor, Malaysia (phone 07–234534). The guide service is *World Express Tours*, 114 Middle Road, #05-01, Singapore 0718 (phone 3363877). If you know for sure in advance that John will be your guide, take him See's chocolates, especially chocolate-covered coconut creams.

Hotel

We stayed at the **Shangri-La,** which is a bit off the main drag and quieter than the hotels on Orchard Street, which is the main drag. If you stay at the Shangri-La, request a room in the Garden Wing, the newer of the buildings (they are building another wing soon). Our rooms were very nice; the service was good.

You should go take a look at the lobby of the **Dynasty Hotel** on Orchard Street—it's the one with the pagoda roof and is quite spectacular.

Raffles is another hotel to go and look at, but don't stay there. It's seen better days. The best idea is to go in the late afternoon and have a Singapore sling in the Palm Court. I thought their sling tasted a lot like strawberry soda. It's something you've got to do, though.

Restaurants

We did get some very good food in Singapore. Try the local eateries for lunch—they are a lot of fun. The government has strict health laws (no surprise) so you don't have to worry too much about getting sick.

Golden Phoenix, Equatorial Hotel.
Another Chinese restaurant which we thoroughly enjoyed. Very casual; lots to eat and lots to look at. Be sure you order the smoked Szechuan duck; also good was the chicken cashew and the fried noodles with shrimp and chilis.

Muthu's Curry Restaurant, 76/78 Race Course Road, in the India section of town, phone 2932389 or 2937029; also at 32 Klang Road, phone 2929460.

This is an Indian restaurant where the entire meal is served on a big banana leaf, and you can eat it all with your fingers, if you want. I still don't know exactly what it is I ate, but I do know it was delicious. Messy. You can get silverware if you want it. Our guide said Muthu's is better than Banana Leaf Apollo, which gets written up in all the books. Best for lunch.

Omar Khayam, 55 Hill Street.

Runs hot and cold, so we were told. Gets good reviews in most guidebooks.

Oriental Gourmet, 21, Unit 0700, Ming Arcade, Cuscaden Road.

This Cantonese restaurant is semicasual and we found the food OK, but not great.

Rasa Singapura, by the Singapore Handicraft Center on Tanglin Road,

is a great place for lunch. Our guide said it is the best of the food-stall restaurants in the city. When you get there, stake out a table and have one person sit and hold it. Everyone else then runs around to all the various food stalls and orders what he wants, which gets delivered to your table (remember your table number), at which point you pay. Be sure you get sugar cane juice. It's all delicious, fun, and cheap.

Shang Palace, Shangri-La Hotel.

Our guide said the food here is mediocre and caters to tourists.

Our guide recommended the following restaurants, which we did not try. *Ramayana,* Plaza Singapura on Orchard Road, for Indonesian cuisine. The *Inn of Happiness* at the Hilton Hotel International. The *Mandarin Singapore,* a revolving restaurant that *is* good. The *Belvedere* at the Mandarin Hotel. *Aziza* for Malaysian-style food. The *Villa Saujana,* out of town, which is a large estate with formal gardens, offering dinner and a floor show (the dinner is not good, the floor show is great, the atmosphere is very good; reservations in advance for groups). *Peking Mayflower,* International Building, 360 Orchard Road, for Cantonese food. The *Rang Mahal* at the Oberoi Hotel for Indian cuisine. For Thai food, you might try *Chit Pochana* at the Tai Pan Hotel; the one in Bangkok is excellent. For Malay food, the *Tsui Hung Village* at the Asia Hotel. Some hotels, such as Raffles and the Mandarin, offer dinner shows on various evenings, so you can get a little culture with your food. Generally speaking, in these situations, the songs and dances surpass the meal.

Sightseeing

There are a couple days' worth of things to see in Singapore, and you'll be well off with a guide and driver. Many of the sights are quite a ways out of the city; traffic is reverse flow, so you probably would not care to drive yourself around.

The Botanic Gardens and Orchid Nursery are right in the downtown area, and are very beautiful. If you're a jogger, this is the place for you early in the morning.

Change Alley is also no longer with us.

Chettiar, Hindu temple, is the richest of its kind in the city.

Chinatown is out of business—the government decided to move it all into modern high-rise buildings.

The Chinese Gardens can be seen along the way to or from the bird park. If you go on a Saturday, you will be dumbfounded by the number of wedding parties there, taking pictures. We saw at least thirty such parties. All the brides wear big, fluffy, frilly, ruffly gowns. They all arrive in cream-colored Mercedes which are strewn with satin ribbons and have a bride doll glued to the hood. They compete with each other for pictures in the most ideal spots in the park (which is huge). How they can stand to do this in the heat of the day with all those clothes on is beyond me. Our guide said it's customary to get married early in the morning, go to this garden for pictures, then have a big bash in the evening. We've never seen anything like this. The gardens, by the way, are beautiful.

The Crocodile Farm has crocs of various sizes and styles, sitting on top of each other in little cement pens, awaiting their bleak future. Next to the farm is a shop (what else?) and guess what they sell?

The Japanese Gardens are somewhere in the vicinity of the Chinese Gardens, but we were too gardened-out to go see them.

Jurong Bird Park is a long drive out of town. It's a large park and very well maintained. Very interesting and of course home to every exotic bird you ever wanted to see. Good for kids. Be sure you go to the "night house" (near the entrance) to see the owls and bats—possibly the highlight of the whole park.

Mt. Faber, the highest point in the city, affords views of the area. From here you can get cable cars over to Sentosa Island; this gives you good views of the harbor area, but there's nothing much to do on the island.

The National Museum,
which was closed for repairs when we were there, has the Haw Par Jade Collection, supposedly the best in Asia.

Serangoon Road, is Little India, good for walking.

Sri Mariamman, Hindu temple, is the oldest of its kind, in Chinatown.

Sri Perumal Temple is Hindu, with a very elaborate and interesting facade and roof.

The Sultan Mosque on Bussorhal Street.

The Temple of 1000 Lights has a huge seated Buddha.

Thandayuthapani Temple on Tank Road is advertised as the "dazzling new Hindu temple and the grandest in Southeast Asia."

Thian Hock Keng is a Hokkien Taoist Temple, the oldest Chinese temple in the city.

Tian Fu Gong is the most famous Chinese temple.

Forget about going to the *pewter "factory"* and store, unless you are dying to buy pewter. It's a tourist trap.

Likewise and even more important, completely forget about going to the *gem-cutting "factory."* In your life you have never seen such ugly, schlocky merchandise; almost laughable.

Forget about going to the *Coralarium* on Sentosa Island.

Don't bother with the *Malay fishing village*—it looked like nothing and not worth the effort to get there.

Under no circumstances should you go to the *Instant Asia Show* at the Singapore Cultural Theatre. It lasts about forty-five minutes, which is forty minutes too long. Actually it starts out OK with some live musicians and a Chinese lion dance, but quickly slips into out-and-out tourist trappery, canned music, and a totally ridiculous number with a snake charmer. We didn't see the *Singapore Experience,* which is a forty-five-minute film about Singapore at the same theater. I'm glad we missed it if the other is any example.

If you see *Tiger Balm Gardens* in Hong Kong, you can skip the one in Singapore. Our guide said you could skip it even if you didn't see the one in Hong Kong.

He also said the *Harbor Tour* was not memorable.

Singapore River and *Statue of Raffles:* OK.

Shopping

We didn't have more than a couple of hours to devote to shopping, so I can't be of much help. If you're going to Hong Kong, save the shopping for there. *Orchard Street* is where all the best shopping is, most of it in large malls. Most of the shops we saw in these malls were on the tacky side, with clothes you wouldn't probably buy at home. There were exceptions, of course. We liked the *Metro Grand Department Store* by the Dynasty Hotel; on the upper floors were some very good buys on silk clothes, and some nice and inexpensive shoes on the main floor.

You can bargain in smaller shops, but not in the department stores or hotel arcades.

Shopping in Chinatown and Change Alley is a thing of the past. There is a *Thieves' Market* every afternoon from 2:00 to 6:00 and on Sundays, but we didn't get to it. There are also shops on Arab Street and in Little India.

Changi Airport is very large, modern, and beautiful. Take your luggage to security control before checking in. The airport is about a forty-minute drive from Orchard Street.

Epilogue

If I left out your favorite country it's only because I haven't had time to get there yet. If I live to be ninety I probably won't see all the places I have on my list. Once you are bitten by the travel bug, as I have been, there is no cure. On the way home from one trip I am already planning where to go next. Terminal wanderlust, I think it's called.

The reality is that few of us will ever be able to endlessly travel off into all the sunsets on this Earth. Even if we could, we'd be too exhausted to appreciate them.

One of the delights of having dined especially well is savoring the meal at a later time. So it is with travel. However wonderful a particular trip may be, it becomes even more so, in memory, as time passes. The best parts of it become better, and the negative aspects become things to laugh about, learn from, or forget altogether. Every experience, both negative and positive, can only give you a better understanding of your own history and who you are in relation to the rest of the world.

It's all out there for us—let's go get it!

Personal Travel Notes